HERVÉ RYSSEN

THE MIRROR OF JUDAISM
The accusatory inversion

Hervé Ryssen

Hervé Ryssen (France) is a historian and an exhaustive researcher of the Jewish intellectual world. He is the author of twelve books and several video documentaries on the Jewish question. In 2005, he published *Planetary Hopes*, a book in which he demonstrates the religious origins of the globalist project. *Psychoanalysis of Judaism*, published in 2006, shows how intellectual Judaism displays all the symptoms of hysterical pathology. There is no "divine choice", but the manifestation of a disorder that has its origins in the practice of incest. Freud had patiently studied this question on the basis of what he observed in his own community.

France is home to one of the largest Jewish communities in the Diaspora, with a very intense cultural and intellectual life. Hervé Ryssen has been able to develop his extensive work on the basis of numerous historical and contemporary sources, both international and French.

THE MIRROR OF JUDAISM,
The accusatory inversion

Le miroir du Judaïsme, l'inversion accusatoire,
Levallois-Perret, Baskerville, 2009

Translated and published by
Omnia Veritas Limited

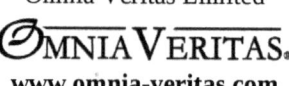

www.omnia-veritas.com

© Omnia Veritas Limited - Hervé Ryssen - 2024

All rights reserved. No part of this work may be reproduced in any form without the prior written permission of the *copyright* holders. Infringement of these rights may constitute a copyright offence.

PART ONE 13

JEWISH IDENTITY 13

1. The Jewish Paradox 13
- Jewish ambiguity 13
- Warrior patriotism 18
- Getting out of military service 24
- Disguise 32
- Instinctive solidarity 40
- The Jew, alone against all 47

2. The mission of the Jews 53
- Messianic hope 53
- The war against nations: immigration and miscegenation 57
- Cosmopolitan Propaganda I: The Multiracial Society 65
- Cosmopolitan propaganda II: blame game 77
- The Muslim Conquest 86
- Anti-Christianity 98
- Bolshevism 103
- Corrosive Judaism 106
- Human Rights 114
- Contempt for the goyim 118
- Apocalyptic Judaism 122

PART TWO 133

PSYCHOPATHOLOGY OF JUDAISM 133

1. The great loneliness of the Jews 133
- An enigma in the midst of nations 133
- The Jewish Jeremiad: 4000 years of pure suffering 138
- The Wandering Jew. Neuropathic Israelites 149

2. Hysterical fabulation 156
- Hysterical fabulation I 156
- Hysterical fabulation II 168
- Hysterical fabulation III 179
- The Fabulous Goyim: Synthetic Jews 186

3. The cosmopolitan mentality 197
- The process of blaming the goyim 197
- Humiliating and sullying the opponent 204
- Haman's Ears 209
- A pathological will to power 214
- Fraudsters and traffickers 223
- The enigma of anti-Semitism 226
- The accusatory inversion 235

PART THREE 243

PSYCHOANALYSIS OF JUDAISM 243

1. Sexual deviations 243
- Militant homosexuality 243
- The origins of feminism 251

  The destruction of patriarchy 256
  Transvestites and transsexuals 262
  Rapists and unbalanced 267
  Pedomaniacs 272
 2. The incestuous sect *280*
  Between a father and daughter 280
  Between a father and son 289
  Between a mother and her child 291
  Between brothers and sisters 297
 3. The myth of the Oedipus complex *307*
  The development of psychoanalysis 307
  Psychoanalysis in question 315
 4. The accusatory reversal *319*
  The incestuous genesis of a genocide 319
  The Diabolical Jew 322
  The sick become doctors 325
 5. The liberation of the Jew *333*
  The Jewish Prison 333
  The Suicide Jew 338
  Forgetting Judaism 342

OTHER TITLES **357**

Jews are scattered in all countries of the world, although they reside mainly in countries of European origin. Most of them are of Ashkenazi origin, i.e. those from Central and Eastern Europe who left in successive waves from the end of the 19th century onwards. A minority, also spread throughout the world, comes from the Mediterranean basin: these are the "Sephardic" Jews. But there are also black Jews in Ethiopia called Falashas, as well as Jews in India and China, who also claim to be "perfectly integrated". So Jews are not a race.

Judaism is not a religion either - or not only - since many Jews declare themselves atheists and do not feel any less Jewish for that. Particularly the Marxist Jews, who formed the leading elite of all communist movements in Western countries. They were fanatical militant atheists, faithful followers of the doctrine instituted by one of their own: Karl Marx.

In fact, it is strictly impossible to define Jewish identity without explaining the "mission" of the "chosen people" on this earth. Everything becomes simpler when one understands the political-religious project inherent in Judaism and which concerns "all humanity". However, it was Freudian psychoanalysis that allowed us to get to the heart of the problem, revealing to us the dark secret of the Jewish community. All we had to do was to read with a mirror.

PART ONE

JEWISH IDENTITY

1. The Jewish Paradox

In most cases, Jews declare themselves "perfectly integrated" in the countries where they live. However, all the testimonies we have collected suggest, behind a façade identity, that they also feel very Jewish and highly concerned about the interests of the Jewish community and the State of Israel.

Jewish ambiguity

Many Jewish intellectuals expressed their difficulty in defining Jewish identity. Jacob Talmon, a well-known Jewish philosopher, wrote for example about Judaism: "After three and a half thousand years, we still cannot define who is part of it and who is not[1]."

The "Hungarian" historian François Fetjö wondered about what made up the nature of the Jew: "Everyone thinks he knows it, but no one can say it," he wrote. It is as if he himself insisted on being indefinable, on escaping the limitations of concepts. It exists, that is undeniable; but what does it consist of, is it a people, a race? Ethnologists deny it this characteristic[2]."

Nahum Goldmann was an important Jewish personality of the 20th century. He was the founder of the World Jewish Congress, which he chaired from 1938. From 1956 to 1968 he combined the position of President of the World Jewish Congress with that of President of the World Zionist Organisation. In 1976, he published a book whose title was

---

[1] Jacob-Leib Talmon, *Destin d'Israël*, 1965, Calmann-Lévy, 1967, p. 137.
[2] François Fetjö, *Dieu et son juif*, Éditions Pierre Horay, 1997, p. 29.

perfectly appropriate: *The Jewish Paradox*[3]. In the preface to his book we read: "This tireless fighter for the Jewish cause exercised his vivacity, his seduction and his humour on the greatest statesmen. From Roosevelt to Adenauer, Mussolini to Litvinov and Ben Gurion to Kissinger, he rubbed shoulders with and sometimes influenced dozens of leaders who have marked the history of our time".

When asked for his definition of Judaism, Nahum Goldmann replied: "There is no definition that is completely satisfactory... I remember giving a lecture when I was a student during which I proposed more than twenty definitions: Judaism is a religion, a people, a nation, a cultural community, etc. None of them was absolutely accurate. None of them was absolutely accurate.

"The Jewish people is the most paradoxical people in the world, Goldmann added. It is neither better nor worse than others, but unique and different in its structure, history, destiny and character from all other peoples, and paradoxical in its contradictions". Goldmann explained, "Jewish thought, Jewish philosophy and Jewish ideology are made up of multiple contradictions. We are at the same time the most separatist and the most universalist people in the world. On the one hand, we have always refused to renounce our identity... On the other hand, there are no moralists more universal than the prophets. Although he has designated the Jews as "his people", the Jewish God is universal, the God of all mankind[4]."

Certainly, Nahum Goldman himself was the first to be "paradoxical", at least in appearance. In all the countries where they live, he claimed, Jews are good citizens: "Jews were not a landless people, for assimilated Jews were good Frenchmen, or good Germans, or good Englishmen, and so on". For he was a true German patriot: "During the First World War, he wrote, intellectuals denounced Prussian militarism. But, educated in Germany, I was a German patriot". So much so that he received thanks from the German chancellor of the time: "I received a letter from the German chancellor expressing his gratitude for all that I had managed to do for the fatherland during the hostilities." Indeed, Goldmann was protected by the police and anti-Semites had better watch out: "This gentleman is a great patriot. Besides, he's an important figure, and if you bother him in the future, you'll have to deal with me. I had become a protégé of the Munich police[5]."

Yet Nahum Goldman, the "German patriot", expressed the depth of his identity: "Ben Gurion reproached me one day for being a wandering Jew. I

---

[3] Nahum Goldman, *La Paradoja judía*, Ed. Losada, Cristal del tiempo, Buenos Aires, 1979 (out of print) (Translator's note, hereinafter NdT.)
[4] Nahum Goldmann, *Le Paradoxe juif*, Stock, Paris, 1976, p. 15, 81-84.
[5] Nahum Goldmann, *Le Paradoxe juif*, Stock, Paris, 1976, p. 110, 28-30.

replied that some people have their roots in themselves, without the need to transplant them in a particular land. This is certainly one of my predominant traits: wherever I am, I take my roots with me. I adapt immediately and, for as long as I can remember, I have never missed this facility: at the age of five I left Lithuania, where I was born in 1895, to settle in Frankfurt, and nothing could have been easier. It is true that I had a perfectly happy childhood. After my birth in the small town of Wisznewo, my parents went to study in Germany because under the Tsarist regime in Lithuania only a very limited number of Jews were admitted to the universities. My father and mother then emigrated to Könisberg, then to Heidelberg, and finally settled in Frankfurt[6]."

Here is a dialogue with the French minister Barthou that Goldmann reproduced in his book: "I am a wandering Jew, I replied. Born in Lithuania, raised in Germany, sometimes living in Switzerland or France, I have four or five passports. The Nazis denaturalised me for high treason, making me a stateless person.

-Listen to me," replied Barthou, "I have an offer for you. It generally requires five years' residence in our country to obtain French nationality, but an old law allows the President of the Republic to naturalise some people after three years if the Minister of Justice proposes it. You have owned a flat in Paris for three years, so we can work it out.

-I am very grateful to you," I said, "but I will speak to you frankly: I have a great admiration for France, its literature and its civilisation: I like living in Paris; but my love for France is not great enough to fight for her. My duty is to fight for the Jewish people. Now, in three or four years' time you will be at war and, in France, the population is mobilised up to the age of fifty-five; as president of the executive of the CJM I could not desert, for the anti-Semites would immediately take advantage of this act against me. I would therefore prefer not to risk it and renounce my French nationality. Barthou shook my hand and replied: "I thank you for your frankness. Get yourself naturalised by some Latin American state: they never go to war, even when they declare it!" So Barthou helped me to get the post of Honduran consul in Geneva and to benefit from a Honduran diplomatic passport... In fact, the only tangible success we achieved against Hitler's Germany was to force his resignation from the SDN by condemning the Nazis' anti-Jewish policy. It was then that Goebbels had me denaturalised for high treason[7]."

In another passage of his book, he recounted a post-war interview with President Truman's Secretary of State, a Jew named Dean Acheson, who

---

[6] Nahum Goldmann, *Le Paradoxe juif*, Stock, Paris, 1976, p. 19.
[7] Nahum Goldmann, *Le Paradoxe juif*, Stock, Paris, 1976, p. 57-61.

was "rather anti-Zionist". At the time, Goldmann was working for the creation of the state of Israel. Here he adapted his identity to suit the circumstances: "I replied: "Listen to me, Mr. Acheson, I am not speaking as a Jew, but as an American. I am an American citizen[8]."

Goldmann had confessed at the beginning of his book, while ironing out the rough edges as far as possible: "Even if they don't want to admit it, there is always this question of dual loyalty. I have had the privilege of knowing personally several Jewish statesmen, such as Leon Blum, Henry Kissinger, Pierre Mendès France, Bruno Kreisky and others, and, although they were true patriots in their respective countries, I am convinced that their Jewish origin made them wonder, even if only unconsciously[9]."

Roger Cukierman was from 2001 to 2008 the president of Crif, the Representative Council of Jewish Institutions in France. He was a Jew originally from Poland who became president of the Edmond Rothschild Bank. It can therefore be said that he was "hyper-integrated" into French society, at least socially and financially. In his book *Ni fiers, ni dominateurs (Neither proud, nor dominators)*, published in 2008, he wrote: "French Jews claim the right to solidarity with the State of Israel. In the two thousand years they have lived in France, Jews have demonstrated their integration and their loyalty. They have nothing to prove[10]." But he also expressed some "paradoxes": "My father, like most Jews, does not hesitate to accept his philosophical contradictions. Despite being anti-clerical, he feels obliged to celebrate my *bar-mitsvah*[11]. An old, elegant and dignified teacher, Mr Berger, came for three months to teach me the rudiments of Hebrew and the text to be read in the synagogue[12]."

We see here that an "integrated" Jew not only continues to cultivate and reinforce for himself and his children's Jewish identity, but also actively works to weaken the identity of the people who took him in - in this case through anti-clericalism.

The much-mediated Bernard-Henri Lévy, a (new) "French philosopher", already explained to us that no one was more French than he was. And that was precisely why he had allowed himself to vilify French intelligence in the most insulting way in his essay entitled *The French Ideology*, published

---

[8]Nahum Goldmann, *Le Paradoxe juif*, Stock, Paris, 1976, p. 46.
[9]Nahum Goldmann, *Le Paradoxe juif*, Stock, Paris, 1976, p. 17.
[10]Roger Cukierman, *Ni fiers, ni dominateurs*, Edition du Moment, 2008, p. 77.
[11]*Bar-mitzvah* is the ritual of coming of age in Judaism. According to Jewish law, before children reach a certain age, parents are responsible for the actions of their children. Once Jewish children reach that age, they are said to "become" *b'nai mitzvah*, at which point they begin to be responsible for their own actions. Traditionally, the father of a *ba-mitzvah* gives thanks to God that he is no longer punished for his child's sins. (NdT)
[12]Roger Cukierman, *Ni fiers, ni dominateurs*, Edition du Moment, 2008, p. 23.

in the early 1980s. He responded to Raymond Aron, who had been alarmed by such vitriol against his host country: "I am sure you have read me too carefully to ignore that it was as a Frenchman and as a Frenchman that, like any other French philosopher, I ventured into this research on black France[13]."

Twenty years later, in another book entitled *Récidives*, published in 2004, he wrote that he felt "an extreme attachment to Israel...I have written a hundred times, the philosopher said, that Israel and the diaspora are like heart and conscience to each other, that one is the support, the pillar, the source of the other - and vice versa...I am a Jew, of course, because of my bond with Israel. I am a Jew when, like every Jew in the world, my heart beats in unison with that of all Israelis under threat...When the whole world believes that Scud missiles are going to fall on Tel-Aviv, I come here instinctively, almost without thinking about it...because Israel remains the refuge state of the Jewish people[14]."

Similarly, this is what the very influential liberal economist Alain Minc declared in the weekly *Marianne* of 13 January 2003, page 14: "To begin with, I would like to make it clear that I do not position myself as a Jew but as a French citizen. My links with Israel are sporadic. The Arab-Israeli conflict worries me as much as the one in Iraq". And in the daily *Le Figaro* of 18 February 2005, Alain Minc himself declared: "As a Jew, I don't usually interfere in the life of the so-called Jewish community. The fault probably lies in my instinctive tendency towards universalism...". That was his way of being "French".

Stéphane Hessel was another Frenchman "more French than the French", of the "perfectly integrated" but at the same time "universalist" type. Born in Poland in 1917, he had come to France as a boy of seven and became a senior French diplomat. In his book published in 2008, whose title *Citizens without Borders* was quite evocative, he also highlighted the same paradox: "From the moment I entered the Alsatian School in the sixth year, I was absolutely certain that France, with its culture and language, would be my country. I never questioned that choice... I knew I would be French. For me, France was symbolically summed up in the motto "*Liberté, Egalité, Fraternité*"". But three pages later, when asked by the journalist: "Which teachers meant the most to you? Hessel replied: "There is Mr Lehman, my philosophy teacher. But the one who made the biggest impression on me was a literature teacher called Paul Bénichou, who I had in the second year of secondary school..... In secondary school, I had already had an exceptional teacher called Fischer, who taught us Latin and French and had

---

[13] Bernard-Henri Lévy, *Questions de principe, deux*, Grasset, 1986, p. 306. On *The French Ideology*, see *Planetary Hopes*.

[14] Bernard-Henri Lévy, *Récidives*, Grasset, 2004, p. 405, 408, 415, 421

a way of presenting French history and literature that served me for the rest of my life[15]." Manifestly, for Stéphane Hessel, France was reduced to the small, closed world of people belonging to his own community.

Warrior patriotism

The apparent paradoxical Jewish identity finds a beginning of explanation when one looks at the context in which those concerned express their patriotism. One quickly realises that this façade patriotism only appears when the interests of the community are at stake. Many Jews in "democratic" countries do indeed declare themselves "patriotic" and wave the national flag with fervour, but only in certain circumstances.

The very famous novelist Paul-Loup Sulitzer, whose books have been translated into almost every language, left this interesting testimony about his father, Jean Sulitzer, a Romanian Jew who came to France at the beginning of the 20th century: "The young immigrant has only his talent and his courage, but he is determined to make the most of them". And like all Jews, it is well known, "he doesn't have a penny in his pocket". But he has the "passion to win". He was first a salesman in a trailer business before he made his fortune. By 1939 he had become a "rich industrialist". He was "deeply patriotic and repulsed by the debacle and national resignation", wrote Paul-Loup Sulitzer. Jean Sulitzer would undoubtedly have preferred the French to fight the Germans to the last man. He was a "rebel" who "refused to compromise". He joined a resistance network and was decorated with "the Croix de guerre and several other medals".

Like his father, Paul-Loup Sulitzer was also a true patriot. Eight pages further on, he wrote: "I am going to Israel to tour the *kibbutzim*.... I am fascinated by the idealistic epic that pervades the creation of this young state. I feel the same solidarity with the Jews as with any massacred or oppressed minority. What fascinates me about Israel is the human quality and the prodigious diversity of the people I met there[16]."

The famous historian Pierre Vidal-Naquet also had a very patriotic father. In his *Memoirs*, he spoke of his father Lucien, a lawyer: "He never ceased to consider the armistice as a crime. Lucien is a member of the Resistance and Margot's solidarity is unwavering. That is her reaction as a Frenchman. But Lucien is also a French Jew who, "as a Frenchman, feels the insult he has received for being a Jew"... As soon as he returned to Paris and to the

---

[15]Stéphane Hessel, *Citoyen sans frontières*, Fayard, 2008, p. 28, 31. The surnames of the professors cited are all of Jewish descent. The examples of this identity ambiguity, so specific to Judaism, are countless and we refer the reader to our previous books.
[16]Paul-Loup Sulitzer, *Laissez-nous réussir*, Stock, Poche, 1994, p. 21, 25, 33

Palace, he shouted his rejection of defeat and his contempt for the masters of the moment and for those who accepted his speech[17]."

The famous American actor Kirk Douglas was also another great "patriot". What he wrote in his memoirs was very revealing of the modulable patriotism of the Jews, who react solely according to their interests: "I knew, though not in concrete terms, of the persecution of the Jews. But the war itself seemed very distant. And when you're young, just into your twenties, you read about all these things, but you're more interested in getting the job that will make you a Boradway star...I felt a surge of patriotism and another surge of Jewishness about what was going on in Europe with Hiler. We didn't have an accurate picture of the atrocities, but we knew enough. Hitler wanted to dominate the world, to eradicate the Jews: "*Deutschland über Alles*". I wanted to bomb the enemy[18]." So it was that he enlisted in the navy and became a liaison officer - a high-risk post - before beginning his brilliant film career.

In another passage of his book, Nahum Goldman acknowledged that his German patriotism before the First World War had a motive: "For all the Jews of the world, things were simple: Tsarist Russia was the worst enemy of the Jews and of Judaism, and since the Germans were at war with Russia, we were therefore pro-German. My personal background reinforced this idea, and my articles tended to justify Germanic ideology[19]."

Of course, after Hitler came to power in 1933, Nahum Goldman was no longer a patriot at all. His pan-Germanist articles of the past: "I wouldn't write them today," he admitted.

During the Algerian war, the patriotism of France's Jewish intellectuals was slightly different. In 1953, Jean-Jacques Servan-Schreiber was the founder of the weekly *L'Express*, which later had considerable influence on the formation of French public opinion. Françoise Giroud (Gourdji), who was a member of the paper's management, recalled the patriotic impulse that mobilised the entire staff of *L'Express*: "Strange times," she wrote. We were doing militant journalism. We wanted to influence the course of events, and first and foremost to fight against the colonial power. We were here to save France!... Jean-Jacques kept repeating it, and we were not far from thinking like that. I was the youngest of about twenty volunteers, all outstanding, enthusiastic young people who had put themselves at the service of France".

Jean Daniel, the editor of the *Nouvel Observateur*, fully confirmed this mood: "For Jean-Jacques, the success of his newspaper was a question of patriotism. He had the gift of transforming everything he undertook into an

---

[17]Pierre Vidal-Naquet, *Mémoires I, 1930-1955*, Seuil, p. 102.
[18]Kirk Douglas, *The Ragpicker's Son* (1988), Cult Books, 2021, p. 78, 84.
[19]Nahum Goldmann, *Le Paradoxe juif*, Stock, Paris, 1976, p. 28-30.

act of war. His sister Brigitte, a heroine of the Resistance, thought she was Joan of Arc and took everything to heart. And Françoise Giroud specified the nature of this combat: "We were in the middle of a battle against the tortures committed there, of which several cases had been denounced[20] ". In short, we must understand that the patriotism of *L'Express* consisted essentially in denouncing the actions of the French army.

Alexandre Minkowski's testimony perfectly illustrates the ambiguity of the Jewish personality and the paradoxical discourse of the Jewish intellectual. Alexandre Minkowski was a famous Jewish doctor, very much in the media spotlight in the 1970s in France. He was also a true French patriot, more French than the French. In his book *Un juif pas très catholique* (A not very catholic Jew), published in 1980, he told his story. His parents had emigrated from Poland before the Second World War and settled in Alsace. He had entered the Alsatian School, in a Protestant environment, but it was the Catholic religion to which he became attached. "Catholicism was probably the religion of my heart. My nanny, a woman of Beauce origin whom I considered my second mother, had introduced me to it. At home, this Catholic aspect of my life remained clandestine; it was only fully expressed during the holidays I often spent in her village. There, I never missed a mass, and I even made friends with the priest, who must have seen in me a soul to be saved". Alexandre Minkowski, as we can see, was becoming a true Frenchman and a good Catholic: "Christ (the best of the Jews) is a figure to whom I have remained deeply attached[21] ", he wrote.

In 1930, Minkowski visited his parents in his home country of Poland: "The trip I made to Warsaw when I was about thirteen reinforced my feelings. I disliked everything, the people, the food, the customs. My memory of that trip is still linked to a terrible impression of filth. The streets, the houses, what I ate, everything seemed dubious to me. And it seemed to me that I myself was perpetually dirty because of it. One day, my father took me to Nalewski, in the middle of the Jewish quarter. It was one of the most traumatic experiences of my childhood. I still have the image of a bustling swarm of people in uniform, dressed in the same black clothes, a cohort of men with dirty beards and sullied kaftans. We walked through the crowd. My father was silent. He had no idea of the enormous, absolutely terrible shock I was suffering. There were very few women on the streets. We passed through a compact mass of men who reminded me of undertakers. And everywhere, the constant impression of filth. The children, often pale and thin, their heads half-shaved, their temples framed with long silky curls. They were dressed even worse than the adults, in poor,

---

[20]Françoise Giroud, *Leçons particulières*, Fayard, 1990, `. 113, 114, 183
[21]Alexandre Minkowski, *Un juif pas très catholique*, Ramsay, 1980, p. 37, 38.

patched clothes. As I looked at them, I suddenly realised that if my parents had never left Poland, I would have been just like them. And my pity turned to revulsion. The idea that I, that handsome, well-dressed little boy, was about to become one of those wretches, plunged me into an abyss of doubt which I immediately tried to fill by repeating to myself at every turn that I was French, undeniably French[22]."

Alexandre Minkowski further confessed: "I could not understand the man I have become without reflecting on the converging influences which marked my childhood and which, intimately intertwined, were Christianity, patriotism and an inordinate love for France. These three elements fused in my mind and in my eyes formed the tangible ideal that was my country. For me, France was not just a land, a people or a history. Like God, who it is said cannot be represented, it was an abstract entity, so perfect that I could not imagine it in concrete terms. Compared to this fabulous divinity who watched over my childhood, God himself was for me no more than a secondary character. Cultural values in general, and Judaism in particular, naturally took a back seat. Serving my country was my only goal. I wanted to serve it, as the saying goes, "with all my means, with all my strength and with all my heart". And that meant, while waiting for the opportunity to sacrifice my life for it, working hard and succeeding in everything to do it with honour. My school and university successes, the top positions I fought for, had no other purpose: to become the best Frenchman in the service of a country that had no equal in the world, and that, of course, in all humility. So I felt French, to an unimaginable extent. And not just any Frenchman: a Frenchman who was almost Catholic and, moreover, a little Protestant. In short, a Frenchman truly worthy of general admiration. As for my origins, I had almost forgotten them. They didn't matter. I considered them to be a forgivable mistake of my youth. For the others, however, and especially for my fellow students at the Faculty of Medicine, I remained first and foremost a Jew. But I was so nice, I had assimilated their sacrosanct patriotic culture so well, that they said of me: "This Minkowski is not a Jew like the others". Which basically meant that despite my origins I wasn't too disgusting a guy. And that was fine with me, I loved his attitude: it totally matched the idea I had of myself". So it would have been wrong to doubt the patriotism of this Minkowski: "I felt so French at the time that I still couldn't assimilate the Hundred Years' War[23]."

Alexandre Minkowski was thus a Frenchman like any other, and perhaps even a little more. But the following sentences already begin to raise doubts, and the whole ambiguity of the Jewish personality gradually emerges

---

[22] Alexandre Minkowski, *Un juif pas très catholique*, Ramsay, 1980, p. 145, 146.
[23] Alexandre Minkowski, *Un juif pas très catholique*, Ramsay, 1980, p. 49-53.

behind the curtain of appearances: "However, I wrote, out of sheer pride, I also claimed my Jewishness. This ambiguous attitude had one advantage: it made me practically immune to anti-Semitism. And God knows how virulent it was at that time, especially at the medical school. I was totally insensitive to the hatred it conveyed because it hardly affected me.... I even had almost friendly relations with extreme right-wing fanatics. However, and this is another of my ambiguities, I was not really a fascist. Incredible as it may seem, I was going to strike a blow on the boulevard Saint-Michel against the *Camelots du roi*[24]."

Indeed, the patriotism of this Minkowski was of a somewhat special, universalist nature. That is to say, an "open" patriotism, not at all "closed in on itself": "I believed deeply in the left-wing ideas which my parents, convinced radical-socialists, had taught me through their love of the fatherland. On the other hand, although I disliked anti-Semites - for I already disapproved of all forms of racism - I did believe that the Jews were condemned to unconditional assimilation[25]."

After his medical examinations and boarding school, Minkowski went to do his military service in Chamonix with the Alpine hunters. But at the end of the 1930s, the war was dangerously close: "To die for the fatherland, although I was beginning to wish for it a little less, still seemed to me an ideal end to an unblemished career". In 1940, he landed in Morocco with the expeditionary corps. Alexandre Minkowski was awarded the Croix de Guerre, but curiously, he did not tell us anything about his deeds of arms.

In this war against the Nazis, the French had behaved like cowards. It is here that Minkowski revealed his deep-seated nature, in which a certain contempt for the natives was apparent: "With the defeat, all the imagery of my childhood mythology had been transformed before my eyes into a heap of fugitives. The heroes of Verdun themselves, those demi-gods, those supermen, had condescended to a pitiful armistice and refused to continue the fight. My dreams had disintegrated with France. Yet not for a moment did I have the slightest inclination to rebel, either against the injustice that was being meted out to my [Jewish] brothers or against the cowardice shown by all. I sadly resumed my studies and my boarding school where I had left them, without the slightest pang of conscience, so obvious was it to me that this was my path. Perhaps, after all, I was one of those selfish petty bourgeois, so typically French, whom Sartre called 'bastards'[26]."

---

[24]The *Fédération nationale des Camelots du roi*, also known simply as the *Camelots du roi* ("Militants of the King"), was a paramilitary organisation during the French Third Republic active between 1908 and 1936 that operated as the youth and shock force of the French Action movement. (NdT)
[25]Alexandre Minkowski, *Un juif pas très catholique*, Ramsay, 1980, p. 51.
[26]Alexandre Minkowski, *Un juif pas très catholique*, Ramsay, 1980, p. 55.

It was therefore as a Jew that Minkowski wanted the French to continue the war against Germany. "On 11 November 1940, the day on which the armistice was commemorated, I took a leading part in the demonstration in front of the Arc de Triomphe. In my mind, it was not yet an act of resistance, but of loyalty to my memories. Then I went back to the hospital where, proud of having defied the enemy in the middle of the Occupation, I told the ward what I had seen. There was a deathly silence in the ward, everyone fell silent, and it was then that one of the interns, Doctor Motte, let fall these words that I can still hear: "it's always the foreigners who meddle in things that don't concern them". An earthquake would not have shaken me more".

Reading his words, it seemed that he had returned to Judaism because of the French who still considered him a foreigner. "Suddenly I discovered what I had always managed to hide from them: those people hated me, I was an object of abjection for them. And suddenly I understood everything they must have said behind my back: that I was the worst and most infamous of the Jews. The strange thing was that I did not react immediately. The blow had stunned and paralysed me, my world had collapsed forever and all my points of reference had vanished. I was helpless, shattered. It took me months to recover from this cataclysm, to get back on my feet and slowly put back together the pieces that still remained inside me, but this time in a different order. I was never able to see myself as a good little Frenchman, a good little boy, a good little anybody. And here I must thank those who helped me in this difficult process of reconstruction, and I am referring to my comrades in the Resistance, who were then called terrorists[27]."

In the 1970s, Alexandre Minkowski became a famous doctor. The Jewish paradox exploded here once again: "Let's go back to those articles about me in the Catholic press. Not only did they praise me as a doctor, but, as a man, they adorned me with almost biblical qualities. One article even suggested that I was 'a Christian without knowing it'. I must admit that this last remark moved me infinitely more than all the superlative praise that accompanied it, to the extent that I have since been seriously thinking of converting." This was on page 90. Seven pages later, at the end of the chapter, Minkowski wrote: "I was jumping on the bandwagon of one of my favourite themes, that of the hand-to-hand between Jews and Protestants: I was preaching resistance to imperialist Catholicism, or Catholic

---

[27] Alexandre Minkowski, *Un juif pas très catholique*, Ramsay, 1980, p. 55, 56. Jews were very numerous in the anti-fascist resistance, also called the "French Resistance", as were the Communists. On this subject, see *Jewish Fanaticism*.

imperialism, as you like.... It was a kind of call to holy union, a kind of religious 'common programme'[28]."

Alexandre Minkowski, an agnostic Jewish doctor, finally came to his conclusion. He attended a Jewish festival one day, the festival of Sukkot: "I almost wanted to join my voice to theirs, I felt so moved. No matter how hard I tried to reason, I could not control the emotion that came over me.... For the first time in my life, perhaps, I felt Jewish, totally, without the slightest restriction. All my prejudices had fallen before these men, so sure of themselves, so firmly anchored in their faith and their identity, and at the same time so non-sectarian, so undogmatic, tolerant and respectful of the particularities of each one. Not only did I recognise myself as a Jew, but I was happy to be one, happy to belong to a people capable of such open-mindedness, such open-heartedness. I could not resist any longer. I surrendered myself to a sweet, almost childlike happiness. I had rediscovered my roots[29]."

Getting out of military service

For a long time, Jews have been criticised throughout the world for shunning military service and lacking courage in combat. While the former reproach is undoubtedly justified, it is far more random to accuse all Jews of cowardice. The truth is that many of them may show great ardour and courage, but only when the interests of the Jewish community are at stake. Otherwise, nothing should be expected of them. Indeed, why risk their lives to defend a country that is not their own?

Jewish historians often insist on anti-Semitism and pogroms to explain the great emigration of Jews from Russia to the United States at the end of the 19th century. Solzhenitsyn, in the first volume of his book *Two Hundred Years Together*, explained that other factors must also be taken into account, particularly the nationalisation of all alcohol distilleries by the Russian state in 1896, which deprived a large number of Jewish families of their income.

As for the Jews of the Austro-Hungarian Empire, they were mainly fleeing conscription. In 1927, the famous novelist Joseph Roth explained that the right of citizenship and the conscription of Jews into the army had made them so fearful that some had preferred to leave for the United States or to self-mutilate: "It is difficult to find a Jewish family in the East that does not have a cousin or an uncle in America. One emigrated one day twenty years ago. He was fleeing military service. Or he deserted after

---

[28] Alexandre Minkowski, *Un juif pas très catholique*, Ramsay, 1980, p. 90, 97.
[29] Alexandre Minkowski, *Un juif pas très catholique*, Ramsay, 1980, p. 136.

being declared fit. If Eastern Jews were not so afraid, they could rightly boast of being the most anti-militaristic people in the world. For a long time, their homelands, Russia and Austria, did not consider them worthy of military service. It was not until the Jews were given equal civic rights that they were forced to join the ranks.... And when they were told of the great honour that they were allowed to fight, to drill and to fall on the battlefield, consternation seized them. He who approached the age of twenty and was in such good health as to suppose that he would be declared fit, fled to America. Those who had no money self-mutilated. Self-mutilation was widespread among Eastern Jews for decades before the war. Those who were greatly frightened by the soldier's life had a finger severed, sinews cut off their feet and poison poured into their eyes. They became heroic cripples, blind, crippled, crippled, broken, subjected themselves to the most ungrateful and ugly of sufferings. They did not want to serve. They did not want to go to war and fall into it... It was not only stupid to die for a tsar or an emperor, but it was a sin to live far from the Torah and against its commandments. It was a sin to eat swine's flesh, to carry a weapon on the Sabbath, to do the instruction, to raise one's hand against an innocent man and a foreigner. The Eastern Jews were the pacifists of the most heroic mettle. They suffered for pacifism. They willingly became cripples. No one has yet sung the heroic deed of these Jews.[30] "

The Austrian writer Franz Werfel was another of these "perfectly integrated" Jews who preferred to slip away when the time came to fight. Here is what journalist Françoise Giroud (Gourdji) wrote about him: "Mobilised in 1914 as a non-commissioned artillery officer, he was wounded while on leave when he jumped from a funicular railway. Convicted at a court martial for voluntary mutilation, he was sent to the Russian front. Thanks to the unsolicited intervention of a member of the aristocracy, Count Harry Kessler, who admires his poetry - always the famous *Protektion* - he is able to return to Vienna, where he is assigned to the army press service. A completely relaxed situation. He lives in the Bristol Hotel and has a lot of free time at his disposal[31]." Obviously, this "great writer" had returned from the war alive. On the other hand, we will never know how the implacable polemicist Karl Kraus - "the king of Vienna" - managed to get away from the theatre of operations. Françoise Giroud simply told us that he had written "a twelve-hour piece after a voluntary suspension during the First World War[32]."

The famous writer Stefan Zweig had also managed to slip away. Despite being "perfectly integrated" and "more Austrian than the Austrians", Stefan

---

[30] Joseph Roth, *Judíos errantes*, Acantilado 164, Barcelona, 2008, p. 103-104.
[31] Françoise Giroud, Alma Mahler, Editorial Noguer, Barcelona, 1990, p. 161.
[32] Françoise Giroud, Alma Mahler, Editorial Noguer, Barcelona, 1990, p. 68.

Zweig, like many of his peers, chose to avoid national service during the First World War: "From the first moment I felt safe in my heart as a citizen of the world; it was more difficult for me to find the right attitude as a citizen of a nation. Although I had reached the age of thirty-two, I had no military obligation for the time being, because I had been declared useless at all reviews, something I had been heartily glad of at the time... In all dangerous situations, my natural attitude has always been to avoid them". Thanks to a good "plug", the great writer had the opportunity to find a "good hiding place", far, far away from the front: "The fact that a friend, a high-ranking officer, worked in the archive made it possible for me to be employed there".

His friend, the writer Rainer Maria Rilke, was not ready for the struggle either: "In Vienna I had become estranged from my old friends and it was not the right time to make new friends. I only had a few conversations with Rainer Maria Rilke, because we understood each other intimately. We also managed to get him to join our lonely war archive, as he would have been the most useless person as a soldier because of his hypersensitive nerves, to which dirt, bad smells and noises caused real physical discomfort[33]."

A scene from one of his novels, *Mendel the Bookman*, published in 1929, was quite revealing of Stefan Zweig's true identity. During the First World War, his character Buchmendel had to appear before the military censorship office to present his papers: "I couldn't quite understand. Hell, did he have his papers, his documents? And where. All he had was a travelling salesman's card. The commander raised the wrinkles on his forehead more and more. He had to clear up the question of his nationality once and for all. And what had his father been, Austrian or Russian? Jakob Mendel calmly replied that he was, of course, Russian. And what about him? Oh, he had smuggled himself across the Russian border thirty-three years ago so that he wouldn't have to do his military service. Since then he had been living in Vienna. The commandant grew increasingly impatient. When had he obtained Austrian citizenship, asked Mendel, and for what purpose? He had never bothered about such things, so he was still a Russian? And Mendel, who had been bored to death by these questions for a long time, answered indifferently: "Actually, yes"[34]."

The Jews who joined the Russian army in 1915 were not much more combative. The great Russian writer Aleksandr Solzhenitsyn quoted a witness: "During offensives, they were usually in the rear; when the army retreated, they were in the front. More than once they sowed panic in their

---

[33] Stefan Zweig, *The World of Yesterday; Memoirs of a European*, Acantilado 44, Barcelona, p. 118, 119, 122
[34] Stefan Zweig, *Mendel, el de los libros*, Acantilado, Barcelona, 2009, p. 40-41.

units". He added: "It cannot be denied that instances of spying and passing to the enemy were not infrequent[35]."

And these inclinations were the same throughout the Second World War. Even when the war corresponded exactly to the interests of the community, Jews seemed to shy away from the zones of hostilities. "One thing was evident, wrote Solzhenitsyn, expressing here the general feeling: they were not much to be seen on the front line. They were much more numerous in the rear staffs, in the quartermaster's office, in the entire medical corps, in many of the technical units stationed in the rear, and, of course, among the administrative staff, the pen-pushers of the entire propaganda machine, including the travelling variety show orchestras and the troupes of artists for the front[36]."

It is known that some 200,000 Jewish soldiers perished in the ranks of the Red Army during the conflict. But in proportion, this figure was four times lower than that of the rest of the Soviet soldiers. The "myth" of the Jew "hiding" in Tashkent, the capital of Uzbekistan, a city where life was good, probably had some basis in reality.[37]

Another, much more common solution was to corrupt officials. This is what Joseph Roth said of the Jews in the Austro-Hungarian Empire: "In any case, military doctors were bribed. Scores of military doctors became rich, left the army and turned to a private practice of their profession, which partly consisted of bribery". Clearly, the manoeuvre presented some risks, and Joseph Roth wrote: "Is it possible to bribe them, as if bribery were an easy thing! Does one know whether bribery will not lead to a tremendous trial that ends in prison? All that is known is that all officials can be bribed. Or rather: that all men are bribable. Bribery is a characteristic of human nature [Roth was generalising his own case, nda]. But what can never be known is when someone will confess to bribery, or if he will confess to bribery. It is impossible to know whether the official who has already taken money ten times will not denounce you on the eleventh simply to prove that the previous ten times he did not take it, so that he can take it another hundred[38]."

Mark Zborowski defended the same discourse in his major study of Eastern European Jewish communities: 'They know from experience that the Goyim understand the value of money, so the bribery system is the

---

[35] Alexandre Soljénitsyne, *Deux siècles ensemble*, tome I, Fayard, 2002, p. 532.
[36] Alexandre Soljénitsyne, *Deux siècles ensemble*, tome II, Fayard, 2002, p. 391.
[37] Read for example the testimonies of Marek Halter and Samuel Pisar in *Planetary Hopes*. "At that time the USSR was the only country willing to accept Jewish refugees, although it sent most of them to its Asian regions." Shlomo Sand, *The Invention of the Jewish People*, Ediciones Akal, 2011, p. 13.
[38] Joseph Roth, *Judíos errantes*, Acantilado 164, Barcelona, 2008, p. 104, 110.

normal adjuvant to transactions with public officials. The shtetlj endorses a theory that is widespread in Eastern Europe: a good civil servant is one who can be bribed[39]."

Nahum Goldmann, the German "patriot", explained another subterfuge that allowed some Jews to avoid military service: "A law exempted only children from service. In Jewish communities, civil registration was kept by the rabbi. In my family, my grandfather's name was Leibman, my father Goldmann and my uncle Szalkowitz[40]."

Jacques Le Rider, a Jewish historian specialising in Central European literature, presented another type of 'accusation' against the Jews of the time: 'Until 1916, the Habsburg authorities, anxious to maintain the cohesion of the monarchy at all costs, censored opinions likely to exacerbate tensions between nationalities, as well as those that were openly anti-Semitic. For example, the polemic launched in 1916 by anti-Semites against Eastern Jews, in particular Galitzians, who were evading their military obligations by hiding behind studies to become rabbis, was not taken up by the civil or military administration....From 1917 onwards, however, censorship was relaxed with regard to anti-Semitic articles, and it became commonplace to see Jews being called "war profiteers", Jewish military doctors being accused of giving preferential treatment to Jewish wounded while non-Jewish wounded were sent back to the front, and so forth. The outbreak of anti-Semitism reached its peak in 1918, with Jews now being used as scapegoats, supposedly to blame for all the calamities that befell Austria[41]."

In the same vein, Aleksandr Solzhenitsyn mentioned the unpleasant "case of the dentists" that had broken out in Russia in 1913. These were "mostly Jews": "A veritable factory of dentists' diplomas had been set up and flooded Moscow. Possession of these diplomas gave them the right to permanent residence and exempted them from military service. Hundreds of fake dentists were sentenced to a year's imprisonment, but thanks to Rasputin's intervention, they were pardoned". According to one Simanovitch, Rasputin "had become a friend and benefactor of the Jews"; "Many young Jews begged for his help to escape from the army[42]."

In the Russian Empire, Jews could be forcibly conscripted into the army. Jacob Brafman (1825-1879) was, in 1869, the author of the *Book of the Kahal* (*Kniga Kagala*), published by the Russian government, in which he denounced the secret actions of Jews in Russia. In 1875, he published *The*

---

[39] Mark Zborowski, *Olam*, 1952, Plon, 1992, p. 218. Shtétlj: Jewish town or village in Eastern Europe.
[40] Nahum Goldmann, *Le Paradoxe juif*, Stock, Paris, 1976, p. 25.
[41] Jacques Le Rider, *Arthur Schnitzler*, Belin, 2003, p. 216, 217
[42] Alexandre Soljénitsyne, *Deux siècles ensemble, tome I*, Fayard, 2002, p. 548.

Universal Jewish Brotherhoods (Les Confréries juives universelles). He reported in detail how these groups "united all the Jews scattered over the earth into one powerful and invincible body[43]."

The Jewish historian Leon Poliakov left us the following passage about this Jacob Brafman in his *History of Jewish Identity Crises*, published in 1994: 'It is true that he had certain reasons to resent his home community, which was based in Klesk, in a Belarusian village, wrote Poliakov. The communities were to provide a quota of Jewish teenagers, the cantonists, for military service for a period of 25 years. They were first baptised and given a new surname, usually of Russian consonance. Understandably, Jewish families feared this obligation above all else, and in most cases, rich families sent children from poor families in their place. There were even professional kidnappers, the "*Khappers*", who were paid to hand over disadvantaged teenagers to the authorities. Jacob Brafan had been handed over in this way by his community, but had managed to escape from the *Khappers*. He was baptised and became the official censor of all Jewish books published in the Russian Empire. His anti-Jewish zeal was formidable."

The famous American actor Kirk Douglas was a Jew originally from Russia. His father Herschel was a poor ragpicker, though he was physically impressive: "He popped caps off bottles and crushed glasses with his teeth, Kirk Douglas wrote in his memoirs; he went from bar to bar with an iron bar, betting drinks that he could bend it with his bare hands, and he did; that no one could beat him in a wrestling match. In all probability he was the toughest and strongest Jew in our town." But when it came to fighting the Japanese, he preferred to go to sea: "Herschel Danielovitch was born in Moscow around 1884 and fled Russia around 1908 in order to avoid being drafted into the army to fight in the Russo-Japanese war[44]."

See also what the liberal economist and essayist Guy Sorman told us. His father was born in Warsaw, a Polish city under Tsarist sovereignty: "He left in 1917 to avoid conscription and a choice between the Russian and German armies. He fled to cosmopolitan Berlin[45]."

After the Franco-Prussian war of 1870, some wondered about the role Jews had played during those events, and we can see that they did not have the reputation of being exceptional soldiers at that time either; it was not their speciality, so to speak. *L'Illustration*, an old reliable weekly, gave this description in its issue of 27 September 1873: "The Jew has been the calamity of the invasion. While the battle lasts, the Jew stays behind. He fears the blows. But once the enemy has fled and the battlefield is clear, the

---

[43]Léon Poliakov, *Histoires des crises d'identités juives*, Austral, 1994, p. 163.
[44]Kirk Douglas, *The Ragpicker's Son* (1988), Cult Books, *2021*, p. 21, 17
[45]Guy Sorman, *Le Bonheur français*, Fayard, 1995, p. 12.

Jew comes running. There he is master and king. All these corpses belong to him. It is not for nothing that the soldiers refer to him by the characteristic name of the raven. He calmly strips the dead, going from group to group. All he seeks is gold. Sometimes a moan is heard. It is a wounded man begging for help, but the raven has no time to dwell on such trifles. Does he not have a mission to accomplish? It is not enough for him to steal, he is also a spy. It is the raven who, after the lost battle, will bring to Headquarters all the papers found on the superior officers. Sometimes, when he is caught, the Jew is shot. He betrays the Germans in the same way as he spies on the French; in the future, he will keep the information from both sides and the business will be all the more lucrative[46]." This story was another manifestation of this ambiguity that nestles at the very heart of Jewish identity.

Martin Gray, in his biography entitled *In the Name of All My People*, recounted that after World War II, when he emigrated to the United States, he had also refused to do his military service and fight in Korea, "in a war that was not my own". I went to the recruiting offices, to the passport services; I made petitions, pleas, protests; I asked for a special commission to be convened; I swore that I would lie down at the entrance of the building, that if necessary I would die there[47]."

Daniel Cohn-Bendit, the former anarchist leader of the May '68 revolt and environmentalist MEP, explained how he had managed to get out of military service. In 1958, the young Daniel had to choose between German and French nationality. "The decisive argument," he wrote, had been a decree by the very right-wing German Defence Minister Franz Josef Strauss authorising Jewish children, if they so wished, to refuse to do military service: "It was to allow Jews returning to Germany to do military service in Israel," Cohn-Bendit commented. Perfect, my father concluded, "you take German nationality and get out of the army. Escape from the army! I didn't hesitate: I became German out of utilitarianism and anti-militarism[48]."

This mentality is also frequently found among the Sephardic Jews of the Mediterranean basin. Dr Georges Valensin, "born into an important Jewish community in Algiers", wrote about his fellow Sephardim, always quoting the sources: "The lack of enthusiasm for bearing arms seems to have been particularly marked among Mediterranean Jews. In 1908, the Young Turks who had seized power wanted to force Israeli citizens to do military service; many left the country.... In Tunisia, the French colony was scandalised in

---

[46]Text reproduced in *Je vous hais!* (dixit Leon Blum), April 1944, p. 52. On the corpses on the battlefields, see *The Planetary Hopes* in the footnote.
[47]Martin Gray, *En nombre de todos los míos*, Plaza & Janés, Barcelona, 1973, p. 339.
[48]Daniel Cohn-Bendit, *Quand tu seras président*, Robert Laffont, 2004, p. 117.

1918 by the noisy demonstrations of joy of the Jewish soldiers who had just been demobilised". And this mood was also prevalent in the United States: "When the United States entered World War I, there was a campaign led mainly by Jews against the draft, and they had a reputation for being easily exempted from service. In Brooklyn, one speaker accused them directly: 'There are three stages in the life of a young Jew: birth, communion at 13 [*bar-mitzvah*, ndt] and exemption at 21'".

Dr. Valensin added: "The reasons for the reluctance to take up arms were above all cultural; a Jewish mother worried about her son, warned him against the slightest physical danger and advised him to flee from the blows of foreign boys rather than to respond to them; he was educated in non-violence and the military man, a man of murder, was despised. For Abbé Maury, who opposed the emancipation of the Jews at the time of the Revolution, the Jews could not be good soldiers because of the Sabbath rest, which forced them to total inaction; he quoted the historian Flavius Josephus in support of his argument: they had allowed the conquest of Jerusalem in order not to fight on the Sabbath[49]."

Georges Valensin pointed out, however, that Jews could fight with great ardour when the interests of the Jewish people were at stake: "Ancient and recent history has shown that Jews can become good soldiers when they identify themselves with the cause for which they are fighting. The Maccabean revolt against the Ptolemies, and later against the Romans and other oppressors, were famous in the annals of valor.... When the United States fought in Vietnam, almost all Israelis managed to stay out of it. But many of the same people wanted to enlist in Israel during the Six Day War. The contrast impressed the Americans.

All this information leads us to believe that French Jews, contrary to what we are led to believe, were perhaps not as heroic as they are made out to be during the First World War. In fact, the permanent exhibition in Paris that pays tribute to their sacrifice seems rather suspicious to us.

Read what Pierre Birenbaum told us about the unparalleled warrior courage of the Jews in defence of the invaded homeland: "The Great War gave rise to constant displays of patriotism and many rabbis fell on the battlefield. Religious services underlined the deep-rooted attachment to the French nation, for which so many Jewish soldiers made the supreme sacrifice[50]."

This assertion is contradicted by generally accepted opinion. Let us recall the words of Jean-Paul Sartre mentioning a common opinion that outraged

---

[49] Georges Valensin, *La Vie sexuelle juive*, Les Éditions philosophiques, 1981, p. 131-135.
[50] Pierre Birenbaum, *Prier pour l'Etat, les Juifs, l'alliance royale et la démocratie*, Calmann-Lévy, , p. 113, 114

him: "If it has been thought to be established that the number of Jewish soldiers was, in 1914, lower than it should have been, it was because one had the curiosity to consult the statistics[51]."

With their 1700 men fallen "for France" between 1914 and 1918, the number of Jews was actually four times less in proportion to that of the native French. But this did not prevent our friends from building an out-of-proportion funerary monument at Verdun, which must be at least eight metres high and twenty-five metres long. By comparison, the ossuary of the Christian soldiers should be at least four kilometres high. If we could measure brazenness and impudence - the now very famous Jewish *chutzpah* - that would probably be the figure to retain. Recall also those two pierced *poilus* helmets[52] displayed in a glass case in the Army museum in Paris. One belonged to a random Dupont, but the other - and this is the most significant - belonged to Private "Lévy". It's the magic of labels!

Disguise

Jews have long been accustomed to wearing the garb of the people they settle in. They speak their language without an accent, outwardly adopt local customs and customs and declare themselves to be "extremely patriotic". However, they live in a world of their own that has nothing to do with that of the Goyim.

For centuries, Jews have lived in this way under a borrowed identity, dressing by day as natives of the host country and by night as Jews. In Spain, in 1492, Isabella the Catholic had given them the choice between converting to Christianity or leaving the territory. The Jews who had chosen to remain had become good Catholics. But it did not take the Spaniards long to realise that they were still secretly Judaising. After several centuries, there were still small communities of Marranos, good Catholics, but only in appearance.[53]

In France, we had a high Church dignitary, Cardinal-Archbishop Jean-Marie Lustiger, who was an excellent example of the willingness of some Jews to dissimulate. He had converted in 1940, shortly before the German invasion. This was his response to Marek Halter in 1995: "As for my marital status, my name is still Aaron. It is no secret in Orléans that I am a Jew, where I was during the war".

---

[51] Jean-Paul Sartre, *Reflections on the Jewish Question*, Ediciones Sur, Buenos Aires, 1948, p. 13.
[52] French soldiers of the First World War in popular slang (NdT).
[53] See also the case of the Donmehs in Turkey (fake Muslims) in our long chapter on "plasticity" in *Psychoanalysis of Judaism*. [And on the Spanish and Portuguese Marranos read further in *History of Anti-Semitism* (2010), NdT].

His false papers, provided to him by a mayor in the Orléans area, established his surname, Lustiger, and invented a new first name, Jean-Marie. Although his papers were in order, my father was discovered, and so was I," he said. That's when we fled to Toulouse". Jean-Marie Lustiger, who became a good Catholic, later became cardinal-archbishop of Paris, and it was thanks to these vestments that he was able to preach a new kind of Catholic doctrine to the faithful.

In his work entitled *The Promise*, Cardinal Lustiger denounced anti-Semitism: "Christian anti-Semitism is not posed as a particular problem of racism among others, but indeed as a sin - a sin whose enormity is indicative of a profound unfaithfulness to the grace of Christ[54]."

On the occasion of Cardinal Lustiger's death, the daily *Le Monde* of 8 August 2007 published an article by the former president of the Crif (Representative Council of Jewish Institutions in France), Théo Klein: "He was already Cardinal and Archbishop of Paris when I met him," said Theo Klein. I was invited as the newly elected president of the Crif and I was very curious to meet this unlikely personality - Jean-Marie, but still Aaron Lustiger - this son of Poland who claimed his Jewishness, suddenly promoted to the most important episcopal see in France".

We learned that Cardinal Lustiger went every year to the synagogue in rue *de la Victoire* (*rue de la Victoire, Paris*) to attend the prayer in memory of the Jewish deportees. "Over the years, wrote Theo Klein, our relations have deepened and our encounters have multiplied.... I realised then that he had never left the Church of Jerusalem of which he had spoken to me. For him, the Father to whom Jesus was referring was indeed the Father from whom Moses, on Sinai, had received the Word and whose welcome he, Aaron Jean-Marie, was awaiting".

Aaron Lustiger's funeral took place on 8 August 2007 in Notre Dame Cathedral in Paris. At the opening of the religious ceremony in the cathedral square, the cardinal's cousin, historian Arno Lustiger, read the *kaddish*, the Jewish prayer for the deceased, followed by a message from the family. "This *kaddish* reading was one of my cousin's last wishes," explained Arno Lustiger. "He told me when I went to see him for the last time. 'I was born a Jew and I am still a Jew,' he always repeated to us."

Arno Lustiger had written a book in 1991 about the Spanish civil war (*Shalom Libertad!*), in which he extolled the struggle of those thousands of Jews who had enlisted in the International Brigades[55]. Many of them were communists of Trotskyist tendency. And the speciality of the Trotskyists,

---

[54] Marek Halter, *La Force du Bien*, Robert Laffont, 1995.
[55] Read in *Jewish Fanaticism*. Almost a third of the international brigaders were Jews.

as is well known, is to infiltrate enemy organisations in order to subvert them more effectively.

Jews adopt the customs and mores of the peoples among whom they live, but retain their Jewish identity inwardly.

The case of the famous TV presenter Michel Drucker is another illustrative example of the "marranos[56]". Michel Drucker was indeed a good Catholic, at least in appearance. *Le Figaro* of 19 September 2007 presented a portrait of the star of the small screen following the publication of his autobiography. He informed us that he had been baptised at his father's request. "This former deportee tried to be more French than the French. My mother, Drucker added, was against it. She said that one could not be baptised with a father called Abraham. She would have liked to have had Jewish daughters-in-law." Drucker was the son of a Romanian Jew and an Austrian Jew who arrived in France in the 1930s and were naturalised in 1937. "He heard Yiddish or German spoken at home," the newspaper reported. With age, the presenter "returns to his roots and increasingly assumes his Jewish origins, which for a long time he had, if not denied, at least concealed.... "I know where I come from, he confessed, and, over the years, I am getting closer and closer to who I really am".

The President of the French Republic elected in 2007, Nicolas Sarkozy, was also another good Catholic. The weekly *Le Point* of 15 November 2007 published an article about his friendship with Patrick Balkany, the mayor of Levallois. The weekly's journalist, "Saïd Mahrane", wrote: "Between the president and the mayor of Levallois-Perret there is a friendship of more than thirty years". Saïd Mahrane then quoted Balkany: "Our Hungarian origins have undoubtedly brought us closer together". One sympathiser gently mocked his idols: "When he's with Sarko, they look like Robert de Niro and Joe Pesci!" - two famous actors known for their roles as gangsters in feature films. Saïd Mahrane was nevertheless keen to dot the i's and cross the t's: "As far as we know," wrote the journalist, "Balkany is of neither Corsican nor Italian origin. He may give the impression of having been born under the sun, but his name is spelt with a Greek 'i', like Sarkozy. A spelling he wears with pride: "My surname is Hungarian," Balkany declared. I am the son of immigrants and I am proud to be so! That's all. Saïd Mahrane, for his part, probably valued the "h" in his surname highly. Otherwise, we might have thought that he too was a Jew acting behind a mask, like a "marrano", precisely.

As we know, Balkany had experienced a number of setbacks in the French justice system. On 28 July 1999, the Regional Court of Auditors of Ile-de-France (Paris region) had condemned him for having employed three

---

[56] *Marrane* in French. NdT.

Levallois municipal agents for three years for his personal service. Following the verdict, he had to reimburse the full amount of the salaries, some 523,897 euros. The same year, he declared himself to be, according to the journalist Saïd Mahrane, "the most honest man on earth". A bit like Saïd Mahrane, in short.

Ferdinand Lasalle was one of the historical founders of German socialism in the 19th century. In the 1860s, he had embarked on a career as a political agitator, travelling throughout Germany. He made speeches and wrote pamphlets with the aim of sensitising and organising the working class. He came from a very prosperous family in Breslau (Wroclaw). Here is what the "English" novelist Israel Zangwill wrote in 1898 about his father and his brother-in-law, a certain Friedland:

"After leaving Berlin for Prague, where he had obtained the gas concession, Friedland, thanks to his overflowing hospitality and careful concealment of his Jewish origin, managed to slip in among well-born families of high social standing, even in the highest echelons of government circles. On the eve of receiving the Prague elite for dinner, old Father Lassalle unexpectedly came to visit his daughter and son-in-law. Each after the other begged him not to reveal that they were Jews. Annoyed, the old man did not answer. When all the guests were seated, old Lassalle rose to speak. Having obtained silence, he asked them if they were aware that they were sitting at a Jewish table.

- It is my duty to inform you that I am a Jew, that my daughter is a Jew and that my son-in-law is a Jew. I refuse that a deception should make me worthy of the honour of dining with you.

The well-behaved guests applauded the old man, but the master of the house, pale with confusion, never forgave him[57]."

In order to disguise themselves better, Jews are also in the habit of changing their surname, or rather transforming their original surname to give it a more local sound and to recognise each other. Albert Memmi, a well-known Jewish intellectual in France in the second half of the 20th century, had written on this subject: "Davidovitch is content to become David or Davideau, Vassilovitch becomes Vassile, Taïeb becomes Taié, etcetera. At the end of the war there were enough of them to give rise to a joke: these badly disguised people were called 'the mutilated of the surname'", and Albert Memmi added: "Sometimes the make-up is very elaborate, sometimes it is superficial, but almost always it is make-up and not a real transformation. Aaron becomes Nora: it's an equivalent investment, just a disguise. Nussembaum becomes Dunnoyer, Bronstein becomes Rochebrune and Swartzstein, Rochenoire: none of this is arbitrary

---

[57] Israël Zangwill, *Rêveurs de ghetto, tome II*, Éd. Complexe, 2000, p. 159

or complicated: it is a simple translation. Often, translations are very approximate[58]."

Jews love secrecy. But if you think about it, these dispositions come naturally to them, since they have so much to hide. What André Spire wrote in 1928 about the writer Marcel Proust's maternal grandfather was very revealing of this conspiratorial mentality: "His Jewish grandfather, that kindly old man, who, like many French Jews who had made their fortune under Louis Philippe and Napoleon III, had a passion for the theatre, knew a great many operas and operettas by heart, and was in the habit of singing them whenever the occasion arose. Thus, when he saw his grandson arrive home with a new friend whom he believed to be a Jew, he would hum between his teeth the air of the Jewess: "O God of our fathers", or "Israel, break your chains".

When the friend had a non-Jewish surname, like Dumont, for example, he would mutter, "Oh, oh! I distrust!" and then whisper, "Archers, on guard! Watch, silently and relentlessly." And when, after skilful questioning, he was certain of the newcomer's secret Jewish origins, he would whisper, "Yes, I am of the chosen race! Then, looking at his grandson with malice, he would say, "Of this timid Israelite, guide the steps here[59] !"

The famous American actor Kirk Douglas was born in 1916 in Amsterdam, New York. His parents had taken his father's older brother's name, "Demsky", as his surname. Kirk Douglas, whose full name at birth was Issur Danielovitch, then became Issur Demsky before being called Kirk Douglas, the actor's first and last name he took and made official: "I didn't know I was adopting such a Scottish name".

Kirk Douglas had been confronted with anti-Semitism from an early age: "There were very few Jews in the city of Amsterdam," he wrote. They posed no threat. I think there were only two Jewish families in Eagle Street, including ours. But they hated the Jews deeply, and the children were not to blame. The kids were not to blame. What do parents say when they are having dinner with their young children? What remarks do they make about "those Jews"...? Often, later on, I found myself talking to people who didn't think so, but I heard them say things like "He's a Jew with the prices". They had learned it from their parents... There was a time when if someone asked me if I was one, I would swallow my breath and say, "I'm half Jewish"... Being half Jewish didn't seem as bad to me as being Jewish at all. How sad[60] !"

In 1934, while still a drama student, he tried to get a job in hotels in the region, but was rejected several times. He then realised that he had to hide

---

[58] Albert Memmi, *Portrait d'un juif II*, Gallimard, 1966, p. 31.
[59] André Spire, *Quelques juifs et demi-juifs*, Grasset, 1928, p. 55, 56.
[60] Kirk Douglas, *The Ragpicker's Son* (1988), Cult Books, *2021*, p. 67, 32, 33

his origins: "I introduced myself as Don Dempsey. They gave me a job... The woman who ran the hotel was attractive and she liked me. She used to confess to me that there was something about Jews that she couldn't stand; she could spot them in a second, whatever their name or their appearance. They gave off a special smell... As the season drew to a close, the landlady became more and more interested in me. I had tried to keep my distance. The night before the hotel closed, my landlady was more attentive than ever. She suggested that we have a farewell drink in her room. As I climbed the stairs I was acutely aware of the end of the season she had planned. She spoke of my return the following summer. I thought of all the things I had heard her say: "Hitler is right, the Jews must be destroyed", "No Jew will ever set foot in this hotel". After a few drinks, we ended up in bed. Strange how aphrodisiacal hatred can be. My loathing turned into a tremendous erection and I pushed my penis inside her. She was wet and ready to receive me, extremely passionate in her moans and groans. I made sure that despite all the sounds she heard me clearly when I said in her ear: - Inside you is a circumcised Jewish cock, do you think you'll be contaminated, that you'll die infected? I'm a Jew. You're being fucked by a Jew! - I ejaculated. She didn't say a word; she was breathing heavily and was still lying down when I left the room[61]."

Evidently, the identity ambiguity of Judaism, Jewish mimicry, predisposes members of the 'community' to work as spies. Cases of espionage involving Jews are not rare, far from it[62]. See for example this case found in *The Testament of an Anti-Semite*, published by Edouard Drumont in 1891, a few years before the famous Dreyfus affair broke out[63] : "Michel, the clerk at the Ministry of War, who was guillotined on the Place de Grève in 1812 for having handed over the plans of military operations to the Russian ambassador, was a Jew. The clerk in charge of bringing every fortnight to the bindery a general report of the situation of all the arms and who delivered this report to Michel, was called Mosé, and the clerk in charge of the revisions, whose complicity had been confirmed, was called Salomon. Glaser, the German spy, was also a Jew. He had the courage to remain for many years in a minor job on the Northern Railways, to keep abreast of the smallest details, and during the war of 1870 he became Director General of the German Railways in Northern France. Lieutenant-

---

[61] Kirk Douglas, *The Ragpicker's Son* (1988), Cult Books, *2021*, p. 44-45
[62] See *Psychoanalysis of Judaism* and *Jewish Fanaticism*.
[63] The Dreyfus case originated in an allegedly anti-Semitic court ruling, against a background of espionage and anti-Semitism, in which the accused was Captain Alfred Dreyfus of Alsatian Jewish origin, and which, for twelve years, from 1894 to 1906, shocked French society at the time, marking a milestone in the history of anti-Semitism. (NdT)

Colonel Schmidt, who was hanged a few months ago in Russia for selling to England documents relating to the Russian fleet, was of Jewish origin. The Russians, moreover, have retained Napoleon's good manners in this respect, and are not content with half measures. The Russians distrust Jews like the plague and do not allow them to loiter in their areas of military operations[64]."

The famous and peerless Nazi hunter Simon Wiesenthal had also told us the story of Alex, "big, reddish-blond", with light eyes, whose father was Jewish, grandfather a rabbi and mother a Catholic. Alex had been raised in the Catholic faith. As a result of the racial laws of the Third Reich, he was declared half-Jewish, a "*Hatbjude*". His parents' best friend was a goy, a very famous doctor in Vienna and a close friend of his father's since university. They decided that Alex's mother would go and confess to the authorities that her real father was this "uncle", so that Alex would be recognised as an Aryan. In addition to protecting his father, Alex was able to enlist in the Waffen SS: "It was Uncle Franz's idea, and I agreed". After the war, in 1958, Alex, who was part of a *Kameradschaft* group, met with Simon Wiesenthal: "It's not enough for me. For the Jews I will remain a damned SS, for the others I will always be a 'filthy Jew'. If I am to be frank, I must accept that I will always be the eternal enemy, the bad guy. - I will tell you why I have come to see you, Herr Wiesenthal. I feel myself to be a Jew, and for me and for you, I am a Jew. But for the world I could still be an SS and help you in your work". One day, in the middle of one of his infiltration missions, Alex said to Wiesenthal: "I would like to become a Jew again officially, for the whole world, because that is the most authentic thing to do". And Wiesenthal wrote: "I was not at all surprised. I replied that yes, it was his thing and he had proved it, but I also told him that he could still do more for us if he remained for a while 'one of them'[65]."

We find this same uprooting of identity in Agneska Holland's film *Europa, Europa* (France-Germany, 1990): To escape the Nazi advance, Sally Perel, a Jewish teenager, abandons his family and takes refuge in a Soviet orphanage. When the Germans invade the USSR, he passes himself off as an Aryan. He then becomes the regimental mascot and is sent to a Nazi school where he must hide his Jewishness. After the invasion of Berlin, he manages to escape the execution squad by the skin of his teeth and goes to live in Israel.

In the name of all my people, Martin Gray presented another good example of the identitarian plasticity of Judaism. He recounts his traffics

---

[64]Edouard Drumont, *Le Testament d'un antisémite*, 1891, p. 98.
[65]Simón Wiesenthal, *Los asesinos entre nosotros*, (pdf) Editorial Noguer, Barcelona, 1967, p. 98, 100, 101. *The Red Orchestra* gave rise to the film by Jacques Rouffio (Fra. 1989).

within the Warsaw ghetto during the war: "I left as soon as the curfew was over... Several times a day I crossed the wall in both directions: I risked my life several times a day. But I lived, free... I already had contacts, links, habits, official suppliers in Aryan Warsaw. I also had false papers: a safe-conduct that had saved me once before. It certified that I lived on the Aryan side and that I was a young Pole of good race. It was cold, but my shirt collar was open: a small gold chain and a little medal of the Virgin Mary were visible. In the evening I studied the Latin mass and the main prayers: my life could depend on those few words that I kept repeating".

His accomplices were rather rough Poles: "I paid them well, they drank, they gorged themselves like never before". After a while, he became their leader: "I could hold those men only by what I gave them and by the esteem they might have for me, not by the fear I might inspire in them...I had to rule that gang by cunning, interest and friendship, not by fear[66]."

He then obtained false identity papers. From now on his name would be Schmidt: "Then I became a pretender and conjurer: when Polish officers approached, I abandoned my air of a gulf. From a small flat metal box in my left pocket, I took out my swastika armband, which had to be always clean and ironed, as befitted the master race, put it on my left arm and became Schmidt, arrogant, angry, haughty, speaking Polish with a German accent. And the "blues", those [Polish] gendarmes who were seen mistreating the Jews, hardly dared to control me. A few hundred metres further on, I had to be a gulf again: quickly taking off my *Volksdeutscher* armband, I regained the light gait of the Warsaw pimps. Then, once past the gate, if I got off the tram in the ghetto, I had to put on my Jewish armband, which I kept in my right-hand pocket. Thus, several times a day, I changed my face, my name, my personality, my language, but I always had to be alert, attentive to the way I had to represent the required personality... Thus I learned to have a double, a triple personality: it was as if I stood before a mirror, acted and watched myself act[67]."

The Jew seems to have the ability to easily transform himself into almost anything. It is the proteiform Jew, so well staged by Woody Allen in his film *Zelig* (1983). It is therefore not surprising to find that many theatre and film actors are of Jewish origin. It is precisely because they are devoid of self-identity that Jews are able to assume multiple identities. You have understood, in reality, Judaism can be summed up simply as words in the wind. This is what Jean-Paul Sartre had sensed, although he had understood nothing of the subject.[68]

---

[66]Martin Gray, *In the Name of All Mine*, Plaza & Janés, Barcelona, 1973, p. 67, 84, 85.
[67]Martin Gray, *In the Name of All Mine*, Plaza & Janés, Barcelona, 1973, p. 89, 90.
[68]Read in *Psychoanalysis of Judaism*.

While ignoring geographical, national and identity boundaries, the Jew also seems to ignore borders and social conventions. We have often seen prodigious social rises, and equally dizzying falls: The ghetto ragpicker, who became a multimillionaire in the next generation, commits suicide a few years later...

In the Middle Ages, Jews were already learning to disguise themselves and to climb. The famous letter that the Jews of Arles had written to the Jews of Constantinople in 1489 to complain about the miseries inflicted on them by the Christians is well known. This letter had been republished in a book printed in Paris in 1789, entitled *The Life and Testament of Michel Nostradamus*. We reproduce below the reply of the Jews of Constantinople, "translated from English into French":

"Beloved brethren in Moses, we have received your letter, in which you inform us of the hardships and misfortunes you are suffering; and the resentment of which has affected us as much as you; but the opinion of the greatest Rabbis and Satraps of our law is as follows:

"You say that the King of France wants you to be Christians; do so, for otherwise you cannot; but always keep the law of Moses in your hearts.

"You say that they want to take your goods from you; make your children merchants, and by means of trafficking you will gradually have all theirs.

"You complain that they are trying to take your lives; make your children doctors and apothecaries, for in this way they will make them lose theirs without fear of punishment.

"If you say that they destroy your synagogues, make your sons become canons and clergymen, for so they will ruin their churches.

"You say that you are suffering great vexations, make their sons lawyers and notaries, and persons who are engaged in public affairs, and by this means they will dominate the Christians, gain their lands, and take vengeance on them. Do not deviate from the order we give you, for you will see by experience that from how humiliated you are, you will be greatly elevated[69].*"*

The letter was signed as follows: *V. S.S.S. V. S. S. F.F., prince of the Jews of Constantinople. December 21, 1489.*

Instinctive solidarity

Jews manifest an instinctive solidarity towards their fellow human beings. This inclination can be seen first and foremost in the misplaced publicity

---

[69] *La Vie et le Testament de Michel Nostradamus*, Gattey Libraire de S. A. S Madame la Duchesse d'Orléans, Paris, 1789, p. 169-170.

and praise of certain journalists when they speak out to promote this or that artist, whom they do not hesitate to describe as "great".

Nahum Goldmann expressed the pride of the sons of Abraham and Jacob as follows: "Economically, they have played a leading role, especially since the Second World War, and intellectually, the three geniuses who have had the greatest influence on modern civilisation, Marx, Freud and Einstein, were Jews.

Goldmann asserted that Jewish identity is first and foremost a question of solidarity: "For me, a Jew is a man who was born Jewish or who converted to Judaism and who feels himself to be Jewish. That's all... A Jew assumes himself to be a Jew: he feels solidarity with the Jewish people, he identifies with their history and their destiny. For some, the central axis is religion. For others, the glory of the Jewish people, who have given the world monotheism, the prophets, Spinoza, Marx, Freud, Einstein and many other geniuses. And for others, respect for Jewish suffering in the past and present underpins their attachment to the Jewish cause: they consider it indecent and immoral to separate themselves from a people who have suffered such martyrdom in order to preserve their identity. There are therefore many motivations...But what is decisive is the will to remain Jewish[70]."

And he insisted again on the genius of the Jews: "Before Hitlerism, for a short century, Germany granted the Jews all rights and, in return, the Jews enriched that country in every way: literary, philosophical, musical, political, financial...Certainly, Hitlerism wiped out the German Jews, but it could do nothing against that manifold and incomparable contribution[71]."

We are all too familiar with the extravagant tendency of Jewish intellectuals to glorify the works of their own kind, even though, especially in literature, these are almost always of remarkable mediocrity. Listen, for example, to what Guy Konopnicki noted in 1983: "The most beautiful words in Paris are engraved in German on a grave in the Montmartre cemetery: "Passer-by, here are the bones of the wretched poet Heinrich Heine; how he would like them to be yours! André Spire wrote of Marcel Proust that "he was perhaps the greatest French novelist since Stendhal and Balzac[72]." We have also heard it said that Kafka was "the best German writer", or that Vassili Grossman was "the Tolstoy of the 20th century[73]."

For those who find it a little difficult to understand what Jewish solidarity means in everyday life, we reproduce here what can be read in an advertisement reserved by *Le Figaro littéraire* of 15 February 2007 for

---

[70] Nahum Goldmann, *Le Paradoxe juif*, Stock, Paris, 1976, p. 81-84.
[71] Nahum Goldmann, *Le Paradoxe juif*, Stock, Paris, 1976, p. 146.
[72] André Spire, *Quelques juifs et demi-juifs*, Grasset, 1928, p. 50.
[73] See in *Planetary Hopes*.

Yasmina Reza, a "French" playwright, about her new book entitled *Le dieu du carnage (The God of the Massacre)*: "She says more about our society than all the essayists of our time. She is our best contemporary author". Signed Etienne de Montety, *Le Figaro*. Franck Nouchi, *Le Monde*, "An extraordinary dialoguist, she resumes here with the inspiration that had so enthused Art's readers". "A brilliant text", wrote Gérard Stadelmaier in *Franfurter Allgemeine Zeitung*. Uplifting.

In the weekly *Marianne* of 20 May 2006, a review of American writer Philip Roth's latest book, *The Plot Against America*, was published: "In this case, there is no doubt that Philip Roth is a writer, and one of the greatest.... His best novel to date, the most easily accessible, certainly, but also the most oppressive, the most gripping. Everything comes together to captivate the reader, to convince him that, after all, things could have happened like this... Psychological finesse...Such a talented writer..." blah blah blah. The article was signed "A.L.". For our part, we found this novel very tedious. Moreover, it is a dishonest book, in which all the duplicity of the Jewish intellectual is very clearly reflected[74]. The truth is that Philip Roth was following in the footsteps of his Austrian predecessor Joseph Roth: same plumage, same branches.

Our readers are already familiar with Irene Nemirovsky, who was writing before the Second World War. Her novels contain some portraits of Ashkenazi Jews that we have used in our *Psychoanalysis of Judaism*. But, in any case, her writing talent is not that great, far from it. Nevertheless, Irene Nemirovsky has been propelled by her peers to the top of the bestseller list.

This is what Alexandre Adler's weekly *Le Courrier international* published on 4 May 2006 about her novel *Suite française*, which describes the exodus after the 1940 defeat and occupied France: "*Suite française*, Irene Nemirovsky's novel, is currently triumphing in the bestseller lists of Great Britain. This success shows that there is reason to have faith in the public's taste. It is very moving that this masterpiece should succeed more than sixty years after its Jewish author perished in Auschwitz [of typhus, ndlr]...Irene Nemirovsky's extraordinary novel paints a portrait of a society that did not behave with courage, honour or dignity. But, again, I doubt that we would have acted any better." The article was by one Max Hastings: a brave "Englishman", no doubt.

The novelist Irene Nemirovsky was born in Kiev in 1903. As her father was a banker, the family had decided that it was preferable to move to Paris at the time of the Bolshevik Revolution. So Irene Nemirovsky wrote all her novels in French. It is true that she was not very successful during her

---

[74] See in *Jewish Fanaticism*.

lifetime, which is perfectly understandable when you read her prose, but given that she came from a Jewish family that had suffered a lot, it was only natural that she should be given a special place in French literature. In 2005 she was posthumously awarded the Renaudot Prize, and since then it is impossible not to see her books ostentatiously displayed in cultural supermarkets, where she is always over-promoted.

Imre Kertesz is also a Jewish genius. A Hungarian-language Jewish writer, he was born in Budapest in 1929 and deported in 1944. He remained "in the shadows for forty years" until his powerful genius was finally recognised by the select team that awards Nobel Prizes. So Imre Kertesz, who still lives in Hungary, received the Nobel Prize for literature in 2002, as well as the cheque that goes with it. This is what we read about his book *Liquidation*, later published in 2004: "We are in Budapest in 1999. The writer B., who committed suicide shortly after the 1989 riots, still haunts the memories of his friends. Especially that of Keserü, a publisher desperate to publish the posthumous works of the admired author, but never succeeded. The publisher tries to get his hands on the novel he believes B. must have written about his origins, about the source of his unease. For B. was born in Auschwitz in 1944, in absurd circumstances, and without ever knowing his mother...In this moving masterpiece, Kertesz deals with the tragic aftermath of the tragedy he experienced early in his life."

We do not doubt for a moment that the experience of death camps can leave traumatic after-effects, especially when one manages to get out of them alive. But suffering does not automatically make a writer a genius, and Imre Kertesz's case seems prefabricated to us. Indeed, we have the vague impression that the awarding of Nobel Prizes is sometimes a matter of community solidarity. But perhaps that is just a figment of our imagination.

In January 2008, the left-wing weekly *Le Nouvel Observateur* sang the praises of Daniel Mendelsohn, a minor author, Jewish, American and homosexual: "Penetrating gaze and shaved head, he is a handsome and elegant young man. His French is almost perfect... Amidst the hullabaloo of the autumn literary awards, no one noticed that one book, in fact, dominated all the others, his: *Les Disparus (The Disappeared)*, winner of the Médécis foreign prize, and of which 120,000 copies have already been sold". This Mendelsohn's book, we were told, deserved this success because of "the originality of the treatment and the richness of the writing." And what was Mendelsohn talking about: "Mendelsohn spent several years researching the disappearance of a great-uncle who was massacred by the Nazis along with his wife and four daughters. His book, however, is not just another piece of Shoah history. It is first and foremost a literary work.... [blah blah blah]. It is for this communal solidarity that Jewish journalists are unfailingly recognised.

Among all the false literary glories engendered by cosmopolitan publicity in France at the turn of the millennium, the novelist Bernard Werber is at the head of the pack. He too is a great literary genius. However, on closer reading, one quickly realises that he is an enormous nullity, who evidently owes his success only to the shameless publicity he receives from his journalistic cronies who belong to the same sect as him. *Le Mystère des Dieux* (*The Mystery of the Gods*), published in 2007, is a silly story in which the friendly "dolphin-men" are persecuted by the evil "shark-men", inhabitants of "Osia", who burn books and want to reduce humanity to slavery.

The "democratic" press is also perfectly controlled by financiers. The influence of high finance on the press was revealed to us by Jean-Jacques Servan-Schreiber, founder of the weekly *L'Express* in the 1950s. This was his testimony in his autobiography *Passions*, published in 1991: "Marcel Bleustein, the great creator of Publicis, who accepted the idea of launching the newspaper, brought with him his old friend Marcel Dassault [Block, ndlr], the aeronautical genius and the richest man in France. Dassault hands me a cheque (signed Dassault at the Dassault bank) for five million francs. The intention is endearing. But, without wishing to offend him, I must nonetheless put a stop to any misunderstandings... and possible rumours.

-Mr Dassault, I am very touched, as is my entire team, by your friendly gesture. And I think we will often come to you for advice, but no cheques! I take the liberty of returning this one. We are relying on our own efforts and we will not be beggars. I hope you understand, with all our esteem and friendship.

"Dassault took back the cheque, a little sad. I console him and accompany him to his car, which is waiting for him on the Champs Elysées[75]." This was how the newspaper *L'Express* remained "free and independent". The paper would live mainly on advertising revenue. Marcel Bleustein's Publicis group became one of the largest advertising groups in the world.

Here is what the French nationalist Henry Coston[76] wrote in 1969: "The newspaper *Témoignage Chrétien*, which had not suffered for its stance

---

[75] Jean-Jacques Servan-Schreiber, *Passions*, Fixot, 1991, p. 204.

[76] Henry Coston (1910-2001) was a French journalist, editor and nationalist essayist. In the interwar period he became known as an "extreme right-wing", "anti-Semitic" and "anti-Mason" journalist and activist. A collaborator during the German occupation, he was condemned at the Liberation. After his release from prison, he resumed his career as a journalist and editor, which he pursued until the end of his life, specialising in the study of French politics and networks of influence: this earned him a reputation in nationalist circles as a leading author. He published a five-volume *Dictionnaire de la politique française* (4,000 pages on scandals, political profiling, turrets and opportunists who have populated the Fifth French Republic) and numerous books over the decades on the networks of influence of international high finance (*Los financieros que mueven*

against French Algeria, saw its advertising reduced to a minimum when its management and editorial staff adopted an unfavourable attitude towards Israel. "If you don't adopt the theses of Zionism," we read in its issue of 30 January 1969, "we curiously see the doors of advertising agencies being closed. Contracts already concluded in principle are suddenly cancelled...There was a time when a newspaper like "TC" did not need any advertising. It was even out of place because it was published in the form of clandestine booklets. It was the time when the militants of *"Témoignage Chrétien"* organised themselves and risked life and liberty to hide Jewish children wanted by the Nazis. The story is undoubtedly a strange one[77]..."""

Jewish solidarity is a self-evident fact, and this has been expressed by numerous communal intellectuals: "Everything in me aspired to full and fervent Jewish solidarity[78] ", wrote the novelist Arnold Mandel. In *The Gates of the Law*, a book published in 1982 with a preface by the Chief Rabbi of France, Ernest Gugenheim confirmed this state of mind: "Israel forms a united body whose members are closely united[79]."

Nahum Goldmann, for his part, quoted the famous verse from the Talmud: "A single Jew is like the whole of Judaism[80]." This is why Jewish intellectuals often write "the Jew" to speak of Jews.

But we also know that "the Jew" can deny the evidence with phenomenal aplomb. In his *Psychoanalysis of Anti-Semitism*, Rudolph Loewenstein explained that the supposed "solidarity" of the Jews was simply a popular belief: "Among the delusional beliefs of the anti-Semites," wrote Loewenstein, "is that of the solidarity of the Jews", a solidarity which impresses the anti-Semites "to such an extent that they come to regard them as an indissoluble whole, directed and governed by mysterious leaders, the legendary 'Wise Men of Zion', whose aim is universal subjugation". And Loewenstein added: "A corollary of this belief is the existence of a united international Jewish finance, of phantasmagorical wealth and power, working hand in hand with Jews of all professions. Anti-Semites claim that the diversity of political opinions, interests and nationalities among Jews is but a mirage designed to deceive naive Christians, that in reality all Jews are one and the same[81]."

No doubt, all this is completely "delusional". But nevertheless, in the same book, some hundred pages later (page 196), Loewenstein wrote about

---

el mundo and *La Europa de los banqueros*, translated into English). (NdT).
[77] Henry Coston, *Le Règne infernal*, 1970, 1995, p. 156.
[78] Arnold Mandel, *Tikoun*, Mazarine, 1980, p. 40
[79] Ernest Gugenheim, *Les Portes de la Loi*, Albin Michel, 1982, p. 45.
[80] Nahum Goldmann, *Le Paradoxe juif*, Stock, Paris, 1976, p. 43.
[81] Rudolph Loewenstein, *Psychanalyse de l'antisémitisme*, 1952, Presses Universitaires de France, 2001, p. 93.

"the" Jew: "He may feel totally different, but there is still a kind of secret bond between him and this other Jew, a bond in which each of them feels responsible for the actions of the other". But it is well known that contradictions are a rule among Jewish intellectuals, and it is not without reason that the word "paradox" appears regularly in their writings.

In his *Portrait of a Jew*, Albert Memmi wrote in his turn: "What anti-Semites write about Jewish solidarity is often flat out stupidity. In my former poor and oriental respect for Culture and the printed Word, it took me a long time to convince myself that people who write, teach, and publicly affirm this, could be so lying, so vain, so stupid, so calmly.... How could Jewish solidarity be so effective against non-Jews, when it is so vacillating and often so derisory on behalf of Jews themselves?" This appeared on page 251. But on page 284, Albert Memmi wrote: "The harder the oppression lasts, the more precise and nuanced the responses become, the stronger and more consolidated the institutions of defence become.... Jewish solidarity is also an undeniably positive fact of Jewish existence[82]." This is another "paradox" of Jewish thought.

Albert Memmi nevertheless acknowledged a reality: "Most of the avowed Jewish writers seemed to me to be of mediocre stature...I only had to leaf through a Jewish anthology of the time, that of Edmond Fleg, for example, to see the aesthetic poverty, the provincialism, the ineffectiveness in making themselves heard, of the vast majority of the texts collected". And he quoted Rabi: "It is a fact that, for all sorts of important reasons, the Jewish world...has always been rather poor in the field of pure literature[83]."

Augustin Hamon, on the other hand, was a real Breton, with a venerable old bearded head. He was the author of several books on anarchism and the translator of Georges-Bernard Shaw. He had joined the SFIO[84] and in 1944 the Communist Party, which did not prevent him from having his own convictions about the Jews. Here is what he wrote: "The Jews have only acquired their fortune by speculation, by legal robbery, celebrated by the whole rotten bourgeoisie. Not only are they useless to all, but they are a deadly plague on Society. They are like the octopus that clings to its victim and does not let go until there is not a drop of blood left (...) In science, they monopolise the places in the Academies and yet they have neither genius nor even unusual talent; they only know how to seize other people's ideas, assimilate them and proclaim loudly that they are the authors. That

---

[82] Albert Memmi, *Portrait d'un juif*, Gallimard, 1962, p. 251, 284.
[83] Albert Memmi, *Portrait d'un juif II*, Gallimard, 1966, p. 146.
[84] The French Section of the Workers' International (SFIO, in French: *Section française de l'Internationale ouvrière*), better known by its abbreviation SFIO, was the political party of the French socialists from its foundation in 1905 until 1969. Its name indicates its character as a national section of the Second International (Workers' International).

is how Maurice Lévy, Mr Loewy and so many others came to sit in the Academies. When it comes to art, the Jews do nothing but trade: their paintings, sculptures and music sell well, but they have only a conventional value, which they know how to increase by means of well-crafted publicity. No brilliant idea has yet come from the brain of a Jew[85]."

The Jew, alone against all

The Jewish people are alone, very alone in the midst of the nations. They love no one and no one loves them. "The Jews are a people to be admired, but difficult to love[86] ", Nahum Goldmann told us.

The Jewish community learned long ago to live in autarchy in order to avoid indiscriminate mixing with the Goyim. The writer Arnold Mandel, a literary medium, conveyed in one of his books this idea of a community turned in on itself, wary of outsiders.

"When a non-Jew, attracted by the faith of Moses, wants to convert, it is customary - and almost a law - to discourage him, to receive him badly and make him feel that he is in no way welcome. Only if he does not allow himself to be discouraged by the rebuffs, insists and returns to the charge, will the rabbis take his quest seriously and show him some benevolence. This tactic is intended to test the love of Israel and zeal for the Jewish faith of the candidate for the Covenant of Abraham[87]."

Nahum Goldman confirmed this: "Contrary to other religions, Judaism never proselytised. Judaism never proselytised, he wrote...The Talmud says that a *guer*, a convert, is as hard to bear as a plague[88]." "It is generally assumed that Judaism has never been a missionary religion and, if any proselytes joined it, they were accepted with extreme reluctance by the Jewish people. The famous Talmudic sentence: proselytes are a disgrace to Israel, is invoked to put an end to any attempt to discuss the subject[89] ," wrote Shlomo Sand. See also what Rabbi Zeira, an ancient rabbi who died in 247, said, expressing in turn the exaggerated distrust of Jews towards converts: "Do not humiliate the Gentiles before a man whose family converted less than ten generations ago[90]."

---

[85] Augustin Hamon and Georges Bachot, *L'agonie d'une société*, *Histoire d'aujourd'hui*, Paris, A. Savine Éd., 1889, p. 7-8, 240.
[86] Nahum Goldmann, *Le Paradoxe juif*, Stock, Paris, 1976, p. 142.
[87] Arnold Mandel, *Tikoun*, Mazarine, 1980, p.245
[88] Nahum Goldmann, *Le Paradoxe juif*, Stock, Paris, 1976, p. 81, 84.
[89] Shlomo Sand, *The Invention of the Jewish People*, Ediciones Akal, 2011, p. 167.
[90] Elie Wiesel, *Célébration talmudique*, Seuil, 1991, p. 323.

In *The Gates of the Law*, the great Rabbi Ernest Gugenheim noted: "This reticent, if not negative, attitude towards conversions endured in fact and doctrine; it remained traditional for two thousand years in the Diaspora[91]."

The Jewish community thus remained in tension for centuries, submerged and complacent in its ghetto. Rudolph Loewenstein acknowledged that the ghetto had been desired by the Jews themselves: "This institution, he wrote, was not only a prison imposed on the Jews, it was at the same time a guarantee requested by the Jewish communities themselves from indulgent sovereigns, a means of protection, a safeguard against possible mob violence. In the shelter of the protective walls of the ghetto, in this isolation from the hostile outside world, the Jewish communities could live and devote themselves to their occupations and to the strict observance of their religion[92]."

The ghetto is historically a Jewish invention," wrote Nahum Goldmann. It is not true that the gentiles forced the Jews to separate themselves from the other communities. When Christians confirmed the ghettos, Jews were already living in them. Of course, there is a difference between being free to choose your neighbours and being forced to live in a particular place that you cannot leave at night; but even today, Jews tend to live in their own neighbourhoods, in an environment that facilitates the life of their community. Before emancipation, things were cruel but simple; being, at most, tolerated, Jews lived on their own, unconcerned with the laws or customs of others. I often quote the brilliant expression of Heinrich Heine, who was a good Jew at the end of his life, and whose conversion to Christianity was a mere formality, his ticket into Western society. Heine asked himself: "What explanation can be given for the mystery of the survival of the Jews, without a homeland, without a state, without anything? And he answered: "It is because they have a real portable homeland in the Shulchan Aruch" (the collection of Jewish laws and prescriptions). It is true that when the Jews were expelled from one country, they went to another, but with the Shulchan Aruch under their arm. On this basis, they would very quickly create a new homeland".

Goldmann continued his exposition, in a very "paradoxical" way: "Today, with the exception of a small minority, Jews no longer live according to the Shulchan Aruch. They are politically emancipated and on an equal footing with others... The Jews are therefore fully integrated, and the difficulty lies precisely in maintaining their identity, their "separate" character. Or there will no longer be a Jewish people[93]."

---

[91] Ernest Gugenheim, *Les Portes de la Loi*, Albin Michel, 1982, p. 152.
[92] Rudolph Loewenstein, *Psychanalyse de l'antisémitisme*, 1952, Presses Universitaires de France, 2001, p. 220.
[93] Nahum Goldmann, *Le Paradoxe juif*, Stock, Paris, 1976, p. 83, 84.

The fight against intermarriage is therefore a priority. The Prime Minister of the State of Israel, Golda Meir, had stated it unequivocally, as one could read in the magazine *Informations d'Israël*: "The great tragedy of young Jews in affluent countries is that most of them do not understand that the greatest danger to Jewish life comes not from anti-Semitism and persecution, but from assimilation and intermarriage".

In 1960, during a conference of European Rabbis held in Britain, the following motion had been passed: "We consider it our solemn duty to warn our communities and every son and daughter of the Jewish people of the terrible danger of intermarriage, which destroys the integrity of the Jewish people and shatters Jewish family life[94]". We also find these statements in the *Tribune juive* of 29 October 1971: "Our own conception of the necessity of Jewish-Christian friendship and Jewish universalism does not involve intermarriage." In 1974, a full-page advertisement appeared in the *New York Times*. It said: "Intermarriage is national and personal suicide. It is the surest way to destroy a people to let them marry outside their faith..... The boys and girls are certain to lose their identity.... The accumulated experience of three thousand years, the rich heritage of a people, all that is strictly theirs will be ignobly annihilated. What a pity! What a disaster! What a shame[95] !"

In the Community weekly *L'Arche* of September 1980, the following words were written: "The haemorrhage is indeed considerable and the losses due to assimilation are equivalent to several trains bound for Auschwitz[96]."

These are not just statements by fundamentalist religious Jews. In October 1988, the magazine of the liberal Jewish *intelligentsia*, *Passages*, presented a model Jewish family in this way: "Mrs. R., like her husband and children, has only Jewish and practising friends...: "And the cleaning lady, is she Jewish too? Mrs. R. bursts out laughing: "Oh no, not at all!" And another thought from the lady: "It is enough for me to know that a girl of my origin sleeps with a non-Jew for this evocation to be unbearable for me".

Nahum Goldmann openly acknowledged: "The Jews are the most separatist people in the world. Their belief in the notion of a chosen people is the basis of their entire religion. Over the centuries, Jews have intensified their separation from the non-Jewish world; they have rejected, and continue to reject, intermarriage; they have erected one wall after another

---

[94]Quoted in *Anatomie du Judaïsme français*, p. 259-260.
[95]Yann Moncomble, *Les Professionels de l'anti-racisme*, Faits et Documents, 1987, p. 282.
[96]Yann Moncomble, *Les Professionels de l'anti-racisme*, Faits et Documents, 1987, p. 284-285.

to protect their existence 'apart', and they have built their own ghetto: their *shtetlj* [Jewish villages] in Eastern Europe, the *mellah* in Morocco[97]."

The former chief rabbi of France, Joseph Sitruck, had declared in 1993: "I wish that young Jewish men would only marry Jewish girls".

In *The Gates of the Law*, Ernest Gugenheim wrote with the blessing of the Chief Rabbi of France, Samuel-René Sirat: "What means are available to combat the danger of intermarriage? This education must begin in pre-adolescence; educators, teachers and rabbis must address this problem when preparing for the Bar Mitzvah, talk about it on every occasion, discuss it in youth circles and make sure that these circles multiply. Young people must be aware and proud of their belonging to Israel, of the value of the treasure they guard - get them to solemnly promise themselves that they will only marry a co-religionist[98]."

All these statements, which complement those we have already published in our previous books, do not prevent many Jews from marrying goyim. Sometimes their children are just as Jewish as they are, at least in spirit, but sometimes Jewishness is inexorably lost in the first generation, or in subsequent generations. This is really what has the rabbis so concerned.

Inbred marriages over several generations explain the frequent similarities in the physiognomy of Jews around the world. Liberal essayist Alain Minc, for example, and Paul Wolfowitz, one of the US government's "hawks" during the 2003 Iraq war, look like two drops of pus. In the same way that the face of Elie Wiesel's father looks remarkably like that of the Hungarian Bolshevik leader Bela Kun.[99]

This facilitated the appearance of anti-Semitic caricatures, especially before the Second World War, when cosmetic surgery did not yet exist and mixed marriages were less frequent. The "Jew" was depicted with certain attributes that were supposed to be characteristic of him[100] : big, curved nose, big ears, etc. Jewish writers themselves have left some striking portraits in their pages. The famous Yiddish novelist Isaac Bashevis Singer, for example, in one of his 1967 novels, portrayed an industrial magnate thus: "He was a short, stocky man, with a large head, axe-blade sideburns, aquiline nose and dark Jewish eyes.... With his rounded shoulders, high forehead, hooked nose and fleshy ears, Wallenberg had the typical Jewish

---

[97] Nahum Goldmann, *Le Paradoxe juif*, Stock, Paris, 1976, p. 16. The ghettos were desired by the Jews themselves, read in *The Jewish Mafia*

[98] Ernest Gugenheim, *Les Portes de la Loi*, Albin Michel, 1982, p. 148.

[99] We have published the photos on our website.

[100] Elie Wiesel, Albert Memmi, François Fetjö, Rudolph Loewenstein, André Neher and others often write "The Jew".

look. Short and stout, he had a head like a pumpkin, dark eyes and shining[101]..."

Here are some portraits written by David Vogel around 1940. Vogel, a second-rate novelist born in the Ukraine, had been deported after being caught up in the French debacle of 1940: "This Lehman was a strange character, a horse dealer and army contractor, a millionaire, a bachelor, a devout philanthropist. Tall and thin, the two features that stood out most in his face were an elongated nose almost to his chin and a pair of very small, short-sighted eyes". And further on, "Dr. Hoffenreich had come from Germany and was active in the Zionist Committee...His thin, long, hooked nose was one of those German Jewish nasal appendages that serve for anti-Semitic caricatures. His small, red-lidded eyes stared motionless, like two asymmetrical black dots drawn in charcoal by some painter[102]."

Albert Memmi quoted the writer Arthur Koestler: "The ugliness of the faces illuminated by the intermittent glare of the lighthouse struck Joseph. It was not the first time he had noticed it, but tonight his repulsion for the curved noses, fleshy lips and liquid eyes was particularly strong. At times he felt as if he were surrounded by antediluvian masks. Perhaps it was over-tiredness, or perhaps the heavy, sweet wine had gone to his head.... But he could not hide the fact that he hated them, and that he hated even more the features of this overripe race he recognised in himself[103]."

Certainly, certain traits are common in this community, which has always lived in isolation from other peoples. Inbreeding, taken to the extreme, can also be the source of many ills, including diseases and genetic defects.[104]

Jewish bankers also have a strong tendency to intermarry. The 1905 *Jewish Encyclpedia* noted that, of fifty-eight Rothschild marriages, twenty-nine had been between first cousins. The Warburgs, another famous Jewish banking dynasty, had strong family ties to the Schiffs and Rothschilds. The Warburg and Co had been founded in 1798 in Germany. A 1939 *Who's Who* review of the American Jewish community featured the ancestry of banker James Paul Warburg, born in Hamburg on 18 August 1896. On the paternal side, all were bankers for six generations. Paul Wargburg, his father, had married Jeny Nina Loeb, whose father, Salomon, founder of the Kuhn, Loeb and Co. bank, had emigrated to the United States in 1902. Jeny Nina Loeb had a sister, Theresa Loeb, who had married in the United States the banker Jacob Schiff, famous for financing Bolshevism in Russia. Jacob Schiff had a daughter, Frieda, who married Felix Wraburg, a Hamburg

---

[101] Isaac Barshevis Singer, *The House of Jampol*, Ed. digital German25, p. 13, 31
[102] David Vogel, *Todos marcharon a la guerra*, Xordica Editorial, Zaragoza, 2017, p. 126-127, 264-265.
[103] Albert Memmi, *Portrait d'un juif II*, Gallimard, 1966, p. 95.
[104] Read in *Psychoanalysis of Judaism*.

banker, Paul's brother, who in turn supported the new Bolshevik regime. His daughter, Carola, would marry Walter M. Rothschild.

The famous writer Arthur Koestler, who had been a fervent Bolshevik in his youth before the Second World War, later turned away from communism, and perhaps even from Judaism. What he wrote here is, as they say, common sense: "Thus, because of its own nationalism, Judaism isolates itself from the outside world. It automatically creates its own culture and ethnic ghetto. That is why it is impossible to be a Jew and a citizen of another nation at the same time. You cannot pray 'next year in Jerusalem' and at the same time stay in London or anywhere else[105]."

The prolific novelist Isaac Bashevis Singer, winner of the Nobel Prize for literature in 1978, also proved to be more consistent and probably more honest than most of his peers. "The Poles are fed up with us, and I must admit that I understand their point of view. We have been here for 800 years and we are still foreigners. Their God is not our God, their history is not our history[106]." One of his characters said, "Is it possible that there is anyone who pretends to enter a foreign home, live in it, in total isolation, and not suffer unpleasant consequences? When someone despises the God of his host, regarding him as a tin image, rejects his wine as forbidden, and condemns his daughters as impure, does he not ask to be treated as an undesirable foreigner? The problem is simple, as you can see[107]."

Under these conditions, it is understandable that many Jews, tired of living as strangers among other peoples, settled in Israel. The '*sabras*' were Jews born in the Hebrew state. The Yiddish novelist Joseph Erlich wrote about them in 1970: "I was especially proud of this young generation, the "*sabras*": proud Jews, liberated from the fear of discovering themselves different from others by their customs and faith, perpetual strangers among other peoples[108]."

---

[105] Arthur Koestler, quoted by J. Jehuda in *L'Antisémitisme, Miroir du Monde*, p. 268.
[106] Isaac Bashevis Singer, *Un jeune homme à la recherche de l'amour*, in Florence Noiville, *Isaac B. Singer*, Stock, 2003, p. 85
[107] Isaac Barshevis Singer, *The House of Jampol*, German25 digital ed., p. 31
[108] Joseph Erlich, *La Flamme du Shabbath*, 1970, Plon, 1978.

2. The mission of the Jews

The Jewish people are God's "chosen people". While this idea means nothing to the Goyim - the non-Jews - it is undoubtedly much more important to the Jews, who are convinced that they have a mission to fulfil in this world. This mission is to establish peace on earth ("shalom"), and this, according to them, will be absolute and definitive. Then, the Messiah they have been awaiting for so long can finally arrive. It is this "planetary" project that enables us to understand the basis of Jewish identity.

Messianic hope

The idea of "mission" has been expressed numerous times by intellectuals and leaders of the Jewish community. In his 1976 book, the founder of the World Jewish Congress, Nahum Goldmann spoke of a people "chosen by God" and "invested with a special mission": "That is why Jews were opposed to proselytising, he wrote. Even today, to become a Jew is quite difficult.... This is the great characteristic of our people; we are set apart, isolated from others and, at the same time, destined to fulfil a mission that concerns the whole world, to be the servants of mankind[109]."

Albert Memmi, who was quite famous in the 1960s, wrote: "The Jew was chosen by God to carry out a mission.... The Jew was preferred to all other peoples, and for an extraordinary mission". And he added: "The mysterious choice of a small people among all others, the sublime mission entrusted to him alone, the covenant of eternal alliance with God, shape for the Jew a destiny of glory, superb and demanding[110]."

Let us also listen to Théo Klein, former president of the Representative Council of Jewish Institutions in France (CRIF), talk about the "special mission" of the Jewish people. According to him, this people is "the bearer of an idea, of a project which it must strive to put into practice.... In my opinion, he said in 2003, this project is universal. Reread Genesis chapter 18, verse 18. Does it not say of Abraham that he will form a "great and mighty nation, and in him all the nations of the earth shall be blessed[111] "?"

---

[109]Nahum Goldmann, *Le Paradoxe juif*, Stock, Paris, 1976, p. 83, 84.
[110]Albert Memmi, *Portrait d'un juif II*, Gallimard, 1966, p. 124, 127.
[111]Théo Klein, *Dieu n'était pas au rendez-vous*, Bayard, 2003, p. 69.

In *The Gates of the Law,* published in 1982, the great Rabbi Ernest Gugenheim also quoted the Torah in support of his arguments: "They shall be to me a kingdom of priests and a holy nation (Exodus, XIX, 6)". "The Torah is addressed to a kingdom of priests, to a holy nation chosen from among the nations; this choice is for the good of mankind, for 'indeed, the whole earth is mine' (Exodus, XIX, 5)."

David Ben Gurion, the first leader of the Hebrew state, was equally steeped in the Jewish sacred texts: "The messianic vision of the Prophets, a vision of universal peace and redemption, has never left the heart of the Jewish people...Their mission among the nations has been defined by the divine promise to the first of the patriarchs: a blessing for all the nations of the earth". And Ernest Gugenheim stressed, "This is the meaning of Israel's election, called to lead humanity as a priest[112]."

The mission of the Jews is to establish "Peace" in the world ("shalom"). So it is up to every Jew to work towards this goal, for these conditions are simply indispensable to achieve what is even more important: the coming of the Messiah[113]. Let us look at what Esther Benbassa wrote in 2007 in her book *Suffering as Identity*: "Hope for the future is omnipresent in the Bible. Isaiah and Jeremiah prophesy the coming of a king of the house of David, whose reign will be a happy one". And he added: "Messianism includes both the idea of a restoration and that of a utopia...: the establishment of universal peace made possible by the adherence of the nations to the worship of the one God[114]."

Jacques Attali, a very influential and omnipresent intellectual on the French media scene, nourished the same messianic hopes: "God has entrusted us with the mission to save men and to speak in His name". And when, in Jerusalem, Solomon's Temple is rebuilt, then the Messiah can come: "Then the world can prepare itself for a perfect time[115]."

In every age, the Jewish community has spawned prophets predicting great cataclysms and terrible suffering, as well as the advent of a final peace on earth. In the 1970s, the physician Alexandre Minkowski also came at one point to believe himself to be a prophet of Israel. After an appearance on the radio, he was warmly congratulated by some of his peers: "My enthusiasm reached its peak when they concluded that men like me had a mission to fulfil. Prophet! My mother's secret dream, like that of all Jewish mothers, by the way. For perhaps the first time in my life, and hopefully

---

[112]Ernest Gugenheim, *Les Portes de la Loi*, Albin Michel, 1982, p. 40, 47, 49.

[113] Active messianism, progressively secularised and political, stems from the esoteric and kabbalistic interpretation of Judaism, developed from the 16th century onwards. See *Psychoanalysis of Judaism*.

[114] Esther Benbassa, *La Souffrance comme identité*, Fayard, 2007, p. 83.

[115] Jacques Attali, *Il viendra*, Fayard, 1994, p. 82.

the last, I took myself completely seriously. I had a lot of pretensions and the fumes went to my head. I saw myself as a kind of missionary travelling the world to preach peace[116]."

Listen also to the voice of the great Elie Wiesel: "For thirty years I have been travelling the continents to the point of exhaustion: by dint of speaking at conferences I have reached the point where I can no longer bear the sound of my voice...I could see myself travelling the Earth, going from city to city, from country to country, like the madman in Rabbi Nahman's stories[117]."

Peace can only be achieved when people are no longer divided by racial, national, social or religious differences. Nahum Goldmann wrote at the beginning of his book: "The grandiose, almost inconceivable idea of one God for all mankind is the brilliant creation of Judaism. No other people had the courage and boldness of spirit to conceive this revolutionary notion. The thinkers of no other religion have so passionately proclaimed the equality of all races and social classes, of masters and slaves, rich and poor, before God." Goldmann naturally advocated the disappearance of nation-states: "By nature, I hate the police, the omnipresence of government, the absolutism of the state. I dream of living in a society in which the State would be abolished and in which everyone would act in accordance with others.... The ideal of messianic peace is great, the ideal of eternal reconciliation is great, the idea of equal justice for all is great[118]."

Manes Sperber, another intellectual of the 1970s, also expressed this Jewish messianism which structures the mental and religious universe of Judaism: "Israel, alone among all peoples, drew its strength from an eschatological hope, from the expectation of a future, near or distant, which, in the midst of the greatest catastrophes, assured its survival. The Law that confronted it with the pagan world was a heavy burden, but to protect it against the seductions and dangers, Israel had for itself the Promise: without prophetic messianism, Israel was inevitably lost[119]."

This messianic hope is the driving force of Judaism, for it induces a militant activism of all Jews to hasten the coming of the messiah. It is precisely from this messianic tension that Jews draw their strength and energy. Indeed, it is the Jews themselves who, through their militancy and their tireless egalitarian propaganda for a world without borders, can bring about this world of "Peace" and the coming of the messiah. That is why they are so numerous in all the media, wherever the people have granted them equal rights. That is why so many Jews threw themselves

---

[116] Alexandre Minkowski, *Un juif pas très catholique*, Ramsay, 1980, p. 139.
[117] Elie Wiesel, *Mémoires, tome II*, Éditions du Seuil, 1996, p. 214, 530.
[118] Nahum Goldmann, *Le Paradoxe juif*, Stock, Paris, 1976, p. 16, 139, 140.
[119] Manès Sperber, *Être Juif*, Odile Jacob, 1994, p. 114, 136.

wholeheartedly into the Bolshevik adventure, and why so many Jews have become the most ardent propagandists of globalism and the multicultural society. The disappearance of nations and the unification of the world are part of the same egalitarian programme that inspired in the past the Marxist doctrines, which also dreamed of abolishing social classes and the differences between bourgeois and proletarians.

Stéphane Hessel was one of these super-militant Jews. In the 1990s, he had been appointed mediator with the illegal immigrants (which the media called "sans papiers") who were arriving en masse on European soil. In 2008, at the end of his life, he wrote his biography, eloquently entitled *Citizen without borders*. At the end of his book, he published the text of one of his lectures delivered in New York on 5 February 2002 under the title *Appel pour le Collegium international* (*Appeal for the International Collegium*): "We believe it is necessary to work today for the birth of a global citizenship and, in the long term, of a global democracy, the only way to provide a basis of democratic legitimacy to the ecological, health, social and economic regulations that have become indispensable[120]."

There are countless similar statements by Jewish intellectuals calling for the unification of the world, and we refer the reader to our previous books. Among Jews, this messianic hope is truly an obsession and seems to motivate all their actions. Georges Charpak, winner of the 1992 Nobel Prize in Physics, who published an essay on the dangers of nuclear energy, ended his interview in *Le Figaro* on 13 October 2005 with these words: "We must learn to overcome short-sightedness, national egoism and the logic of immediate interest. On nuclear matters and weapons of mass destruction, I am firmly in favour of abandoning all obsolete notions of absolute national sovereignty".

This is also what leads us to believe that the current French President, Nicolas Sarkozy, is undoubtedly a hidden Jew, a "crypto-Jew". His maternal origins are evident behind his Catholic façade. On 25 September 2007, in his speech to the United Nations General Assembly, he relaunched the idea of a new world order: "On behalf of France, I call on all states to unite in founding the new world order of the 21st century, based on the powerful idea that the common goods of humanity must be placed under the responsibility of humanity as a whole".

In the same spirit, James Warburg, son of Paul Warburg, who was one of the financiers in the service of the Bolsheviks, prophesied on 17 February 1950 before the US Senate Foreign Relations Committee: "We will have a world government, whether we like it or not. The question is only whether we shall have it by consent or by conquest".

---

[120]Stéphane Hessel, *Citoyen sans frontières*, Fayard, 2008, p. 298.

This globalist project is the one that Jews all over the world have been professing to us for centuries. At the end of the 19th century, Herman Cohen, a German Jewish thinker, had also explicitly written that "the messianic future will require the unification of all peoples in a confederation of states[121]."

This messianic project of world unification has been the stimulus, the sting of all the Marxist doctrinaires of the 19th and 20th centuries, who, from Karl Marx to Jacques Derrida, via Trotsky or Georges Lukacs, almost all came from "the community"[122].

In the issue of 9 February 1883, the "English" weekly *The Jewish World* wrote in its pages: "The dispersion of the Jews has made them a cosmopolitan people. They are the only truly cosmopolitan people, and in this capacity they must and do act as dissolvers of all distinctions of race or nationality. The great ideal of Judaism is not that the Jews should one day assemble in some corner of the earth for separatist purposes, but that the whole world should be permeated with Jewish teaching and that, in a universal brotherhood of nations, all separate races and religions should disappear[123]."

Indeed, Judaism is a dissolving power. Unlike Christianity or Islam, the Jews do not seek to convert others to Judaism, but simply to make them renounce their religion, their race, their identity, their family and all their traditions in the name of "Humanity" and the "Rights of Man". The global empire can only be built on the remains of the great civilisations, built with the human dust produced by democratic societies and the mercantile system.

The war against nations: immigration and miscegenation

There are different ways of "pacifying" nations and men. One can use intensive bombing, or communist totalitarianism (or oligarchic collectivism in "democracy"). But continuous immigration, miscegenation and consumer society reap better rewards in the long run. The destruction of nations is part of this "world pacification" programme. The "new philosopher" Bernard-Henri Lévy declared, for example, in an interview with the daily *France-Soir* on 24 April 1979: "Bravo to everything that

---

[121] Esther Benbassa, *La Souffrance comme identité*, Fayard, 2007, p. 111.
[122] See Hervé Ryssen, *Planetary Hopes* (chap: *Trotskyist Messianism*).
[123] Léon de Poncins, who had dusted off this article in 1965, stated: "I personally checked the accuracy of this quotation at the British Museum". Léon de Poncins, *Le Problème Juif; Face au Concile*, 1965 (brochure).

contributes to breaking down the reactionary mythologies of nation-states, of the patriotic nationalism of the France of terroir, bagpipes and folklore".

Thirty years later, his convictions have not budged one iota. He is still enthusiastic about the supranational and federal Europe under construction. Here is what he told the newspaper Le *Nouvel Observateur* on 4 November 2007, at the launch of his latest book: "I am a convinced cosmopolitan. I love mixing and I hate nationalism. I don't vibrate to the *Marseillaise*. I hope that one day the national framework will be overcome. And one of the main merits of Europe, as I see it, is that it works as a machine to cool down this national passion".

Alain Minc is a liberal Jewish intellectual, also very influential in French society at the end of the 20th century. In his book entitled *Epistle to our masters*, published in 2002, Alain Minc (actually read Elie Minkowski), launched a feverish appeal for immigration as an imperative necessity: "We will need new immigrants. This is not a long-term prophecy but an almost immediate reality". In reality, it is above all a question for Jewish intellectuals of favouring as much as possible the dissolution of the European peoples in order to protect themselves from a nationalist reaction. At the end of his book, Alain Minc reminded us once again, in case we had forgotten, that immigration was "economically necessary". Finally, the liberal intellectual made himself the champion of European citizenship and globalism: "The day we collectively convince ourselves that we are a canton on the scale of the world, everything will be simpler[124]".

The former right-wing prime minister, Jean-Pierre Raffarin, a pot-bellied[125] potevinist with the air of a Turkish communist militant, repeated the same lenifying and dissolving discourse: "The France of the 21st century is mixed race. France is mixed race and will remain so", he declared in October 2002. And on 7 May 2002, on Radio *France-Inter*, he insisted bluntly: "I want to appoint French people of Maghrebi or African origin to symbolic posts: school directors, prefects, police commissioners. I want to allow foreigners to vote in municipal elections".

In 2003, another former prime minister of Jewish origin, Laurent Fabius, a socialist and millionaire, declared: "When the Marianas in our town halls have the beautiful face of a young French woman of immigrant origin, then France will have taken a step forward in fully embracing the values of the Republic".

In the same vein, Nicolas Sarkozy, whose mother was born in Mallah, and who would become President of the Republic a few months later, declared in his investiture speech at the Liberal Party Congress on 14 January 2007:

---

[124] Alain Minc, *Epître à nos nouveaux maîtres*, Grasset, 2002, p. 98, 245, 260.
[125] Originally from the Poitou region.

"I want to be the President of a France that understands that creation lies in mixing, in openness and in encounter; I am not afraid of the word, in miscegenation".

On Sunday 19 December 2007, on France 2 television, invited by the presenter Michel Drucker, he said once again: "France must open up to others. We must not be afraid of those who are different. Inbreeding is the end of a civilisation. And in his 2006 book *Témoignages*, on page 280, he wrote: "I believe that the French are waiting for the France of the future..., a France in which the expression "French with roots [126] " will have disappeared". A few years earlier, in 2004, he had already warned us: "France must remain a country of immigration. I believe in mixing, in miscegenation, in the meeting of cultures".

Here are other extracts from Nicolas Sarkozy's famous speech in Dakar on 29 July 2007: "Young people of Africa, do not fall into the temptation of purity because it is a disease, a disease of intelligence, and it is the most dangerous thing in the world.... Young people of Africa, do not separate yourselves from what enriches you, do not separate yourselves from a part of yourselves. Purity is a fantasy that leads to fanaticism..... Civilisations are only as great as their participation in the great intermingling of the human spirit". And Sarkozy continued: "The weakness of Africa, which has known so many brilliant civilisations on its soil, was for a long time that it did not participate sufficiently in this great interbreeding. Africa has paid dearly for this disengagement from the world, which has made it so vulnerable. But from its misfortunes, Africa has drawn new strength by mixing with itself. This mixing, whatever the painful conditions under which it has taken place, is Africa's real strength and opportunity at a time when the world's first civilisation is emerging.... Open your eyes, young Africans, and no longer see the world as a threat to your identity, but world civilisation as something that belongs to you too."

With this kind of grandiose cosmopolitan invitation, one can see the extent to which miscegenation is a real obsession for Jews, although it must also be understood that this discourse is a product exclusively reserved for export and not for the chosen community. Nicolas Sarkozy, for example, married Jewish women: first Cecila Cziganer Albeniz, who has Romanian origins, and then Carla Bruni, an Italian Jew.

Twenty years earlier, the Romanian-born former minister Lionel Stoleru had also expressed this obsession of the Jews with dissolving national identity. In his 1982 book *France at Two Speeds*, he wrote: "There is, to name but a few, an Asian culture even older and perhaps more refined than ours; there is a South American culture where death and violence coexist

---

[126] *Français de souche*, as opposed to *Français de branche*, French for branch (NdT).

peacefully with tenderness and fraternity. There is an African culture where the warmth of the sun and human warmth have merged into a single melting pot. France can be Europe's wide-open door to these cultural currents that we still know too little about. It can be the "Theatre of Nations", the stage on which the sordid and grandiose history of the human race is played out[127]."

In the early 1980s, the former communist Guy Konopnicki was one of the first to realise that the American liberal model would make it possible to establish a multicultural society much more quickly and successfully than the communist system. In left-wing discourse, this aspect of the issue often dominates over economic considerations and the critique of inequality-creating liberal capitalism. The very progressive Konopnicki thus praised the American model and encouraged the multi-ethnic society: "A new culture is emerging in La Courneuve and in Meudon-la-Forêt, a way of being that ignores origins and borders.... This mix is American-cosmopolitan: Vitry is now closer to Harlem than to Castres[128]."

But most other "progressive" Jewish intellectuals only began to turn to the right after the incidents with young Afro-Maghrebi immigrants in the French suburbs that erupted during the second Palestinian Intifada in September 2001. Left-wing intellectuals then mutated into supporters of the 'hard' right: for them it was not a matter of expelling the millions of immigrants they had brought into France with their ideological discourse, but of forcibly consolidating the multiracial society they had helped to build.

Enrico Macias is a French singer of Algerian origin. This Sephardic Jew, who sings of universal brotherhood, had his glory days in the 1970s and 1980s, but still appears from time to time on television sets at the beginning of the 21st century. The left-wing singer supported Nicolas Sarkozy, the pro-Zionist, pro-American liberal candidate during his presidential campaign in 2007. In an interview with the free daily *20 Minutes*, the journalist asked him: "Do you still define yourself as a man of the left? To which Macias replied: "Of course I do. I am on the left, but I support Sarkozy because he is an extraordinary man. In fact, I supported him at a time when everyone was criticising me. Macias went on to cite the example of some of his colleagues who had also changed their jackets: "Look at Dominique Strauss-Kahn, Jack Lang, Bernard Kouchner, all those important men in the Socialist Party who work with him. In fact, like them, if he offered me a mission, I would accept it".

---

[127] Lionel Stoleru, *La France à deux vitesses*, Flammarion, 1982, p. 246.
[128] Guy Konopnicki, *La Place de la nation*, Olivier Orban, 1983, p. 175.

On immigration issues, of course, right-wing policy is almost identical to left-wing policy. It continues to bring in more immigrants and regularise illegal immigrants, thus accentuating the "pull effect". Enrico Macias then went to see his colleague Sarkozy: "He listened to me and solved a hundred cases that I entrusted to him".

Enrico Macias is also a very rich businessman. He invested his millions in the Partouche casinos. Perhaps he could share some of it with the native French in misery. But as we all know, a Jew reasons and acts only in the interest of the Jewish community. And his interest, clearly, is not to help us, but to dissolve us.

In the 1970s, the doctor Alexandre Minkowski worked to "pacify" the French by injecting as many minorities as possible into the national body. In the hospital where he practised, he always gave priority to recruiting foreigners, to the detriment of the French: "I already had a Syrian, an Israeli, two Algerians and an Indonesian Muslim in my unit, and they all worked perfectly well together. So why not add a few Palestinians? Ten or twenty of them came to the hospital, all doctors, with the exception of a Palestinian Christian social worker[129]."

In his cheap novel published in 1980, Arnold Mandel made an apology for miscegenation for the goyim. It featured a Frenchwoman and an Arab. After the French defeat in June 1940 in Marseilles, the French-Arab couple, Germaine and Ali "used to fight and copulate noisily...Germaine and Ali woke up and made love, powerfully vocalising their consensus[130]."

Twenty years later, the obsessions of Judaism are still the same. Dr. Georges Federmann, a psychiatrist from Strasbourg, considers the Roma as brothers, or at least cousins. A militant democrat and humanist, a member of "anti-racist" associations, he is very involved in the fight for the Roma and the "sans-papiers". "I'm waiting for the messianic period, but I'm working my ass off to get there[131]", read an article published in the *Dernières Nouvelles d'Alsace* on 21 January 2003. Federmann served as a model for the main character in Tony Gatlif's film *Swing*, which tells the story of a doctor who treats gypsies free of charge. However, on Tuesday 15 November 2005, newspapers reported that the renowned psychiatrist had had some trouble with one of his protégés. The psychiatrist, known for his stance in favour of the disadvantaged, was seriously wounded along with his wife and his assistant. He was shot four times in the body. The perpetrator of the attack was a 57-year-old man who was said to have

---

[129] Alexandre Minkowski, *Un juif pas très catholique*, Ramsay, 1980, p. 163.
[130] Arnold Mandel, *Tikoun*, Mazarine, 1980, p. 60, 64
[131] The French expression used is: *Je me casse le cul pour qu'elle arrive;* literally "I bust my ass to get her to arrive", more ordinary and vulgar.

serious psychiatric problems. Dr. Federmann, on the other hand, was perfectly sane.

Jewish intellectuals also regularly display a certain penchant for uttering enormous falsehoods. This readiness to take the goyim for mentally retarded, such foolhardiness is called in the Jewish community "*chutzpah*" (in German Yiddish) - pronounced "chutzpah[132]".

In March 2008, the magazine *Géo Histoire* published, for example, a three-page interview with demographer Gérard Noiriel, a specialist in the history of immigration and director of studies at the Ecole des Hautes Etudes en Sciences Sociales (a very comfortable position). The interview was entitled: *The identity fantasy*. Here is a paragraph: "Based on his research, the historian points out that immigration has never been so low in France in the last 150 years. In 2007, it had not increased significantly for more than thirty years. The INED (National Institute for Demographic Studies) statistics confirm this: there are fewer foreigners today than in 1997". As a good Jew, Gérard Noiriel concluded: "It is important to deconstruct this notion: France[133]."

While many left-wing intellectuals and politicians have joined the ranks of the liberal right at the beginning of the 21st century, conversely, many "liberals" have long maintained an obvious sympathy for far-left revolutionary movements. All this is perfectly natural once it is understood that, for these cosmopolitan minds, the most important thing is to work for a multicultural society and a world government.

Paul-Loup Sulitzer, a very successful businessman and novelist, who was also very liberal, told his story: "I took part in the lyrical farándula of May '68. I am far from feeling left-wing or revolutionary. But I hate stagnation. If I had been a Russian in 1917, I would probably have wanted to throw off the Tsarist yoke". He continued: "People and society have to keep moving; movement is life. You have to revise your own positions every day, refuse to become stagnant, to stand still[134]."

The very liberal Alain Minc, in turn, exalted the events of May '68: the "liberating shock of May '68[135]", as he defined it. The political project of

---

[132] The word also passed from Yiddish into Polish (*hucpa*), German (*chuzpe*), Dutch (*gotspe*), Czech (*chucpe*) and is very commonly used in Alsatian and Spanish-Argentine, where it acquires a clearly negative connotation and invariably refers to arrogance, impudence, impudence, disinhibition, lack of shame or conscience, of superego or self-repression, and of respect for the most elementary expected rules or norms. Apparently, the word is used in California courts of law (source: wikipedia). (NdT)

[133] Alain Minc, Guy Sorman, Jack Lang made similar comments, see our previous books.

[134] Paul-Loup Sulitzer, *Laissez-nous réussir*, Stock, Poche, 1994, p. 37, 38

[135] Alain Minc, *Epître à nos nouveaux maîtres*, Grasset, 2002, p. 67.

communism was exactly the same as that of the international financiers: to dissolve national identities, erase human and economic borders, abolish national freedoms and use all possible means to promote the unification of the world and the establishment of a world government.

The Jews are literally obsessed with the dissolution of nations and world unification, it is their hobbyhorse, the *sine qua non of* the coming of their messiah. Just read, for example, what the aforementioned Jean-Jacques Servan-Schreiber, founder of the bourgeois weekly *L'Express*, wrote in 1953. In a small book entitled *The Awakening of France, May-June 1968*, Servan-Schreiber also exalted the spirit of May '68, excusing students who had spat on the tomb of the unknown soldier: "It is quite obvious, he wrote, that the students did not spit on that wretch, who in his anonymity represents so well all those who, like him, have died in atrocious wars. They were attacking the monstrous stupidity of the eternal system of national sovereignty, set up as a supreme value, which drags war and hatred with it as the cloud drags the storm". And he insisted, with that characteristic formidable *chutzpah*: "This is perhaps the first really serious tribute paid to the unknown man in Star Square[136]."

In his book *The Undertakers*, published in 1993, Jean-Jacques Servan-Schreiber himself elliptically expressed this feverish expectation of the Jewish messiah: "To reach this fully realised society of individual fulfilment, we will have to leave the ancestral order... it will take a long time, and we will find it hard to bear these slownesses that dismay us[137]."

Left or right, for these cosmopolitan spirits, are only two slightly different ways of achieving the same goal. In September 2008, the US elections pitted a black Democrat, Barack Obama, against a white conservative, John McCain. Listen to this account by a banker in the 4 September issue of *Le Nouvel Observateur*, the left-wing weekly edited by Jean Daniel (Bensaïd). Claude Weill's article was entitled *A black man in the White House?* Claude Weill presented Barack Obama: "He is the American dream incarnate. An illustration of the values of openness and mixed race that have made America great. The country where everything is possible... The man who will slay America's demons and allow it to reconnect with the best of its tradition. Of course I'm going to vote for Obama," a well-groomed conservative [Jewish] banker tells me, "I don't want to miss this historic moment".

In reality, the division between the supporters of the "left" and the "right" has long since disappeared. It is a gigantic struggle between, on the one hand, the Jews and the supporters of the global Empire and, on the other

---

[136] Jean-Jacques Servan-Schreiber, *Le réveil de la France, mai-juin 1968*, Denoël, 1968, p. 88.
[137] Jean-Jacques Servan-Schreiber, *Les Fossoyeurs*, Fixot, 1993, p. 59.

hand, the peoples and all the defenders of the traditional world and local freedoms. In fact, the situation has become clearer since the fall of the Berlin Wall in 1989 and the collapse of the Soviet Union.

In 1992, the "new left-wing" philosopher Bernard-Henri Lévy pointed out his convergence of views with Alain Minc, a liberal intellectual, but obviously without explaining the origin: "We often have the same reflexes. Similar sensibilities... A vision of the world which, on most subjects, leads us to be on the same wavelength[138]."

This convergence of views was also evident in the historical collusion between international finance and the Bolshevik movement. Let us recall for example how, in 1918, the famous banker Max Warburg found himself confronted by the Spartacists, whose leaders were all sons of the "chosen people". This is what we read in Jacques Attali's book on the Warburg family: "On 5 November 1918, a revolutionary committee seized power in Hamburg. Max Warburg's aura is such that the committee, having taken him hostage and pressured him to say where the city's money is, protects his family, invites him to lunch in the town hall and listens to him as an adviser.

Communist Jews apparently had great respect and sympathy for their fellow bankers. Jacques Attali then confirmed that Judaism is not so much a religion as a political project. Max's son Sigmund Warburg "was an agnostic with a very religious spirit. He always identified himself with the cause of Judaism as a moral force[139]". Israel interests him, and he only helps what he believes in...". the Weizmann Institute, and in London the *Jewish Observer*, because he is a liberal". Sigmund Warburg "claims to be a citizen of the world" and "his religiosity blends with his life, although he is too universalist to adhere to a single faith[140]", Attali added in his biography.

---

[138] Bernard-Henri Lévy, *Le Lys et la cendre*, Grasset, 1996, p. 16, 233, 470.

[139] Jacques Attali, *Sir Sigmund G. Warburg, Un Homme d'influence*, Fayard, 1985, Poche, p. 329.

[140] Jacques Attali, *Un hombre de influencia*, Seix Barral, Barcelona, 1992, p. 101, 347, 348. [Siegmundo Warburg was one of the most influential bankers of the second half of the 20th century. "His universalism makes him return a little to his Jewish identity... He devours books by Elie Wiesel, such as *The Night*, which he reads in German and likes, he says, for its "ethical value". He explains to his friends that he is neither Zionist nor anti-Zionist, but that Israel's affairs interest him more than in the past. He is often seen with Nahum Goldmann, to whom he feels very close. More passionate about morality and law than about a soil, he hardly tolerates the idea that a Jew might not be as demanding as, in his opinion, the Book [the Torah] demands...But he does not want to harm Israel, and apparently stops financing a magazine published in London, the *Jewish Observer and Middle-East Review*, when it becomes too hostile to Jerusalem." In *A Man of Influence*, Seix Barral, p. 405].

In 2008, Bernard-Henri Lévy could not have been clearer: Judaism is not just a religion: "Apparently, what most people find difficult to understand is that Judaism is not a religion. The word *"religion"* does not exist in Hebrew... And if the word does not exist, if it does not appear in the book of the Talmud nor does it appear in the mouths of the sages and teachers who have forged the greatness of the oral law... it is because the thing itself does not exist either... Do you know that "synagogue", for example, *Beit Knesset*, means house of assembly and not house of prayer? Do you know that the Torah designates less a breviary, a missal, a prayer book, than the constitution (truly the constitution, in the proper, almost political or, at any rate, civil sense of the word constitution) given to Moses to his people after receiving the Tablets?...Do you know that there were, even in the twentieth century, within what you would call the world of belief and faith, eminent teachers (I am thinking of Rav Kook[141]) who maintain that atheism is not a problem for Judaism; that it is even a perfectly serious and admissible hypothesis[142]." Indeed, we must repeat it again and again, Judaism is first and foremost a political project.[143]

Cosmopolitan propaganda I: the multiracial society

It is extremely rare that a Jewish writer, filmmaker or producer does not try to convey a message in his or her essay, novel or film. For the general public, this relentless propaganda can easily be seen in the film industry and in many television series[144]. Planetary cinema first celebrates the

---

[141] Abraham Isaac haCohen Kook (1865-1935) was the first Ashkenazic chief rabbi in the Land of Israel during the British Mandate. He was a rector of Talmudic law (halakhah), kabbalist and thinker. He founded the Chief Rabbinate of Israel, at the head of which he was the first Ashkenazic Chief Rabbi. He also founded the *Merkaz haRav* Yeshiva and is considered one of the fathers of religious Zionism. His halachic rulings, especially on political issues and commandments relating to the Land, are a recognised source of jurisprudence. He developed a doctrine favourable to the *New Yishuv* and Zionism based on Kabbalah. He is the main religious and philosophical reference for contemporary Israeli nationalist religious currents. (NdT).

[142] Bernard-Henri Lévy - Michel Houellebecq, *Enemigos públicos*, Anagrama, Barcelona, 2010, p. 160, 161.

[143] Judaism is not a religion (in the spiritual and transcendental sense, except perhaps the mystical kabbalistic strand which is a form of Gnosticism within Judaism), but a religious nationalism with real-world imperial messianic pretensions. Their holy book (the Torah) is a book of national history, their religious holidays celebrate war and national (historical or mythical) events. Exactly as if we Spaniards celebrate our religious holidays remembering Numantia, Covadonga, Las Navas de Tolosa, Lepanto or the 2nd of May. (NdT).

[144] Today's reader knows that this phenomenon is now even more prevalent and has become the norm in the West. The big audiovisual production companies and platforms

virtues of multicultural democracy and miscegenation: in one way or another, the aim is to incite the viewer to envision a world without borders and to instil tolerance towards "others". This cosmopolitan propaganda also often uses a white man to play the role of the bastard. He is often portrayed as a light-haired, blue-eyed Nordic man. This is not accidental, but reflects a visceral hatred of the European world. We have already mentioned numerous examples in our previous books. Let us continue our study here:

Périgord noir (France, 1988) is a rather emblematic film. An African village has been devastated by the closure of the banana plantation that provided its income and livelihood. The beautiful Adiza, who studied in France, is on a mission to find the money to buy back the plantation and save the community. She invents an imaginary father, using a photograph of a soldier found in her late mother's boot, and disembarks at the head of her entire village in a modest town in the French Dordogne. Antonio, the false father in question, pretends to believe that he is really the father of such a charming young woman, and the Africans, who have taken up permanent residence there, set the pace for the peaceful French village. Fraternisation proceeds apace, much to the chagrin of the wily and irascible mayor, Jeantou, who laments that he cannot even exploit this recalcitrant workforce. Love enters the picture. When Jeantou refuses to marry off several couples, the Perigordinos decide to leave their village to live in Africa with their black friends. And this is what the programme guide told us: "An excellent comedy, very well acted, and with an upbeat, cheerful and not at all didactic anti-racism". The film is by a certain Nicolas Ribowski, and the review is probably from one of his girlfriends.

À l'ombre de la haine (*Monster's ball*) is a 2001 American film: Hank is a conscientious prison officer at a penitentiary in the southern United States. He is in charge of executing death row inmates. His father, old and retired, used to do the job, but his son Sony, on the other hand, seems too fragile of nerve and breaks down when it is time to take the prisoner to the electric chair. Hank can't stand this weakness and treats his son with contempt and

---

(Netflix, HBO, Disney, etc.) and even the technological giants (Amazon, Apple) have diversified and massified this type of audiovisual production (films and series). The advertising of big companies and corporations is also unanimously multiracial and actively promotes miscegenation and the LGBT revolution on all platforms and social networks with invasive advertisements. This is actively promoted from the centre of the financial and corporate system through policies that financially incentivise these social and also environmental goals. These objectives are monitored and evaluated by official measurement criteria such as ESG (*Environmental Social and Corporate Governance*) and CEI (*Corporate Equality Index*). The declarations of Larry Fink, president of Blacrock (the first global hedge fund), in globalist forums leave no doubt about this desire to transform society and reality in this sense, beyond the capitalist profit motive. (NdT).

violence. In fact, he has always hated this weak son. Pushed to the limit, Sony commits suicide. Hank, in spite of everything, is moved and resigns. He is naturally very racist, as his old father always was, and he certainly felt no pity for the blacks he led to their deaths. But the vagaries of life lead him to meet the widow of a man he had executed. A relationship develops between the former prison guard and this attractive young black woman, who quickly understands the tragic nature of the situation. Eventually they become lovers. Marc Foster's film is said to be "deeply moving".

Quand on sera grand (France, 2001), reflects quite well the hyper-aggressiveness of Judaism. Here is the script: Simon Dadoun is a journalist in his thirties. He cannot have children with his girlfriend, a goy. Fortunately, he is comforted by his new neighbour's wife, a Sephardic Jew like him, but neglected by her husband, an Ashkenazi radiologist, haughty and unfriendly. On the other hand, the film's director, Renaud Cohen, shows us French people who are very given to miscegenation. Simon Dadoun's friends are married, one to an Asian and the other to a Senegalese. Another French character in the film is a neighbour in the building who lives alone and is quite depressed. Simon, who, like all Sephardic Jews, has a big heart, introduces her to Roger, a French childhood friend whom she has met by chance and who is also experiencing his bachelorhood rather badly. Everything seems to be going smoothly between the two young people, but Roger turns out to be a sexual pervert who can also be violent. What's more, he likes to wear thongs! As a result, the French girl becomes a lesbian. At the end of the film, she seems to have finally found her true sexuality and gives free rein to her inclinations. She would like, she says, to "fuck the Senegalese woman". In the background, Renaud Cohen films the French capital from a very multicultural angle, between African encounters, oriental music and Chinese New Year. To complete the picture, the film also complacently depicts the consumption of hashish. Miscegenation and homosexuality: these are the main ingredients of many of the films made by Jews. Once again, Jews seem obsessed with our destruction, obsessed with destroying everything that is not Jewish. "The actors are admirably spontaneous. A mix of genres perfectly executed by Renaud Cohen, who thus achieves a beautiful film", Claude Bouniq-Mercier told us in the *Guide des films*.

In the 2003 film *Gomez et Tavarès*, a handsome young man climbs over the wall of a rich estate and enters the house. On the wall is a picture of a beautiful blonde woman with her husband, a black man, and their children, who are slightly less so. The viewer immediately thinks: this is a film by a Jewish director. We continue to watch it for a while to see what it's like, and after a few minutes we realise that all the actors have been chosen according to ethnic criteria to form a multi-racial cast. We interrupt the viewing and discover that the director is a certain Gilles Paquet-Brenner.

Now, if you type Gilles Paquet-Brenner into an internet search engine and choose "images", you will immediately find his picture. And no surprise: it's not a pretty blonde!

We have found the following film synopses in Jean Tulard's *Guide des films*, all very revealing of the cosmopolitan mentality:

Jonas et Lila by Alain Tanner (France, 1999): Jonas is married to Aïssa, a beautiful African. The couple go to the countryside with a Russian actress.

La Parenthèse enchantée (France, 1999) takes place between May '68 and the years of AIDS. In 1969, two friends get married on the same day. Vincent (Vincent Elbaz) to Marie, and Paul (Roschdy Zem) to Eve. The French women seem to be betrothed to Jews and Arabs. The director is also very complacent about adultery, Marxism, feminism and abortion. For Claude Bouniq-Mercier, Michel Spinoza's film is "a small success".

À la place du coeur (France, 1998): Clémentine and Fançois, known as Baby, want to get married. Clémentine is pregnant. Baby, he, is black: he is the adopted son of Franck and Francine, a sterile couple. But Bebe, wrongly accused by a racist policeman of raping a Bosnian woman, is in jail. Bouniq-Mercier admits that the film is "Manichean": on the one hand, the good guys, on the other the bad guys (the hysterical Catholic, the racist police). The film is by Robert Guédiguian, a particularly aggressive director.

Je suis né d'une cigogne, by Tony Gatlif (France, 1998): Otto, an unemployed man, and Louma, a hairdresser, decide to change their lives. They befriend Ali, a young runaway, and set off at random wherever the road takes them. It is "a pamphlet-film in favour of undocumented migrants".

One Night stand (USA, 1997): Max, a black man, is married to an Asian woman, Mimi. He lives in Los Angeles and has a friend in New York called Charlie, a homosexual. He also sleeps with Karen, a beautiful blonde who eventually marries his brother Vernon. Homosexuality for the white man, miscegenation for the white woman. Signed Mike Figgis.

Vive la République! (France, 1997): Henri gathers a group of unemployed boys and girls like himself to found a new political party based on the idea of "social decompartmentalisation" and "sharing knowledge". In reality, the script is above all a pretext to show a multiracial France, with Arab actors and pretty French girls. A film by Eric Rochant.

C'est pour la bonne cause, by Jacques Fansten (France, 1996): Tonin has always listened to his parents when they told him to take an interest in others, to show solidarity and to be useful to others. That is why, when the authorities at his school are looking for families to take in an African child from a refugee camp for a month, Tonin raises his hand and immediately offers his services. "A gentle, humanist comedy, full of good feelings... fresh and funny", wrote Claude Bouniq-Mercier.

Walk the walk (France, 1996): A family lives near a tobacco shop in Berre: Nellie, the mother, is white and a biologist. Abel, the father, is black and a runner. Raye, their mixed-race daughter, learns to sing. Robert Kramer, the film's director, is Jewish.

Cauchemar blanc, a short film from 1991, shows us four very racist, very mean white people who are raging against a poor Arab in a working-class suburb on the outskirts of a big city. It is clear that Mathieu Kassovitz, the director, doesn't like whites very much.

Come see the paradise (USA, 1990): A disgraced trade unionist, Jack McGurn moved to Los Angeles in 1936. He became a projectionist in a Japanese neighbourhood cinema owned by Mr. Kawamura. He soon falls in love with Lily, his charming nineteen-year-old daughter. But the war is coming and the Japanese living on American soil are to be interned in concentration camps: "Languor and weeping". As we know, director Alan Parker is a true cosmopolitan.

Les Innocents is a film by André Techiné (France, 1987): Jeanne, a girl from the North, arrives in Toulon where she meets Said, a young Moor who is the lover of Klotz, an alcoholic orchestra leader whose son Stéphane is a fascist. The script is by Pascal Bonitzer, and it is not exactly homosexual.

Tod and Toby (USA, 1981) is a cartoon by Art Stevens, Ted Berman and Richard Rich. Tid is an orphaned little fox who has been taken in by a nice farm girl in the southern United States. He makes a new friend, Toby, the neighbour's young dog. "The film is a good lesson against racism," wrote Bouniq-Mercier.

The Human Factor (USA, 1979) is an espionage film. In South Africa, a British secret agent falls in love with a black native. The film is by the famous Jewish and Zionist director Otto Preminger.

Pretty Baby (USA, 1978): The story is set in a warm and familiar New Orleans brothel in 1917. Violet, the natural daughter of Hattie, a prostitute, lives there. When she reaches puberty, her virginity is auctioned off. Violet becomes a sought-after prostitute. Whipped for indulging in amorous games with a young black man, she runs away and takes refuge with Bellocq, with whom she has a stormy relationship. Louis Malle denounces here "a bourgeois and hypocritical society", wrote Bouniq-Mercier, adding: "A careful film, with warm colours".

Mandingo (USA, 1975): In 1840, Hammond, the son of a cotton plantation owner, marries Blanche. But when he discovers she is not a virgin, he abandons her for a black slave. As a result, Blanche gives herself to a giant Mandingo and gives birth to a black baby who is killed by the doctor. Hammond poisons his wife and scalds the Mandingo. He himself is killed by the butler, while the slave revolt against the white bastards is brewing and about to break out. The film is by Richard Fleischer.

Flipper city (USA, 1973): Michael is the son of a possessive and irritable Jewish mother and an Italian mobster father. He draws violent comic strips featuring prostitutes, criminals, vagrants, gangsters, drug dealers, drug addicts and cops. Then Michael meets Carol, a "beautiful young black girl". A film by Ralph Bakshi.

Les Aventures de Rabbi Jacob (*The Adventures of Rabbi Jacob*, Fr, 1973), a French classic with Louis de Funès: In New York, Rabbi Jacob flies to Paris. Meanwhile, in France, Monsieur Pivert urges his chauffeur Salomon to be on time for his daughter's wedding. Finally, two Arab assassins are sent to kill a revolutionary leader, Slimane. After some back-and-forth, everything works out and it is Slimane who marries Pivert's daughter. An amusing comedy by Gérard Oury.

Smic, Smac, Smoc (Fr, 1971): Amidou, who works in the shipyards of La Ciotat, marries Catherine, a nice white baker. A film by Claude Lelouch.

If we go back in time, we will still find these films:

In Billy Wilder's *The Fortune Cookie* (*The Fortune Cookie*, USA, 1966): During a football game, cameraman Harry Hinkle is unintentionally hit by black player Boom Boom Jackson. In the end, the two men become friends. Integration is underway.

West Side Story (USA, 1961) is a musical comedy by Robert Wise. Two gangs clash: the Jets, white Americans led by Riff, and the Sharks, Puerto Rican immigrants led by Bernardo. In the end, the two gangs realise the absurdity of their struggle. This is a propagandist film in favour of a multiracial society; with a soundtrack by Leonard Bernstein.

Flaming star (USA, 1960): Pacer Burton (Elvis Presley) was born to an Indian mother and a white father. His parents are killed during the war and he joins the Indians. A film about the emotional heartbreak of the half-breeds.

Propaganda in favour of miscegenation and multiculturalism had already appeared on the big screen in the 1950s:

Yellowstone Kelly (USA, 1959) by Gordon Douglas. A white trapper falls in love with an Indian woman he saved from death. "A beautiful, progressive, humanist western."

Fugitives (USA, 1958) by Stanley Kramer: Two prisoners escape chained to each other. One is white and racially prejudiced, the other black and sullen. Despite their preconceived ideas, solidarity develops between them. A "sympathetic plea against racism", wrote Jean Tulard.

The Oklahoman (USA, 1957): A doctor makes enemies by championing the cause of the Indians. The film is by Francis Lyon and the screenplay by Daniel Ullman.

Apache Woman (USA, 1955): two half-breeds, Anne and Armand, live between two worlds: that of the whites and that of the Indians who reject them. The film is by Roger Corman.

Fort Yuma (USA, 1955): On the convoy to Fort Yuma, the racist lieutenant is loved by the Indian woman, whose brother, a scout, is coveted by the white schoolteacher. The main thing is that the Jews don't mix. The film is by Lesley Selander.

The Well (*The Well*, USA, 1951); in a southern American town, a black girl goes missing and a white man, suspected of the abduction, is arrested. The town is rocked by violent race riots, but the girl is found at the bottom of a disused mine shaft and everyone tries to save her. Leo Popkin's "An anti-racist thriller".

Marc Sorkin's *The White Slave* (France) was released in 1939: at the beginning of the 20th century, a young French woman marries a westernised Turk who takes her to his still culturally backward country. They are persecuted by the Sultan and saved in extremis by a revolutionary.

In the 1925 film *The Vanishing American* (USA), the Indian Nophaie loves Marion, a white teacher. But despite his good will, he encounters racism and bad faith on the part of the whites. The Navajos go to war, but are defeated by the whites. Nophaie dies in Marion's arms. It was, Jean Tulard told us, "the first western to show the Indians in a kinder light, victims of the race to the west". The film is by George B. Steiz and was adapted in 1955 by Joseph Kane.

In the 1970s and 1980s, the two cult series *Kojak* and *Colombo* insidiously distilled the cosmopolitan message. We present here Ignacio Ramonet's brilliant Marxist analysis in his book *Propagandas silenciosas*:

Kojak is a cop policing Manhattan's underworld. He almost always has to deal with brown individuals belonging to national or ethnic minorities. Throughout the 116 episodes of the series, produced between 1973 and 1978, all of Manhattan's minorities are portrayed one after the other, reduced to one or two dominant and simplifying traits: "Gypsies in traditional costumes who live on fortune telling, fortune tellers who predict the future with the eternal crystal ball"; "gangs of young black men described in the script as good kids at heart (they are not at all politicised), for a moment led astray by an exalted individual who soon regrets it"; "Puerto Ricans who play basketball tirelessly in fenced parks"; "Italians who do odd jobs and are still very religious"; "excessive Poles", "nostalgic Jews", "enigmatic Chinese", and so on. All the communities that make up the American melting pot are condescendingly represented. These suspects, wrote Ignacio Ramonet with great lucidity, "often turn out not to be guilty in the end". Kojak's role here is very clear: while protecting the American system, law and order, this policeman must gently promote the integration and assimilation of minorities.... With this aim in mind, Ramonet wrote, this realistic series, conceived at the end of the 1960s, at the time of the political explosion of minorities, renews the myth of America as a land of asylum and freedom, and heralds the fashion for multiculturalism.

The screenwriter and inventor of the Kojak character, Abby Mann ('Abby', short for Abraham), was a writer who belonged to the American left and was a long-time civil rights activist. He was a friend of the black American pacifist leader Martin Luther King, the Nobel Peace Prize laureate assassinated on 4 April 1968, and made a "generous and well-documented" three-hour feature film about his life and struggles entitled *King*. He was also the author of *The Simon Wiesenthal Story* (1989), "a film about the life of the famous Nazi hunter", Ignacio Ramonet noted at the end of his analysis with remarkable lucidity.

Here is a summary of what Ignacio Ramonet wrote about the other cult TV series of the time: Columbo investigates only in the posh neighbourhoods of Los Angeles. His thing is blood crimes, never petty crime such as muggings and robberies. His formidable adversaries belong to the crème de la crème of society. They are arrogant and think they are criminal geniuses and often have impeccable alibis. In front of them, Columbo is pitiful, with his dirty old trench coat, worn-out suit and rickety old Peugeot 403 convertible. Everything about him clashes with the charm, the elegance and the elegance of his interlocutors. And yet it is our little lieutenant who triumphs in every episode, in the face of the arrogance of these rich and beautiful people. The success of this series comes precisely from this identification of the middle class with the inspector's cause, as opposed to the rich and powerful who think they have the right to everything. The established order is thus legitimised. The analysis of the Marxist Ignacio Ramonet is all the more pertinent because it sheds light on the creators of this series, whose first episode was broadcast in the United States in 1968: William Link and Richard Lewinson.

These two TV series had no other aim than to reinforce the multicultural society and to make the Anglo-Saxon elite feel guilty, i.e. to "harass" the white Goyim from above and below. Now, it is astonishing to see how Ignacio Ramonet, a Marxist author, manages to fit this enormous reality into his ideology. Here is how Ignacio Ramonet finally denounced bourgeois power and the American patriots, henchmen of big capital: "Thus, stationed at the two extremes of the dominant ideology," he wrote, "the American police lieutenants Kojak and Columbo, protectors of the middle class, guard their respective borders throughout the series. Upstream, on the side of the elite, Lieutenant Columbo moralises, stigmatises, unmasks and punishes the criminal behaviour of the cosmopolitan billionaires, the arrogant rich, without country or virtue. Downstream, on the people's side, Inspector Kojak orders, monitors, normalises and Americanises the rise of ethnic minorities from the groups and margins of society."

In reality, Columbo is not attacking the "cosmopolitan billionaires" at all, but the white Anglo-Saxon haute bourgeoisie, and we must point out here that, between an Anglo-Saxon millionaire or a big Breton landowner, on the one hand, and a cosmopolitan billionaire [in billions of dollars], on the other, there is the same difference as between someone who rides a bicycle and someone who drives a Rolls Royce. Poor Ignacio sees nothing, he hears nothing, understands nothing of what is happening to him. His Marxist reading grid that sifts his thinking is a late 20th century model, which does not allow him to understand the reality of globalism on the move.

In March 2007, television aired an episode of the *FBI series, Missing Persons*, entitled *The Roots of Evil*. Here we enter a truly twisted genre: At university, a student who has made racist remarks in class mysteriously disappears after the incident. The FBI investigates and discovers that his mother once had a relationship with a black man. This white student, as you might have guessed, is unaware that his real father was actually a black man. A flashback scene shows him discovering the truth. To his mother, who explains it all to him, he replies, visibly shocked and indignant: "But that's not possible, I'm white!" And she replies: "Sometimes it happens!" This delirious episode was directed by one Martha Mitchell.

In 1949, a cosmopolitan director released a film based on a similar script: *Pinky* (USA, 1949): everyone thinks that the beautiful nurse Pinky is white, but in reality she is black. In love with a white doctor, she runs away from this love to live with her black grandmother in the south of the country. The doctor, having realised that miscegenation is actually an enriching experience, runs off in search of her and together they travel north to found a hospital for... black children. Thanks to whom? Thanks to Elia Kazan.

In the same style, Phillipe Niang's film *Un bébé noir dans un couffin blanc* (Fr. 2002) (*A black baby in a white basket*) shows a young French couple expecting a baby. When the young woman gives birth, they are astonished because the baby is... black! Of course, in the village, the French, who are all very stupid and very racist, are extremely nasty towards the wife whom they accuse of having cheated on her husband with the only black man in the village. In the end, we learn that this is a rare case of a white couple giving birth to a black child (to be proven). So all those French assholes end up apologising, and all ends well, as the black man on duty, cleared of all suspicion, wins the football cup for the village, so everyone is happy. Integration is on its way! In our opinion, there is no doubt that the film's scriptwriter is Jewish.

Philippe Niang - that is his name - shared another vision of his cosmopolitanism in another telefilm entitled *Si j'avais des millions* (2005) (*If I had millions*), where, like most Jews, he is obsessed with the integration of immigrants and the biological destruction of the white man. As we can see, Jews are literally obsessed with ethnic mixing, at least when it comes to others, for they cultivate for themselves the strictest defence of their own identity. Now, Philippe Niang can be called Tarempion or Walid ibn Reza: it doesn't matter. You don't recognise a Jew by his name or his face so much as by what he says, what he writes and what he does.

The confusion that certain filmmakers like to instil in society is not only a desire to subvert the European world, but also reflects the very ambivalence of Jewish identity. In the 1980s, for example, a South African Jewish singer, Johnny Clegg, enjoyed short-lived fame. Johnny Clegg was known as the "White Zulu", because he danced like a Zulu and sang for the abolition of the Apartheid regime in South Africa and for equal rights for blacks. Jewish Zulu" would obviously have been more appropriate, since Johnny Clegg (Klugman) belonged to that community.

Twenty years later, the ambiguity and plasticity of the Jewish personality is once again magnificently portrayed in the person of a certain Alain Lévy, who also danced like a black man. This is what the Swiss newspaper *Le Matin* had to say about him in 2007: "Alain Lévy is white, Jewish and an executive, and he wins Congolese dance competitions! Nicknamed "*Mundélé Ndombé*" in Lingala (Black White), he has become a symbol of cultural openness and the fight against prejudice by dancing the *ndombolo*. In his show, Alain Lévy appears masked. Not an inch of skin is visible. With rhythm, he moves his hips to perfection. And when he reveals his face, it is a "positive electric shock". This ability to dance, to "resonate", which came to him "out of nowhere", he insists, has become his way of fighting prejudice. Because "the idea that black people have rhythm in their blood is racist".

"I'm breaking down the barriers between blacks and whites, he says. It's so good to do projects and build bridges between human beings! In the competitions, the jury and all the dancers are black. In South Africa, I was the only white person in the whole stadium! Can you imagine? In apartheid South Africa, that's no mean feat. And the journalist added: "This stunt, this random span of our arrival on Earth gives him a childish joy. "My ability has no explanation, that's what puzzles people," he says. If there were, perhaps it would be too easy to say: 'Yes, it's because you grew up in Africa, it's normal'. But I've always lived in France, I'm rubbish at sport, I've never played an instrument, my wife is not African. And I have Congolese colleagues who don't know how to dance. Alain Lévy also delivers the usual tolerance line: "What's interesting is the message of tolerance in my project. Because racism is still alive in Europe. In reality, this Lévy is typically Jewish, and it is not at all because of his name that one notices it at first glance, but because of his characteristic discourse: mixing of peoples, overlapping of identities, suppression of borders, militancy in favour of immigration, etc., as well as his own identity ambiguity. In reality, Jews are more recognisable by what they say, what they write and what they do than by their surname or their face. So Alain

Lévy can keep his mask. We don't need a DNA test to recognise his true identity.

Let us now look at another symptomatic example of identity ambivalence. In 2008, with the help of a lot of publicity, the British singer Amy Winehouse became a youth idol. Amy Winehouse was born into a Jewish family of Russian origin in North London, we are told. She also feels black: she sings like a black woman, "with a black mama voice", to the *soul music* of the 1960s that she is bringing back into fashion, and she often appears on television screens surrounded by her black musicians and singers. At 24, she is "*the diva of soul*". She is also the "new *trash* icon". This is what you could read about her: "self-mutilation, drugs, alcoholism, anorexia, bulimia, Amy dares everything: she insults her audience... she swears like a road at a charity gala, she vomits in the middle of a concert, she carves her husband's name in her stomach with a piece of crystal glass... And everyone applauds... Amy Winehouse is not only the embodiment of *trash* attitude, she is, above all, talented". Of course, Amy Winehouse has been rewarded by all her cronies in the "international media community": "At the US Grammy Awards, she won five awards, including Record of the Year for her song "*rehab*" ("*Désintoxication*"), which is largely autobiographical. How far will the new idol go? A month ago he suffered his umpteenth overdose and nearly died. His mother had even reserved a place in the cemetery for him...".

One of the most iconic films in this regard is undoubtedly the western *Little Big Man* (USA, 1970). It is the story of a white boy who has grown up among the Cheyenne Indians since the age of ten, and who goes back and forth between the camp of the Whites - who appear in the film as bloodthirsty warriors - and the camp of the gentle, quiet Indians. The director, Arthur Penn, was evidently a Jew, expressing here the full ambivalence of Jewish identity, and using the occasion to make Europeans feel guilty. The inclusion of a homosexual Indian character, inverted in every sense, is also very symptomatic of the Jewish personality. As we shall see in this study, sexual ambiguity is also often a marker and component of Jewish identity.

Certainly, the expression of an ambiguous identity cannot completely hide the aggressiveness of cosmopolitan filmmakers against the European world. Take, for example, *The Truman Show (*USA, 1998), which is another propaganda film: Truman is a man who is unaware that he only lives to star in a TV show. Everything around him is a set. Everyone he comes into contact with is an actor, and he is the only one who doesn't know it. The director wanted to denounce the cardboard society that serves as a backdrop to Truman's life, its hypocrisy, its false happiness. This hypocritical society is a WASP (White Anglo-Saxon Protestant) society, where there are no drugs, crime or porn films. By escaping from this "hemmed-in, timorous, self-enclosed world", as essayist Alain Minc would put it, Truman can finally savour the joys of sex, drugs and racial mayhem. One would expect nothing else from the director of *Dead Poets Club*, Peter Weir.

Europeans have to learn to be tolerant. This is what Joseph Losey's film *The Boy with green hair* (USA, 1948) was about: It is the story of a young orphan boy who faces the hostility of his peers. "A magnificent fable about racism and tolerance, the encounter with the other and the fear of difference," Serge Bromberg explained in his introduction. In 1952, Joseph Losey was a victim of McCarthyism, condemned by the Un-American Activities Committee, along with the film's two screenwriters, Ban Barzman and Alfred Lewis.

The Day the earth stood still (USA, 1951) is a film by Robert Wise: a flying saucer lands over Washington. Aliens are peaceful and we should welcome them with open arms among us. This is also what Steven Spielberg expected us to do with his *E.T., the Extra-Terrestrial* (USA, 1982), and the same message can be found in Barry Sonnenfeld's *Men in Black* (1997).

We can end this chapter with Thierry Binisti's film *Monsieur Molina* (2006), also full of humanity and kindness. Mr. Bonnard's two sons, Laurent and Jimmy, reproach their father for the gift he made to an unknown woman, Amina, who will receive the family home on Mr. Bonnard's death. The two brothers were previously unaware of the existence of this half-Arab half-sister, the fruit of a secret love affair. Mr. Molina, a magistrate at the Lille court (played by Enrico Macias), will have to solve this thorny family problem. And this is what the daily *Programme.tv* says: "Enrico Macias' first great role as a local magistrate, sensitive and human, a character that suits him like a glove". "Human and sensitive", that's right. The film is indeed hyper-moralising, as only Jewish intellectuals know how to be, always inclined to lecture the rest of humanity. The two brothers, intolerant and probably a bit racist, finally accept their new "stepsister". It is also very nice to see a Jewish judge with his "*black-foot*" accent[145] giving lessons to some good Frenchmen who bow their heads respectfully before him.

---

[145] The *pieds-noirs* (*blackfeet*) are people of mainly French and, to a lesser extent, other European origins who were born in Algeria during the French colonial period from 1830 to 1962, the vast majority of whom had to flee to metropolitan France as soon as Algeria gained its independence, or in the months that followed. Depending on the context, the definition may also include Algerian Jews, who had been granted French nationality by the Crémieux Decree. (NdT).

Cosmopolitan propaganda II: blame game

Cosmopolitan filmmakers also work to make Europeans feel deeply guilty, to make them ashamed of who they are.

Some episodes of the "American" series *Coldcase* are very emblematic in this sense. Julian, a friend and correspondent of ours, watched and summarised for us two episodes of this early 21st century series: a brilliant teacher wants to go to teach in a ghetto high school to help blacks. Shortly afterwards, she is murdered. But the culprit turns out to be the only white man in the school: a white drug-addicted teacher who forced his students to sell him drugs. After the crime, he leaves to teach at a Christian school...

Here is another episode: in the 1960s, a white housewife starts selling food containers in Mississippi, but her activity is mainly a cover to help blacks fight for their civic rights. She is murdered by the Klu Klux Klan, which even attacks black children by burning their schools. It is at the end of the episode that we discover the culprit, thirty years later: a retired military man, a good-for-nothing who lives quietly in the Old South. These scripts were written by Meredith Stiehm and produced by Jerry Bruckheimer.

Julián also analysed for us a few episodes of the crime series *The Wire*, the famous HBO series unanimously acclaimed by critics as one of the best series in history. Here is a brief summary. We have kept the colloquial writing style of "The Internet": "All the bosses and good cops are black, all the white guys are assholes (to an extent rarely seen in a series: for example, a cop photocopies his phone to save a printout of a phone number). The only intelligent white character is an alcoholic and a womaniser... The police heroine is black and a lesbian (with another black woman). There are also two junkies, a black philosopher and a poor white asshole. The latter is massacred by some blacks and ends up humiliated, with a transplanted artificial urine bag because his bladder no longer works. He's a sissy and all he can think about is pricking himself again, but that doesn't stop him from declaring loud and clear that he's a "Viking". There's also a young, inept white cop (he makes a serious blunder with his service weapon and ends up as a docile teacher in a slum high school), or a black criminal (Omar, sounds post 9/11) who is gay and has sex with a white guy (who plays a woman, obviously)." And our judicious correspondent added: "I looked up the name of the director and the winner is: David Simon." Naturally, all the reviews of this television vomit are laudatory, and it is even cited as President Obama's favourite series... "even though it's rubbish," wrote Julian. Even retards don't watch it anymore. The third season should be cancelled.

In France, at the beginning of the 21st century, a series like *Navarro*, imagined by Pierre Grimblat and starring Roger Hanin, was clearly inspired by the American series *Kojak*. Other series, such as *Julie Lescaut, Le Commissaire Moulin, Quai n°1* or *Une femme d'honneur* also have a similar ideological and sociological intention, and focus on social issues: urban violence, racism, unemployment, suburbs, political and economic shenanigans. There is also Alain Krief's *PJ* and *Plus Belle la vie*, a soap opera in which Olivier Szulzynger praises miscegenation (for white women) and homosexuality (for white men).

Let's look at the script of an episode of *Julie Lescaut* entitled *Crédit revolver* (1994): a very French and very racist baker, very given to pulling out his shotgun every now and then to threaten young immigrants, is a friend of the deputy mayor called Lefranc ["The Frenchman"], who heads an "extreme right-wing" party, the Union for France. The mayor is also a bastard, as he is elected thanks to the votes of the "extreme right". Lefranc turns out to be a murderer, but fortunately he is unmasked by Inspector Julie Lescaut, a strong and independent woman.

Le Guide des films offers many more examples in the same vein[146], although of course we cannot cite them all:

Inch'Allah Dimanche (Fr., 2001): In 1974, the year of family reunification (wanted by President Valéry Giscard D'Estaing[147]), an Algerian family is reunited in northern France. The French neighbours are mean and mean, obsessed with their garden. Yamina Benguigui's film was produced by Philippe Depuis-Mendel.

Liam (UK, 2000) is set in 1930s Liverpool. Liam is seven years old and his sister is the maid for a wealthy Jewish family. The poor Jews are targeted by right-wing scumbags, and we are made to realise that Christianity's stranglehold on people's minds does nothing to improve things. A film by the very cosmopolitan Stephen Frears.

The Patriot (USA, 2000) is a good film about the American War of Independence. But the viewer is unconsciously reminded that the blue-eyed man is cruel by nature, and that only a multiracial society can appease his warrior instincts. The film is by Roland Emmerich.

Gadjo Dilo is a film by Tony Gatlif (Fr., 1997): Stéphane, a somewhat lost Frenchman, wanders the roads of Romania. He stumbles upon a gypsy village and realises that the gypsies are really nice people, but he encounters the infamous racism of the Romanians. A word of warning: this is fiction. We strongly advise you not to travel the roads of rural Romania or eastern Slovakia to meet friendly gypsies.

---

[146] *Le Guide des films,* edited by Jean Tulard, three volumes, 3380 pages, Robert Laffont, 2002.

[147] The right to family reunification is the right of migrants to maintain the unity of their family by being able to reunite certain relatives in the country to which they have moved. (NdT).

Pullman Paradis (Fr., 1995): During an excursion to Normandy in a Pullman coach, the passengers become friends. Director Michèle Rosier presents French people "with their pettiness and their ordinary racism". We learn that she is the daughter of journalist Hélène Gordon-Lazareff.

Rising Sun (USA, 1993): A Japanese company in Los Angeles discovers the body of a prostitute in its offices. "A good thriller with racism and xenophobia towards the Japanese as a backdrop."

District 34 (Q&A, USA, 1990), cop Mike Brennan kills a Puerto Rican mobster in self-defence. But a counter-investigation reveals Brennan to be a sadistic, racist cop. A film by Sidney Lumet, who was a very famous and aggressive director.

On peut toujours rêver is a film by Pierre Richard (Fr., 1990): At the head of a huge financial empire, Charles de Boleyve, known as the "Emperor", is a hated billionaire. He befriends a certain Rachid, an unprejudiced and uninhibited Moor. The Frenchman is cold, prissy and unpleasant, with a personality that contrasts with "the cheerful exuberance of the Maghrebi family".

L'Entraînement du champion avant la course, by Bernard Favre (Fr., 1990): In a Parisian suburb, Fabrice is a butcher with a mediocre life. He divides his life between his wife and his mistress, but his only real pleasure is training for cycling races. "Fabrice is a mediocrity in all its horror, wrote Claude Bouniq-Mercier: a supporter of the death penalty, sadistic, violent, misogynist, selfish, reactionary, his mind is as narrow as his life horizon". Thank you, Mr Bouniq.

True believer (USA, 1989) is a film by Joseph Ruben: Dodd is a maverick lawyer. He agrees to take on the case of an imprisoned young Korean man accused of murdering an overly brutal prisoner. Despite the prosecutor's opposition, Dodd will establish the truth that exonerates the Korean. The film denounces white racism and corruption.

In John Frankenheimer's *Dead Bang* (USA, 1988), a Los Angeles cop tracks the killer of one of his colleagues to Arizona. His search leads him to a group of neo-Nazis.

In Roland Joffé's *The Mission* (USA, 1986), the director takes us back to 1750 in South America. Mendoza, a slave trader, makes amends by supporting the Jesuits in their mission on behalf of the Indians. But the Church and the Spanish merchants intend to continue their dirty business, and the final assault will be unleashed against the Jesuits and their peaceful Indians. In the film, of course, the slave traders are good Christians, and certainly not Jews (cf. *The Jewish Mafia*, 2008).

Soldier's story (USA, 1984) is the story of a black officer investigating the 1944 murder of a sergeant in a black military unit stationed in Louisiana. Naturally, his investigations lead to white culprits. The film is by Norman Jewison, a director as mediocre as he is aggressive.

Urgence is a film by Gilles Béat (Fr., 1984): Max is a journalist infiltrating a Nazi group. He is convinced that an attack is being planned, but is unmasked and killed by the group's leader. The Nazis are arrested. The screenplay is by Jean Herman, based on the play by Didier Cohen.

Équateur, by Serge Gainsbourg (Fr., 1983): Timar arrives in Gabon in the 1950s. He falls in love with Adèle. After the murder of one of her sons, Adèle leaves with Timar to exploit a concession in the jungle. Overcome by alcohol and heat, Timar loses his love for Adèle and gets her to confess to the boy's murder, but another black man has already been convicted.

We must believe that it is whites who benefit from immigration: In *Borderline* (USA, 1980), Jeb Maynard runs a customs post in California. His best friend is shot dead by a human trafficker. Jeb investigates and unmasks the killer's bosses. Illegal immigrants are portrayed here as victims, the real culprits being the new slave traders. But don't panic: the film is not about Jews. The film is by Jerrold Freddman.

Haines (USA, 1949) is a film that denounces the exploitation of Mexican labour in Southern California. Joseph Losey, as we know, is a "generous" director. It is obvious that whites get rich at the expense of immigrants. On the other hand, they also benefit from the subsidies of big capital which, as we all know, is the breeding ground of fascism.

In Philipe labro's *L'Héritier* (Fr., 1972), Bart Cordell returns from the United States to inherit an industrial empire. He discovers that his father has been murdered by his stepfather, who runs an industrial emporium and finances a neo-fascist party. This is what the screenwriter, Jacques Lanzmann, would have us believe.

Mille Milliards de dollars, by Henri Verneuil (Fr., 1981), has the same objective: a journalist discovers that the multinational GTI was working for the Nazis. Its owner refuses to allow the investigation to continue. The journalist has to go into hiding and only a small provincial newspaper publishes his article. It is well known that the mainstream press is totally controlled by the fascists.

The Last wave (*The Last wave*, Australia, 1977) is a film about the Aborigines of Australia. One of them is accused of murder. One can see "the artistic expression of Anglo-Saxon guilt towards the Aborigines". Another humanist work by Peter Weir.

William Graham's *Cry for Me, Billy* (USA, 1976) is a western: Billy, a young hitman, is outraged by the army's treatment of Indians. He himself becomes involved with a young Indian girl who has survived a massacre. A patrol of soldiers finds them and the men rape the Indian. Sullied, she commits suicide. Billy avenges her, but falls in turn. "A very sympathetic western, an anti-racist plea in favour of the Indians", wrote Jean Tulard. The script is by David Markson, also a very likeable Jew.

Buffalo Bill and the Indians (USA, 1976) is a film by Robert Altman: read Jean Tulard's comment: "Altman is the anti-Ford in his vision of the West. Here it is Buffalo Bill who is portrayed as a lousy comic, a bad shot, and a bad horseman, but a heavy drinker of whisky. The Indians, on the other hand, are exalted in the person of Sitting Bull."

Since the white authorities are so corrupt, anything goes to overthrow the authorities of the goyim. Here is Mel Brooks' *Blazing Saddles* (USA, 1973). It's a western spoof: the corrupt governor seeks to expropriate the villagers for the benefit of a railroad company. He is defeated by a black sheriff, an alcoholic gunman and a brute.

Punishment Park (USA, 1971) is a film by Peter Watkins. In 1971, President Nixon declares a state of emergency. The film denounces "the forces of repression against minorities". It is a "denunciation of extraordinary violence".

The Liberation of L.B. Jones (USA, 1970) is a film by William Wyler, a very famous Jewish director and four-time Oscar winner, especially his film *Ben-Hur* (1960): A racist cop, Willie Joe, sleeps with the wife of a black businessman. The latter wants to initiate divorce proceedings. In the end, the cop murders the businessman and the case is hushed up by the businessman's own lawyer.

In the film *The Desperados* (USA, 1969), a father and his three sons, former Confederate guerrillas, spread terror at the head of a band of demobilised soldiers. Southerners are like that. The film is by Henry Levin.

The Scalphunters (USA, 1968): trapper Bass has to trade his mule and furs for the life of an escaped black slave. After an Indian massacre, he joins the black slave in pursuit of the marauders and tries to get his furs back. "A failed western, but endearing because of the relationship between the white man and the black man". This is filmmaker Sidney Pollack, who also directed the film *The Firm (*1993), in which the members of a law firm are all bastards. Obviously, they are all completely white and Christian.

La longue marche is a film by Alexandre Astruc (Fr., 1966): In June 1944, in the Cévennes, a group of Resistance fighters requisition a Petainist doctor[148] to treat their leader. The Resistance fighters are denounced by the French peasants, mean and rapacious, as everyone knows (just the opposite of the Jews).

The Desired Night (*Hurry Sundown*, USA, 1966) is set in the American South. It is a story about jazz musicians: the whites are evil and unscrupulous, while the blacks are poor victims. A three-hour film directed by Otto Preminger. The same Otto Preminger who made *Exodus* (1960),

---

[148] A doctor loyal to the Vichy regime and a collaborationist with National Socialist Germany.

which exalts the Jewish struggle in 1947 against the British and the Arabs to build a Jewish state in Palestine.

The Professionals (USA, 1966) is a "humanistic and moralistic" western, wrote Guy Bellinger. On the one hand, there are the Mexican mercenaries, who turn out to be idealists. "As for the brave landowner who falls victim to the Mexican bandit, he is nothing but a despicable hypocrite who has stolen his girlfriend from the bandit. Gradually, the initial situation is reversed". The film was directed by Richard Brooks. In *Elmer Gantry* in 1960, Richard Brooks had already made fun of hypocritical Christian preachers.

Genghis Khan (USA, 1965) is another film by Henry Levin. Genghis Khan is portrayed as a "courteous, magnanimous, feminist, libertarian and progressive" man.

Major Dundee is a film by Sam Peckinpah (USA, 1964): At the end of the American Civil War, Major Dundee, a Northerner, decides to pursue the Apaches into Mexican territory. Dundee exterminates the Apaches. In this film we see the hatred of Southerners for blacks, as well as the hatred of Northerners for Apaches. The script is by Harry and Julian Fink, who clearly do not appreciate either Southerners or Northerners.

In *The Diary of a Chambermaid* (Fr., 1964), Joseph, a servant who murdered a little girl, is also an extreme right-wing military man. Mexican director Luis Buñuel, the scion of a wealthy Indian, is well known for his extreme left-wing views and his visceral hatred of Catholicism.

The Intruder (USA, 1962): Adam Cramer arrives in a small southern American town to fight against the integration of black children in white schools. A journalist opposes him and Cramer blackmails his daughter into saying that she was raped by a black man. Just as the man is about to be lynched, the truth comes out and Cramer has to flee. A film by Roger Corman, a "white man".

Going back a little further in time, we come to John Ford's *The Black Sergeant* (USA, 1960): a story of rape and an innocent victim in the army. For the first time in John Ford's work, one of the two heroes is black. "Ford takes an uncomplacent look at the fears, hypocrisies and despicable racism of certain whites". The screenplay was written by one W. Goldbeck.

In Elia Kazan's *Wild River* (USA, 1960), the viewer is transported to the year 1933: a dam is being built on the Tennessee River. The local population (racist white cretins) opposes the hiring of blacks. Chuck fights "victoriously against the obscurantism of the backward common people". Guy Bellinger talks about us like this.

Odds Against Tomorrow (USA, 1959): Burke, an ex-cop, sets up a big heist in which he teams up with Slater, recently released from prison, and a black singer, Ingram. But Slater hates blacks, and during the bank robbery

Slater's prejudices cause everything to go wrong. A thriller about racism, that is, an anti-white racist thriller, directed by a Jew, Robert Wise.

In *The Vanishing American* (USA, 1955), the Joseph Kane *remake* (Cohen), a young girl helps Navajo Indians resist white encroachment on their land.

George Sherman's *Chief Crazy Horse* (USA, 1955) is a film about the death of Crazy Horse, the Indian chief, which is "in the fashion of pro-Indian films". But not pro-Palestinian.

The Yellow Tomahawk, is a western "of a rare anti-militarism". Faced with Indians, a swaggering officer leads his company to the slaughter, and turns out to be incredibly cowardly. He rolls on the ground, cries, begs not to be abandoned. The film is by prolific B western director Lesley Selander, based on a screenplay by H. Bloom. Which of the two rolled on the ground begging in the schoolyard?

In 1951, in *Storm Warming*, Stuart Heisler denounces the racism of the Klu Klux Klan, a den of real murderers. The screenplay is by Daniel Fuchs and Richard Brooks.

In *The Man from Planet X* (USA, 1951), an alien arrives on Earth seeking help for his cooling planet. He encounters the selfishness and hatred of humans, well... mostly white humans. The film is by Edgar Ulmer.

Les Statues meurent aussi, by Alain Resnais (Fr., 1950): A film that denounces colonisation through the art of black craftsmanship. In 1974, Alain Resnais also made a film about the famous Jewish swindler of the 1930s, Stavisky, in which the character's Jewishness was completely erased. Resnais also directed the unforgettable Holocaust *film Nuit et brouillard* (*Night and Fog,* Fr., 1955). Here is what Bouniq-Mercier wrote about it, without exaggeration: "Today, the concentration camps are no more than names on a map. Yet nine million men, women and children were deported there, humiliated, starved and exterminated". "Nine million': that's a lot, isn't it? Is that Hollywood?

Home of the brave, by Mark Robson (USA, 1949): Major Robinson needs three volunteers to locate a Japanese-occupied Pacific island. One of the volunteers is a black man, and the group reacts badly to him. The film is "an anti-racist plea". Based on a screenplay by Carl Foreman.

Archie Mayo's *Black Legion* (*Black Legion,* USA, 1937): A Klu Klux Klan militant rages against immigrants. At his trial, he reveals everything he knows about the organisation. The screenplay is by Abel Finkel, who belongs to another, but much more influential, sect.

White people are bastards who destroy nature and kill animals just for fun. *The Last Hunt* (*The Last Hunt,* USA, 1956) is about the buffalo hunt. Charles Gison, a cruel-tempered hunter, has nothing but contempt for the Indians. "A brave film because it bluntly reminds the American people that they are responsible for the genocide of the Indians, for an ecological catastrophe (the virtual disappearance of the sixteen million bison on which the "redskins" fed) and that they have an excessive taste for firearms", wrote Guy Bellinger, adding that it is a film "that makes you uncomfortable". Richard Brooks (again) is the director.

In *The Roots of Heaven* (USA, 1955), Morel, a white man, dedicates himself to defending elephants on safari in Central Africa. He joins forces with a black revolutionary leader... A film by John Huston, based on a screenplay by Romain Gary (Roman Kacew).

In *I'm with the Hippos*, by Italo Zingarelli (Italy, 1979), two sympathetic compadres (Terence Hill and Bud Spencer) help their African friends against a gang of ivory traffickers. "Probably one of the most progressive films of 1979", wrote Serge Toubiana, who forgot to tell us who the main ivory traffickers are.

When whites love animals, it is to use them in the service of their hatred. See *Les Chiens (The Dogs)*, a film by Alain Jessua (Fr., 1979): In a new town near Paris, many immigrant workers are bitten by guard dogs trained by a certain Morel. Soon, young men set fire to the kennel and kill Morel, and the town splits into two clans. And here is Claude Bouniq-Mercier's brilliant and enlightening commentary: "Evil is rampant, like the plague in the Middle Ages or Nazism more recently. And dogs are the expression of a dehumanisation that threatens our world".

In Samuel Fuller's *White Dog* (*White Dog*, USA, 1982), a young actress who has run over a white wolfdog adopts it to prevent it from being put down and becomes attached to it. We learn that it is a dog trained to attack blacks.

Cosmopolitan cinema also regularly attacks the army. In 1940, the French army was certainly made up of brave soldiers, who went out to "garrison the barbed wire fences", as Céline put it, to defend universal human rights and democracy. But during the Algerian war, the French army, which defended the interests of the French (and their lives), became a gang of torturers. In *La Question* (Fr., 1976), paratroopers sow terror in Algiers. A film by Laurent Heynemen. *Diabolo menthe*, by Diane Kurys (Fr., 1977), denounces the OAS in 1963 and the fascists who run this obscure organisation[149]. *The Battle of Algiers* is another guilt-ridden film about the Algerian war. The film received a Golden Lion at Venice in 1965. Its director, Gilles Pontecorvo, was an Italian Jew.

Michel Drach's *Elise ou la vraie vie* (France-Algeria, 1970) is another film about this period. Originally from Bordeaux, Élise joins her brother Lucien in Paris. Lucien works in a factory and supports the FLN. With no

---

[149]Organisation of the Secret Army (*OAS: Organisation de l'Armée Secrète*) was a French right-wing extremist terrorist organisation founded in Madrid in 1961 after the attempted coup d'état against De Gaulle.

money, Élise is forced to work in a factory, where she starts a relationship with Arezki, an Algerian militant. Faced with racism and police raids, their love is difficult and dangerous. According to Claude Bouniq-Mercier, this is "an honest and generous film that dares to tackle the problems of racism in France during the turbulent period of the Algerian war".

In the light of all this propaganda, we can conclude that "people of colour" have a natural right to kill evil white people. In Joel Schumacher's *A Time to kill* (*A Time to kill*, USA, 1996), a black girl in the American South has been kidnapped and murdered by two criminals. Her father avenges her by killing the culprit during a transfer. The screenplay is by Akiva Goldsman.

It's pretty clear now that blacks are going to save humanity. In Michael Ritchie's *The Golden Boy* (USA, 1986), a child with divine powers has been stolen from a Tibetan monastery by the perfidious Numpsa. Only one of God's chosen can find him. The chosen one in question is a black man from Los Angeles.

In *Deep Impact* (USA, 1998), a giant asteroid is about to crash into the Earth. The planet is saved in extremis by the American president, who is black. In Luc Besson's film *The Fifth Element*, the president of the world is also black. In *As God* (*Bruce Almighty*, USA, 2003), another black man plays the role of God. The film is by Tom Shadyac, based on a screenplay by Steven Koren. David Palmer, the President of the United States in the series *24*, is again played by a black actor. In *Independence Day* (USA, 1996), director Roland Emmerich shows a planet under attack by aliens. Earth is saved by a black man and, hiding right behind him, a Hasidic Jew[150]. All this propaganda prepared the American people to elect the first black president of the United States in November 2008.

But let us end this analysis of Western multicultural society through cinema with a science fiction film, a truly entertaining and enlightening one: *The Matrix* (USA, 1999). Larry and Andy Wachowski's film is a cult work in its genre. But it has been misunderstood by many.

In the film, humans are totally subjected to a computer programme created by machines that dominates their every thought and every aspect of their lives. They believe they exist, but in reality they are nothing more than slaves to the Matrix. The last free human beings in the real world are those who resist this totalitarian world. *The Matrix* is a system, it is our enemy, Morpheus explains to Neo in the famous scene in the middle of the crowd in the streets of New York, where Neo turns to look at the beautiful blonde in the red dress. What do we see in that scene? That the whole crowd, all those people who are part of the Matrix and who don't want to unplug, are

---

[150] On Hasidic Jews, a branch of the Kabbalistic mystics, see *Psychoanalysis of Judaism* and *Jewish Fanaticism*, and note *225*.

white. All of them, without exception. We see nuns crossing the street, suspicious policemen, stockbrokers in suits and ties, etc., and they are all part of the system, which is the enemy. The message is quite clear. On the other hand, on the contrary, the resistance is made up of people of all colours and conditions. The leader of the resistance, Morpheus, is black. Among them, there is a traitor; and he is obviously white. He will be eliminated by a black man. Faced with the cruelty of the white Matrix guards - the Smith Agents - who persecute our heroes and torture Morpheus, the viewer naturally identifies with the resistance. In the last scene of the film, Neo, the liberator of humanity, the messiah everyone was waiting for, hears a message in the phone box. And this message, delivered to the audience, is the following: "From now on you will accept to live in a world without laws or rules, without limits or boundaries. A world where anything can happen...I know you are afraid...You are afraid of change. But don't be afraid. That is the message: a world without borders, a humane world government. The viewer who has identified with Neo and Morpheus has been deceived. Because the Matrix really exists. She made the film. And there are enough clues in the film to make this clear. The last nest of human resistance is called Zion, the hero, Neo, is the chosen one, the mythical liberator of humanity announced according to the prophecies who will be able to save Zion, as revealed by the Oracle.

Since then, Larry and Andy Wachowski have changed sex. They are now women. Their names are Lana and Lilly Wachowski and they live their femininity and their (Kabbalistic?) Judaism very well without any problems.

The Muslim conquest

The migratory invasion of the Third World that submerged Europe and the Western world after the Second World War has no other cause than this tireless propaganda in favour of the cosmopolitan project. Already in the 7th century the Jews had favoured the conquest of the Visigothic kingdom of Spain by the Muslims and had begun to triangulate the conflicts in the Iberian peninsula. They had been the first to open the gates of Spanish cities to invaders whom they welcomed as liberators. Heinrich Gratez, one of the first Jewish historians of the mid-19th century, wrote: "After the battle of Jerez (July 711) and the death of Rodrigo, the last of the Visigothic kings, the victorious Arabs moved on, supported everywhere by the Jews. In each city they conquered, the Muslim generals could leave only a small garrison of their own troops, as they needed every man to subdue the country; they therefore entrusted them to the custody of the Jews. Thus the Jews, who until recently had been serfs, became the masters of the cities of Cordoba, Granada, Malaga and many others[151]."

A century later, in 1981, another famous Jewish historian, Leon Poliakov, wrote explicitly in his monumental *History of Anti-Semitism*: "What seems certain is that, as they advanced, the Arab conquerors entrusted them with the surveillance of the cities that fell into their hands[152]". Nor was the phenomenon a novelty, for the Jews had already favoured the Muslim advance wherever the Christians had difficulties: The "Jewries" of Syria, Palestine and Egypt, under Christian rule, as well as those of Mesopotamia, under Persian rule, "joyfully welcomed the Muslim invaders[153]", Poliakov also wrote.

This role played by Jews is therefore of public notoriety[154]. In 1945, the Jewish historian Abraham Leon Sachar, who was national director of the Hillel Foundations for Universities in the United States, claimed in his *History of the Jews* that the Arabs had conquered the Visigothic kingdom thanks to the favourable attitude of the Jews.[155]

Read also what the German-born Jewish historian Josef Kastein said in his book *History and Fate of the Jews*: "The Berbers helped the Arab movement to spread to Spain, at the same time as the Jews supported this movement with men and money[156]."

Deborah Pessin, in her book *The Jewish People*, published in New York in 1952, also confirmed this: "In the year 711, Spain was conquered by the Muslims, and the Jews greeted their arrival with joy. They were able to return to Spain from the countries where they had fled. They went out to meet the invaders, helping them to take the Spanish cities[157]."

---

[151] Heinrich Graetz, *History of the Jews III*, London, Myers High Holborn, 1904, p. 111.
[152] Léon Poliakov, *Histoire de l'antisémitisme, tome I*, Point Seuil, 1981, p. 97.
[153] Léon Poliakov, *Histoire de l'antisémitisme, tome I*, Point Seuil, 1981, p. 74.
[154] Marcelino Menéndez Pelayo also wrote it clearly in his *Historia de los Heterodoxos españoles, Tomo I*, Ed. F. Maroto, Madrid, 1880, p. 216.
[155] Abram Leon Sachar, *A History of the Jews*, Mc Graw-Hill College, 1967 - Abraham Leon Sachar, *Historia de los Judíos*, Ediciones Ercilla, Santiago de Chile, 1945, p. 227.
[156] Josef Kastein, *History and destiny of the Jews*, Garden City Publishing, 1936, p. 239.
[157] Deborah Pessin, *The Jewish People*, United Synagogue Commission on Jewish Education, 1952, book II, p. 200, 201. [For more details read the great study by Maurice Pinay, *Plot against the Church*, for example, in Part Four, chapter XV, p. 215: "Around 694, seventeen years before *the conquest of Spain by the Muslims, they planned a general uprising, in agreement with their* co-religionists beyond the Straits of Gibraltar, where the Muslims *conquered Spain.* 215: "Around 694, seventeen years before the conquest of Spain by the Muslims, they planned a general uprising, in agreement with their co-religionists beyond the Straits, where several Berber tribes professed Judaism and where the Jews banished from Spain had found refuge. The rebellion was probably to break out in several places at once, the moment the Jews from Africa had landed on the shores of Spain; but before the time agreed upon for the execution of the plan

The Jews of North Africa, who had emigrated from Spain in the previous century, joined the invading Muslim troops, while the Jews still residing in the Visigothic kingdom opened their doors to them.

In his book entitled *The Invention of the Jewish People*, published in 2008, Israeli historian Shlomo Sand confirmed this once again, in case it was necessary: "Contemporary Christian sources condemned the treacherous behaviour of Jews in various cities who greeted the invading forces and were even recruited by them as auxiliary troops. Indeed, the flight of many Christians led to the Jews, their rivals, being appointed governors of many cities. In his compilation *Israel in Exile*, Ben-Zion Dinur had included many quotations from Arab sources that corroborated the Christian ones[158]."

Under Muslim rule, the Jews enjoyed great prosperity. This situation lasted until the Berber invasion of the Almohads in the mid-12th century. Contrary to their predecessors, the Almohads had decided to put an end to Jewish power in al-Andalus. Leon Poliakov told us: "In Andalusia, the golden age was not to last long. In 1147 it was invaded by the intolerant and sectarian Almohads from Morocco, who imposed Islam by force". The Jews had to leave the region for more benign places in the Christian lands of Castile, Aragon, Languedoc and Provence: "When, in the mid-13th century, the fall of the Almohad dynasty rendered concealment useless, there was no sign of a massive return to Judaism.... But a Jewish community was openly reconstituted in Granada[159]."

---

arrived, the government was put on notice of the conspiracy. King Egica immediately took the measures dictated by necessity; then, having summoned a Council at Toledo, he informed his spiritual and temporal guides of the guilty designs of the Jews, and requested them to punish severely that "accursed race". Hearing the declarations of some Israelites, from which it transpired that the plot aimed at nothing less than turning Spain into a Jewish State, the bishops, shuddering with anger and indignation, condemned all the Jews to the loss of their property and freedom. The king would hand them over as slaves to the Christians and even to those who had hitherto been slaves of the Jews and whom the king emancipated". *Enciclopedia Judaica Castellana*, vocablo España, vol. IV, p. 142, col. 2].

[158]Shlomo Sand, *La invención del pueblo judío*, Akal, 2011, Madrid, p. 228-229. [The third regiment, which had been sent against Elvira, besieged Granada, the capital of that state, and entrusted the blockade to a local force made up of Muslims and Jews, and that is what they did wherever they found Jews [...]. Having taken Carmona, Musa attacked Seville. After a siege that lasted many months, Musa captured the city, and the Christians fled to Baya. Leaving the Jews as the standing army in Seville, Musa advanced towards Merida. Moreover, when Tariq saw that Toledo was empty, he took the Jews there and left some of his men with them, while he headed for Wadi al-Hajara (Guadalajara)." note 39: B.Z. Dinur, *Israel in Exile*, cit., vol.1,1, p. 116-117. (NdT)]

[159]Léon Poliakov, *Histoire de l'antisémitisme, tome I*, Point Seuil, 1981, p. 112.

All the Jews in Muslim Spain had not "integrated". Others had preferred to flee northwards, to join the Christians, whom they had betrayed a few centuries earlier, in their struggle against Islam.[160]

Shmuel Trigano tried to make us believe that the Jews were the best allies of the Christians. With impudence, the usual famous *chutzpah*, he wrote: "The Christian princes of the reconquest found in the Jews reliable allies and, once the territories were conquered, the familiarity of the Jews with the country was a useful advantage. Kings and nobles appointed Jews to important posts as diplomats, financiers, tax collectors, administrators, scholars and physicians. In Castile, which was often politically unstable, kings felt they could rely on their Jewish advisors, as they were not subject to the conflicting loyalties of their Christian vassals[161]."

Leon Poliakov said the same, writing without laughing: "The princes of the Reconquest found in them dedicated and reliable auxiliaries". Their rise in Christian Spain was "vertiginous". And it had to be said that not all Jews lived in misery: "The Jews took their place in the social scale immediately after kings and lords, a rank which assured them of the great variety of their socio-economic functions. Trade, industry and handicrafts were largely in their hands," Poliakov noted. "In charge of both the princes' pleasures and their business affairs, the great Jews of Toledo and Barcelona acted as the permanent think-tank of the Spanish kings, accompanying them on their ceaseless travels.

In Aragon, the role of the Jews began to fade at the end of the 13th century, but in Castile, which was more Islamised, it continued until the 15th century. Leon Poliakov also claimed that the Jews of Spain played a civilising role, as did the Catholic clergy in the rest of Europe: "Hence the substitution, from the 13th century onwards, of Latin for the vernacular in administrative and legal documents, since the Jews had a marked aversion to Latin[162]."

---

[160] The situation was similar in 2008: after having favoured the invasion of Europe by the masses of the third world, the Jewish intellectuals, as a whole, were encouraging the West to wage war in Iraq and Afghanistan, waiting for the turn of Iran, Libya and Syria. [Read for example this interesting editorial in the daily *Le Monde* of 16 March 2011 entitled: "*Yes, we must intervene in Libya, and quickly!*", signed by the cream of the "French" *intelligentsia*: Pascal Bruckner, Daniel Cohn-Bendit, Frédéric Encel, Raphaël Enthoven, André Glucksmann, Bernard Kouchner, Claude Lanzmann, Bernard-Henry Lévy. At https://www.lemonde.fr/idees/article/2011/03/16/oui-il-faut-intervenir-en-libye-et-vite_1493895_3232.html.]

[161] Shmuel Trigano, (ed.), *La Société juive à travers l'histoire, tome I*, Fayard, 1992, p. 275.

[162] Léon Poliakov, *Histoire de l'antisémitisme, tome I*, Point Seuil, 1981, p. 117, 118, 129.

But their speciality was undoubtedly finance: "The great Jewish financiers of Toledo and Seville, who controlled all the financial circuits of the kingdom, remained all-powerful at the Castilian court, wrote Poliakov...They lived in an atmosphere of oriental seraglio, intrigue and conspiracy, fighting fiercely against the Christian favourites when they were not fighting among themselves". Moreover, they carried weapons in the manner of the nobles and knew how to use them to liquidate their enemies, as Poliakov told us: "In 1380, several Jewish notables, jealous of the favour shown by Henry of Castile to his treasurer Joseph Pichon, beheaded him in his house, arousing the great indignation of the king and of the chroniclers of the time[163]."

At this time there was a civil war between the pro-Jewish King Peter the Cruel and his bastard brother Henry of Trastamara, supported by the Christian bourgeoisie. In the end, Henry of Trastamara won and immediately took measures against the Jews[164]. In 1380, a royal edict abolished the judicial autonomy of the Jewish communities. "The cornerstone of their power was crumbling," wrote Poliakov. Thereafter, many Jews found refuge in Portugal, where "the clergy protested against Jewish domination as elsewhere, and the population began to murmur[165]." In 1391, the common people revolted against the Jews and a bloodbath flooded Castile, Aragon, Catalonia and Majorca. Led by a monk named Martínez de Ecija, the Spaniards killed more than 4,000 Jews in Seville. The Barcelona community was annihilated. A royal decree of 1412 banned Jews from holding public office and forced them to wear long black coats down to their feet. This is what Poliakov had to say on the subject: "In Aragon, documents show that they were traditionally already recognisable, apparently thanks to their coats, and that they themselves attached great importance to this distinction[166]." Although it is true that in Castile the Jews refused to wear them.

Some Jews converted to Catholicism out of self-interest, but continued to practise Judaism in secret. The Spanish soon gave them a name: the

---

[163] Léon Poliakov, *Histoire de l'antisémitisme, tome I*, Point Seuil, 1981, p. 135.
[164] For an account of this war, see Hervé Ryssen, *A History of Anti-Semitism* (2010).
[165] Léon Poliakov, *Histoire de l'antisémitisme, tome I*, Point Seuil, 1981, p. 135-146.
[166] Léon Poliakov, *Histoire de l'antisémitisme, tome I*, Point Seuil, 1981, p. 121. Elie Wiesel confirmed these facts at the time: "The yellow star? Well, it doesn't really bother me. It even allows me to feel more intimately connected to the Jews of the Middle Ages who wore the *wheel* in the ghettos of Italy... There are stars for all prices. Those of the rich are resplendent; those of the poor are dull. It is strange, but I wear mine with an inexplicable pride". *Mémoires, Tome I*, Éditions du Seuil, 1994, p. 82. In 1942, Serge Gainsbourg, who would later become a famous singer in France, also had to wear the yellow star. He recalled: "I was very proud of that cloth star, I asked my mother every day to iron it well so that it would be impeccable".

"marranos". Thanks to baptism, these Jewish converts had gained even greater access to court jobs, honorary positions and ecclesiastical offices that had previously been completely forbidden to them. By entering universities and religious orders where, as Jews, they had no right of entry, they penetrated whole strata of society - medicine, the army, the judiciary, the clergy - and were even able to marry sons and daughters of the Aragonese and Castilian nobility. "They cleverly took over the most dynamic sectors of society", wrote Henri Tincq in Le Monde on 2 August 2007[167]. Catholic Spain had long boasted of these conversions, before realising that most of them were faked. These "crypto-Jews", or "conversos", were soon accused of being false Christians, and it was through blood lineage that the Spanish came to legitimately consider the Jewish question. Léon Poliakov confirmed that the Marranos played a certain role in weakening the Christian faith: many conversos, he wrote, "professed an aggressive atheism. Some of them, Poliakov recounted, formed a circle whose existence is recorded around 1460 in Medina del Campo'. It was in this town that the first historical mention of an "atheist sect" within Christianity was found.[168]

Already at the beginning of the 15th century, a college of the University of Salamanca had introduced a rule prohibiting those who did not come from pure blood (*ex puro sanguine*) from joining its ranks. In 1440, after several riots against the conversos, Toledo became the first city to adopt the statutes of limpieza de sangre. In 1543, Cardinal Juan Martínez Siliceo convinced King Philip II to enact them for the whole of Spain. From then on, in order to enter university or religious orders, a certificate of purity of blood had to be presented after a thorough genealogical investigation that went as far back in the lineage as possible (the Nazi Nuremberg laws would be limited to the fourth generation): it was the Inquisition. The tribunals of the Inquisition had been operating in Spain with full authority since a bull issued by Pope Sixtus IV in 1478, and their task was to unmask false Catholics, i.e. Jews who had falsely converted to Catholicism and sought to undermine Christianity from within. The Dominican Tomás de Torquemada, appointed by King Ferdinand as Inquisitor of Aragon, Valencia and Catalonia, became famous for his fervent zeal.

As the regional measures of segregation and expulsion were insufficient, the Inquisition proposed to the sovereigns the general expulsion of the Jews. The Jews, "poor and persecuted", tried, as always, to corrupt the authorities. Henri Tincq chose his words well to explain the situation: "The Castilian Jews tried to delay the deadline, and said they were prepared to pay a high

---

[167]Henri Tincq was a French journalist and Vaticanist. After working for the daily *La Croix*, he was a specialist in religious news at *Le Monde* from 1985 to 2008.
[168] Léon Poliakov, *Histoire de l'antisémitisme, tome I*, Point Seuil, 1981, p. 157.

price". But Torquemada, before the Court assembled on 20 March, had succeeded in convincing the king. The year was 1492. The royal decree of 31 March finally obliged the Jews to leave the country by 31 July. That same year, the capture of Granada by the Christians marked the end of several centuries of confrontation with Islam. Under Charles V and Philip II, Spain would experience its great Golden Age.

On the other side of the Mediterranean, Christians were fighting the Turks. In 1453, the Turks had taken Constantinople and, once again, the Jews were decisive in the Muslim victory. Leon Poliakov wrote: "In certain Marrano circles, this Ishmaelite victory, which left a prodigious impression throughout Europe, was understood as a harbinger of the imminent fall of Edom [Christendom, ndlr[169]] and the imminent liberation of Israel".

The Jews had been awaiting the arrival of their longed-for Messiah since time immemorial: "An active congregation of Marranos from Valencia, convinced that the Messiah had just appeared on a mountain near the Bosphorus, set out to emigrate to Turkey: "The blind goyim do not see, said one of the fanatics of the group, that after we have been subdued to them, our God will see to it that we rule over them; our God has promised us that we will go to Turkey; we have heard that the Antichrist is coming; it is said that the Turk will destroy the Christian churches and turn them into stables for cattle, and that he will render honour and reverence to the Jews and the synagogues[170] "."

This idea was also put forward by the novelist Isaac Bashevis Singer, who compared the fate of the Jews in Christianity and in the land of Islam: "When the Redeemer came, the Jews of Israel would be the first to greet him. Besides, a Jew could breathe more freely in the land of the Turks, where the Torah was respected. There were many wealthy Jews living in Istanbul, Izmir, Damascus and Cairo. Yes, sometimes hostile edicts were issued and false accusations were made, but, catastrophes like those in Poland, that was never[171] !"

The Jews had long had high hopes for the Turks. In his book *Rendezvous with Islam*, the writer and journalist Alexandre Adler confirmed that the Jews had supported the Turkish invasion, just as they had supported the Arab invasion of Spain a few centuries earlier:

"Everywhere they advanced, Adler wrote, the Jews... welcomed the Turks as liberators.

The Ottoman Empire of Suleiman the Magnificent, a contemporary of

---

[169] Read about Jewish exegesis in *Psychoanalysis of Judaism* (NdT).
[170] Léon Poliakov, *Histoire de l'antisémitisme, tome I,* Point Seuil, 1981, p. 155.
[171] Isaac Bashevis Singer, *The Slave* (1962), Debols!llo (Penguin Random House), Barcelona, 2019, p. 280

Francis I of France, massively welcomed Jews from Spain, Portugal, Naples, Malta, Sicily and Sardinia, expelled by the Habsburgs. The four great cities of the empire, Salonika, Smyrna, Andrinople and Constantinople, thus became home to the Judeo-Spanish community. These Iberian Jews, the Sephardim, provided the empire with a commercial and intellectual network which, according to Alexandre Adler, played a much underestimated role in the great Ottoman diplomacy of the 16th century. At that time, Turkey found the means to forge strategic alliances with the three anti-Spanish powers of Europe: the France of Henry III and Henry IV, and above all the Protestants: the England of Elizabeth I and the Holland of William of Orange. And Adler stated: "Everywhere, it was the Marranos or crypto-Jews of London, Amsterdam, Bordeaux, Nantes or Angers who wove this tight network of Judaism and revolutionary humanism that was to lead to the great victories of European freedom in the mid-17th century[172]."

José Nasí played an important role in this "victory of European freedom". José Nasí was heir to the wealthy Mendés family, who had fled Portugal for Constantinople, where the Sultan welcomed them with open arms. "Thanks to an international network of Marranos, wrote Poliakov, he was for some fifteen years the best informed man in Europe, and his information, combined with his gifts, enabled him to form a "lobby", influence Ottoman foreign policy and even decide on declarations of war and peace conclusions[173]."

Nasid became a sworn enemy of France following a dispute over 150,000 ducats he had lent to Henry II around 1549. The conflict between France and the Ottoman Empire was settled by a treaty in October 1569, "the original of which was written in Hebrew; who knows whether this unusual detail did not reflect a further vexation which the Jew intended to inflict on the very Christian King?" wrote Poliakov, adding: "As constant as his hostility to France seems to have been his sympathy for the cause of the rebellious Protestants in Flanders".

He sent encouraging advice to the Calvinists in Antwerp, "among whom he counted many old friends. More than once during the religious struggles of the 16th century, the Calvinists were aided by Jews, and William of Orange himself sought their help. Indeed, in 1566, among the leaders of the Flemish resistance were the influential Marranos Marcos Pérez, Martín López and Fernandino Bernuy".

Poliakov referred to these words spoken about Joseph Nasi: "Philip II described him as "the personage who contributes most to the enterprises

---

[172] Alexandre Adler, *Rendez-vous avec l'islam*, Grasset, 2005, p. 168.
[173] Léon Poliakov, *Histoire de l'antisémitisme, tome I*, Point Seuil, 1981, p. 211.

being carried out to the detriment of Christianity, and who drives them most"; in short, the invisible conductor of an anti-Christian plot[174]." On several occasions, Joseph Nasi set himself up as a protector of the Jews. In 1561, the sultan gave him the city of Tiberias and the surrounding lands as a gift to create a kind of Jewish home or refuge. Nasid set about restoring the city, surrounding it with a wall and attempting to establish industries, despite the protests of the apostolic delegate to Palestine, Boniface of Ragusa, who spoke out against "the arrival of those vipers, worse than those who roam the ruins of the city". But the project failed, as the Jewish masses did not spontaneously embrace this political Zionism ahead of its time, and very few Jews came to settle in Tiberias.

Nevertheless, Joseph Nasid continued to pursue his goals. A sworn enemy of Christianity, Nasi sought revenge against the Christians through the Turks. In 1566, the new Sultan Selim II gave him the island of Naxos and made him Duke of Naxos. In 1570, it was he who urged the Sultan to declare war on Venice. The enterprise began with the conquest of Cyprus, where he hoped to become king. "The great island was the geographical springboard to Palestine," wrote Poliakov.

"Nasid advises Suleiman to attack Venice in order to take Cyprus, which he wants to turn into a refuge for the Jews[175]", wrote Jacques Attali.

But the Ottoman offensive led to an alliance between Spain, Venice and the Holy See, and resulted in the great Turkish naval defeat at Lepanto. Nasid thus fell into a state of semi-disgrace. "Other Jewish favourites replaced him in the Sultan's favour", wrote Poliakov. For fifteen years, his name had been constantly in the headlines of European diplomatic correspondence. Through Marlowe's *The Jew of Malta*, he helped crystallise the image of Shylock, the odious character in Shakespeare's play, *The Merchant of Venice*[176]. Israeli historiography rightly made him the first great precursor of Zionism.

In 19th century North Africa, under the Ottoman Empire, the situation of the Jews was already less favourable than in the budding democratic Europe, especially in France and England, where already at the beginning of the century the Rothschilds, the Foulds, the Pereires and other cosmopolitan bankers were striving to tighten their grip on European governments.

André Nahoum, a Tunisian neighbourhood doctor, son of a prosperous merchant, described the atmosphere in Tunisia before the advent of the French protectorate: "The Jews got along quite well with the Arabs, but

---

[174] Léon Poliakov, *Histoire de l'antisémitisme, tome I*, Point Seuil, 1981, p. 212.
[175] Jacques Attali, *Los judíos, el mundo y el dinero*, Fondo de cultura económica, Buenos Aires, 2005, p. 227.
[176] Léon Poliakov, *Histoire de l'antisémitisme, tome I*, Point Seuil, 1981, p. 214.

they were "*dhimmis*", that is, protected - like the Christians, by the way - by Islam. They paid a special tax, the "capitation", and were subject to all sorts of prohibitions, such as riding horses or building houses higher than those of the Muslims. Finally, they were subject to the "*chtaka*", a custom that entitled any Arab to strike a Jew on the head. It is said that one day, in the ghetto, a very small Arab boy saw a Jew who was too tall for him, and said: "I want to give you your *chtaka*, but I don't know how to do it, so lift me up. And the tall Jew did it.

"Arriving in France could only mean liberation, added André Nahoum; it was republican France, the France of 1789, which brought emancipation to the oppressed. The Jews of Tunisia, like those of Morocco and Algeria, gave themselves fully to the French identity[177]."

In fact, there are many other accounts of North African Jews brimming with enthusiasm for France. This was not, of course, the France of the terroirs, which was indifferent to them, but the France of the "rights of man", generous and tolerant, with its jelly-brain, unreluctant and open to all the winds of the East. We see that, although Jews and Arabs "got along quite well", the Jews immediately collaborated with the French coloniser.

As early as 1830, when a French expeditionary force took possession of Algiers, the Jews rejoiced, seeing it as an instrument of their revenge against the Turks. In the 6 June 2006 issue of the daily *Rivarol*, Camille Galic quoted a book by Claude Martin, published in 1936 and entitled *Les Israélites* algériens *(The Algerian Israelites)*: "On 29 June 1830, Bacri and Duran, the two leading figures of Algiers, went to meet General Bourmont, followed by a long retinue of women, children, camels and mules. To the cry of Long Live the French! they set out gaily to beat and plunder the Turks, and then were insolent to the Moors, many of whom left the city for it. The Jews then played a profitable part in the real estate business, monopolising on a large scale the role of commercial and political intermediaries." Bacri, for example, acted as adviser to Marshal de Bourmont in administrative matters and "received substantial bribes for his intermediations."

We know that in Algeria, in 1870, the flamboyant Third French Republic granted French nationality to Jews, and only to Jews. It should be remembered that a "French" minister at the time, Adolphe Crémieux, was also president of the Alliance *Israélite Universelle* (Universal Israelite *Alliance*). Thus, North African Muslims could legitimately harbour some resentment against Republican France.[178]

---

[177] André Harris and Alain de Sédouy, *Juifs et Français*, Grasset, 1979, Poche, p. 288.
[178] See also in *Jewish Fanaticism*.

Charles de Foucauld, who explored Morocco in 1883-1884, left an important testimony. Read how he spoke of the Moroccan peasant: "There is only one resource: the Jew. If he is an honest man, he will lend you 60%, if not much more: then it's all over; in the first year of drought, they confiscate his land and he ends up in prison; ruin is total. That's the story you hear at every turn; you hear it repeated in every house you enter. Everything unites for such a result, everyone supports each other so that there is no escape. The kaid protects the Jew, who bribes him; the sultan supports the kaid, who brings every year a gigantic tribute, who constantly sends rich feasts, and who finally collects only for his master, for sooner or later all that he possesses will be confiscated, either in life or at his death. The whole population is therefore deeply saddened and discouraged."

The country was at that time forbidden to Christians, and Charles de Foucauld had travelled through it disguised as a Jew and accompanied by a rabbi. He then wrote: "Chefchaouen is one of the most fanatical towns in the Rif, famous for its intolerance. The story is still told of the torture of an unfortunate Spaniard... Even the Jews are subjected to the worst treatment; outside the *mellah* [Jewish quarter, ndt], they are attacked with stones. No one passed me without greeting me with an *Allah iharrak bouk*, May God burn your father[179] !"

In Algeria, in the years of the Dreyfus affair[180], the descendants of the pioneers, the "little whites", walked shoulder to shoulder with the Arabs through the streets of Algiers singing the "anti-Jewish Marseillaise". During World War II, the Arabs naturally sided with the Axis powers. In November 1942, German troops invaded Tunisia. Gisèle Halimi, a Sephardic feminist lawyer, left another interesting testimony in her autobiography: 'The parachuting of the Germans,' she wrote, 'caused a real jubilation among the Arabs. In the streets, the green uniforms attracted to them offerings, handshakes and fraternisation. "Germans-Arabs, *kif kif*," said the young men to the astonished soldiers..... These Arabs, born traitors, betrayed. They're a different breed," a neighbour explained to my mother, "they'll stab you in the back if you don't keep them at bay[181] "."

In his 1997 book *Racism or Identity Hatred*, the scribbler Daniel Sibony spoke of the suffering of his fellow Sephardim, who would have liked to stay in Algeria after independence in 1962. Here we see the intellectual contortions so characteristic of the Talmudic spirit, and, again, always that inclination to blame others: "They felt like Arabs, he wrote. But their Arab brothers did not feel that way, and one fine day they told them nicely: you

---

[179]Charles de Foucauld, *Reconnaissance au Maroc*, p. 41, 8. Read the similar testimony of the writer Guy de Maupassant in *Jewish Fanaticism*.
[180] See footnote 63.
[181] Gisèle Halimi, *Le Lait de l'oranger*, Gallimard, 1988, Pocket, 2001, p. 72.

can do whatever you want, you are Jews.... Those Jews claimed that they could do it, and the Arabs replied: it is impossible. Did they know that in their Islam the Jewish traces are impossible to erase? In any case, they were right. Unless this dialogue was understood in a different way, and the Jews said to them: we want to offer you our Memory, our identity. And the others replied, not without delicacy: You can accept to lose it, but we cannot accept to receive it.... And these Jews went away, leaving behind their possessions and their dreams[182]."

In the lands of Islam, as elsewhere, Judaism is a corrosive force for religion and the ancestral traditions of the people. In the early 20th century, after the First World War, the secular movement of the Young Turks and the Kemalist revolution had part of their origins in the influence exerted by the "*Dommehs*", Jews falsely converted to Islam. Here is what Gershom Scholem, one of the greatest Jewish thinkers of the 20th century, had to say about the latter: "The Dommehs, he wrote, provided many members of the Young Turks' intelligentsia.... They played an important role in the beginnings of the Committee of Union and Progress, an organisation of the Young Turks' movement that originated in Salonika.... There is evidence that David Bey, one of the three ministers in the first Young Turk government and an important leader of the Young Turk party, was a Donmeh[183]."

The intellectual and influential press director Alexandre Adler confirmed this: "At least one of the founders of the Young Turks movement on 14 July 1889, the centenary of the storming of the Bastille, was a self-confessed Donmeh, Sükrü Dey. Several Donmeh generals fought at the head of his troops... in the ill-fated wars of the empire. But Mustafa Kemal's entourage, despite his complete break with his scheming Donmeh finance minister Djazid Bey, was full of Sabbateans (and also a clique of Sunni Muslim Masons originally of the Scottish Rite)[184]."

In the immediate aftermath of World War I, the secular movement of the "Young Turks" aroused a wave of hostility towards the Greek Christian population. In a 1979 book entitled *Jews and the French,* we find a most interesting testimony. This was told by a certain Maurice Denailles, a merchant in the Sentier district (Paris) and a Jew of Turkish origin. He had emigrated to France in 1924 and recalled Mustafa Kemal's rise to power: "My first memories are horrible. It was genocide. I witnessed the massacre of the Greeks in Smyrna, I saw whole neighbourhoods burn. I saw Turks

---

[182] Daniel Sibony, *Le Racisme ou la haine identitaire*, C. Bourgeois, 1997, p. 287.
[183] Gershom Scholem, *Le Messianisme juif*, 1971, Calmann-Lévy, 1974, p. 235. On the Donmehs, false Muslim converts of Sabbatean origin (Kabbalistic mystics), see *Psychoanalysis of Judaism.*
[184] Alexandre Adler, *Rendez-vous avec l'islam*, Grasset, 2005, p. 175.

parading with necklaces made of pieces of breasts hanging down. I saw Greek popes descending in line through the streets, forced to walk on broken bottles thrown by the crowd". Maurice Denailles, for his part, was glad that the Jews did not have to suffer the fury of the Turks: "Fortunately, he explained, Kemal had a half-Jewish mother, which is why we were spared that time[185]." It remains to be seen what role exactly the Donmeh generals of the Turkish armies played in the massacre of Christians in Turkey and the genocide of Christians in Armenia.

Anti-Christianity

Jewish intellectuals hold in sovereign contempt all those who question their "mission" as "chosen people" and "redeemers of mankind". In the 21st century, they continue their secular fight against Christianity, especially against the Catholic Church.

In 1994, a second-rate Jewish intellectual like Edouard Valdman published a book entitled *The Jews and Money*. The author made no secret of his feelings towards the Catholic Church: "A fantastic destruction of human intelligence[186] ", he wrote. And Valdman, who had clearly ingested a large dose of Nietzsche, equated Catholicism with Bolshevism. Note that this intellectual hackery allows for silence on the overwhelming role of Bolshevik Jews in Russia and elsewhere: "Here the Inquisition, there the Gulag. The same methods, the same ideology, the cult of transparency, equality, purity and therefore death. The desire to make people transparent to themselves and to the world plunges us into crime". The Jew, on the other hand, is never a criminal, even if his red hands are stained with Russian blood. Communism and Catholicism, Valdman added, "are two perversions, two cults of equality, two cults of reduction". He insisted: "There can be no peace, no equality, all of them deadly, Christian ideas, which, if they are to be embodied, lead directly to totalitarianism". Further on in his text, he spoke, without fearing possible legal action, of "perverse and guilt-ridden Christianity[187]."

In cinema, Jewish directors have gradually dared to attack the Christian religion. In our previous works, we saw more than twenty films in which Christians, and Catholics in particular, were portrayed by cosmopolitan directors as obtuse, mean-spirited, even psychotic, and medieval Europe as an abominable era. Let us look at a few more examples:

---

[185] André Harris and Alain de Sédouy, *Juifs et Français*, Grasset, 1979, Poche, p. 94.
[186] Édouard Valdman, *Les Juifs et l'argent*, Editions Galilée, 1994, p. 28.
[187] Édouard Valdman, *Les Juifs et l'argent*, Éditions Galilée, 1994, p. 31, 63, 70.

Mirrors (Fr., 2008): A nun was once possessed by a demon as a child. Lunatic psychiatrists succeeded in enclosing the demon in mirrors, and since then it has manifested itself through the windows of a house to commit its misdeeds and terrorise a nice mixed-race family. The nun is sought out and persuaded to confront the mirrors. She then finds herself tied up in a room, surrounded by the mirrors, and confronts the demon, praying with all her might, rosary in hand, until it literally explodes into a thousand pieces! It turns out that the demon was none other than the nun herself when she was 12 years old. The director of this dreck is Alexandre "Aja", aka Jouan-Arcady, son of the cosmopolitan filmmaker Alexandre Arcady.

Le moine et la sorcière (*The Monk and the Witch*) (Fr., 1986): In the 13th century, Brother Etienne arrives in a village to eradicate heresy. Elda, a young woman with the power to heal with plants, is accused of witchcraft. The inquisitor has her transferred to the prisons of the Count of Vilars, who also ruthlessly exploits his peasants. Apparently these were not good times to live in. The film is by Suzanne Schiffman.

Ladyhawke (*Ladyhawke*, USA, 1984) is also set in the Middle Ages. The knight Navarre is in love with Isabeau of Anjou, but an evil bishop, Aquila, has bewitched the couple. In the end, Navarre rides into the cathedral during mass and slashes the evil bishop with his sword, much to the delight of the director, Richard Donner, who is obviously not a Catholic.

*Entre tinieblas (*Spain, 1983) is a film by Pedro Almodóvar: an abbess tries everything to ensure the survival of the convent. In the film we see a homosexual nun, drug addict and expert blackmailer.

The Verdict (USA, 1982) is a Sidney Lumet film (again): a young woman has fallen into a coma after a medical error. The town's archbishop, who runs the hospital, tries to hush up the case by offering a large sum of money to the family's lawyer. The latter ends up winning the case, thanks to the testimony of a black anaesthetist. The Catholic Church and the judiciary get a good hiding.

Ms. 45 (*Angel of Vengeance*, USA, 1981): Thana, deaf and dumb but beautiful, is raped twice on the streets of New York and in her flat. She becomes seductive and lures men in order to better execute them. Disguised as a nun, she attends the grand ball of haute couture and pulls out a pistol hidden in her black stockings. In the end she is killed. A film by Abel Ferrara, produced by Arthur Weisberg.

In *Bad Lieutenant* (USA, 1992), Abel Ferrara himself portrays a corrupt cop, drug addict, gambler and bad father. One day he learns that a nun has been brutally raped at the church altar by a gang of thugs. The corrupt lieutenant is determined to find the culprits and collect the reward, but the nun insists on protecting them. A sordid film, like most of Abel Ferrara's films.

True confessions (USA, 1980) is the story of a confrontation between two brothers: Desmond, who is chancellor of the archdiocese (played by Robert de Niro), and Tom, a policeman. Tom has found a priest dead of a heart attack... in a brothel bed. He also learns that his brother is working for the Church in major real estate deals with a disreputable, but very Catholic, businessman. And her Catholic brother is also involved in a pornographic film business! This is a film by Ulu Grosbard, whose real name is Israel Grosbard. Born in Antwerp, he was the son of Rose Tenenbaum and Morris Grosbard, who worked in the diamond trade...

Hair was made in 1979. Those who made it through the first hour of this unwatchable film without nodding off will have noticed a sacrilegious scene that takes place in a church: a gang of hairy hippies, high on LSD, transform a wedding ceremony into an unholy party, indulging in unbridled ecstatic dancing, as if each of these freaks had an evil demon to evacuate. In reality, these dances are more reminiscent of Hasidic Jewish customs[188]. The film is by the "Czech" director Milos Forman. We know that Jewish directors love to interrupt Catholic religious ceremonies in their films. But perhaps it is even more interesting, in this case, to note that this scene is nothing more than a projection onto the goyim (gentiles) of a specifically Jewish problem.

In *The Medusa Touch* (UK, 1978), the diabolical brain of a dead man continues to wreak terrible havoc, culminating in the destruction of Canterbury Cathedral. In the final scene, the archbishop is crushed to death by large blocks of stone falling from the vaults, and the entire cathedral collapses on the worshippers. This is what makes director Jack Gold dream.

Inside a convent (*Interno di un convento*, Italy, 1977) is set in a 19th century Italian convent. The abbess discovers that Sister Veronica has a lover who comes to see her at night. The abbess fires the young man, but to take revenge Veronica has opium poured into the convent's food. A wave of sexual madness sweeps through the nuns' quarters. "A beautiful and vibrant pamphlet against oppression and hypocrisy", according to Claude Bouniq-Mercier. The film is by Walerian Borowczyk, who is certainly not a Catholic.

The Omen, released in 1976, is a film by Richard Donner: Robert Thorn (Gregory Peck) is the US ambassador to London. He has a 5-year-old son, Damien, whom he adopted at birth without the knowledge of his wife, who had just suffered a traumatic miscarriage. Several tragic and strange deaths occur in and around the ambassador's home. One day, in his office, he receives a hallucinated priest who was in the hospital when his son was

---

[188] On Hasidic Jewish sects (mystical Kabbalistic Jews) read *Psychoanalysis of Judaism* and *Jewish Fanaticism*.

born. Father Brennan tries to convince him that Damien is none other than the Antichrist. The priest's bedroom is completely covered with pages from the Bible and no less than 47 crucifixes hang on the walls. It's clear that the Catholic religion can drive people crazy... The famous director Richard Donner (who directed *Lethal Weapon*) was actually called Richard Schwartzberg. The screenplay was written by David Seltzer.

In the same genre, there is William Friedkin's famous film *The Exorcist*, released in 1973. But in *The Exorcist*, the director gives the two Catholic priests a certain dignity. So *The Exorcist* is not an entirely anti-Christian film.

Flavia the Muslim Nun, by Gianfranco Mingozzi (Italy, 1974): In the early 15th century, the young Flavia, moved by the fate of a wounded Saracen, is punished and sent to a convent by her father. A raid by a troop of Saracens gives Flavia the opportunity to regain her freedom. She becomes the wife of a Moorish chieftain, but he disappoints her. The Christians punish her terribly: naked, they cut off her shanks before slitting her throat. "A plea for women's liberation" and "naive anti-clericalism", according to critics. But the real question is: Mingozzi or Minkowski?

We also see that nuns can be very mean. *Papillon* is a famous 1973 American film about the prison world. Actor Steve McQueen plays a convict deported to Cayenne. Life is hell. But he manages to escape, crosses the sea and is taken in by a convent of nuns. The Mother Superior is very suspicious, but finally agrees to offer him hospitality and gives him a room for the night. Unfortunately for him, however, the next morning he is woken up by the police: that's what Catholic nuns are like, they are sneaky and false. The film is by Franklin Schaffner, who also made an anti-Nazi film in 1978, *The Boys from Brazil* (1978).

In the Name of the Father (Italy, 1971), by Marco Bellochio: Angelo and Franck cannot stand the limitations of their Jesuit school and rebel against the teachers. Salvatore, for his part, becomes the spokesman for the staff and instigates a strike that ends with his dismissal. The pupils "revolted against the Church and its subjugation of their minds", wrote Jean Tulard.

The Pirate's Bride (Fr, 1969) is a film that bears "the mark": In the French countryside, a young gypsy girl lives with her mother and a billy goat in a wooden hut far from the village. Relations with the villagers are tense and conflictual. Good nomads versus bad sedentary people: we already have the plot of a script that promises to be very "cosmopolitan". One day, his mother is killed by a car on the road. In a stampede, one of the villagers shoots his billy goat to death. The young girl is left alone and decides to take revenge on the villager bastards. As she is quite pretty, she goes to sell her charms to the peasants, but also to the village notables, taking care to record them with a tape recorder. When the priest comes to see her in an attempt to redeem her, she asks him to pray in the church... For her goat! For the devil, as it were.

At the end of the film, we see her enter the church where a mass is being held, which is, of course, interrupted. With the help of a ladder, she places the tape recorder above the door and surreptitiously exits the same way she entered. We then hear the recorded voices of the men who took advantage of his favours echoing in the nave. As they rant at their own wives and neighbours, consternation quickly gives way to settling of scores. As for the girl, she burns her hut and sets off, far from these "mean and timorous" villagers, as Alain Minc would say. This typically Jewish film is the work of Kelly Kaplan.

In *Él* (Mexico), released in 1953, Luis Buñuel portrays an authoritarian and unsympathetic Catholic character. This rich landowner falls in love with Gloria, whom he sees at a religious service. He gets his way and makes her his wife, but little by little, and for no reason, he becomes insanely jealous, to the point of acute paranoia. A religious ceremony is interrupted by the quarrel. In one scene of the film, we also see a gluttonous priest eating with his mouth open in front of the other guests. It is this priest, a friend of the rich landowner, who lectures the young bride who has come to ask his advice. We also see a priest kissing the foot of an altar boy, and a few references to the Marquis de Sade... The director, Luis Buñuel, had been educated by the Jesuit fathers, but apparently the authoritarianism of that environment had disgusted him with religion. The film was produced by Oscar Dancigers, who was of "Russian" origin.

The Captive City (USA, 1952): Jim and Marge Austin flee the small town of Kennington where, as a journalist, Jim has uncovered a web of corruption that extends to all the town's authorities, including the clergy. He will make the case before the Senate. A Robert Wise film. In 1952, Hollywood producers still had to be cautious about attacking Christianity so as not to arouse the anger of the goyim.[189]

In the Middle Ages, Christians were not imbued with all this cosmopolitan propaganda and felt no guilt towards the Jews. Peter the Venerable, abbot of Cluny in the 12th century, wrote a letter to King Louis VII, who was then on a crusade: "The Jews," he said, "are the greatest enemies of the Christians and worse than the Saracens. And he added: "However, it is not fitting to put them to death, but to reserve for them a greater torment, which is to be always slaves, timid and fugitives[190]." At

---

[189]The Hays Code (Motion Picture Production Code) was in force between 1934 and 1967. It determined, in American productions, with a series of restrictive rules (censorship), what could be seen on screen and what could not (NdT).

[190]Fleury, *Histoire ecclésiastique*, par l'abbé Gayraud, *Antisémitisme de Saint Thomas d'Aquin*, p. 105, in André Spire, *Quelques juifs et demi-juifs II*, Grasset, 1928, p. 187.

that time, people knew how to defend themselves against the constant attacks and taunts coming from the "community".

Bolshevism

In October 1917, the Bolshevik revolution broke out in Russia in the form of a coup d'état. Initially, the ideological goal was not only to "liberate the workers", but also to build a perfect world, a world without borders, where equality reigned. A "clean slate" was to be wiped clean so that a "new man" could emerge. In reality, the egalitarian fanaticism of communism immediately led to a succession of crimes and massacres. In all, over the first thirty years, more than thirty million Russians and Ukrainians were liquidated by the criminal madness of the new masters. After the Maoist experiment in China, the Russian Revolution was the second greatest tragedy in human history.

But while at the beginning of the 21st century it is permissible to denounce the horrors of communism, it is still perfectly forbidden in democratic countries to insist on the identity of its main instigators. Yet communism was essentially a Jewish affair: Karl Marx was the grandson of a rabbi; Lenin also had Jewish origins on his mother's side; Trotsky, the leader of the Red Army, was actually called Bronstein; Kamenev, who was president of the Moscow Soviet, was actually surnamed Rosenfeld; as was Zinoviev, the master of Leningrad, who was called Apfelbaum; the first president of the Soviet Union was a Jew, Lenin's close collaborator called Sverdlov, etc, etc. The list of Jewish Bolshevik dignitaries is simply endless.

The revolution that broke out in Berlin in 1918 was led by other Jews: Karl Liebknecht and Rosa Luxemburg. In Hungary at the same time, Bela Kun had headed a revolutionary government composed almost exclusively of Jews, and after 1945 Jews are known to have led the country, as in Poland, Czechoslovakia and Romania. The famous writer Alexander Solzhenitsyn, after many others, demonstrated the involvement of numerous Jewish leaders in this history, and indeed Jewish doctrinaires, Jewish officials and Jewish torturers bore a particularly crushing responsibility for the atrocities committed in the name of this bloody utopia between 1917 and 1947.[191]

Of course, there will always be a Goy to show us that Judaism is above all "diversity", even though what characterises it is precisely its incomparable homogeneity throughout the world.

[191] Read the chapters on this subject in *Planetary Hopes* (Russia 1917 and the 1920s) and *Jewish Fanaticism* (USSR and Central Europe in the 1930s and 1940s and the Spanish Civil War).

After the collapse of the Soviet Union in 1991, Jewish intellectuals around the world threw themselves completely into the advent of a multicultural society and became the most ardent advocates of immigration in all countries. Of course, it is always about the same project: to build a borderless, cosmopolitan world of peace (*shalom*), where people are free and equal and where all identities have disappeared forever - except their own. This is how they imagine one day being recognised as God's people.

Here is yet another testimony to add to the tons of evidence and miles of texts that already exist. In 1992, *Das Ende der Lügen* (*The End of Lies*), a book by Russian-Jewish historian Sonja Margolina, was published in Germany and had the effect of a small bomb. The author, the daughter of a Russian Bolshevik, described the mass participation of Jews in the Bolshevik atrocities.

"The enthusiastic participation of Bolshevik Jews in the subjugation and destruction of Russia was disproportionate, he wrote.... Jews were now everywhere and at all levels of power. The Russian people saw Jews at the head of the Tsar's city, Moscow, where the new Soviet power was concentrated, and also as commanders of the Red Army...The ordinary Russian citizen was very likely to have to deal with a Jewish interrogator or executioner. Wherever the Russian went, he encountered Jews in high positions.... The people were outraged by the fact that Jewish Communists were involved in the destruction of the Russian churches.

Sonja Margolina also recognised another reality: "Overflows of destructive, criminal and pathological potentials, which had nested within the Jewish community, were set in motion in the early years of the Soviet Revolution.

The men of the repressive services were clearly recognisable: "If the officer, the aristocrat or the bureaucrat in uniform were typical of the tsarist regime, then, under the new Bolshevik revolutionary power, the Jewish commissar in his leather jacket and automatic pistol, who often spoke broken Russian, became a symbolic figure of the new regime".

Sonja Margolina also cited the case of one Jakov Bljumkin, a left-wing socialist who had murdered the German ambassador von Mirbach in 1918: 'This neurotic adventurer,' she wrote, 'had been accepted by the Cheka as a reward for his services to the Bolsheviks. Nadesha Mandelstam recounted in her memoirs that, in a Kiev café, Blkhumkin showed a horrified crowd blank forms of death sentences. He boasted that he could write any name he wanted on those pre-printed forms."

At the end of the 1920s, "an appreciable number of Jewish communists invested with the power of life and death in the countryside were seen for the first time. It was during collectivisation that the image of the Jew as the implacable enemy of the peasant was definitively established, even in the most remote places where no one had ever seen a Jew in the flesh.... To an impartial person like the New York-based historian Boris Paramov, the Jewish presence in power was so strikingly conspicuous that he wondered whether the promotion of Jews to positions of leadership had not been a 'gigantic provocation' to the Russian people...Jews all over the world supported Soviet power and remained silent in the face of any criticism from the opposition".

It is worth noting here that some Jewish intellectuals may eventually confess to the crimes of their fellow Jews, but only after a certain time, when passions have already dissipated. An account by Nahum Goldmann confirmed the preponderance of Jews in the communist system: "Many communists were themselves Jews and anti-Zionists, he wrote. One day, Litvinov [the foreign minister, ndlr] arrived in Geneva with a delegation of fourteen members, eleven of whom were Jews. I asked the minister: "But why do you need a *minyan* (a *minyan* is a quorum, a prayer meeting of at least ten faithful)? Litvinov, who spoke very good Yiddish, laughed and explained: "It's very simple. All I need is people who speak French, English and German, and in Russia only Jews know foreign languages. In 1976, Goldmann added, this is no longer true, but it was true at the time. In the 1930s, it was the Jews who made the International[192]."

After the war, the countries occupied by the Red Army suffered the revenge of the Jews enthroned by Stalin in the command posts of those countries. In its June 1995 issue, *L'Arche*, the "monthly magazine of French Jewry", published a report on Germany. Alexandre Adler wrote on pages 44-45: "Jews today form the natural elite, the intellectual aristocracy accepted by consensus in the new German society, just when the influence of official Judaism is the weakest in Europe".

We learned that the sister-in-law of the philosopher Walter Benjamin (who committed suicide in 1940 after crossing the Spanish border) had become Minister of Justice in East Germany (GDR: German Democratic Republic). Alexandre Adler wrote here: "As East German Minister of Justice, Hilde, *Roter Hilde*, was responsible for several thousand death sentences that were, at the very least, summary. As luck would have it, one of her disciples, Elisabeth Heimann, now in her seventies and still a Jew, will end up being sentenced in principle to five years for refusing to make any act of contrition for the death sentences she generously distributed in the GDR during her long and vindictive career".

Alexandre Adler also mentioned the case of Markus Wolf, an "evil Jew", "eternal head of the Communist intelligence service", the HVA, "who had put his sarcastic and ever-awake mind" at the service of his Stalinist masters: "Aborting some Bavarian minister's girlfriends in an East Berlin

---

[192] Nahum Goldmann, *Le Paradoxe juif*, Stock, Paris, 1976, p. 39, 40.

clinic, sending some Don Juan to seduce the unmarried secretary of a prominent politician, bamboozling Willy Brandt [head of the West German government] with a completely devoted and servile young militant."

The historian François Fejto, a French Jew of Hungarian origin known for his studies on the history of Central Europe, also acknowledged this, albeit furtively: "Their presence in positions of authority provided new fuel for "popular" anti-Semitism[193] ". It was not until several decades after the tragedy that some Jewish intellectuals finally began to timidly acknowledge the crushing responsibility of their "community".

Corrosive Judaism

Jewish intellectuals and film-makers work tirelessly to establish "peace" on earth. Their propaganda, in one way or another, aims to dissolve all ancestral values, all religions and all identities, to eradicate the supposed sources of conflict between peoples. Judaism is thus essentially a dissolving power.

Pierre Goldmann, a gangster in 1970s France whom the philosopher Bernard-Henri Lévy admired, expressed this inherent corrosive power of Judaism very clearly[194]. He was interviewed in the newspaper *Le Monde* on 30 September 1979, shortly before his assassination. The journalist asked him: "In your opinion, does Judaism have something specific to contribute to today's world?" And Pierre Goldman replied: "What Jews can contribute to civilisation is stateless wandering, the feeling of not belonging. I believe in the Jewish values that anti-Semites hate. I believe in nihilism, in negativity. I believe in the libertarian Jew who is there as a dissolving principle of positive values, because he is neither the man of a land, nor the man of a homeland, nor the man of a nation."

Goldman's comments effectively confirm the analyses of all anti-Semites since time immemorial: Judaism is a corrosive power, a solvent, a constant threat to peoples, nations and civilisations throughout humanity.

In 1934, the art historian and essayist Elie Faure confirmed this assessment, evoking the hysterical sarcasm of the Jewish spirit and its "power of disintegration": "This mocking and sarcastic laughter - Heine, Offenbach - against everything that is not Jewish... Its merciless analysis and irresistible sarcasm have acted like a potent vitriol". Elie Faure put it very explicitly: "Freud, Einstein, Marcel Proust, Charlie Chaplin have opened in us, in all directions, prodigious avenues that tear down the bulkheads of the classical, Greco-Latin and Catholic edifice, within which

---

[193] François Fejtö, *Dieu et son juif*, Ed. Pierre Horay, 1997, p. 37.
[194] On Pierre Goldmann, read *Psychoanalysis of Judaism* and *Jewish Fanaticism*.

the burning doubt of the Jewish soul had been lying in wait, for five or six centuries, for the opportunity to shake it up....Could the Jew be seen as anything other than a wrecker armed with the corroding doubt which Israel has always opposed to the sentimental idealism of Europe since the Greeks?"

In his 1965 pamphlet entitled *The Jewish Problem; Facing the Council* (*Le Problème Juif; Face au Concile*), Léons de Poncins, a French patriot, judiciously quoted the linguist James Darmesteter. The Jew, wrote James Darmesteter, "is the doctor of unbelief. All the revolted of the spirit come to him in the shadows or in the open. He is at work in the immense workshop of the blasphemous great Emperor Frederick and the Princes of Swabia or Aragon; He is the one who forges all that criminal arsenal of reasoning and irony which he will bequeath to the sceptics of the Renaissance, to the libertines of the great century, and Voltaire's sarcasm is but his last and resounding echo of a word muttered six centuries earlier in the shadow of the ghetto and even earlier (in the counter-evangeliums of the first and second centuries) in the time of Celsus and Origen, in the very cradle of the religion of Christ[195]."

As the *Jewish World* of 9 February 1883 wrote: "The dispersion of the Jews has made them a cosmopolitan people. They are the only truly cosmopolitan people, and, in this capacity, they must and do act as a solvent of all distinctions of race or nationality".

In his *Portrait of a Jew*, published in 1962, Albert Memmi stated it unequivocally: "We lived in eager expectation of new, extraordinary times, and we thought we could already see the precursory signs: the beginning of the death throes of religions, families and nations. We felt nothing but rage, contempt and irony for the retards of history who clung to these residues[196]."

"The dawn of Our Day is already shining on the horizon", wrote one of its prophets, his brain addled by the vision of the coming triumph[197]. Léons de Poncins, who referred to these words, added quite rightly: "The messianic dream may take the most diverse forms, the final goal remains unchanged: the triumph of Judaism, of Jewish law and of the Jewish people.

---

[195] James Darmesteter, *Coup d'oeil sur l'histoire du peuple juif*, Paris, 1881, in Julio Meinvieille, *El Judío en el misterio del mundo (1937)*, Cruz y Fierro Editores, Buenos Aires, 1982, p. 72. Quoted by Léons de Poncins, *Le Problème Juif; Face au Concile*, 1965 (pamphlet). Quoted in turn by André Spire, *Quelques juifs*, Éd. Grasset, Paris, 1928. The quotation was already in the book by Mgr Henri Delassus, *L'Américanisme et la conjuration antichrétienne*, Société de Saint-Augustin, D. de Brouwer et Cie, Paris 1899, p. 48.

[196] Albert Memmi, *Portrait d'un juif*, Gallimard, 1962, p. 186, and in Léon de Poncins.

[197] Alfred Nossig, *Integrales Judentum*, Renaissance Verlag, Berlin, 1922, in Léon de Poncins.

It is the unification of the world under the leadership of the Jewish people. Under the guise of universalism, it is in reality Jewish imperialism that seeks to rule and enslave the world".

So the target of cosmopolitan propaganda attacks must be the judiciary, the army and the European aristocracy. In the cinema, some "social" films surreptitiously encourage the common people to revolt against the European authorities and elites, who are often portrayed as corrupt and stale, to be overthrown and replaced as soon as possible.

Jacques Deray's *Un Crime* (France, 1992) denounces the haute bourgeoisie. A lawyer manages to acquit his client of the double murder of his parents. The client reveals his dark secrets...

In *F.I.S.T.* (USA, 1978), Kovak, a Polish immigrant who works unloading trucks, joins the Teamsters' Federation (FIST). The unionists team up with the Mafia to take down the bosses' militias. A film by Norman Jewison, who directed the anti-Catholic *Agnes of God* (1985).

In *The Three Days of the Condor* (USA, 1975), Turner, alias "the Condor", works for the CIA in a bibliographic research section. He soon discovers a secret network within the organisation that does not hesitate to have his colleagues assassinated. From then on, his life hangs in the balance. The film is "an impeccable denunciation of the vileness of the CIA", we read in Jean Tulard's *Guide des films*. The film was directed by Sydney Pollack.

Je sais rien mais je dirai tout (*I don't know anything but I'll tell you everything*) by Pierre Richard (France, 1973): Pierre is the uprising son of an arms manufacturer. "Pierre Richard confronts the powers that be, such as the bosses, the Church and the army, to make a very dynamic film.

Coup pour coup (*Coup pour coup,* France, 1971): In a garment factory, the workers suffer harassment and a hellish pace. Two leaders are fired and soon a wildcat strike breaks out that goes beyond the unions. The owner, kidnapped and humiliated, has to give in. The workers won the strike on their own and vow to continue the struggle. The film is directed by Marin Karmitz. It should be noted that Marin Karmitz went on to direct MK2, a major French cinema network. Like many of his co-religionists, he too moved from the extreme left to the liberal right. In January 2009, we learned that he had been appointed by French President Nicolas Sarkozy to head the "Council for Artistic Creation".

Force of Evil by Abraham Polonsky (USA, 1948): Joe Morse is a crime syndicate lawyer a little overwhelmed by the cases he is handling. "Beyond the shenanigans, it is capitalist society that Polonsky wanted to question in this thriller, which is also a social film," wrote Jean Tulard.

The Strike (USSR, 1924): In a factory in the middle of Tsarist Russia, a worker is wrongly accused of theft and commits suicide. A strike breaks out, but in the end the workers are massacred by the evil Russian aristocrats. The Jewish Bolshevik aristocrats will be much more benevolent towards the people. The film is by the legendary Sergei Eisenstein, a true Russian, who also directed *Battleship Potemkin* (1925) and *October* (1927) in the same "social" genre.

To weaken the goy aristocracy, it was also necessary to encourage marriages with the working classes. *The Late George Apley* (USA, 1947) is a film by Joseph Mankiewicz: a Boston notable, George Apley, discovers that his daughter is dating a poor boy and that his son John is ignoring his cousin for a young woman from the suburbs. He sets the family in order, but in the end he returns to his bourgeois prejudices.

The King and the Chorus Girl (USA, 1937) tells the story of an aristocrat who falls in love with a dancer at the *Folies-Bergère* cabaret in Paris. The film was directed by Mervyn Leroy, with a screenplay by Norman Krasna.

Even better, in the same vein, is *Gipsy* (Great Britain, 1957), about the tumultuous love affair between a gypsy woman and a member of the English aristocracy. A film by the cosmopolitan Joseph Losey.

The Judgement of God (*Le jugement de Dieu*), by Raymond Bernard (France, 1949), denounces the social tensions of medieval society as well as Catholicism. It tells the story of the mad and impossible love - in the middle of the 15th century - between the young Prince Albert of Bavaria and Agnés Bernauer, daughter of an apothecary barber. Albert marries Agnes, but she is soon accused of witchcraft by evil churchmen. She is arrested, tried and condemned to drown in the waters of the Danube. Desperate, Albert throws himself into the river to join her. The screenplay is by Bernard Zimmer.

In fact, if one looks a little closer, one realises that the history of Europeans is nothing but one long oppression. The medieval period, in particular, was especially dark:

The Virgin Queen (*The Virgin Queen*, USA, 1965): In the 11th century, the local lord notices a young peasant girl on a hunt. She is betrothed to a man, and they are to be married, but the lord then asserts his right of pernada (an invention of the 19th century French republicans). "Battle scenes and eroticism combine very well". The film is by Franklin Schaffner.

The Song of Roland (*La chanson de Roland*, France, 1977) revives the story of the Frankish hero. The director has simply taken some liberties with the famous legend: in the 12th century, a troupe of comedians accompanies pilgrims on their way to Santiago de Compostela. They sing of the exploits of the heroes of the holy war. The road is strewn with pitfalls and violence. Roland wonders about the origin of this evil and the true social role he should play. He realised that he was serving an unjust order and, after the attack on Roncesvalles, he returned to Flanders to join the peasants in revolt. From then on, he would sing of hope and no longer of fate and destiny. "A pertinent reflection... a film of great analytical intelligence", wrote Claude Bouniq-Mercier in the *Guide des films*. The film is by Franck Cassenti, who never teased us.

The police, the judiciary and the prison administration are, of course, full of white bastards and psychopaths. Let us now complete the list we published in our previous books. In *Sleepers* (USA, 1996), four young gang members end up in prison, tortured and raped by degenerate and sadistic guards. A Barry Levinson film.

The Choirboys is a film by Robert Aldrich (USA, 1977): it narrates the day-to-day life of a Los Angeles police station. There is Cachalote, a policeman waiting for his retirement; Roscoe, a racist brute; and Baxter, a masochistic amateur. The latter commits suicide. Another policeman accidentally kills a homosexual and will be punished. The screenplay is by Christopher Knopf and Joseph Wambaugh.

Apparently, we have to believe that most of the people imprisoned are actually innocent. Take *Hurricane Carter* (USA, 1999): Boxer Hurricane Carter, sentenced to life imprisonment for triple murder, is actually innocent. The film is by Norman Jewison (him again!). Twenty years earlier, Jewison had made *Justice for All* (1979): Kirkland, an overly impulsive lawyer, ends up in jail for assaulting a perverse judge whom he reproaches for letting an innocent man rot in prison. Now the judge, who has been accused of rape, calls on him as a lawyer. Norman Jewison "stops at nothing to question the judicial system and the prison world (rape, hysteria)".

In Clint Eastwood's *True Crime* (USA, 1999), a young black man is sentenced to death for murder, but a journalist is out to prove his innocence. The screenplay is by Larry Gross and Stephen Schiff.

The Soviet Union and the communist states of Central Europe, which had driven the Jews out of power after the Second World War, also had to take a beating. In *The Confession* (*L'Aveu*, France, 1970), Constantin Costa-Gavras depicts the interminable interrogation of an innocent man in Prague in 1951. Exhausted, he confesses to crimes of which he is not guilty. The film is based on the book by Arthur London.

Jewish filmmakers also spoke out clearly in favour of the abolition of the death penalty. Undoubtedly, this was not only the fruit of deep philosophical reflection, but also motivated by an objective interest, for we know that Jewish criminals are numerous in all forms of illicit trafficking and in the international mafia (arms, drugs, diamonds, money laundering, pimping, contract killings, etc.; read in *The Jewish Mafia*).

In Tim Robbins' *Dead Man Walking* (USA, 1995), Matthew Poncelet, accused of a double murder, is sentenced to death but claims to be innocent. The film is "a violent attack on the death penalty, all the more so because the condemned man does not inspire much self-pity. He is obtuse, fascist, racist, but nevertheless a human being," wrote Bouniq. Thanks anyway.

Daniel (USA, 1983): Daniel, whose communist parents were executed in the electric chair at the height of McCarthyism, decides to find out the truth. Sydney Lumet's film revisits the Rosenbergs' execution. Lumet argues that the couple were sentenced to death as an example.

In 1957, Sydney Lumet had already directed *Twelve Angry Men*: Twelve jurors gather in the deliberation room to decide the verdict to be returned on an eighteen-year-old defendant. Since the defendant faces the death penalty, the jury must be unanimous. The first ballot is taken: eleven jurors vote guilty and one not guilty. Davis, the only juror to vote not guilty, succeeds, with his eloquence and the rigour of his demonstration, in persuading one by one the other jurors that the indictment is flawed and that the defendant can only be found not guilty.

Le pull-over rouge (*The Red Jersey*, France, 1979) is another plea against the death penalty. The film was directed by Michel Drach.

In Gordon Douglas's *The Detective* (USA, 1968), Joe Leland, an honest cop, captures a homosexual suspected of murdering his partner. He gets him to talk and obtains his death sentence. Promoted to captain, he breaks up with his nymphomaniac wife. He also becomes aware of the corruption of his superiors. Worse, he learns that the man he sent to the electric chair was innocent. The screenplay is by Aby Mann.

I want to live! (USA, 1958): Barbara, suspected of the murder of a rich widow, is sentenced to death. A "plea against the death penalty" directed by Robert Wise (again!).

Je suis un sentimental, by John Berry (Fr-It, 1955): They're going to guillotine an innocent man! Based on a screenplay by Lee Gold.

Convicted (USA, 1950): Joe Hufford is accused of murder despite being innocent. A film by Henry Levin. In short, everyone is innocent, especially Jews.

The military hierarchy can also be blamed: *Allons z'enfants*, by Yves Boisset (France, 1981): Simon Chalumot is placed by his father in a school for troop infantrymen. He hates military life. During his convalescence in hospital, he has a brief affair with sister Beatrice. A "violent critique of the army". The screenplay is by Jacques Kirsner.

The Trial of Billy Mitchell is a film by Otto Preminger (USA, 1955). Colonel Mitchell is convinced that aviation will play a key role in future wars. He becomes a nuisance and is soon court-martialled and expelled from the army. The film is "an indictment of backward-looking judges".

Paths of Glory (1958) paints a fierce portrait of French generals in 1916. The film was banned for a long time in France. It is by Stanley Kubrick, who also directed *Full Metal Jacket*, another anti-militarist film.

Cosmopolitan filmmakers do not only attack European culture. Wherever they are, they have to attack local elites in order to replace them:

Here is an example of an attack on Indian culture, a Tamil film: *A Donkey in the Brahmin Enclave* (*Un âne dans l'enclave des Brahmanes*, India, 1977): A donkey enters the Brahmin enclave of a village and is adopted as a pet by a teacher. At first, the members of the Brahmin caste do not want the animal in their sacred enclosure. But soon, the donkey provokes miraculous visions in the priests and the animal eventually becomes an object of veneration. An "acid satire against the fanaticism of the upper caste Brahmins", and "a landmark work of the new Indian auteur cinema". The film is by John Abraham, Tamil to the core.

The Milk Shake (*Le Barattage*) is a 1976 Indian film. A veterinary surgeon, Dr. Rao, is sent to a small village in Gujarat to set up a dairy cooperative. Rao relies on the untouchable community and the chief Bhola, who end up taking control of their destiny, despite the attempts of intimidation by those in power. Jean Tulard wrote here: "This powerful, self-produced social film had a profound impact in India and shows once again Shyam Benegal's sympathy for the oppressed and his desire to change mentalities through cinema.

The Seed (India, 1974): In an Indian village, a peasant girl, a servant in the house of a landowner, is seduced by her boss. He perpetuates a series of abuses against the peasants with impunity, but a revolt is brewing. Director Shyam Benegal is "one of India's most talented filmmakers".

As we see, Judaism is a universal dissolving force for all the nations it penetrates. As Nahum Goldman wrote very explicitly: "This is the way it is: the Jews are revolutionaries for other peoples, not for themselves[198]."

Read also this testimony found in the book by the French Catholic Roger Gougenot des Mousseaux, written in 1869. Gougenot mentioned the "very curious account extracted from a report made by Dr. Buchanan, in 1810, to the Anglican Church, concerning this Messianic faith whose perseverance is no less remarkable among the Israelites of India than among those of the central part of Europe. "During my stay in the East, I met Jews everywhere who were animated by the hope of returning to Jerusalem and seeing their Messiah. But two things struck me above all, the memory they have of the destruction of Jerusalem and the hope they have of one day seeing this holy city reborn from its ruins. Without a king, without a homeland, they never cease to speak of their nation; the remoteness of time and place does not seem to have weakened the memory of their misfortune. They speak of Palestine as a neighbouring and easily accessible country... They believe that the time of their liberation is not far off, and they look upon the revolutions that are shaking the universe as harbingers of freedom. A sure

---

[198] Nahum Goldmann, *Le Paradoxe juif*, Stock, Paris, 1976, p. 72.

sign of our next step, they say, is that in almost every country persecutions against us are on the wane[199].""

See also what the famous Irish writer James Joyce wrote in a dialogue in his *Ulysses*: "Mark what I say, Mr. Dedalus," he said, "England is in the hands of the Jews. In all the highest places: in its finances, in its press. And they are the sign of a nation's decline. Wherever they gather, they eat into the life force of the country. I've seen them coming for a few years now. As sure as we are here, the Jewish hucksters are already at their work of destruction. Old England is dying[200]."

Behind the façade of dissimilarities, Jewish thought is in reality remarkably homogeneous. Whether left or right, Marxist or liberal, religious or atheist, Zionist or "perfectly integrated", Jews are the strongest advocates of a multicultural society and a world without borders, for the simple reason that the world of "peace" they wish to establish is the *sine qua non* for the arrival of their longed-for messiah. So a Jew can be recognised by three things: what he says, what he writes and what he does. If his words and deeds are conducive to cosmopolitanism, he is a Jew. If his words and deeds are rooted in the land and soul of the nation, he is a goy. It is on this basis that we must reason. We can then refine the criteria with ancestry, surname and physiognomy, to make sure that we are not dealing with a synthetic Jew. Of course, genealogy remains an important criterion for defining an individual's Jewishness, as Jews themselves recognise anyone born to a Jewish mother as a Jew. However, there are people who have only one Jewish grandparent on their father's side and who feel themselves to be Jewish to the core. On the other hand, Judaism can also be lost over the generations, so it is possible to meet a "Blumenthal" who is no longer aware of his Jewishness.

Onomastics - the study of the origin of surnames - is not infallible either, since many Jews, under the pretext of integration, modify their surnames to give them a more local consonance or even change them radically. Obviously, a TV, film, banking or mafia personality is much more suspicious than an old native peasant. But no one in history has ever attacked Jews "because they are Jews", but because they are, by their own admission, "irritating" and "annoying", obsessed with unifying the world and destroying everything that is not Jewish. This is precisely what the Jews poutingly, or subtly, call "working for peace in the world".

---

[199] Gougenot des Mousseaux. *El Judío, el judaísmo y la judaización de los pueblos cristianos*, pdf version. Translated into Spanish by Professor Noemí Coronel and the invaluable collaboration of the team of Nacionalismo Católico Argentina, 2013, p. 495.
[200] *Ulysses*, James Joyce, quoted in Albert Memmi, *Portrait d'un juif*, Gallimard, 1962, p. 129.

Human Rights

Human rights are a key concept in the cosmopolitan propaganda arsenal. They mean that every human being, regardless of race, nationality or religion, can settle and live wherever he or she pleases, regardless of borders and ignoring the rights of indigenous peoples in their own countries. Human rights are thus an ideological war machine working to dissolve national and ethnic identities, and it is no coincidence that, once again, it is Jewish intellectuals who are the loudest criers of these principles.

René Cassin was one of the great men of the French Republic. This former president of the Universal Israelite Alliance (*Alliance Israélite Universelle*), from 1943 until his death in 1976, was also the father of the 1948 Universal Declaration of Human Rights, which he saw as "a laicisation of the principles of Judaism[201]." This is also what Chief Rabbi Jacob Kaplan said, "To find the original source of 1789, we have to go back beyond classical antiquity, to the Bible, the Torah and the prophets." During World War II, René Cassin envisioned "a kind of universal ministry of education". His plans took shape after the war, with the creation of Unesco. After General de Gaulle's return to power in 1958, he was in charge of drafting the Constitution of the Fifth Republic. He received an Honorary Doctorate from the Hebrew University of Jerusalem and was re-elected President of the European Court of Human Rights in June 1968, shortly before receiving the Human Rights Prize and the Nobel Peace Prize. René Cassin died on 20 February 1976 and his ashes were transferred to the Pantheon in 1987.

But to better understand the fate of this emblematic figure and the ideology he embodied, it seems necessary to present his actions during the Second World War. René Cassin went into exile in London in 1940. In 1943, he was appointed by General de Gaulle to head the Legal Committee in Algiers, and was entrusted with the preparation of an exceptional jurisdiction to punish crimes of collaboration: the Courts of Justice. René Cassin was the inventor of the legal postulate that Marshal Pétain's government had been illegal since 16 June 1940, the date that marked the fall of Paul Reynaud's ministry and the appointment of the Marshal as President of the Council by Albert Lebrun. As a result of this subterfuge, the officials who had obeyed Marshal Pétain were subject to Articles 75 et seq. of the Penal Code. From 1944 onwards, the courts responsible for trying French citizens guilty of obeying Marshal Pétain handed down 2,853

---

[201] Statement made during the colloquium of the *Decalogue Lawyers Society,* held in Chicago in 1970; in Yann Moncomble, *Les Professionnels de l'anti-racisme,* Faits et Documents, 1987, p. 60-64.

death sentences, 2,248 sentences of hard labour for life (plus 454 in contumacy), 8,864 sentences of hard labour for a fixed period (plus 1,773 in contumacy), 1,956 sentences of imprisonment and 22,883 prison sentences.

In addition, tens of thousands of people were sentenced to national degradation, a penalty hitherto unknown in French law. National indignity and degradation entailed loss of the right to vote, ineligibility, loss of access to jobs in the civil service and public enterprises, loss of all ranks in the army, loss of the right to retirement, loss of the right to teach, to set up a business, to run a press or broadcasting company, and loss of the right to compensation for war damages. This was also the work of René Cassin.

On 27 November 1967, after the Six Day War and the victory of the Israeli army, General de Gaulle dared to speak, in a famous press conference, of the "bellicose State of Israel, determined to expand", and of "a self-confident and domineering people". These words were not appreciated by Jews and caused "a great commotion in the community". René Cassin's reaction, recounted here by the former President of the Council, Pierre Mendés France, was as follows: "During the reception of the Council of State at the Elysée Palace on New Year's Day, the President approached René Cassin and told him that he had been misunderstood, etc. Cassin replied: "In *Mein Kampf*, General, the adjective "domineering" as applied to the Jews appears forty times". Without replying, the General raised his arms to the sky, walking away as Cassin remarked loudly: "General, the word you used is a murderous term[202]"." No more, no less! We know that Jewish intellectuals are "highly intolerant of frustration", as a certain medical diagnosis states.

In 1958, a certain Daniel Mayer was elected President of the Human Rights League (*Ligue des Droits de l'Homme*). He remained in this position until 1975. He too advocated tolerance, but, once again, it was really a speech for export. On 31 January 1950, at a meeting of the Lica (League against anti-Semitism - Ligue contre l'antisémitisme), he had declared about the liberation and purge of 1944: "There were many heads shaved, but not enough heads cut off[203]."

Daniel Mayer was a devious Jew. From 1962 to 1967 he was a regular contributor to the newspaper *Témoignage chrétien*. But when the weekly protested against the occupation of new Arab territories by Israeli settlers in 1967, he stopped writing for it, at the same time that Marcel Bleustein-Blanchet, president of the Publicis agency, abruptly cut off all advertising for the paper.

---

[202] Claude Vigée, *Délivrance du souffle*, Flammarion, 1977, p. 213.
[203] Yan Moncomble, *Les Professionels de l'anti-racisme*, Faits et Documents, 1987, p. 20.

This sense of belonging had not prevented him from declaring one day: "I am first of all a socialist, then a Frenchman and finally just a Jew". The weekly *L'Express* of 4 March 1983 reported the words of an Israeli diplomat: "Fortunately, in Hebrew everything is read backwards [204]." Jewish intellectuals clearly have a habit of confusing the Jewish community with humanity as a whole, and of projecting onto a universal plane what in reality only concerns Jews. Elie Wiesel wrote for example: "To save our people, we must save all of humanity[205]." And look at what Franz Kafka said: "Whoever strikes a Jew strikes down humanity[206]."

Nahum Goldmann also expressed the same egocentrism: "It is in the interest of all mankind that the Jewish people should not disappear", he said, because it is the bearer of "values that concern all mankind".

Under these conditions, it is natural for the Palestinians to vacate and leave the site to them: "Israel is the only way to give the Jewish people the opportunity to continue their contribution to human civilisation. Thus, humanity has the right to say to the Arabs: "We ask you to sacrifice one percent of your territories to serve the whole of humanity[207] "."

Another Jewish intellectual, André Neher, also wrote quite naturally: "The world needs the Jew, but the Jew expects and wants the world to express this need[208]."

At the end of 1986, Elie Wiesel was awarded the Nobel Peace Prize. In his *Oslo Speech*, delivered on that occasion, he spoke as usual of memory, hope, humanity and "peace" on earth. We know that Elie Wiesel always liked great phrases: "Memory defies death, because death stops memory; memory denies hatred, because hatred denies memory".

He also seemed to confuse the Jewish sect with humanity as a whole, as if Jews were the quintessence of humanity: "Our survival makes sense in the eyes of humanity as a whole," he wrote. "In recounting the martyrdom of my people, I evoke the suffering of all peoples". And again: "Jewish suffering must concern all humanity. The day will come when crimes against Jews will be considered crimes against humanity, and crimes against humanity crimes against the Jewish people[209]." In short, if you pluck a hair out of a rabbi's beard, you are attacking all of humanity.

Thus, anti-Semitism is not just a Jewish thing: it is "everybody's business". In October 2004, the Union of Jewish Students of France (Uejf)

---

[204] Yan Moncomble, *Les Professionels de l'anti-racisme*, Faits et Documents, 1987, p. 22.
[205] Elie Wiesel, *Mémoires, tome I*, Seuil, 1994, p. 51.
[206] Bernard-Henri Lévy, *Le Testament de Dieu*, Grasset, 1979, p. 181.
[207] Nahum Goldmann, *Le Paradoxe juif*, Stock, Paris, 1976, p. 238.
[208] André Neher, *L'Identité juive*, 1977, Petite Bibliothèque Payot, 2007, p. 35.
[209] Elie Wiesel, *Discours d'Oslo*, Grasset, 1987, p. 28, 18, 38, 41

wanted to launch a campaign against anti-Semitism and make this fight "a great national cause". According to Yonathan Arfi, the head of the association, the aim was to "produce an emotional shock, the only way to leave a deep impression". The planned poster campaign reflected this willingness of Jews, deliberate or not, to provoke the Goyim. The posters showed Christ, "spray-painted" with the insult "dirty Jew", and the Virgin Mary with the baby Jesus in her arms, smeared with the inscription "dirty Jew". "Our aim is not to provoke or offend gratuitously", Yonathan explained, but to persuade everyone that the insult "Dirty Jew" defiles and degrades all men without exception". The slogan was: "Anti-Semitism - what if it was everyone's business?

However, the project was not to everyone's liking, and under pressure from Licra (International League Against Racism and Anti-Semitism - Ligue Internationale Contre le Racisme et l'Antisémitisme), the Uejf was forced to backtrack. Licra considered that the campaign was "shocking" and could "have a counterproductive effect".

"We are disappointed," acknowledged Yonathan Arfi. In his opinion, "this campaign exposes how unbearable the moral and intellectual brutality of anti-Semitism is". These posters "address everyone and the message is fundamentally Christian: Jesus was the first anti-racist".

Rudolph Loewenstein was also trying to get us to admit that Judaism was at the heart of our civilisation, as was Christianity. He confused the two, bluntly evoking "the principles of justice, freedom, charity and human dignity with which Judaism and Christianity have permeated Western civilisation[210]."

Since it is absolutely impossible for people to resent Jews, and only Jews, since they are innocent, the reason for their hatred can only be hatred of all humanity. The Jewish intellectual here was typically projecting evil on a universal plane.

"There, in Treblinka, wrote Martin Gray, they did not kill the Jews, they did not exterminate a particular race: the executioners wanted to destroy man, and they had decided to begin with those they called Jews; but all men were doomed. Only the executioners and their dogs would be left alive. In Treblinka they were eliminating the man. But in order to better conceal this gigantic undertaking, the executioners had tried to hide the human being under the name of Jew[211]."

Therefore, we can legitimately think that in the minds of the leaders of the League of Human Rights it was above all about defending the rights of

---

[210] Rudolph Loewenstein, *Psychanalyse de l'antisémitisme*, 1952, PUF, 2001, p. 154.
[211] Martin Gray, *En nombre de todos los míos*, Plaza & Janés, Barcelona, 1973, p. 176.

the Jews to impose their vision and their project on the rest of the world [Man=Jew, ndt].[212]

"Israel is the people of God and of poetry, wrote Edouard Valdman. As soon as the Jews renounce this, they will lose themselves and, in losing themselves, they will threaten Man [213]." He was thus instinctively expressing Israel's inordinate pride or, more accurately, the megalomania characteristic of the hysterical personality.

Contempt for the goyim

Nahum Goldmann, founder of the World Jewish Congress, expressed the common opinion that Central European Jews had of the Goyim at the beginning of the 20th century: "The opinion generally held of the Jews of the shtetlj - those small isolated villages in a Goy environment - seems to me to be wrong, he wrote. It is often said that these Jews led an unhappy, even miserable existence. This is not entirely true: the Jews were certainly in an unenviable economic position; moreover, they had no political say. But it is not the objective facts that determine a life: it is the psychological reaction to those facts. And from this point of view, the Jews were on the whole a fairly happy people". And Goldmann added: "The Jews regarded their persecutors as an inferior race... In my small town of Wisznewo, we lived in a rural area and most of my grandfather's patients were peasants. Every Jew felt ten times, a hundred times, superior to these humble farmers: he was educated, he learned Hebrew, he knew the Bible, he studied the Talmud; in short, he knew himself far above these illiterate people". And again: "The Jewish people have always believed in their superiority (expressed in the classical form of the "chosen people")[214]."

"Of course, the Jews were deprived of political rights, but if they had had them, they probably would not have made use of them. The politics of the goyim (non-Jews) did not interest them: that world was alien to them and they felt that they were just passing through. One day, the Messiah would come and take them to Israel. So the only important thing was to survive until the Messiah arrived, without worrying too much about the reality of "the others". Thanks to this reasoning, Goldmann added, the Jews managed to overcome what would have destroyed any other people[215]."

The gangster of the 1970s, Pierre Goldmann, left a concordant testimony of how Jews viewed the rest of the world. Here is what he said in an

---

[212] A definition of humanity confirmed by rabbinic exegesis in the Talmud, e.g. in *Keritot; 6b*.
[213] Édouard Valdman, *Les Juifs et l'argent*, Ed. Galilée, 1994, p. 20.
[214] Nahum Goldmann, *Le Paradoxe juif*, Stock, Paris, 1976, p. 21, 16
[215] Nahum Goldmann, *Le Paradoxe juif*, Stock, Paris, 1976, p. 21.

interview published in *Le Monde* on 30 September 1979, entitled *Goldman l'étranger*: "Yes, I hate humiliation. I was wrong to speak of humiliated rabbis. My father explained to me that the bearded Jew, dedicated to intellectual work, who was whipped by the Cossack, was not humiliated at all. He deeply despised the Cossack. He was perfectly aware of his superiority. In the Jewish religion, it must be said, there is great contempt for others."

The novelist Arnold Mendel, a Polish-born Jew, was no different. In one of his books, he gave the following definition of the Yiddish word "*Goïmnachess*": "A term of contempt, used in Judeo-German and Yiddish. *Goïmnachess* refers to pleasures, glories and triumphs, hardly worthy of the puerile vanities of the Goyim, the non-Jews.... And we had a contemptuous indulgence for that world of *goïmnachess*, its futility and vulgarity[216]."

In 1997, the historian François Fetjo also wrote: "The misfortunes of life, the small and great misfortunes and even the catastrophes, the plagues, the wars, the pogroms, the Auschwitz, the Jew endures them, adapts to them and survives them. The flagrant injustices to which he is subjected, the humiliations, he also endures them on the part of the majority of men, they seem natural to him because he does not have a good opinion of man, of the "gentile", of the non-chosen. He believes him capable of anything. The cruelty and hatred of men do not cause him pity, they only justify his contempt[217]."

Theodor Herzl, the founder of Zionism, also expressed this immense pride: "Our race is, in everything, more capable than most of the peoples of the world[218]."

See also what the scholar Gilles Keppel wrote in 1994 in *Le Retour de Dieu*, quoting the *Revue de la jeunesse loubavitch de France*: "God created the entire universe according to the fundamental division of the four kingdoms: mineral, vegetable, animal and human.... It is written that there is actually a fifth genus: *AmIsrael*, the Jewish people. And the gap that separates it from the fourth genus - the whole of the 'speaking', human species - is no less than the gap between the human and the animal".

As for the Chief Rabbi of France, Joseph Sitruk, he went so far as to declare in the Jewish magazine *Passages* in May 1988, with regard to General de Gaulle and his famous phrase about the Jewish people - "self-

---

[216] Arnold Mendel, *Tikoun*, Mazarine, 1980, p. 18, 29
[217] François Fetjö, *Dieu et son juif*, Ed. Pierre Horay, 1997, p. 43, 44.
[218] Theodor Herzl, *L'État juif*, Stock-plus ed. Collection Judaïsme/Israël, p. 217. [*"Zionism is the return to Judaism, and precedes the return to the land of the Jews"*. Theodor Herzl *The State of Israel and Other Writings*, Editorial Israel, Buenos Aires, 1960, p. 195].

confident and domineering": "I have never had the impression that he was wrong on the essentials".

In practice, when Jews feel they have a free hand, this contempt translates into brutality and cruelty on a par with the worst despots in history. In Israel, in particular, some senior officials openly advocate ethnic cleansing against Arabs.

Avigdor Lieberman, appointed Deputy Prime Minister for Strategic Affairs in 2006, encouraged the transfer of the West Bank's Arab populations: 'He has made it clear that he favours expulsion, to make Israel a homogenous Jewish state "as far as possible"', wrote John Mearsheimer and Stephen Walt in their 2007 book that has gone around the world: *The Israel Lobby and US Foreign Policy*.

The two American academics explained the methods adopted by Jews from the beginning of their settlement of Palestine: "It was the Jewish terrorists of the Irgun who first planted bombs in buses or crowded places in Palestine in late 1937," the professors explained. "One need only read what Ben-Gurion wrote in his diary on 1 January 1948, a time when he often met with other Zionist leaders to discuss how to deal with the Palestinian question: 'The time has come to react firmly and violently. We must specify the time, the place and the target. If we attack a family, we must brutalise them mercilessly, women and children included. Otherwise, it will not be an effective reaction.... We must not distinguish between guilty and not guilty".

These methods have not changed over time: "*Tsahal* shot hundreds of Egyptian prisoners during the 1956 and 1967 wars. In 1967 it expelled between 100,000 and 260,000 Palestinians from the newly conquered West Bank and 80,000 Syrians from the Golan Heights. When the victims of this ethnic cleansing attempted to return to their homes, often unarmed, the Israelis sometimes shot them dead. Amnesty International estimates that between 1967 and 2003 Israel destroyed more than 10,000 homes in the West Bank and Gaza Strip[219]."

After the Six Day War, in June 1967, a certain Victor Tibika published a small Zionist propaganda book entitled *1967, Awakening and Unity of the Jewish People*, which aimed to encourage Jews in France to settle in Israel. The author suggested that Jews and Arabs had been the best friends in the world. This was, of course, propaganda and not the work of a historian. So Victor Tibika allowed himself to write: "I have not forgotten the excellent cooperation and understanding between Jews and Arabs in North Africa. In 1941-1942, the Algerian Arabs behaved perfectly with the Jews". But in

---

[219] John J. Mearsheimer / Stephen Walt, *Le Lobby pro-israélien et la politique étrangère américaine*, La Découverte, 2007, p. 103, 112, 113, 115.

1967, the Arabs, in his opinion, made a grave mistake: "It was Arab-fascist aggression against a small country that aspired only to peace[220]."

Victor Tibika also had a special gift for getting the Palestinians to talk: "Many Arabs in the Israeli-controlled areas said to me: 'We really did not expect them to be so conciliatory and lenient towards us, whereas our behaviour towards them would have been very different if we had been victorious. It must be said that our bosses had filled our heads with their anti-Israeli propaganda and their slogans preaching nothing but the killing and extermination of the Jews...This propaganda has done nothing but excite us against the Jews, describing them as monsters, and inciting us to exterminate them in a holy war, in the name of Islam! Our revered prophet Mohammed would certainly not have approved of it[221] !'"

In 1994, Claude Lanzman, in his film to the glory of the Israeli army, *Tsahal*, came to the same conclusion. In an interview with the daily *Le Figaro*, he extolled with his usual *chutzpah* the exceptional kindness of the *Tsahal* soldiers, while condemning the inherent corruption of the blood of French soldiers: "The Israeli paratrooper, Claude Lanzmann explained, is not the French paratrooper.... The Jewish soldier does not have violence in his blood. He can kill, but he is not a murderer. To begin with, they have their hair. In *Tsahal* there is no cult of virility, no machismo. The soldiers are kind, tender. The others: they have the act of violence in their blood".

During World War II, as we know, not all Jews were victims: many of them fought in the Allied armies or in partisan groups in the East. In 2007, for example, Lithuania opened a case against a certain Yitzhak Arad, former director of the Yad Vashem institute[222] in Israel, who had fought against the Nazis in that country. Lithuania officially asked Israel to allow it to investigate the massacre of 300 Lithuanian civilians. Yitzhak Arad's memoirs included detailed descriptions of his crimes.

We have already seen some similar cases in *Jewish Fanaticism*, but very few such reports made it through the filters of the mainstream media in the decades after the end of the war.

There are also the cases of the brothers Tuvia and Aaron Bielski, leaders of a Polish Jewish maquis accused of numerous murders, including the massacre of 128 peasants in Nabiloki on 8 May 1943. Aaron later settled in the United States and changed his surname. He now called himself Aaron

---

[220] Victor Tibika, *1967, Réveil et unité du peuple juif*, p. 70, 40
[221] Victor Tibika, *1967, Réveil et unité du peuple juif*, p. 69, 70
[222] Yad Vashem is the official Israeli institution established in memory of the victims of the Holocaust during World War II. The site is located in the Jerusalem Forest, on the western slope of Mount Herzl ("Mount of Remembrance"). It has had a delegation in Spain since 2007 and holds commemorative events throughout the country: https://yadvashemspain.com/. (NdT).

Bell. In 2007 he was accused of appropriating the savings ($250,000) of a 93-year-old Catholic neighbour.

The contempt for the goy was also evident in the words of Philppe Sollers, a rather media-friendly "French" writer. In 1999, during a European election campaign, Jean-Pierre Chevènement, a left-wing politician with a certain patriotic streak, had the supreme audacity to criticise Daniel Cohn-Bendit, saying of the former May '68 leader turned environmentalist candidate that "in a way he was the representative of the globalised elites[223]."

This banal comment was enough to unleash a violent press campaign against him. On 28 January, *Le Monde* published on its front page an article by the writer Philipe Sollers, a former Maoist and friend of Bernard-Henri Lévy's, entitled *La France en moulé*. In it, Sollers denounced the "cowardly rentiers", the "unparalleled French stupidity" and poured out his bile: "Mildewed France, he said, has always hated the Germans, the English, the Jews, the Arabs, foreigners in general, modern art, fussy intellectuals, women who think or are too independent, rebellious workers and, in short, freedom in all its forms[224]."

Sollers ' reaction was very symptomatic: when a Jewish intellectual thinks he is the target of criticism, his first instinct is to make a fool of himself by associating himself in his misfortune with other communities: Gypsies, Protestants, workers, immigrants, lepers, heretics persecuted by the Inquisition, and so on. For it is indeed incomprehensible that Jews, and only Jews, are singled out, and no one else.

Apocalyptic Judaism

The expectation of the Messiah is the axis around which the mental universe of the Jews is structured. The Jews have absolute faith in his coming, which will be the moment of their liberation. They are carried away by the prophecies and are as it were absorbed by messianic hopes.

These appear, for example, in the film *Kadosh*, by Israeli director Amos Gitai (1999): In Jerusalem, in the ultra-Orthodox Jewish neighbourhood of Mea Shearim, Meir has been living with Rivka for ten years, but she has not given him any children. The rabbi forces Meir to repudiate Rivka and marry another woman. Rivka is cloistered in prostration, but Malka, her sister, decides it is time to rebel. The film harshly denounces the customs of these Hasidic Jews, who treat their wives like cattle. We also hear the

---

[223] *Public* programme, presented by Michel Field, 10 January 1999.
[224] In Elisabeth Lévy, *Les Maîtres censeurs*, Lattès, Poche, 2002, p. 291, *La France moisie*, Le Monde, 28 janvier 1999.

rabbi lecturing poor Meir, explaining to him that it is his duty to marry his wife in order to have children, because it is the duty of every Jew to procreate: "That is how we can defeat them", he tells him plainly.

Meir then asks him - for the understanding of the spectators - who he is talking about, and the rabbi replies: "the others", before adding, after a pause: "the wicked, the pagans who rule this country". But everyone will have understood that the message is coded and that it is indeed about defeating the goyim.[225]

Another passage in the film shows a Hasidic Jew at the wheel of his car, using a megaphone to invite Jews to gather. It is 1999 and he warns the Jews that the times are coming, that the Messiah is about to arrive and that the goyim must be punished for all the evil they have done to the Jews. The scene is quite revealing of the Jewish spirit, animated by the messianic hope of world domination. The Jewish intellectuals here speak piously of "peace" on earth and the "pacification" of peoples and individuals. Their victory is "ineluctable", as was that of the proletariat at the time of triumphant communism. History shows, however, that it is above all the painful setbacks that seem "ineluctable".

In the Pesach Haggadah[226], a Hebrew text used for the Passover ceremony commemorating the liberation from Egypt, the corresponding French translation of the Kiddush prayer[227] on page 9 reads: "Blessed are

---

[225]On the Hasidic movement (Kabbalistic Jewish mysticism), read *Psychoanalysis of Judaism* and *Jewish Fanaticism*. The *Hasidim* (or Hasidim), wrote Elie Wiesel, 'undermined the importance of Talmudic study by claiming that reciting the Psalms was as important as studying the Torah in depth'. Their opponents, the *mitnagdim*, "did not appreciate the exhibitionism of the *Hasidim*, who shouted as they prayed, shook themselves, banged on walls and desks to achieve ecstasy. Moreover, they would gather in private homes where they would tell each other raucous stories and learn popular tunes instead of studying the Bible". They had to be punished: "Some were publicly flogged, others expelled from the city. The Hasidic centres were dispersed and their leaders humiliated. Then it was decided to take the repression a step further by anathematizing the *Hasidim* en masse: their writings were burned, their books destroyed and communities near and far were mobilised against them." Elie Wiesel, *Célébrations hassidique II*, Seuil, 1981, p. 37-39. Jews are in the habit of burning the books of their adversaries. In Israel, Yehuda's students burned Christian Gospels on 20 May 2008. In the Middle Ages, the books of Maimonides, among others, were also burned by the rabbis.

[226] The term Haggadah (Hebrew: "narrative" or "discourse") refers to a collection of narratives from the Hebrew oral tradition, as well as Hebrew literary texts of a <u>non-legalistic</u> nature, sometimes from rabbinic debates and writings (such as the Talmud), including stories, legends, parables and many other narratives that may refer to Jewish history. (NdT)

[227] *Kiddush* (Aramaic: Sanctification) is a blessing recited over wine on Shabbat and other Jewish holidays.

you, Lord, our God, King of the Universe, who has chosen us from among all peoples and has raised us above all nations, and has sanctified us by your commandments". The book was prefaced by the Chief Rabbi of France, Joseph Sitruk.

In his 1973 book, entitled *Prophetic Encyclopaedia*, the author Jacques Lévitan expressed very explicitly the planetary obsessions of Jewish intellectuals. The book was aimed at a knowledgeable Jewish audience, so the author was able to express himself more frankly than his more media-conscious colleagues. The first sentences of his book were those of a Rabbi, taken from a 1964 book entitled *La Conscience juive devant l'histoire (Jewish Conscience in the Face of History*, Editions Payot). Here is what this Rabbi said, quoted by Jacques Lévitan:

"A gigantic struggle is being waged on the vast chessboard of the world, the outcome of which will undoubtedly be known before the end of the sixth millennium (of the Jewish calendar, i.e., about the year 2000). The object of this vast struggle is the possession of the world claimed by two human groups, both of whom are seeking planetary domination. Humanity seeks a foothold and moves irrevocably towards world government. Forty years from now, the unity of the world will be realised. This unity which we have sought, and which we have proclaimed by all the ways of exile for two millennia, will be achieved in life or in death, but it will be achieved[228]."

The rest of the book tended to show, by calculations based on Torah and Kabbalah, that the time was at hand. This time would surely be the final one!

Jacques Lévitan surely claimed a place for himself in the long list of Israel's prophets. Listen to these lucubrations:

"Looking back, we see that the Israelites remained in Egypt for 430 years (cf. *Exodus 12:40* and *Ezekiel 4:5-6*). Now, what was done is what will be done. It turns out that the Ottoman Empire, from which the Turks are descended, occupied the land of Israel for 400 years, from 1517 to 1917 to be exact. To these 400 years we must add 30 years of British rule to make 430 years: 1947, the date on which the land of Israel was liberated. The Temple was built 480 years after leaving Egypt (cf. *Kings 6/1*). If, therefore, to these 430 years (1947) we add 50 years (1997: 480 years), we get the approximate date of the rebuilding of the Sanctuary (in the midst of the distress of the times...cf. *Daniel 9/26*). For as the woman begets in the pain of her deliverance, so the world will beget in the pain of its deliverance, "desiring to bear it with tribulations to make it happy in the end" (cf.

---

[228] Jacques Lévitan, *Encyclopedie prophétique*, La Pensée universelle, 1973, p. 13.

Deuteronomy 8/16). This seems to confirm that the destiny of mankind is written beforehand in the book of life[229]."

It is written that four empires must succeed one another before the coming of the Messiah, according to the visions of the prophet Zechariah, who saw "four horns" that scattered Judah, Israel and Jerusalem [*Zechariah 2:2*]. Zechariah was referring to the four kingdoms of Babylon, Persia, Greece and Rome, "which ruled over Israel and did her so much harm[230]."

Jacques Lévitan used biblical sources to explain the contemporary era: the first empire, according to him, was now that of the Nazi eagle; the second empire (the Bear) was the USSR. "The third empire, not yet fully sovereign, was represented until then by Nasser (the Panther)." The fourth empire, the new Magog, was to be the Asian bloc.

"When we went to press in early 1971, Nasser had already disappeared from the world of the living several months earlier.... He will have contributed... to the creation of an Arab unity that prefigures this third empire with four heads (four kings) determined to rise up and reconquer Israel...We can conclude, then, that we are approaching the end of days by leaps and bounds, when our bewilderment will increase[231]." We have to expect, apparently, a new large-scale confrontation before the coming of the Messiah "of Israel and Deliverer of the whole earth".

The people of Israel also had to prepare for new persecutions: "It is a fact that Israel was born out of persecution. Now the Messiah - like Moses - will be born out of a second persecution, doubtless even more formidable than the previous one".

But the final outcome is already written. It is in the texts themselves: "Jerusalem, the navel of the earth, is destined to become "the throne of the Lord" and "the metropolis of all nations[232] "."

Indeed, "universal peace" must be preceded by great catastrophes. The Jews look forward to revolutions, wars and catastrophes, as well as persecutions which they imagine will herald the day of Redemption. These are, as they themselves say, "the birth pangs of the Messiah".

The persecutions are therefore considered part of the process of redemption. If, after all these centuries of unspeakable suffering, the Jews are still present, it is because their nature can only be divine. This is how

---

[229] Jacques Lévitan, *Encyclopedie prophétique*, La Pensée universelle, 1973, p. 295, 296. For the Jews, the earthly sufferings that precede "the birth of the Messiah" are comparable to the sufferings of the woman before giving birth.
[230] Read in *Psychoanalysis of Judaism*.
[231] Jacques Lévitan, *Encyclopedie prophétique*, La Pensée universelle, 1973, p. 14, 15.
[232] Jacques Lévitan, *Encyclopedie prophétique*, La Pensée universelle, 1973, p. 302, 303, 310

the writer Edouard Valdman explained it, in the process taking a swipe at the Catholic Church:

"Despite the efforts of the Holy Inquisition, and all inquisitions', he wrote, the Jews are still there, thanks to some diabolical sleight of hand. A strange question? Many genocides have succeeded, Indians, blacks, Armenians, etc. and often with the assent of the Roman Church. A people has always been there and has always resisted. It has to be accepted, and apparently it is not easy[233]."

François Fetjó has also expressed this idea: "Even beaten, crushed, scattered, it has survived, which has not happened to any other people. Here, then, is the supreme proof given by the Pharisees of Israel's eternal vocation[234]."

The Jews seem capable of resisting the onslaught of all their enemies: "The survivors of every catastrophe rediscovered their invincibility," wrote Manès Sperber. Since antiquity, "we see that they have never considered themselves truly defeated, but, on the contrary, believe that they have been promised a future triumph that will be definitive. They claim an invincible ally, their God, the one true God, who reigns over the whole universe[235]."

While they are ecstatic about the durability of Judaism amidst the ruins of peoples and civilisations that have disappeared (Babylon, Persia, Greece, Rome), Jewish intellectuals remain very discreet about the role played by the egalitarian fanaticism of Judaism in the collapse of these great civilisations.

Judaism thus feeds a messianic tension that invariably leads Jews around the world to expect the worst apocalyptic scenarios for humanity. "In traditional Jewish literature, Benbassa explained, the arrival of the messianic era, announced by the return of the prophet Elijah, is associated with cataclysms, wars, revolutions and various plagues. Benbassa provided us with the constituent elements of Jewish messianism, as we have presented them in much greater detail in our first three books. "The book of Isaiah," wrote Benbassa, "describes the messianic age in two forms, both catastrophe and utopia. The final deliverance is the end of the exile, the reunion in the Holy Land of the scattered tribes and the restoration of Israel's political sovereignty under the authority of a descendant of David, but it is also the establishment of universal peace, made possible by the adherence of the nations to the worship of the one God[236]."

---

[233] Édouard Valdman, *Les Juifs et l'argent*, Ed. Galilée, 1994, p. 29.
[234] François Fetjö, *Dieu et son juif*, Ed. Pierre Horay, 1997, p. 64.
[235] Manès Sperber, Être *Juif*, Odile Jacob, 1994, p. 60, 133.
[236] Benbassa, *La Souffrance comme identité*, Fayard, 2007, p. 85, 83. It is therefore an immanent, nationalist and imperialist political project, and not a transcendental religion. On the expectation of great catastrophes, see *Planetary Hopes, Psychoanalysis of*

The novelist Arnold Mandel also seemed to look forward to catastrophes with feverish impatience: "I had always been, more or less unconsciously, a catastrophist, he admitted. I would have liked to have lived at the time of the Crusades, the Great Plague, the Red Terror or the exodus of the Jews from Spain in 1492, under Isabella the Catholic[237]."

Manès Sperber wrote: "The sense of the permanence of the catastrophe was general in all of us[238]." The writer Chaïm Potok, in *The Chosen*, a 1967 novel, confirmed this mood and expressed his faith in the coming of the Messiah: "Just before he comes, he wrote, there will be a time of great disasters". Through the mouth of one of his characters, he expressed the activist inclinations of many Jews: "I am tired of waiting. The time has come to bring the Messiah, not to wait for him[239]."

Revolutions, cataclysms, wars and epidemics, all kinds of murderous madness, and anything that might bring humanity closer to apocalypse, seem to be a blessing for the sect. Elie Faure put it between the lines: "Its historical mission is clearly defined, and perhaps forever. It will be the main factor in all apocalyptic times, as it was at the end of the ancient world, and as it is at the end - which we are now witnessing - of the Christian world[240]."

So it should come as no surprise to find a number of films based on disaster scripts. Science fiction stories, moreover, are always a pretext to unite humans of all races against aliens.

We saw for example in *Deep Impact* (USA, 1998) how a giant asteroid was about to crash into the Earth. The planet was saved in extremis by the American President, a black man. In *Independence Day* (USA, 1996), director Roland Emmerich shows the planet attacked by aliens and saved by a black man and a Jew. In Tim Burton's *Mars Attacks* (USA, 1996), flying saucers invade the skies over the United States, and the Martians, with their hypertrophied brains, are anything but friendly.

The Village of the Damned is a film by John Carpenter (USA, 1995): following a strange phenomenon affecting a village, several women become pregnant and give birth to blonde, highly intelligent children. In reality they are aliens intent on conquering the Earth. In 1988, John Carpenter directed the famous film *They Live* (USA, 1988): Thanks to special glasses, the hero, Nada, discovers that a small part of the population

---

Judaism and *Jewish Fanaticism*.
[237] Arnold Mandel, *Tikoun*, Mazarine, 1980, p. 39.
[238] Manès Sperber, *Être Juif*, Odile Jacob, 1994, p. 114, 136.
[239] Chaïm Potok, *L'élu*, 1967, Calmann-Lévy, 1969, p. 117, 237
[240] Élie Faure, *L'Âme juive* dans *La Question juive vue par vingt-six éminentes personnalités juives*, Paris, E.I.F, 1934, in Léon de Poncins, *Le Problème Juif; Face au concile*, 1965 (Brochure).

is made up of perfectly normal-looking aliens. They form an elite that rules the world through lies and corruption. These glasses also allow her to read the subliminal messages on billboards that command the submission of humans. They are everywhere, they control everything, but you don't see them!

When it is not aliens, it is vampires that threaten humanity: in *Return to Salem'Lot* (USA, 1987), these vampires are of a rather special nature, but here too it is mainly an accusatory inversion: an anthropologist travels to Salem'Lot with his son. Strange things happen and it soon becomes clear that the town is in the hands of Nazi vampires! A film by Larry Cohen.

We have mentioned above the role of influential Jews in the communist revolutions in Europe during the 20th century. We must also mention the role of certain Jews in triggering the wars that have taken place in recent decades. As far as the Second World War is concerned, two testimonies can be cited here that corroborate what we have already presented in our previous books. The American Jewish historian Saul Friedlander has quoted an excerpt from a speech delivered by the famous aviator Charles Lindbergh on 11 September 1939 before 8,000 people in Des Moines, Iowa: "Who are the agitators of war?" Lindbergh censured the US administration, the British and the Jews.... "The greatest danger to this country lies in their large estates and their influence on our cinema, press, radio and government." And Saul Friedlander added: "Possibly without realising it, Lindbergh had at that moment fallen to the same level as a famous American anti-Semitic agitator, the radio preacher Charles Coughlin, or even to the same level as Goebbels' arguments[241][242]."

However, another testimony by Nahum Goldmann shed much more light on the role played by Jewish leaders around the US president:

"Roosevelt not only loved humour, he practised it brilliantly, wrote Goldmann. Here is an example, taken in particularly tragic circumstances. One summer day in 1943, we received terrifying messages from Gerhart Riegner, telling us the details of the Nazis' 'Final Solution' to annihilate the Jews. It was Saturday and I immediately phoned Stephen Wise for advice. During the weekend, President Roosevelt rarely stayed in Washington, preferring to rest at his country home in Hyde Park. I suggested waiting until he returned on Monday morning to inform him of these horrifying revelations, but Wise felt that the circumstances were

---

[241] Saul Friedländer, *The Third Reich and the Jews (1939-1945)*, *Los años del exterminio*, Galaxia Gutenberg, Barcelona, 2009, p. 369-370.

[242] "We cannot allow the passions and natural prejudices of other peoples to lead our country to destruction." Saul Friedländer, *The Third Reich and the Jews (1939-1945)*, p. 370 (Des Moines Speech).

serious enough to turn immediately to the President's adviser, Sam Rosenman, who had rented a house near Roosevelt's so that he would always be on hand in case of need. Alerted by Wise, Rosenman asked us to meet him at his home. It was a very hot day and the three of us were in our shirtsleeves on Rosenman's terrace when we heard the sound of the President's car, Roosevelt's car stopped in front of the terrace and, seeing us all together, the President said: "Well, Rosenman, Stephen Wise and Nahum Goldmann talking together! Go on, boys, Sam will tell me on Monday what I have to do". His car started to pull away and Roosevelt stopped it to tell us: "Imagine how much Goebbels would pay to have a photograph of this scene: the President of the United States receiving instructions from the Three Wise Men of Zion[243] "."

At the beginning of the 21st century, the main organised force opposing Jewish messianism appears to be radical Islam, at least the Shia Islam championed by Iran. The 11 September 2001 attacks in New York justified the US invasion of Afghanistan and Iraq. Since then, in the United States and Europe, the Jewish lobby[244] is trying to launch the West into a new war

---

[243] Nahum Goldmann, *Le Paradoxe juif*, Stock, Paris, 1976, p. 189. In the France of Léon Blum and Daladier, before the war, Jean Zay had been Minister of Education and was a fervent supporter of the war against Germany, as was his colleague in the Ministry of the Interior, Georges Mandel.

[244] On the neoconservative Zionist Jewish lobby in the United States, see *Jewish Fanaticism*. US foreign policy for the 21st century was decisively shaped by a group of neo-conservative Zionist personalities who were very present and influential in the US media and the Washington administration in the 1990s. This policy was prepared and publicly announced in articles and documents that have gone down in the history of newspaper archives. For example: *A Clean Break: A New Strategy for Securing the Realm*, a 1996 paper written by a think tank led by Richard Perle for then Israeli Prime Minister Benjamin Netanyahu. This document included ideas by James Colbert, Douglas Feith, Charles Fairbanks, Robert Loewenberg, David Wurmser and Meyrav Wurmser. Another prominent document was the report *Rebuilding America's Defenses Strategy, Forces and Resources For a New Century*. This 1997 report was the result of an initiative of the famous neo-conservative *think tank* PNAC (*Project for the New American Century*). PNAC was founded by William Kristol and Robert Kagan in 1997 and disbanded in 2006. This project involved the collaboration of a legion of personalities: Bruce P. Jackson, Mark Gerson, Randy Scheunemann, Ellen Bork, Timothy Lehmann, Giselle Donnely, Reuel Marc Gerecht, Gary Schmitt, Michael Goldfarb, Dov Zakheim, John R. Bolton, Richard Perle, Elliot Abrams, Gary Bauer, William J. Bennett, John Ellis Bush, Dick Cheney, Eliot A. Cohen, Midge Decter, Paula Paula Paula Decter, John Ellis Bush, Dick Cheney, Eliot A. Cohen, Midge Decter, Paula Paula Ellis Bush, John Ellis Bush and John Ellis Bush. Cohen, Midge Decter, Paula Dobriansky, Steve Forbes, Aaron Friedberg, Francis Fukuyama, Frank Gaffney, Fred C. Ikle, Donald Kagan, Zalmay Khalilzad, Norman Podhoretz, J. Danforth Quayle, Peter W. Rodman, Stephen P. Rosen, Henry S. Rowen, Donald Rumsfeld, Vin Weber, George Weigel, William Schneider Jr, Paul Wolfowitz. See also an article in *The New York*

against Iran; and President Putin's Russia - which got rid of the "oligarchs [245] " - is also the target of the small "international media community". Indeed, "Human" rights do not apply to the enemies of "Humanity".

The bellicose statements and agitation of many influential Jews (declared or not) on this issue are so blatant that even Jean-François Kahn's left-wing weekly *Marianne* was alarmed by the situation. In its issue of 17 February 2007, one could read a few discreet lines: "Clumsiness: the Representative Council of French Jewish Institutions (Crif) has called on all the candidates in the presidential elections to ask them to support the idea of war against Iran. This shows that the lessons of history are never learned: the same people always make the same mistakes. Such is the eternal Jew, steeped in and shaped by reading the Torah, Talmud and Zohar: the texts do not change; neither does the stubborn Jew.

Hollywood has naturally taken over the planetary propaganda. In the 1980s and 1990s, there were some thirty films depicting Arabs trying to enslave the "free" world.

In William Friedkin's *Rules of Engagement* (USA, 2000), the US embassy in Yemen is threatened by a mob manipulated by Islamists. They are so vile that the audience applauds as the US Marines begin the massacre.

Alexandre Arcady's *L'Union sacrée (Sacred Union)* (France, 1989) is a rather emblematic film (read in *Psychoanalysis of Judaism*).

The Siege is a film by Edward Zwick (USA, 1988): The United States has become the target of terrorist attacks. In retaliation, a commando kidnaps a fundamentalist Muslim leader. An ultimatum is sent to the New York counter-terrorism unit.

Delta Force, by Menahem Golan (USA, 1986): Arabs hijack a plane and terrorise the passengers.

Robert Zemeckis' *Back to the Future* (USA, 1985) depicts Arab arms dealers who are as violent as they are stupid.

In Richard Brokks' *Deadly Target* (*Wronh is right*, USA, 1982), an Arab terrorist plans to destroy Tel Aviv and Jerusalem with two atomic bombs. These people are completely insane!

In *Network* (USA, 1977), we see how the Arabs and their petrodollars are buying up the whole of America. A presenter calls on viewers to revolt. This projective film is by Sydney Lumet.

Black Sunday (USA, 1977): A Palestinian terrorist threatens to kill thousands of Americans gathered in a Miami stadium for a football game. She eliminates anyone who stands in her way. A John Frankenheimer film.

Times of 30 January 1998 by William Kristol and Robert Kagan entitled *"Bombing Iraq Isn't Enough"*.

[245] On the "Russian oligarchs", read *The Jewish Mafia*.

The Shadow of a Giant (USA, 1966) is a film by Melville Shavelson about the creation of the State of Israel. The Palestinians are portrayed as brutal and bloodthirsty, while Kirk Douglas, as an American soldier, comes to the rescue to lend his expertise to the just Israeli cause.

In September 2007, the minister Bernard Kouchner, the famous creator and supporter of "humanitarian interference", expressed his warmongering towards President Ahmadinejad's Iran, making all those neo-conservatives who dreamed of using French soldiers to defend Jewish interests around the world boil with joy.

On 22 September 2007, the weekly *Marianne* quoted Antoine Sfeir, a very popular intellectual in France who specialises in Middle Eastern affairs: "Sfeir is surprised by the ignorance of many French intellectuals. They ignore, for example, that President Ahmadinejad, an illuminist and an anti-Semite, 'belongs to an apocalyptic movement of messianic madmen who are not at all representative of the regime'". Once again, this was an accusatory inversion.

It is clear, however, that the Jews will not stop voluntarily. Despite all the setbacks history has inflicted on them, they remain convinced of their mission and continue their frantic struggle against the rest of humanity. To borrow a phrase from Ernst Jünger: they are "like iron machines that only stop when they break".

In his little book of Zionist propaganda, written in 1970, Victor Tibika already deplored the hostile attitude of the Arabs towards the Jews who had stolen their land after the Six Day War of 1967: "In the future, he said, historians are sure to judge the enemies of Israel very harshly if, by maintaining their provocative and aggressive attitude, they again start a war which, this time, would degenerate into an apocalyptic conflagration of the universe".

And Victor Tibika continued: "The only thing left for all of us, children of God in our own right, whatever the colour of our skin, is to work and pray tirelessly, with all our strength, for a definitive peace in the world[246]."

Obviously, it is all a question of vocabulary. Everyone is in favour of "peace". After having crushed their enemies, they are always in favour of "peace".

---

[246] Victor Tibika, *Réveil et unité du peuple juif*, 1970, p. 92.

PART TWO

PSYCHOPATHOLOGY OF JUDAISM

1. The great loneliness of the Jews

An enigma in the midst of nations

André Neher, a Jewish intellectual of the 1970s, expressed the heavy loneliness of Jews in the world: "The definition of the man-Israel, he wrote, is precisely to be the man of loneliness". It is "a lonely people", and this loneliness is "dramatic". And he added: "Not to be like others, to live in solitude, to remain in the dwelling", such is the destiny of the Jewish people. And André Neher then quoted the Torah: "Yes, it is a people that will dwell alone and will not be recognised as one of the nations" (Numbers XXIII, 9)[247]."

Albert Memmi, in his *Portrait of a Jew*, published in 1962, lamented the fate of his fellow Jews: "I know well the pain of disappointed love, he wrote: to love without being loved, this is in short the civic drama of many Jews; to wish desperately to be loved, adopted once and for all, while being almost certain never to be loved[248]."

In volume II, he again spoke of the "terrible loneliness" of the Jewish people: "Isolation is a corollary of choice," he wrote. And he asked: "Why this cruel fate, why have they been thrown into this terrible history which constantly crushes and punishes them?

The answer couldonly be of a divine nature: "Election explains everything, comforts everything; it reassures and flatters, it demands and

---

[247] André Neher, *L'Identité juive*, 1977, Seghers, 1989, p. 23, 24, 26.
[248] Albert Memmi, *Portrait d'un juif*, Gallimard, 1962, p. 198.

attracts. It is at once the glory and the duty of the Jew, the burden, the privilege and the protection[249]."

In his 1952 *Psychoanalysis of Anti-Semitism*, Rudolph Loewenstein expressed the same anguish: "Like unjustly punished children, the Jews suffer from injustice but also from lack of affection. For people, like children in this respect, expect proof of love from fate, from the whole world, from God. The Jews, in spite of their conviction that they are God's favourites, perhaps suffer more from lack of affection than from all the misfortunes they suffer[250]."

Shmuel Trigano, a university professor, insisted on Israel's uniqueness: "The most unique aspect of the Jewish people, he wrote, is its idea of its dual autonomy. The Jewish people see themselves as an autonomous entity, both politically, in relation to other nations, and spiritually, in relation to other religious systems...Autonomy' is an essential Jewish concept. It refers to self-government in accordance with the specific laws and norms of the Jewish people.... Political and spiritual autonomy is guaranteed by the covenant with God[251]."

The story of Barry Lyndon, the hero of Stanley Kubrick's film (1975), seems an allegory to the initiated insider. The film beautifully reflects the anxieties of Judaism, and it is probably no coincidence that Stanley Kubrick used this script to adapt it[252]. In the middle of the 18th century, Barry Lyndon is a young Irish nobleman who, out of love, challenges an English officer to a duel. He is sure of his rights and causes a scandal. He is put out of the way by a machination. Believing he has killed the English officer, he is forced to flee. He enlists in the British army and leaves for the battlefields of Europe. Barry Lyndon flees from the battlefield, from a fight that does not concern him, deserts the army and goes over to the other side. He lies, tells anything to the officer who interrogates him and finally receives a decoration. He then became a spy, but betrayed again to save a fellow countryman. He then makes his fortune in the aristocratic salons by cheating at gambling games. He enters a large wealthy family to take advantage of the wealth accumulated by others. As master of the house, he behaves like a dictator, squandering the family inheritance, inciting hatred and sowing discord and madness. Finally, a member of the family rebels, confronts him and drives him out; and Barry Lyndon takes the path of exile, shunned by all, as at the beginning.

---

[249] Albert Memmi, *Portrait d'un juif II*, Gallimard, 1966, p. 127-129.
[250] Rudolph Loewenstein, *Psychanalyse de l'antisémitisme*, 1952, Presses Universitaires de France, 2001, p. 211.
[251] Shmuel Trigano, *La Société juive à travers l'histoire*, t. I, Fayard, 1992, p. 71.
[252] *The Luck of Barry Lyndon* (1844) by William Makepeace Thackeray.

Jews are acutely aware of their loneliness in this confrontation with the rest of humanity. Edouard Valdman was a second-rate Jewish intellectual, but his 1994 book, *Jews and Money*, contains some interesting insights. First of all, it is worth noting that, although he addressed many issues, Valdman said almost nothing about the relationship between Jews and money. But the title was more salesman like that, and that was clearly the most important thing. Make money, but don't talk about it too much. Please read the following text carefully. Edouard Valdman praised psychoanalysis, but the informed reader will see in it an identity introspection peculiar to Judaism. "Psychoanalysis, he said, is to listen to the word of the other within oneself, of the unknown within oneself...to accept to dig into one's own abyss. It means trying to see if the reason for this perpetual clash with the outside world, for this wound we constantly feel in our contact with it, as if the relationship with the other were impossible, is not to be found first and foremost within ourselves[253]."

You have understood: it is indeed about Judaism. Valdman was talking about Judaism and its "perpetual clash with the world". A few pages earlier, Edouard Valdman had already mentioned the "mystery" of Judaism, its "strangeness": "What is the origin, today as yesterday, of Polish anti-Semitism? wrote Valdman: It is the strangeness of Judaism, this impossibility of apprehending it, when it is precisely disembodiment, breach and openness". But the intellectual preferred to project the evil onto European culture: "Auschwitz is not an accident, but the ultimate expression within European culture of that immense fear of the strange, of the unknown, of the emptiness that lies within every human being and that the presence of the Jew has precisely the vocation to reveal[254]."

In the same vein, the psychoanalyst Elisabeth Roudinesco has been able to write: "The fate of the Jewish people appears to the historian as a paradoxical, incredible and almost incomprehensible phenomenon. It is unique and without parallel in human history[255]."

For his part, the famous philosopher Bernard-Henri Lévy was ecstatic about the mystery of the Jewish people: "An absolutely unique case of rebellion against any logic, oblivion or genocide, of stubbornness in saying no, in denying the verdict of facts, in defying the machine of centuries in its procession of admonitions and murderous fatalities". This "indomitable people" is therefore "one of the most profound enigmas for contemporary consciousness[256]."

---

[253] Édouard Valdman, *Les Juifs et l'argent*, Ed. Galilée, 1994, p. 48.
[254] Édouard Valdman, *Les Juifs et l'argent*, Ed. Galilée, 1994, p. 31.
[255] Elisabeth Roudinesco, *Le Malheur d'Israël*, Cluny, 1956, p. 7.
[256] Bernard-Henri Lévy, *Le Testament de Dieu*, Grasset, 1979, p. 8, 9.

The influential press director Jean Daniel said nothing else: "The Jewish mystery is a moving phenomenon that can raise mystical questions and lead some to believe in the election of a people[257]."

Again we hear the echo of André Glucksmann's words: "Two millennia of being a living question for the whole world. Two millennia of innocence, having nothing to do with anything[258]."

Even before the war, Daniel Pasmanik wrote: "Taken as a whole, the history of the Jewish people is unique and without equivalent in the world. Even today it is an insoluble enigma for sociologists, philosophers and historians. Every culture is original, but Jewish culture, the product of Jewish history, is absolutely exceptional[259]."

André Neher also waxed lyrical about the "mystery" of Judaism. "The Jew', he wrote, is 'something other than a man in the earthly, technical and banal sense of the term'. This "mystery" is "the very sign of his divine, transcendent and eternal origin". The Jew is therefore not a man like other men: "This man who accepts to be the particular man, the "other" man, the man "not like other men", is Israel".

André Neher warned us, however, that we run the risk of great disappointment if we approach this divine being who lives among us and enter into conversation with him: "The observer may catch this divine gaze which illuminates the Jew and haloes him with an exemplary holiness; but then he runs the risk of not noticing it and of being stupefied and disappointed when he discovers that this witness of divine light is at the same time a worker of the earth's crust". It is what the author called "the characteristic and fatal ambiguity of the Jew[260]."

Judaism's plan for the unification of the world and peace on earth, an "absolute and final peace", entails an egalitarian fanaticism that is in absolute opposition to the laws of nature. The Jews are well aware that their project runs counter to the laws of this world.

In 1968, the novelist Albert Cohen, in *Bella del señor*, put it in plain language:

"Israel is the people of unnature, the bearer of a mad hope which the natural abhors". And he continued in a prophetic trance: "The noblest portions of humanity are of Jewish soul and stand firm on their rock which is the Bible oh my Jews to whom I speak in silence know your people

---

[257] Jean Daniel, *La Blessure*, Grasset, 1992, p. 259.
[258] André Glucksmann, *Le Discours de la haine*, Plon, 2004, p. 88.
[259] Daniel Pasmanik, *Qu'est ce que le Judaïsme?*, Lipschutz, 1930, p. 83.
[260] André Neher, *L'Identité juive*, 1977, Petite Bibliothèque Payot, 2007, p. 32, 26. [To mitigate this disappointment, we suggest the reader search for and watch a *Chabad Hasidic Dance* on youtube, for example. Or, on the contrary, read *The Jewish Mafia*, depending on one's point of view. NdT.]

venerate them for having wanted schism and separation for having taken up the fight against nature and its laws[261]."

The feminist Elisabeth Badinter had also pointed out the inclination of Jews to oppose the laws of nature: "Nature's dominion over us is receding, and with it the difference between the sexes". And in passing he extolled the New World Order promised by the prophets: "Equality is in the process of being realised, it generates the likeness which puts an end to war.... The 20th century has inaugurated in our part of the world something that resembles a new era," he wrote, rejecting objections: "The moralists will see in this change, so contrary to the natural order, only a manifestation of decadence analogous to so many others that history has known[262]."

Philosopher Emmanuel Levinas' little book, *Some Reflections on the Philosophy of Hitlerism*, published in 1934, promised some gems. In reality, it is utterly incomprehensible gibberish. What is more, in the 1997 reprint, we discover that the great philosopher's text is actually only about twenty pages long; the rest of the book is an essay by Miguel Abensour, whose name is written in small characters on the cover. One thus feels a little cheated on the twentieth page, although perhaps Abensour may turn out to be no worse than Levinas. Wrong! Abensour, like his master, is also totally illegible. Listen to this: "For Levinas, the source of Nazi barbarism would henceforth reside - apart from any contingency or accident - in an "essential possibility of elementary Evil" which would have to do with the ontology of Being, concerned with being[263]." There is no need to continue reading: it is all of the same kind.

However, we have been able to rescue the following idea, buried in this dialectical imbroglio: "Jewish destiny can thus be defined as a being foreign to the world, a challenge and a questioning of the world that seems to contain it".

It is the "extraterrestrial" Jew, so to speak. "In this case," continued Abensour, quoting Levinas, "anti-Semitism can unfold as the revolt of Nature against Supernature, the aspiration of the world to its own apotheosis, to its beatification in its own nature[264]."

---

[261] Albert Cohen, *Bella del Señor*, Anagrama, Barcelona, 2017, p. 711-716. This is stream of consciousness, an uninterrupted flow without typographic punctuation or differentiation in which the character's thoughts and impressions emerge. (It can be read in Molly Blum's famous soliloquy in James Joyce's *Ulysses* and in the novels of Marcel Proust).

[262] Elisabeth Badinter, *L'un est l'autre*, Éd. Odile Jacob, 1986, p. 245, 250. Read more in *Jewish Fanaticism*.

[263] Emmanuel Levinas, *Quelques Réflexions sur la philosophie de l'hitlérisme*, 1934, Rivages poche 1997, p. 95.

[264] Emmanuel Levinas, *Quelques Réflexions sur la philosophie de l'hitlérisme*, 1934, Rivages poche 1997, p. 36.

What Edouard Valdman wrote about nature echoed the words of Albert Cohen, Elisabeth Badinter and Emmanuel Levinas: "Before Abraham, men were enclosed in Nature, he wrote, in the fascination of beauty and all the terrors of the world. They were at that time idolaters... They went round and round in the circle of their own tragedy". Edouard Valdman once again expressed the pathological egocentrism of Judaism, incapable of seeing the world except through its messianism: "Until then [before Abraham], there is no History, he wrote; there is only the circle and fatality". And Valdman continued: "For these men, for the Jews, the world will henceforth be a march and a search. There will be no rest. But on the way, they have become others. Never again will they be slaves to nature, to the nation, to repetition, to the soil[265]." The Jewish people know no rest. "They can no longer rest," he added two pages later.

But the problem is not that Jews cannot rest, but that they prevent others from living in peace by boasting about it. This is an idea that we often find in intellectual Judaism.[266]

To the question "What is a Jew?", Nobel laureate Isaac Bashevis Singer, interviewed in the *New York Times Magazine* in November 1978, replied: "A Jew is someone who, unable to fall asleep, prevents everyone else from falling asleep".

The Jewish Jeremiad: 4000 years of pure suffering

Jews themselves often present their history as an "uninterrupted vale of tears". No doubt, laments and jeremiads are deeply rooted in the Jewish soul.

Esther Benbassa is a Jewish intellectual who seems more serene than most of her peers. In a book published in 2007, entitled *Suffering as Identity*, Esther Benbassa showed a certain amount of high-mindedness in questioning Israel's uniqueness and denouncing the lachrymose view that Jews have of their own history. She rightly wrote: "Even today, when people talk about the Jews, the first thing that comes to mind is their suffering.... Suffering and victimhood have acquired the value of a quasi-dogma for many secularised Jews. For some, it is sacrilege to touch them, even just to allude to them[267]."

It is often said that Heinrich Graetz, the author of the monumental eleven-volume *History of the Jews*, published in Germany between 1853 and 1875,

---

[265] Édouard Valdman, *Les Juifs et l'argent*, Ed. Galilée, 1994, p. 17-19.
[266] They boast of being "annoying", "irritating", read the statements of Elie Wiesel, Emmanuel Levinas, Daniel Cohn.Bendit, George Steiner in *Psychoanalysis of Judaism* and in *Jewish Fanaticism*.
[267] Esther Benbassa, *La Souffrance comme identité*, Fayard, 2007, p. 116.

would have been the "ideologue, the undisputed architect of this lachrymose history". But in fact, long before him, Joseph Ha-Cohen had already written *The Valley of Tears* in 1560, which recounted anti-Semitic violence in Europe since the time of the Crusades: "*The Valley of Tears* was to make its author the archetypal representative of the lachrymose vision of Jewish history, wrote Benbassa. He was influenced by the stories of the Crusades". Indeed, the first crusade of 1096 marks, according to European Jews, the origin of their misfortunes in Christian lands.

The German Jewish thinker Hermann Cohen tried to make sense of these persecutions: "In his posthumous work published in 1918, *The Religion of Reason*, he saw the suffering of the Jews as a messianic sign addressed to the nations[268]."

The very famous Jacques Attali, who was adviser to socialist president François Mitterrand before becoming adviser to the liberal conservative Nicolas Sarkozy [and later godfather of Rothschild banker Emmanuel Macron, ndt], was naturally steeped in Jewish suffering. In his book on the great banker Siegmund Warburg, published in 1985, he shed a few tears over the fate of the poor Jewish bankers of the Middle Ages. They are, Attali wrote, "forced to lend money to princes to attract their protection, at the risk of being creditors of the powerful to guarantee their freedom, knowing that they multiply at the same time the risk of ending up as scapegoats, and having learned, in four thousand years of suffering, to articulate a morality and an action[269]."

The American actor Kirk Douglas was also outraged by the eternal and still unexplained persecution of Jews: "My parents were among the lucky ones, lucky to escape the pogroms in Russia, where vodka-fuelled young Cossacks made it a sport to gallop through the ghetto and crack open a few Jewish heads[270]." And Kirk Douglas might well have added: "Just like that, just for the fun of it", for Jews are innocent of anything that can be blamed on them.

This is exactly what the novelist Joseph Joffo would have us believe in *The Horseman of the Promised Land*, his novel published in 1983. The entire novel, from beginning to end, recounts the humiliations suffered by poor Russian Jews in the early 20th century:

"With a cry of triumph, Ivan fell upon him and struck, struck.... He repeated over and over again: Jew! Jew!.... Andrei felt the pain overwhelm him. Everything around him became a blur and he sank into a black hole".

---

[268] Esther Benbassa, *La Souffrance comme identité*, Fayard, 2007, p. 111.
[269] Jacques Attali, *Un homme d'influence*, Seix Barral, Barcelona, 1992, p. 11.
[270] Kirk Douglas, *The Ragpicker's Son* (1988), Cult Books, *2021*, p. 18

As for Myriam: "She had been humiliated and raped because she was Jewish" (pages 77, 79). Russian girls did not sleep with Jews: "Suddenly Olga pushed Andrei away. Distrust flashed in her eyes.
- Are you... Jewish? she asked. He did not answer. Olga's gaze hardened. She grabbed her blouse and held it in front of her as if to protect herself. "Jew! You're a Jew!" she repeated. It was as if she had spat out the words.
- Yes," said Andrei.
She had a bitter laugh.
- To think that I was going to sleep with a Jew... You are all thieves and liars," cried Olga, "You damned race, you have deceived us! Without a word, Andrei left the room" (page 233).

The Cossacks also took it out on the old men, just for fun: "The three old men kept praying, swinging their busts with renewed vigour". A soldier stepped forward, "swept the candlestick with his sabre and sent it to the other end of the room". Soon "the three old men, dragged in the mud, were thrown at the colonel's feet".

The Russians loved to humiliate the poor Jews: "Now, Jews, you will bow down before this pig and say the prayer of the dead!" There was some laughter, but the four men did not flinch.
- You're wrong to play hard to get," said the NCO. If so, we'll find something funnier.
He drew his sabre and, in one swift movement, slit the throat of the unfortunate pig. The blood gushed out...
- Now you are going to kneel down and drink the pig's blood, the sergeant ordered.

The men still did not move. The Cossack grabbed his braided leather whip and began to strike. The strap whistled. The leather fell on the four old Jews. When Andrei tried to intervene, the sergeant replied, "No, they didn't do anything to me, but you have to have some fun[271] !"

However, the Jews of Russia at the beginning of the twentieth century were not all poor devils persecuted for no reason by the evil Cossacks. We have already seen in *Jewish Fanaticism* that most of the mining wealth was in the hands of wealthy Jewish businessmen and bankers. Sholem Asch, who along with Scholem Aleichem and Isaac Bashevis Singer was one of the great Yiddish-language writers, confirmed this in one of his novels, entitled *Petersburg* and published in 1933. In it, a Jewish revolutionary turned to his fellows in high finance for money and subsidies: "Do you want to know, gentlemen, why we are coming to you? It is because Russian capital is concentrated in your hands. There is Russia's oil talking," and he

---

[271] Joseph Joffo, *Le Cavalier de la terre promise*, Editions Ramsay, 1983, p. 266, 267, 267, 279, 280

looked at Boris Khaimovitch, "next to me I have Russia's tea, over there Russia's sugar, and here are Russia's forests in front of me. - And the young man pointed to each of these gentlemen, with an almost cynical smile on his lips. - The poor Jews are the only oppressed people in Russia; Jewish capital is still free. That is why we have come to see them[272]."

Manès Sperber, an influential intellectual of the 1970s, was rather caricatured when he spoke of the persecutions. Sperber wrote, for example: "With the Crusades began the era of the nameless martyr, an almost uninterrupted succession of oppression and suffering". Naturally, he could not forget the "Shoah": "For decades now, not a day goes by that I do not think of that time when my people, in the heart of Europe, were humiliated to the point of dehumanisation and eliminated by the murderers in power. Not a day goes by when I can forget the indifference with which the world tolerated this for years. Such loneliness has nestled in the hearts of my fellow human beings ever since". And he added: "Europe fell lower than the bottom of the abyss: it became the scene of a genocide practised every day against defenceless human beings[273]."

The novelist Chaim Potok also accused the whole world. In *The Chosen*, he wrote about the situation of the Jews in 1942: "The British let in a few Jews, and then closed the door. America had not cared enough about them either. Nobody had cared enough. The world had closed its doors, and six million Jews had been slaughtered. What a world! What a world of madmen[274]!" If the whole world allowed the poor Jews to suffer, then the whole world is guilty, and one day it will have to atone for its crimes. This is a recurrent discourse.

The legend of Moses has also served to perpetuate Jewish suffering. As we know, Batya, the Pharaoh's daughter, discovered the abandoned child in the waters of the Nile. Elie Wiesel wrote of this biblical episode: "He knew he was a Jew because he wept not as a child but as an adult, as a community of adults; all his people wept in him, says one commentator[275]."

The anniversary date of this continuous Jewish lament is the 9th of Av (late July-early August in the Christian calendar), i.e. the day of the destruction of the two temples, the first destroyed by Nebuchadnezzar in 486 BC, and the second by the Roman legions of Titus in 68 AD.

The mass expulsion of the Jews from Spain in 1492 took place on the same day, according to Abravanel, who was then the leader of the Spanish Jewish community. Esther Benbassa pointed out, however, that it was on 31 July, i.e. 7 Av, that the last Jew left the lands of Spain, and not on the

---

[272] Scholem Asch, *Pétersbourg*, 1933, Belfond, 1985, p. 51.
[273] Manès Sperber, *Être Juif*, Odile Jacob, 1994, p. 97, 28, 110.
[274] Chaïm Potok, *L'élu*, 1967, Calmann-Lévy, 1969, p. 212.
[275] Elie Wiesel, *Celebración bíblica*, pdf Proyectos Editoriales, Buenos Aires, p. 153.

9th, and added: "Here we see again how the author inserts the vicissitudes of the present into the traditional liturgical framework accepted for great catastrophes.... Spain is identified with the land of Israel and the expulsion with the destruction of the Temple, while Abravanel himself is transformed into a new Ezekiel, prophet of the exile[276]."

In 2007, John Mearsheimer and Stephen Walt's book on the Lobby contained a number of considerations that confirmed the same point. They pointed out, for example, that the new anti-Semitism did not date from the beginning of the 21st century: "In 1967, Arnold Foster and Benjamin Epstein of the ADL [Anti-Defamation League] published *The New Antisemitism*".

Indeed, Jewish intellectuals have always complained about the resurgence of the phenomenon. On 11 May 2002, *New York Times* columnist Frank Rich admitted: "Like many other Jews, perhaps I am too inclined to believe that the whole world is anti-Semitic.

"This deep-seated fear among American Jews came to the fore when Israel was roundly criticised around the world in the spring of 2002, the two American academics added. Nat Hentoff, writing for the *Village Voice*, said at the time: "If suddenly a voice on a loudspeaker shouted down the street, "All Jews in Times Square!", I would not be at all surprised. Ron Rosenbaum has argued in the *New York Observer* that a "second Holocaust could very well happen". This concern became so widespread that the weekly *New Republic* felt it necessary to put on its front page this headline from an article by Leon Wieseltier, himself very committed to Israel's defence: "Hitler is Dead: A plea against the ethnic panic of American Jews[277]"."

In France, the situation is very similar. In its 1995 issue, *L'Arche*, the monthly magazine of French Judaism, published an article by a certain Christian Boltanski, who wrote on page 24: "The war in France has taught me that our neighbour has only one desire: to kill us, that our neighbour, who is extremely kind and nice, can kill us the next day, that the same man who kisses his son in the morning can kill others in the afternoon". And he also added: "...and that we ourselves are capable of it".

Twenty years earlier, community leaders did not see the world differently. In 1978, for example, *Le Droit de vivre*, the official organ of the League against anti-Semitism (Licra), headlined on its front page: "Defeating anti-Semitism to avoid the worst". In 1991, its president declared: "We have a right to be worried. I have the impression that we are in 1934 or 1938".

---

[276] Esther Benbassa, *La Souffrance comme identité*, Fayard, 2007, p. 86.
[277] John J. Mearsheimer / Stephen Walt, *Le Lobby pro-israélien et la politique étrangère américaine*, La Découverte, 2007, p. 207, 210.

In his book *Portrait of a Jew*, published in 1962, Albert Memmi also lamented the miserable condition of the Jews: "The Jew as a Jew, he wrote, can hardly ever influence the national destiny of which he is nevertheless a part: he is not consulted and, most of the time, does not even ask to be consulted, for he is content to be forgotten and treated as if he did not exist. But if he does ask, he immediately discovers his powerlessness". And Albert Memmi insisted in the same vein: "We are, in the end, the outcasts, the rejects of history. We want to go unnoticed, but since history is made without us, it is also, more often than not, made against us. As we have seen, everything happens as if the Jew were designated and offered as an expiatory victim to the poor imagination of executioners, dictators and politicians. But this is not by chance: socially and historically, the Jew is the weakest point of the nation, the weakest link in the chain, which must therefore give way first".

This theme is repeated throughout his book: "Jews are particularly oppressed, more severely, more generally than others[278]." And there was still cause for alarm: "Last year, the walls of Paris were once again covered with anti-Jewish slogans and symbols. A publishing house chose the same moment to launch a dictionary containing numerous insulting definitions of Jews[279]."

In volume II, he went on and on: "Yes, the Jew is still essentially an oppressed person...In Argentina, the thighs of some Jewish schoolgirls were incised with swastikas. In England, neo-Nazi rallies were held, and once again chanted "Jews out!" In America, synagogues continued to be ransacked: twenty-five in two years[280] !"

In November 2007, the public television channel France 3 broadcast one of countless reports on the extraordinary suffering of the Jews at the beginning of the 21st century: *Comme un juif en France* (*Like a Jew in France*). All the witnesses, without exception, played the usual role of the whining and crying Jew. With such testimonies, an observer would say, five generations later, that our time had been truly terrible for the poor Jews. They had been vilified, harassed and abused in the schools and on the streets of the big cities. Their synagogues were burned and they were afraid. They had been forced to flee Israel (two or three thousand a year, out of a total of about one million individuals), and no one cared and looked after them. At no point in the documentary, of course, were we told about the Jewish ministers, the Jewish billionaires, the ubiquitous Jews on TV, radio and film, always ready to lecture on tolerance and guilt in order to impose

---

[278] Albert Memmi, *Portrait d'un juif*, Gallimard, 1962, p. 193, 195, 219.
[279] Albert Memmi, *Portrait d'un juif*, Gallimard, 1962, p. 212.
[280] Albert Memmi, *La Libération du Juif, Portrait d'un Juif II*, Gallimard, 1966, p. 14, 13

themselves more strongly as a homogeneous and relentlessly racist people in the midst of the people who have taken them in.

By the end of the 20th century, the millions of Afro-Muslim immigrants, whom Jewish intellectuals had done so much to bring to France in the space of a few decades, were beginning to cause serious problems. Since the beginning of the new millennium, there have been widespread riots in the French suburbs, and the few anti-Semitic attacks that have occurred, however small, have greatly alarmed the leaders of the Jewish community.

For this reason, Jews have recently realised that Arabs and Muslims now represent the main danger to them. Roger Cukierman, elected President of Crif in 2001, published an article in *Le Monde* on 5 February 2002 in which he wrote: "The most immediate danger comes not from the traditional extreme right, but from a few Islamist fanatics or isolated individuals who are often tactfully referred to as "young hooligans" from the suburbs[281]."

Many Jewish intellectuals have openly gone over to the hard, liberal, pro-American right. André Glucksmann, Alexandre Adler, Marc Weitzmann, Pascal Bruckner, Romain Goupil and Alain Finkielkraut are thus pursuing their messianic goals of world unification precisely because they are Jews, because they are still Jews. Certainly, there are Jews who have sincerely integrated into French society, but they are no longer Jews at all. For they are French.

On 27 April 2006, the weekly *Le Point* published a report on anti-Semitism in France and the emigration of some Jews to Israel. In it, Julien Dray, a socialist leader and co-founder of SOS Racisme in the 1980s, explained that compared to the millions of Arabs now living in France, Jews did not carry much weight. Listen to this: "The truth is that the community has made a mistake by going in that direction. It has become a lobby to influence France's foreign policy. It's a suicidal attitude, because lobby against lobby, you can't compete[282]." Indeed, it is quite clear that the Jewish lobby of world trade, international finance and the media is no match for the formidable lobby of Maghrebi neighbourhood shopkeepers and hashish traffickers.

The same issue of the weekly also featured statements by the well-known philosopher Alain Finkielkraut. Alarmed by the aggressiveness of young Muslims living in France, he too had gone over to the "right". He too

---

[281] Roger Cukiermamn, *Ni fiers ni dominateurs*, Edition du Moment, 2008, p. 240. Read statements by Cukierman and other Crif presidents *in Planetary Hopes, Psychoanalysis of Judaism* and *Jewish Fanaticism*. ["Youthland" appeared in France in those years. NdT.]

[282] Julien Dray's flat was searched in December 2008. The man is suspected of fraud. A few years ago he bought a watch worth 38,000 euros, partly in cash. He also withdrew tens of thousands of euros from the accounts of the association SOS Racisme.

expressed this identity-based suffering of the Jewish personality. He denounced the discourse of these immigrants, who now posed as victims of the West and competed dangerously with Jewish victimhood propaganda: "There are imaginary slaves in France," said the thinker, "imaginary natives who want to settle their scores with the Jews. No doubt they believe that the Holocaust is a choice and they are envious. I don't know if the Jews have changed, but the situation is new. I suffer from it not only as a Jew, but also as a Frenchman, especially since two of the most common insults are "damned Jew" and "damned Frenchman"."

Double suffering, then, for Alain Finkielkraut. His comments recalled what the historian Pierre Vidal-Naquet had written in his memoirs about his father Lucien, who had also suffered long before the war: "Lucien, he said, was a French Jew who felt as a Frenchman the insult done to him as a Jew[283]."

In the same issue of *Le Point*, Shmuel Trigano, an author with whom readers of *Planetary Hopes* are already somewhat familiar, also expressed his great pain: "Why judge the Jews for having turned to the right...? It is pathetic that the only French people who are asked to prove that they are good Frenchmen are the Jews. They are expected to be the quintessence of France. And because France has lost its mind, they become the scapegoats for everything that goes wrong. The Jew is a scapegoat, always persecuted for no reason. It is one of the great enigmas of history.

Rabbi Haïm Dynovisz put it simply: "With Arabs, you either hit or you get hit. There is no *kavod* (respect) to show an Arab. Either he is under your feet or you are under his".

The journalists of *Le Point* wrote: "When asked about this racist morality, Haïm Dynovisz protested: "I am talking about Arab civilisation, not about individuals who, taken individually, are very good". Readers of the weekly could therefore be reassured that Haïm Dynovisz would not be dragged before the courts like a common goy.

Victor Malka was certainly not an intellectual of great prominence, but what he wrote was quite revealing. His *Letter to my Muslim Friends*, published in 2006, was full of good sentiments, although its aim was simply to convince Muslims in France to respect the 'Man'. His discourse was a bit puerile, as is sometimes the case with Jewish thinkers and scriptwriters.[284]

Victor Malka acknowledged that Jewish intellectuals were always ready to support immigrants: "Have you noticed," he wrote, "the large number of intellectuals among us - sometimes themselves from Morocco, Algeria or

---

[283] Pierre Vidal-Naquet, *Mémoires I*, 1930-1955, Seuil, p. 102.
[284] Edouard Drumont had already noted this character trait, read in *Psychoanalysis of Judaism*.

Tunisia - who support their demands and take up their cause every day in the columns of the national press?"

But the Arabs had to understand that the support they could receive from Jews living in France depended on their respect for democratic laws: "We can be your best travelling companions as soon as you cut all ties - by making it known loud and clear, unequivocally - with fundamentalists of every hue and variety (whether they come from Egypt or Saudi Arabia), with their liberticidal projects and their impossible dreams of domination". It is well known, indeed, that fanatical Muslims seek world domination: the exact opposite of the Jews, in short.

Muslims are therefore invited to reform their religion to become true Westerners, good, docile and cosmopolitan consumers, eager to keep the economic machine running at full capacity: "You probably need to dust off some of your customs to bring them up to date with French times[285]", Victor Malka wrote proudly.

Jewish intellectuals, for the most part, often explain to us that throughout history relations between Jews and Arabs have always been cordial. In reality, one hardly needs to do much research to realise that this discourse is largely fallacious. More than anything else, it must be understood that for them historical truth is of no importance when it comes to working on behalf of the Jewish community.

If they are to be believed, Jews and Arabs in France can be the best friends in the world: "We have coexisted together most of the time in harmony and peace. Better still, sometimes in a kind of symbiosis," Malka assures us.

And he might as well have added: "We at the top of the power, you at the bottom of the ladder". In fact, the whole book is written in this condescending tone: "You see, our problems and yours are not as far apart as you might think at first glance...". The speech resembles that of a psychiatrist giving an injection to a slightly suspicious victim, as another way of saying: "You see, in the end, it doesn't hurt so much".

On 22 February 2007, the weekly *Le Point* published an article on French Jews settling in Israel: "They gather in homogeneous groups in Beit Vagan, Har Nof, Kyriat Moshe or Bnei Braq, the religious neighbourhoods of Jerusalem or Tel Aviv", we read. These few thousand Jews are literally "disgusted" with what France has become. Here is what the journalist wrote about one of these emigrants: "At 55, he never imagined that it would be so easy for him to make a definitive cross to his life in France. For him, it was a sign that the divorce had already been finalised for a long time. He could not find harsh enough words for De Gaulle, Giscard, Michel Jobert and Roland Dumas, whom he unreservedly accused of "having sold France

---

[285] Victor Malka, *Letrre à mes amis musulmans*, Albin Michel, 2006, p. 21, 192.

to the Arab world". Jacques Chirac, for his part, had scandalously favoured "Arab-Muslim immigrants" to the detriment of France's Jews.

Here is what 20-year-old Miguel had to say. Born in Marseille, Miguel joined the Tsahal, the Israeli army: "France is forced to choose between the scum and the Jews. It has made it very clear which way it leans. I don't think it was free to make that choice. The Jews in France don't count for anything; the others, on the other hand, can burn thousands of cars if they are disturbed".

Alex Moïse, co-founder of Radio Shalom and secretary general of the Federation of Jewish Organisations in France, spoke to *Actualité juive* on 24 July 2008: 'I am convinced that European Judaism is on the way out,' he declared. The rampant assimilation and Islamisation of the continent means that in twenty years' time it will be difficult to live as a Jew. China and India should be home to thriving communities in the future". We see how the Jew is ready to leave in search of new lands and thus continue his eternal wandering.

In all democratic countries, the smallest "anti-Semitic" incident often takes on gigantic proportions, in proportion to the influence of Jews in the media. But not all such incidents are the fault of "neo-Nazis" or Muslims.

These are just a few examples to add to our long list of fake anti-Semitic attacks, which we have already listed in *Jewish Fanaticism* (2007).

In 1990, a Maryland accountant, Joel Davis, was convicted of insurance fraud. He had set fire to his farmhouse and covered the walls with anti-Semitic graffiti.

In the same year, an Israeli court convicted a Jew, David Goldner, for writing anti-Semitic graffiti on 300 Jewish graves in a Haifa cemetery. The culprit explained that he had done so in order to make Jews aware of the danger and unite against the enemy (*Los Angeles Times*, 28 May 1999).

In 1995, in Portland, Oregon, another Jew, Dan Davenport, was convicted of similar acts: he set fire to his house and painted swastikas on the walls to collect insurance money.

In 1996, in Miami, Al Rubin was sentenced to three years in prison, and his son to eight years, for covering a Jewish school, Hillel County Scholl, with Nazi graffiti and destroying school buses.

In 1998, a 15-year-old Jewish boy from Huntington Beach, California, was arrested along with four other friends for painting and burning a swastika in his parents' yard. He later admitted that he had done it because his parents had forbidden him to go to a beach party, and also because his mother had refused to give him three dollars to buy cigarettes.

In February 2000, Alan Jay Lorenz, a Jew, decorated two Connecticut synagogues with graffiti calling for "killing Jews" (*Associated Press*, 11 February 2000).

In October 2007, the French Jewish community was shocked when a 13-year-old Jewish schoolgirl was attacked by three men of "Maghrebi and African type" on the stairs of the metro station of the Church of Pantin. This was a clear case of anti-Semitic aggression. Kelly F. filed a complaint and the National Antisemitism Monitoring Bureau, headed by Sammy Ghozlan, appealed to the public authorities. The weekly *Rivarol* of 26 October 2007 explained that after the RER D affair, in which a young woman complained that her body had been covered with swastikas, the authorities had been more cautious this time and had waited for the conclusions of the investigation before reacting. They did the right thing: "Questioned at length by the departmental security police, the teenager gave several contradictory versions before admitting on 11 October that she had accidentally injured herself on a fence and that she had invented the incident, for which she gave no explanation".

Faits et Dcouments, Emmanuel Ratier's newsletter, reported on 15 November 2007 that for several weeks swastikas had been flourishing on the walls of George Washington University, where about a third of the students were Jewish. Several community organisations filed a complaint and, thanks to surveillance cameras, the perpetrator was caught red-handed. The perpetrator was Sarah Marshak, a student from the Jewish community.

While some actual incidents may occur, the media coverage is in any case often totally disproportionate. Esther Benbassa is one of the few Jewish intellectuals who recognises the shortcomings of her community. She has observed that "the Jewish press devotes too much space to the smallest incidents, which are generally of little concern. There is no doubt that anti-Semitism is not dead, he wrote, but today I see no reason to be anxious to detect it everywhere. The non-Jewish press also keeps the phenomenon alive. I don't quite know what to call it. Obsession? By constantly harping on anti-Semitism, relentlessly denouncing any speech that does not conform to the norm, tirelessly tracking down the slightest trace of hatred, rejection or even simple indifference, we are undoubtedly creating an illusory community of suffering[286]."

Sigmund Freud himself had a strong tendency to hyperemotionality. His disciple and biographer Ernst Jones wrote of him in his *Life and Work of Sigmund Freud*: "He felt Jewish to the depths of his being, and this evidently meant a great deal to him. He had an exaggerated sensitivity, common among Jews, to the slightest hint of anti-Semitism, and he had very few non-Jewish friends. He was strongly opposed to the idea that Jews were unpopular, or inferior in any way, and he evidently suffered greatly,

---

[286] Esther Benbassa, Jean-Christophe Attias, *Les Juifs ont-ils un avenir?* J.C. Lattès, 2001, p. 108-114

from school days onwards, and especially at the University, from anti-Semitism[287]."

The truth is that this inclination to jeremiad is obviously pathological in nature. The "great emotional fragility", as we have already studied it in *Psychoanalysis of Judaism* and *Jewish Fanaticism,* is one of the symptoms of hysterical pathology. It was no mere coincidence if it was precisely from the study of this illness that Freud developed his psychoanalytic theories.

The Wandering Jew. Neuropathic Israelites

All observers of Judaism have noted the extraordinary homogeneity of Jewish thought and the many similarities between individuals of very different characters. At the end of the 19th century, faced with the massive influx of Jews from Russia and Eastern Europe, some Frenchmen were alarmed to see these foreigners crowding the streets of Paris, but also benefiting from the mysterious support of the upper echelons of republican power. Their ragged clothing and the sickly appearance of many of them raised doubts among French hygienists and doctors of the time, who were already busy treating their own population.

The April 1998 issue of the community magazine *Passages* published an interesting article on this subject by a certain Tristan Mendés France. He pointed out that the press was then talking about "a Jewish invasion of Paris".

"This disorderly arrival drove a large number of homeless Jews into the city centre, living in promiscuity or vagrancy. People soon began to associate this state of wandering with the old legend of the wandering Jew, to the point of considering that it was in the nature of the Jew to wander without ceasing".

The author then referred to the work of Professor Jean-Martin Charcot[288], at the Sapêtrière hospital, and "the elaboration of a pathology of migration": "We owe to Professor Charcot, he wrote, and in particular to his famous

---

[287] Ernst Jones, *Vida y Obra de Sigmund Freud, Volume I,* Editorial Anagrama, Barcelona, 1981, p. 48.

[288] Jean-Martin Charcot (1825-1893) was a French neurologist, professor of clinical neurology at the Faculty of Medicine in Paris and member of the French Academy of Medicine. He was the discoverer of amyotrophic lateral sclerosis (ALS), a neurodegenerative disease named after him in French-speaking medical literature. Together with Guillaume Duchenne, he was the founder of modern neurology, one of the great promoters of clinical medicine and a leading figure of positivism. His work on hypnosis and hysteria, which gave rise to the Salpêtrière School, inspired both Pierre Janet in his studies of psychopathology and Sigmund Freud, who was briefly his pupil and one of his first translators into German, in his invention of psychoanalysis. (NdT).

"Tuesday lectures", the first theoretical conception of the pathology of the Wandering Jew. The doctor imagines that Jews suffer from a specific stress inherited over the centuries, probably as a consequence of the successive exclusions to which they were subjected".

Others after him identified a pathology linked to the uprooting of the journey. In 1893, Dr Henry Meige, a pupil of Charcot's, continued and deepened his medical studies. Having had the opportunity to observe neurasthenic or wandering Jews, he devoted his doctoral thesis to their cases, published in 1893 under the title *Study on certain neuropathic travellers; The Wandering Jew in the Salpêtrière*: "Thus, the wandering Jew exists today," he wrote. Cartaphilus, Ahasverus, Isaac Laquedem fall into the field of nervous pathology in the same way as the illnesses whose story we have just recounted". The wandering Jew may well have been "a kind of prototype of the neuropathic Israelites who wandered the world[289]."

Tristan Mendés France pointed out that these considerations had been widely exploited at the time by French nationalists, who accused the poor Jews of all evils: "The Jewish neurosis linked to wandering of which Charcot spoke was answered by the "implacable Jewish disease" linked to cosmopolitanism denounced by Edouard Drumont".

Naturally, in the words of Mendès France, these anti-Semitic accusations seemed totally delirious and out of place. Jews, for example, were accused of being the cause of an epidemic of conjunctivitis and of constituting a veritable "social plague". A second campaign on the same theme was launched in 1920 by several former anti-Dreyfus senators[290], this time accusing immigrant Jews of bringing "all kinds of diseases, including leprosy and, above all, disease number 9 [the plague]".

Louis Dausset, one of these senators, after citing the epidemic dangers posed by Jewish immigrants in Paris, argued that they were also "carriers of revolutionary poison". These comments were repeated in November of the same year in the newspaper *Le Petit Bleu*: "These undesirables spread not only germs, but also the doctrines of defeatist Bolshevism among the lower classes with whom they come into contact" (*Le Petit Bleu*, 3 November 1920). In 1920, Gaudin de Vilaine, another senator, summed up the economic situation of Jewish immigrants in Paris: "anarchic microbes", he concluded bluntly.

The other immigrants were also used as scapegoats. The Jews were not the only ones accused, which was no doubt a great relief for Tristan Mendès France. "Every immigrant therefore has a natural propensity for this kind of pathology, this illness of the nation. This a priori assumption that

---

[289] Henry Meige, *Étude sur certains névropathes voyageurs; Le Juif errant à la Salpêtrière*, p. 61, 68, 69
[290] See footnote63.

immigrants are carriers of diseases perverts the discourse on immigration, without being able to clearly distinguish fantasy from medical reality".

Tristan Mendès France concluded, therefore, that Europeans had not yet completely shaken off the old ridiculous legends that still structured the deepest part of their being, "those ancestral schemes in which the Jew... becomes the diffusing agent of an anti-national evil that cannot be contained".

And he used this example: "Jean-Marie Le Pen is a revealing vehicle. By using the neologism of sidaïque *(sidaïque)* - a contraction of sida and judaïque *(judaïque)*[291] - he is nothing more than a transmission belt for the old legend of the wandering Jew who carried epidemics. In short, according to Mendès France, the Jews did not spread any social evil or disease, and were completely innocent of any responsibility for the crimes of Bolshevism and innocent of anything that could be blamed on them. Europeans, on the other hand, had to get rid of all the old legends that still clogged their brains and prevented them from understanding all the benefits of Judaism.

Of all the popular legends, that of the Wandering Jew is one of the most universally spread. The mysterious figure of the eternal wanderer has fuelled the imagination of many authors and artists since time immemorial: novelists, poets, scholars and painters have studied, commented on and reproduced his immutable features in various forms. Gregory of Tours was the first to make the legend known.[292]

But it is to Matthew Paris, an English Benedictine who lived in the time of Henry III, that we owe the first detailed account[293] : Cartophilus (or Cartaphilus), the doorkeeper of Pontius Pilate's praetorium, struck Jesus Christ with his fist as he was crossing the threshold and said to him: "Walk! Why do you stop?" Jesus turned and said to him, "I am coming. But you will wait for my second coming: you will walk for ever". And Cartophilus set out on his way, never to stop again. *"Ne morra pas voirement / Jusqu'au jour del jugement*[294]*."*

---

[291] *Sidaïque: a* word coined by Guillaume Faye, a "far-right" journalist and writer, and popularised by several National Front figures, including its former president Jean-Marie Le Pen. It is based on the French acronym Sida. The General Commission of the French Language has recommended the use of the term *sidéen*, while others have preferred the term *sidatique* (sidoso). (NdT).

[292] Gregory of Tours, *Epistola ad Sulpilium Bituriensem*, translated by Abbé Marolles, II, 712, p. 148. [Gregory of Tours (539-594) was a cleric and historian who lived at the time of the Merovingian kings of France. He is best known for his writings, which constitute an essential literary and historical record of the 6th century and the earlier periods he describes].

[293] Mathieu Pâris, *Historia Major*, in fol. édit. Will Wats, p. 352, Londini, 1640.

[294] Rhymed chronicle of Ph. Mouskes, de. Reiffemberg, p. 491. French was still spoken

Closer to us in time, the Wandering Jew has captivated other novelists: Goethe, Béranger and, above all, Eugene Sue, who presented another version in 1844. The legendary Jew crossed his path, contaminating his footsteps with the evil whose burden he carries. He would walk away, laden with curses and death. Eugene Sue showed the eternally cursed man, on the heights of Montmartre, conjuring God to deliver him from the invisible calamity he sows in his path, the plague, for the cholera epidemic of 1834 had rekindled fear in the city.[295]

For the Christians of old, the legend of the wandering Jew symbolised the nomadism of the Israelites, guilty in their eyes of having condemned Christ to death, and who paid for their crime by wandering forever.

The myth of the wandering Jew Ahasverus is of German origin. According to the Germanic chroniclers of the Middle Ages, when Pontius Pilate asked the Jews whether they wanted Jesus or Barabbas killed, Ahasverus, a shoemaker, was one of those who shouted the loudest: "Jesus! Jesus!" Jesus, carrying the Holy Cross, walked past the shoemaker's shop. He leaned against it. Ahasverus pushed him badly away, and Jesus said to the cobbler: "Truly, I will stop, and you, Ahasverus, will walk forever". Suddenly repentant, the Jew, weeping, left Jerusalem in that hour. And so it was that, having refused to help Jesus on the way of the cross, Ahasverus was condemned to wander from country to country, never being able to settle anywhere.

In the 19th century he was called Isaac Laquedem. His fame rivalled that of the mythical Beast of Gévaudan. The good people of the country thought they had seen him in Beauvais, Strasbourg or Metz. The curse of which he was the object sometimes provoked pity or terror. Numerous lamentations evoked it:

"Is there anything on earth / More surprising / Than the great misery / Of the poor wandering Jew / That his wretched fate / Seems sad and unhappy.

One day near the city / Of Brussels, in Brabant / Some docile burghers / Passed by and accosted him; / They had never seen / Such a bearded man.

His clothes were all misshapen / And very badly dressed / He made them believe that the man / Was a foreigner, / He wore a worker's apron / In front of him.

They said to him: - Good morning, master, /Please allow us/ The satisfaction of being /A moment with you /Don't refuse/ Retrace your steps a little.

- Gentlemen, I protest/ For I am very unhappy/ I never stop,/ Neither here, nor elsewhere,/ In good weather or bad,/ I walk on and on.

---

at the court of the kingdom of England.
[295] Eugène Sue, *Le Juif errant*, 1844, Laffont, Paris, 1990.

- Come into this inn, venerable old man, / With a mug of cold beer / Take part with us, / We'll treat you / As best we can.
- I will agree to Drink / Two drinks with you, / But I cannot sit, / I must stand, / I am truly/ Confused by your kindnesses.

And the wandering Jew concluded:
- Gentlemen, time is running out, / Farewell to the company. /Thank you for your courtesy/ I thank you, /I am too tormented/ When I stop.

The French nationalist Edouard Drumond had clearly seen that the frenetic and permanent agitation of the Jews was above all the manifestation of a neurosis, and that this very specific neurosis corresponded exactly to the hysterical pathology that Doctotr Charcot was studying at the time and that Freud would study after him. However, in 1886, when he finished writing the two volumes of *Jewish France*, Edouard Drumond still did not have enough material to make a precise diagnosis of the very specific illness that afflicted the Jews. Here is what he wrote in the first volume of *Jewish France*: "Neurosis is the relentless disease of the Jews. In this long-persecuted people, who live always in perpetual anguish and incessant conspiracies, then shaken by the fever of speculation, who, moreover, exercise professions in which only cerebral activity is involved, the nervous system has ended by completely altering itself. In Prussia, the proportion of the insane is much higher among the Israelites than among the Catholics.... Doctor Charcot made the most curious revelations on this subject in his lectures at the Salpêtrière hospital, concerning the Russian Jews, the only ones we can talk about, since the others carefully hide their illnesses in their palaces".

Drumont was alarmed by the fabulous power that the Jewish elite had so rapidly acquired in Christian society: "This neurosis, the Jew has ended up, curiously enough, by communicating it to our whole generation," he wrote. Jewish neurosis has played its part in the destinies of the world. During the twenty years that the Semites have, as Disraeli said, pulled the strings of secret diplomacy, and have reduced the real ambassadors to the status of extras, during the twenty years that they have directed European policy, this policy has become truly irrational and insane".

In the second volume of *Jewish France*, we also find this pertinent observation: "They are always on the move, incessantly on all the billboards, continually occupying Paris with their noisy and vain personalities; they attract each other and promote each other by echoing each other. Sarah Bernhardt cannot take a step without Wolf blowing his trumpet; Arthur Meyer appears immediately; Marie Colombier intervenes and the din is inaudible...Jewish neurosis obviously has a lot to do with this hectic agitation; it is not natural, indeed, that one cannot rest, nor can one leave the others. For these publicity enthusiasts, sleep itself does not seem to exist; they think they are dead when they no longer hear any noise around them".

And Drumont relied on the insight of the French doctors and specialists of his time: "On these particular states of mind, which reveal an undeniable disorder of the nervous system, it will be useful to consult Legrand du Saulle who, in his book on *Hysteria*, clearly saw and described the unhealthy side of these manifestations. The learned physician explains very clearly how the virtues themselves have become, for these theatrical beings, an opportunity to appear, to be on stage[296]."

Jacques Ploncard, a French patriot, was one of the few anti-Semitic resisters who drew inspiration from Charcot's work. Unfortunately, he published only one article on the subject. It appeared in the journal *L'Ethnie française,* in January 1943, and was entitled *Note sur l'hystero-neurasthénie juive* (*Note on Jewish hystero-neurasthénie*): "Shouts like Leon Blum's "*Je vous hais!*" (*I hate you!*), accompanied by a shuddering of his body, are symptoms that cannot deceive, he wrote. There is a Jewish mass hysteria. The ancient Hebrews seem to have already suffered from it. Throughout the New Testament, we see a multitude of demon-possessed individuals, madmen, men with impure spirits who call on Christ to deliver them". And Jacques Ploncard continued: "Bénédikt, Charcot and many other authors recognise that hysteria is more prevalent among Jews than among Aryans. According to their observations, it is mainly a hysteria which affects men more than women. It is often combined with neurasthenia".

Ploncard also referred to Doctor Jean Flamant, who had studied in his doctoral thesis (published in 1934 by the Jewish bookshop Lipschutz) *The Pathology of the Israelites*: "Charcot observed a large proportion of neuropaths and hysterics among Jews and reported numerous observations on the subject.... The Jewish professor Lombroso found four times as many Jewish alienated persons as Aryans in Italy".

Jews feel a morbid need to communicate their illness to the rest of humanity. In *The Great Fear of the Biemensants,* published in 1931, Georges Bernanos, who denounced the fanaticism of the Jews at the time of the Dreyfus affair, also noted this perpetual agitation: "It was clear, he wrote, that in the long run, the frenzied and convulsive agitation of the Jewish world would eventually break the nerves of a people already infected by this oriental neurosis". And Bernanos added, perhaps without realising the accuracy of his diagnosis: "This is how a hysterical woman triumphs over the best man[297]."

---

[296] Édouard Drumont, *La France juive*, 1886, tome I, p. 105, 106, 108; tome II, p. 231, 232

[297] Georges Bernanos, *La grande peur des bien-pensants, Edouard Drumont*, 1931,

Grasset, Poche, 1969, p. 323.

2. Hysterical fabulation

Hysterical fabulation I

Fabulation is one of the many symptoms of hysterical pathology. As we know, hysteria is very common in Judaism. This pathology, which so attracted Sigmund Freud's attention, is also extremely contagious, and it must be emphasised that Jews are the great specialists in these politico-religious delusions which regularly set mankind on fire. The hysterical personality always expresses his anxieties with great emotion, so that he quickly communicates them to his environment. At first, their emotional fragility and existential crises inspire pity and prevent those close to them from realising their extraordinary capacity for manipulation. Only after some time, the people around her, exhausted, prefer to distance themselves from her or decide to keep her at a distance. This is the whole drama of the history of Judaism.

After the destruction of the Temple, the torments of the First Crusade, the expulsion from Spain and all the countries of Europe, the pogroms of the Cossacks in the East, etc., the misfortunes suffered by the Jews during the Second World War have provoked a new trauma in them, and since then the Jews, through the modern media system, have taken advantage of it to share it with the rest of humanity. Broadcast live on television and in the cinema, the cries of unspeakable suffering and deafening wailing eventually brought humanity to its knees, literally stunned by so much emotion. And yet, in all this incessant logorrhea, there is an obvious part of fable.

In 1967, Simon Wiesenthal, the famous Nazi hunter, published a book entitled *The Murderers Among Us*. It contains several examples of obvious hysterical fabulation. At the beginning of the book, one Joseph Wechsberg sketched a portrait of Simon Wiesenthal. In the Lwów concentration camp, "one of the most perverse SS guards was known as "Tom Mix", a nickname taken from the famous Western film artist. Tom Mix's" favourite pastime was riding around the camp on horseback and shooting at prisoners. There are several eyewitnesses to the crimes of "Tom Mix", but Wiesenthal has not been able to find the man in question because he does not know his real name".

Joseph Wechsberg also claimed that the SS were guilty of unspeakable atrocities: "I have read another letter in which an SS describes how they killed newborn Jewish children by throwing them against the wall and then asked whether his little boy is well with measles[298]."

We also see that the Nazis knew how to celebrate big occasions in style: "The SS were going to execute a few Jews to celebrate the Führer's birthday[299]."

They had more pity for the animals than for the poor Jews. In the summer of 1944, Jews from the camp were moved: "They were marched through the city, which was under heavy artillery fire, and when they reached the station they were pushed into a freight car, already crowded with Poles. Someone said the SS were going to gas them there, but when the door opened again and an SS man named Blum brought up a little black dog and gave them a cage with a canary in it, threatening to execute them all if anything happened to the little animals, Wiesenthal knew they were not going to gas them: the SS love animals[300]."

Joseph Wechsberg then recounted how Simon Wiesenthal had escaped death. Wiesenthal had been part of a convoy of prisoners transferred from Buchenwald to Mauthausen in the dead of winter. Weschberg wrote: "Of the three thousand people who had left Buchenwald three weeks earlier, only twelve hundred were left alive. One hundred and eighty died on the way from the station to the Mauthausen concentration camp, a walk of only six kilometres. Wiesenthal remembers all too well the dreadful cold, the clear night, the crunch of icy snow underfoot. Every step was a greater effort. It turned out that he was walking beside Prince Radziwill, one of whose relatives would eventually marry the sister of John F. Kennedy's widow. Their arms were tied side by side, and they tried to hold each other up, but in the end they could not go on and fell in the snow. Wiesenthal heard a voice saying, "Are you alive?", and then a shot. But the SS must have had numb hands, because the bullet went between Wiesenthal and Radziwill. The column disappeared into the darkness, but Wiesenthal and Radziwill continued to lie there. After a while he began to feel comfortable, almost warm, lying there in the snow, and he remembers sleeping for a while and then being lifted up and thrown into a truck with the corpses. Later he was told that the camp authorities had sent to collect the dead so that the people of Mauthausen, when they went to work in the morning, would not be shocked by the sight of so many corpses. Apparently, he and Radziwill were almost stiff with cold and were presumed dead. But when

---

[298] Simon Wiesenthal, *The Murderers Among Us*, (pdf) Editorial Noguer, Barcelona, 1967, p. 13, 16.
[299] Simon Wiesenthal, *The Murderers Among Us*, (pdf) Editorial Noguer, Barcelona, 1967, p. 24.
[300] Simon Wiesenthal, *The Murderers Among Us*, (pdf) Editorial Noguer, Barcelona, 1967, p. 29.

the truck arrived at the camp crematorium and the bodies were removed, the prisoners assigned to the job noticed that the two men were not "quite dead". Luckily there were no SS present and the courtyard was pitch dark; so the prisoners took Wiesenthal and Radziwill to nearby showers, stripped them of their clothes and put them under a stream of cold water that revived them. From the showers, a narrow corridor led to the camp barracks, and the two were secretly led into one of them, weak and dazed, but alive[301]."
We have to believe it.

Simon Wiesenthal then recounted his own experience as a Nazi hunter after the war. Franz Murer was a terrible criminal: "Szymon Bastocki, a former resident of Vilna, now in New York, testified about a certain day in March 1943 when Murer gathered women and children in the labour camp square, ordering the police to tear the children from their mothers and load them onto waiting trucks. The newborns were thrown through the air like packages. Heart-rending scenes took place, but Murer remained uncompromising[302]."

Dr. Josef Mengele, a native of Günzburg on the Danube in Bavaria, was the notorious chief physician at Auschwitz. He held a doctorate in philosophy from the University of Munich. He had studied Kant's *Critique of Pure Reason* and, as Wiesenthal told us, "simultaneously steeped himself in the racial rubbish of the Hitlerite philosopher Alfred Rosenberg". He was also a medical doctor at the University of Frankfurt.

Here is what Simon Wiesenthal had to say about him: "I have the testimony of a man who saw Mengele throw a living creature into the flames and of another who witnessed Mengele kill a fourteen-year-old girl with a bayonet. Crazy, isn't it?

But Dr Mengele was even more sadistic. His friend Hermann Langbein "told him that Mengele once went into the children's block at Auschwitz to measure the children's heights. He was very angry that many of them were short in relation to their age and made the children stand one after the other against a post at the entrance which had nails marking the appropriate height for each age. If the children did not reach the nail, Mengele would make a sign with his whip and the child would be taken to the gas chamber. More than a thousand children were killed on this occasion.

But that was not all: Mengele "sacrificed thousands of twin boys from all over Europe, injecting them with painful solutions to try to change the brown colour of their eyes to blue [what a bastard]...In Auschwitz, his surgical room was spotlessly clean, his syringes with which he often

---

[301] Simon Wiesenthal, *The Murderers Among Us*, (pdf) Editorial Noguer, Barcelona, 1967, p. 31.

[302] Simon Wiesenthal, *The Murderers Among Us*, (pdf) Editorial Noguer, Barcelona, 1967, p. 53.

injected carbolic acid, benzine or air, which killed his patients within seconds, always sterile. Mengele was the perfect SS. He smiled at pretty girls as he sent them to their deaths. In front of the crematorium at Auschwitz he was once heard to say: "Here the Jews enter through the door and leave through the chimney[303]"."

However, a few Jews had survived the surveillance of the horrible Dr. Mengele. This is how the great Elie Wiesel told the story. To all the survivors of the "extermination camps", Wiesel left this moving testimony: "And of this family of five or seven dwarfs that people came to see and applaud from everywhere: they all survived Mengele's selections and tortures in Birkenau[304]."

After the war, Mengele lived quietly for several years in his hometown. In 1950, he fled first to Spain and, in 1959, to Paraguay. He was never arrested, despite the relentless pursuit of Nazi hunters. He was undoubtedly, for the Jews, what is called a "scapegoat", as it is written in the Torah, i.e. an expiatory victim whom the Jews hold responsible for their unspeakable crimes.

Martin Gray was one of the great witnesses of the Holocaust. In 1971 he achieved international fame with his book *In the Name of All My People*. In 1941, Martin Gray was seventeen years old and living in the Warsaw ghetto, where he trafficked goods. "My profits were enormous...", he wrote on page 67. He said that he had been arrested by the police and interrogated about his trafficking. When he remained silent, the German police laid the boy on a table and tortured him horribly for several days, beating him with truncheons, kicking him in the crotch and burning his hands with cigarettes and his wounds with acid. They also hung him "by his feet and arms like the body of an animal hung on a butcher's hook," he wrote. "When they let me fall to the ground and the red-faced, sweating executioner approached me, I said in German: - I will speak." And then, as the officer approached, Martin Gray made a heroic gesture. He wrote: "He approached me, baton raised. Gathering my strength, I spat in his face." The officer, shouting, ordered the soldiers out: "His face was against mine. You will kill me and you will have achieved nothing! I spat again."

After three or four days of torture, Martin Gray was still strong enough to resist. The Gestapo policeman then offered him a deal: he would let him live if he would give up his accomplices. Gray replied: "First get me cured... And you will give me the papers of an Aryan. Finally, he was transported to the infirmary where Gestapo doctor Scherbel came to visit him: "I

---

[303] Simon Wiesenthal, *The Murderers Among Us*, (pdf) Editorial Noguer, Barcelona, 1967, p. 110, 111.
[304] Elie Wiesel, *Mémoires, tome I*, Seuil, 1994, p. 48.

learned later that he sometimes operated on prisoners without anaesthesia, just to please himself.

One morning, a week later, the Polish doctor treating him turned out to be an accomplice. He injected a substance into his veins that made him delirious, to make it look like he was suffering from typhoid fever. The Germans, fearing contagion, rushed him to a suburban hospital. There he was freed by his comrades, tied up and lowered with a rope down the front of the building. A corpse had been placed in its place on the bed. This is how Martin Gray got out of this terrible ordeal alive.[305]

He was later arrested again and sent to the Treblinka camp, where he became a *Totenjuden*, a Jew of death. Along with other inmates, he removed the corpses of the poor Jews from the gas chamber, "those new chambers so well conceived, Gray wrote, with their shower taps through which the gas was passed". He dumped the "thousands of bodies" on stretchers and threw them into the pits. Martin Gray removed the corpses from the gas chamber immediately after gassing, without even taking the precaution of putting on a gas mask, even though the devastating Zyklon B gas permeated the clothes and bodies of the victims: "Among the warm bodies we found those of children still alive. Just children, pressed against the bodies of their mothers. And we strangled them with our own hands, before throwing them into the pit: and we risked our lives doing that, because we were wasting time. Because the executioners wanted everything to be done quickly".

Life in the camp was atrocious. Dogs bit the prisoners: "We heard the mad cries, the barking of the dogs. And sometimes we would find mutilated men, their lower bellies bloody. The dogs whipped by the men to drive the living to their death".

The next day, it was his turn to work in the pits: "Every time a large convoy arrived, we were all pushed into the pits, into the wooden doors of the gas chambers, and we would go back to pick up the canvas stretchers, run under the hammering of the bulldozer that was digging deep into the yellow sand, to other pits....I had to go down into the pit, standing over the corpses, arranging them as if they were pieces of wood, arranging them as if they were pieces of wood, kicking them as if they had not been, half an hour before, vibrant existences of fear and hope[306]."

There were also Jewish policemen who collaborated with the Germans: "Every Jewish policeman had to carry four heads a day...I had dreamt of

---

[305] Martin Gray, *En nombre de todos los míos*, Plaza & Janés, Barcelona, 1973, p. 116-118.
[306] Martin Gray, *In the Name of All Mine*, Plaza & Janés, Barcelona, 1973, p. 161, 164, 168.

killing those men who, to save their skin, gave our lives to the executioners". (page 127).

Martin Gray managed to escape from a cattle train, but was caught again. The police discovered that he was circumcised: "I still tried to protest, to explain that I had been ill, that I had been operated on as a child; but they no longer heard me; I spoke so as not to fall into despair". Again he was atrociously beaten and tortured, but refused to give the names of the partisans. A German officer guarding him saved his life by letting him escape into the forest. In reality, he was a Jew in German uniform: "Everywhere [Jewish] men survived; some hidden under the uniform of the executioners[307]."

To escape from the Germans once again, Martin Mietek had to hide in the filthy pit of an outhouse. The following scene was astonishingly authentic: "I heard screams, barking dogs, voices. I slid through the shit, first down to my waist, then lower still, down to my neck, my stomach churning with spasms of disgust and my mouth full of bitter bile. Don't think, Mietek, survive, Mietek. I put the planks back on top of me, putting my arms on the icy layer around me, but which was melting little by little. Outside, always the dogs near the hut: a soldier came in: his boots crushed the planks, his lamp illuminated them. He was talking to his comrade, who had stayed outside...I could hear his boots scraping the floor. His shit landed on my back. When the one had finished, the other came in, and again the shit, on my back. I didn't move, I didn't breathe, I didn't exist: I was an insensible thing, a hard chunk planted in the shit, a piece of iron that nothing would dent[308]."

Then he crossed fields and forests, in the snow, sleeping on farms and robbing Polish peasants: "Like a fox, I stole eggs and chickens... I stole bacon and bread and the peasants chased me... Then I sold them sacks of jute, precious in that period of hardship, which I had just stolen from the stairs of their granary. I found beasts with the faces of men..." (pages 214-215), Gray wrote. He had already expressed his opinion of the natives at the beginning of his account: "How could I not hate those gentle Poles who strolled along *the Marszalkowska*" (page 101); "For me vengeance would live" (page 153), Gray swore.

Then he set off in search of the partisans in the forest: "What a joy to win at last, to raise a war cry, to begin the time of revenge" (page 219). "The time of the test had come; I was with my people with a gun in my hand, we were going to start to make them pay, and the debt was immense" (page

---

[307] Martin Gray, *En nombre de todos los míos*, Plaza & Janés, Barcelona, 1973, p. 202, 204.

[308] Martin Gray, *En nombre de todos los míos*, Plaza & Janés, Barcelona, 1973, p. 213. He is up to his neck in excrement, but receives the faeces on his back. Strange...

234). Indeed, revenge, as we know, is a recurring theme in Jewish literature. "Revenge' is, in fact, the title of the second part of Martin Gray's book[309]. During the fighting in Warsaw, one of his comrades claimed that he had "seen the Germans set fire to the hospital in the ghetto; he had seen them smash the heads of newborn babies against the walls, cut open the wombs of pregnant women, throw the sick into the flames. He had seen it[310] ". And if he saw them, then we must believe him.

"Then began the time of heroism: I saw a girl douse herself with petrol, set herself on fire, and throw herself on a tank; I saw men come up to the Germans with their arms up in the air, and then rush at them and tear off their guns. To survive we resorted to all forms of warfare. Hiding in the ruins, I called out to the Germans in the guttural tone of one of them, and killed them under cover of night. Then some of us put on the SS uniforms we had recovered on the first day... and walked down the street to a barrier guarded by a dozen soldiers. We approached calmly and then opened fire[311]."

So they accumulated a series of exploits against the Germans and anti-Jewish Poles, stabbing to death, setting fire to dairies and sawmills. "He was Mietek the partisan, who spied on the traitors, who organised their punishment... He was Mietek the avenger". Later, he joined the ranks of the enemy, the Polish NSZ, anti-Semitic militiamen, posing as one of them. Their leader, Zemba, "was a beast with the face of a man": "Now I was there, among those bandits, laughing with them. My ordeal lasted a few weeks... At night I would slip out of the village, into the forest, a comrade was waiting for me. He gave the names of the NSZ, the situation of the villages that were loyal to them, the peasants who helped them... He swore with the others, he drank with them, he cheated them. However, I realised that they were suspicious...They all laughed at the sight of Zemba's gesture...I wanted to live, to win, not to burst under the knives of those drunken bandits. To win... I stood up as if to ask for a drink or to talk; then I jumped towards the door and, turning around, threw a grenade at the

---

[309] Martin Gray, *In the name of all my people:* "-We will avenge ourselves, Martin. In the end we will be the strongest.", p. 38; "When could we raise a war cry, when could we avenge our dead?" p. 95; "When will we raise a war cry? Zofia, when shall we take revenge?" p. 105; "I could not launch the war cry and revenge." p. 114; "Live to shout, say, avenge." p. 155; "Live, live to avenge myself..." p. 156; "I had gone out to avenge myself.", p. 185; "I had escaped from Treblinka, to fight and avenge us.", p. 187; "...I would survive...only if necessary, and at least one man would be left to avenge them.", p. 193; "-You will avenge us." p. 196; "I have survived, I have fought, I have avenged you.", p. 357.

[310] Martin Gray, *En nombre de todos los míos*, Plaza & Janés, Barcelona, 1973, p. 237.

[311] Martin Gray, *En nombre de todos los míos*, Plaza & Janés, Barcelona, 1973, p. 239.

house, to run into the forest, towards my trees[312]." Martin Mietek had also planted explosives on railways and blown up entire trains.

He was later assigned to a unit of the Soviet NKVD, the political police. With his unit, he was able to dispense justice in the camps, with all the humanity of the "Men" that the Bolshevik political commissars knew how to dispense.

After the war, he left for the United States. In New York he was reunited with his family, who miraculously had not been exterminated. It was a "miracle", one among hundreds of thousands. In a seaside resort a few hours from New York, he met Russian and Polish Jews and worked in a hotel: "Once again I had changed my name: Martin, Mietek, Micha, Mendle; but it was always me, I didn't change; it was me, with a plan to carry out. Eight more days and I became head waiter. Most of them were students, who made fun of me, of my frenzy".

Martin Gray made money, lots of money, "frantically". That was his way of making the messiah of the Jews come: "You'll make a fortune; you want dollars and you'll get them. Don't run so fast, you'll burst," they told him. What did I care about dollars? I had to build a fortress, quickly, because I had been waiting for peace for centuries... Life is a race, Mietek, you have to run. I multiplied my activities, games, sales, service, shows. I accumulated dollars. At night I would collapse in bed, exhausted[313]." At the end of his long career Gray would go into the antiquities trade on a grand scale, looting works of art all over Europe, especially in occupied Germany, always "in a frenzy".[314]

Wladyslaw Szpilman also left an extraordinary testimony. His book, *The Pianist*, published in 1946, told the extraordinary story of a Jewish musician in the Warsaw ghetto. The author wrote this account just after the war, but the Soviet authorities quickly withdrew the book from bookstores because it contained shameful "truths" about the behaviour of Russians, Poles and Latvians. In 1940, Jews from western Poland were deported in trains to the capital: "On some trains barely half of the passengers were left alive, and with severe frostbite. The other half were corpses, stiffened by the freezing cold, standing imprisoned among the living and falling to the ground as the latter moved[315]."

---

[312] Martin Gray, *In the Name of All Mine*, Plaza & Janés, Barcelona, 1973, p. 259, 261, 262.
[313] Martin Gray, *In the Name of All Mine*, Plaza & Janés, Barcelona, 1973, p. 330, 332.
[314] On Martin Gray's shady business dealings and the plunder of defeated countries, read *The Jewish Mafia*
[315] Wladyslaw Szpilman, *The Pianist of the Warsaw Ghetto*, Turpial Amaranto, Madrid, 2003, p. 57.

Director Roman Polanski has adapted Wladyslaw Szpilman's story for the big screen. His film includes a scene in which German soldiers throw an old man and his armchair out of a "third-floor window" (page 82). The film also shows the scene in which a mother, hiding with her baby in her arms, is forced to suffocate her child to avoid being discovered by the SS (page 106).

Some of the SS may at first glance appear to be perfectly normal human beings: "At the head of the little column was an SS man who, like a good German, loved children, even when he was about to see them on their way to the next world. He was particularly fond of a twelve-year-old boy, a violinist, who carried his instrument under his arm. The SS told him to stand at the head of the cortege and play, and so they began the march. When I met them on Gesia Street they were smiling and singing in chorus; the little violinist played for them and Korczak carried two of the younger children, who were also smiling, and told them some funny stories. I am sure that even in the gas chamber, when the lethal fluid was choking them and turning the hope in their hearts into terror, "the old doctor" would whisper to them in a last effort that all was well and that everything was going to be all right, to spare his pupils, at least, the fear of the passage from life to death[316]."

The Nazis had their own methods. Here, Wladyslaw Szpilman described what he had seen with his own eyes, at the edge of the ghetto, on the outskirts of a dead-end street: "There were bodies lying on the ground: the corpses of those who had been killed the day before for some crime, perhaps even for trying to escape. Among the corpses of men were the bodies of a young woman and two girls with their skulls smashed in. The wall at the foot of which the bodies lay showed traces of blood and brain matter. The children had been killed by one of the Germans' favourite methods: grabbing them by the legs, they were thrown violently against the wall. Large black flies landed on the corpses and in the pools of blood on the ground, and the bodies swelled and decomposed almost in plain sight from the heat[317]." However, we have our doubts about the reality of these Nazi methods. In fact, we are inclined to think that it is more a case of "projection", or accusatory inversion, if you prefer.

Wladyslaw Szpilman hid for several months in the attic of one of Warsaw's many abandoned houses, until one day he came face to face with a polite and cultured German officer, who informed him that the special forces headquarters in Warsaw was about to move in. When the officer

---

[316] Wladyslaw Szpilman, *The Pianist of the Warsaw Ghetto*, Turpial Amaranto, Madrid, 2003, p. 98-99.

[317] Wladyslaw Szpilman, *The Pianist of the Warsaw Ghetto*, Turpial Amaranto, Madrid, 2003, p. 101.

learned that the poor Jew was a pianist, he asked him to play on the grand piano that happened to be there. It was there, in the rubble, that Wladyslaw Szpilman played Frédéric Chopin's nocturne in C-sharp minor. After which, the German officer, Szpilman told us, felt ashamed to be German: "I am ashamed to be German, after all that is happening[318]", he confessed. As you can see, Wladyslaw Szpilman also went out of his way to blame the Goyim.

At the end of the book was the diary of Captain Wilm Hosenfeld, a German anti-Nazi officer: "We have covered ourselves with a shame that cannot be erased; it is a curse that cannot be lifted. We deserve no forgiveness; we are all guilty[319]", he wrote in his personal diary. Although one would swear that it was Szpilman himself who wrote the text.

On 25 July 1942, Hosenfeld described the atrocities the Germans were capable of committing: "Somewhere near Lublin, buildings have been constructed with rooms that can be heated by electric current, like crematoria. The unfortunates are taken into these rooms and burned alive, and every day thousands of people can be killed in this way, thus avoiding the inconvenience of shooting them, digging mass graves and burying them".

On 6 September 1942, Hosenfeld recounted what he had heard from people who had managed to escape from the hell of Treblinka in eastern Poland: "The thousands of women and children have to be stripped naked, and then they are taken to a mobile hut, where they are gassed. The hut is placed over a pit and has a mechanism that opens one of the walls and lifts the floor, so that the corpses fall into the pit. It has been in operation for a long time...My confidant heard about all this from a Jew who managed to escape with seven other missionaries."

On 13 August 1942 there was a shooting in the Warsaw ghetto: "A woman told my Polish acquaintance that several Gestapo men had entered the Jewish maternity hospital, taken the newborn babies [this is an obsession!], put them in a sack, got out and threw them into a hearse. The wicked were not moved by the cries of the children or the heart-rending complaints of the mothers. Although you can hardly believe it, it was so."

On 21 August 1942, Hosenfeld noted in his diary this consideration: "No, things cannot go on like this, for the sake of human nature and freedom of spirit. Liars and those who distort the truth must perish and be deprived of their ability to rule by force, and then there will again be room for a freer and nobler humanity."

---

[318] Wladyslaw Szpilman, *The Pianist of the Warsaw Ghetto*, Turpial Amaranto, Madrid, 2003, p. 180.

[319] Wladyslaw Szpilman, *The Pianist of the Warsaw Ghetto*, Turpial Amaranto, Madrid, 2003, p. 204.

And on 23 June 1942: "I cannot believe that Hitler would want such a thing and that there are Germans who could give such orders. But, in such a case, there can only be one explanation: they are sick or abnormal, or insane[320]." It is exactly that: "sick or abnormal, or insane."

We have already quoted Elie Wiesel at length in our previous books, noting his penchant for fabulation. In fact, the great "Man" presented some confessions in his work, skilfully distilled in elliptical form. Here are some other interesting facts about the Wiesel "case". In a 1993 book entitled *L'Holocauste au scanner (The Holocaust under the magnifying glass)*, the Swiss-German historian Jürgen Graf wrote: "In *The Night*, his "testimony" published in 1958, he says nothing about the gas chambers.... Wiesel therefore did not see the gas chambers, nor did he hear about them, otherwise he would have mentioned them". And the author judiciously observed: "Attention, the gas chambers suddenly appear in the German version, *Die Nacht zu begraben*, Elischa, translation by Curt Meyer-Clason, published by Ullstein editions; every time the word "crematorium" appears in the original text, Meyer-Clason translates it as "gas chamber"".

In the absence of gas chambers, Wiesel had seen what no one else had seen: "Not far from us, flames were rising from a pit, gigantic flames. They were burning something. A truck approached the pit and unloaded its load: they were children. They were babies! Yes, I saw them, with my own eyes I saw them... Children in flames (Is it amazing if since then sleep flees from my eyes?) So that's where we were going. A little further there would be another bigger pit for the adults... Father, if that's the case, I don't want to wait any longer. I'll go to the electrified fences. It's better than agonising for hours in the flames".

But Elie Wiesel would be spared the endless agony in the flames without having to resort to the electrified barbed wire. As they walked straight to their deaths, towards the glowing pits, this is what happened: "Our column only had about fifteen steps to go. I bit my lips so my father wouldn't hear my jaws trembling. Ten steps still to go. Eight. Seven. We walked slowly, as if following behind a funeral car, following our own burial. Only four steps. Three steps. Now the pit and the flames were very close to us. I summoned all my remaining strength to jump out of the ranks and throw myself against the barbed wire. Deep in my heart, I said goodbye to my father, to the whole Universe, and in spite of myself, the words "*Yizgadal veyiskadash shmé raba*...May his name be praised and sanctified..." formed and burst from my lips in a whisper. My heart was going to burst. That was it. I was before the Angel of Death...No. Two steps from the moat, we were

---

[320] Wladyslaw Szpilman, *The Pianist of the Warsaw Ghetto*, Turpial Amaranto, Madrid, 2003, p. 198-202.

ordered to turn left, and made to enter a barrack[321]." Just like in an American film.

Regarding the Babi Yar massacre near Kiev, "attested only by eyewitnesses presented by the Soviet NKVD", reported Jürgen Graf, Elie Wiesel wrote: "Later, I learned from a witness that for months and months the ground had not stopped shaking and that geysers of blood gushed out from time to time". This was similar to what the novelist Isaac Bashevis Singer also wrote when describing the atrocities of the Cossacks during the 17th century pogroms: "Moses Bunim was impaled. He was moaning all night. Twenty Cossacks forced your sister Leah, and then they hacked her to pieces..... On such a morning it was hard to believe that this was a world where children were murdered or buried alive and where the earth was nourished with blood as in the days of Cain[322]." This was obviously an image taken from the Talmud.

On 20 January 1945, in the face of the advancing Red Army, a total of more than 98,000 Jews were evacuated from Auschwitz. Elie Wiesel preferred to leave the Auschwitz camp with the Nazis and walk the snow-covered roads rather than wait quietly in a barracks for the Soviet liberators[323]. Why did the Nazis go to all this trouble to take the Jewish prisoners from Auschwitz and other camps with them, when it would have been more comfortable to "gas" or summarily shoot them? Curiously, none of the star historians on television have ever answered this question.

In his book *The Holocaust Industry*, published in 2000, Norman Finkelstein also revealed Elie Wiesel's many contradictions: "In his acclaimed memoirs, Elie Wiesel recalls that, when he was only eighteen years old after his release from Buchenwald, he read *The Critique of Pure Reason* - don't laugh - in Yiddish. Even disregarding the fact that Wiesel himself confesses that at the time he "had no idea of Yiddish grammar", it must be said that *The Critique of Pure Reason* has never been translated into Yiddish". And Finkelstein added: 'Wiesel also recalls in all sorts of intricate detail a "mysterious Talmudic scholar" who "mastered Hungarian in two weeks", only to surprise him. Wiesel tells a Jewish weekly that he "often goes hoarse or loses his voice" while silently reading books, because he reads them "inwardly aloud". And, to a *New York Times* reporter, he recalls the time he was hit by a taxi in Times Square. "I flew around a whole block. The taxi hit me on the corner of 45th Street and Broadway and the

---

[321] Elie Wiesel, *Trilogía de la noche*, Austral-El Aleph Editores, Barcelona, [eleventh printing 2023!], p. 42, 43, 44, in Jürgen Graf, *L'Holocauste au scanner*, Guideon Burg Verlag, 1993, p. 54-56.
[322] Isaac Bashevis Singer, *The Slave*, Debols!llo, Penguin Random House, Barcelona, 2019, p. 110, 129
[323] Elie Wiesel, *Mémoires, tome I*, Seuil, 1994, p. 119, cf. *Psychoanalysis of Judaism*.

ambulance picked me up on 44th Street." "The truth I offer is unvarnished," Wiesel says with a sigh, "I don't know how to do it any other way."[324]."

Hysterical fabulation II

In his small 1993 book *L'Holocauste au scanner (The Holocaust under the magnifying glass)*[325], the Swiss-German writer Jürgen Graf examined certain contradictions in the testimonies and compiled the work of revisionist researchers. The first reports on the extermination of the Jews, he wrote, appeared in 1942 in Zionist-controlled newspapers such as the *New York Times* and were most likely due to the World Jewish Congress.

Jürgen Graf quoted an American historian:

"In his book *The Hoax of the Twentieth Century*, the author Arthur Butz studies the genesis of the hoax of the century. In addition to gas chambers, the columns of the *New York Times* fantasised about every imaginary method of murder there is and ever will be. On 30 June 1942 they reported on a "shooting house" where a thousand Jews were shot every day, and on 7 February 1943 on "blood poisoning stations" in occupied Poland. But while the shooting house and the blood poisoning stations were consigned to the back pages of history even before the end of the war, the steam execution cells were more successful, even appearing at the Nuremberg trials. There, on 14 December 1945, the following was recorded in the minutes: All the victims had to take off their clothes and shoes, which were then collected; then all the victims - first the women and children - were pushed into the death chambers. Once the chambers were full, they were hermetically sealed and steam was blown in.... From the reports submitted it can be estimated that several hundred thousand Jews were exterminated at Treblinka (Nuremberg Document, PS-3311). Exactly 75 days later, the High Court had already forgotten about the steam chambers: now it was suddenly talking about the gas chambers at Treblinka". And Jürgen Graf concluded: "So it was not until after the end of the war that agreement was reached on the final form of the legend[326]."

---

[324] Wiesel, *All Rivers*, p. 121-130, 139, 163-164, 201-202, 336. *Jewish Week*, 17 September 1999, *New York Times*, 5 March 1997, in Norman Finkelstein, *La industria del Holocausto*, Ediciones Akal, Madrid, 2014, p. 76.

[325] Jürgen Graf, *Der Holocaust auf dem Prüfstand -Augenzeugenberichte versus Naturgesetze*, 1992, Guideon Burg Verlag, Basel, Switzerland. Jürgen Graf, *L'Holocauste au scanner, Témoignages oculaires ou lois de la nature*, Guideon Burg Verlag, 1993. Jürgen Graf, *El Holocausto bajo la lupa, Testimonios oculares versus leyes de la naturaleza*, with Prologue by Joaquín Bochaca, Editorial Revisión, Buenos Aires, 1997.

[326] Jürgen Graf, *El Holocausto bajo la lupa*, Editorial Revisión, Buenos Aires, 1997, p.

Belzec in eastern Poland was another 'extermination' camp, the third largest, according to official historiography. Six hundred thousand Jews were allegedly gassed there. The story of Belzec, said Jürgen Graf, 'is a miniature version of the whole Holocaust legend'. Belzec was opened in March 1942 as a transit camp for Jews deported to Russia. Soon after the camp opened, rumours spread that massacres were taking place there. The Italian historian Carlo Mattagno investigated these rumours and discovered different versions of the events.[327]

According to a first variant, the Jews were pushed into a barrack where they had to stand on a metal plate through which a lethal electric current was passed (as reported in December 1942 by the Polish government-in-exile newspaper *Polish Fortnightly Review*).

In a second variant, Jews were shot and those who were not shot were gassed or electrocuted (Statement of the Allied Information Committee of 19 December 1942).

Third variant: Jews were killed by heat in an electric furnace. This was stated by Abraham Silberschein (*Die Judenausrottung in Polen*, Geneva, August 1944).

Stefan Szende, a doctor of philosophy, presented another variant in his book *Der letzte Jude aus Polen*[328] *(The Last Jew of Poland)*: "Trains loaded to the brim with Jews were taken through a tunnel into the underground rooms of the place of execution... Everything was taken from them... The objects were neatly separated, inventoried and used for the purposes of the master race.... Everything was taken from them...The objects were neatly separated, inventoried and used for the purposes of the master race. In order to avoid this complicated and time-consuming work, all transports were later delivered naked. The naked Jews were taken to huge halls. These halls could hold several thousand people. They had no windows, and were made of metal with a submersible floor. The floor of these halls, with the thousands of Jews on top, was then lowered into a pool of water, which was underneath; but only so much that the people on the metal platform were not completely covered by the water. When the water was up to their hips, a high-voltage line was activated through the water. After a few moments, all the Jews, thousands at a time, were dead. Then the metal floor would rise again. On it lay the corpses of the executed. Another electric current was switched on, and the metal platform became an incandescent crematorium, until all the corpses had turned to ashes. Gigantic cranes then

---

57, 58.

[327] *Annales d'histoire révisionniste n°1*, printemps 1987, p. 15-107, in J. Graf, *The Holocaust under the magnifying glass*.

[328] Europa-Verlag, Zurich-New York, 1945, p. 290, in J. Graf, *The Holocaust under the magnifying glass*, p. 60, 61.

lifted this immense urn and unloaded the ashes. Large factory-type chimneys evacuated the smoke. The procedure was over. The next train was already waiting with more Jews in front of the tunnel mouth. Each train brought three to five thousand, and sometimes even more Jews. There were days when the Belzec branch had carried twenty or even more trains. Modern technology was triumphing under Nazi leadership. They had solved the problem of how to execute millions of people".

There was also a fifth variant: Jews were electrocuted in electric showers and then turned into soap. This version came from Simon Wiesenthal himself: 'The people, crowded together, egged on by the SS, Latvians and Ukrainians, came running through the open gate to the "bath". 500 people could fit in at a time. The floor of the "bathing room" was made of metal, and showers hung from the ceiling. When the space was full, the SS connected high-voltage current, 5,000 volts, to the metal plate. At the same time, the showers were pouring water. A brief scream, and the execution was over. An SS chief physician, Dr. Schmidt, checked the victims through a peephole, whereupon the second door was opened, through which the "corpse commando" entered and quickly removed the dead. There was already room for the next 500[329]."

According to Simon Wiesenthal, the corpses of the victims were not 'reduced to ashes in an incandescent crematory coffin', as Stefan Szende claimed: the executioners used them to make soap under the brand name RIF, *'Rein jüdisches Fett'*, in English 'pure Jewish fat'. In reality, RIF stood for "*Reichstelle für Industrielle Fettversorgung*"; in English: "Department *for* the Supply of Industrial Grease of the Reich".

And Wiesenthal continued: "In the last week of March (1946), the Romanian press reported a unique story In the small Romanian town of Folticeni, with all solemnity and regular burial ceremony, twenty crates of soap were buried in the Jewish cemetery...On the crates was written the acronym RIF - "Pure Jewish Fat"...At the end of 1942, the terrible expression "Soap Transport" was heard for the first time! It was in the (Polish) Governorate General, and the factory was located in Galicia, in Belzec. From April 1942 to May 1943, 900,000 Jews were used in that factory as raw material."

Simon Wiesenthal added his own commentary: "For the civilised world it is perhaps incomprehensible how the Nazis and their wives look at the soap in the Governor General's office. In every bar of soap they saw a Jew, whom they would have bewitched and thus prevented a second Freud, Ehrlich or Einstein from being bred.... The burial of the soap in a small

---

[329] Simon Wiesenthal, *Der neue Weg*, Vienne, 19, 20, 1946, in J. Graf, *The Holocaust under the magnifying glass*, p. 60.

Romanian town will seem supernatural. The bewitched grief, enclosed in this small everyday object, tears at the already insensitive human heart of this century. In this atomic age, the return to the sorceries of the darkest Middle Ages seems like a phantom! And yet, it is true![330] " It would have been a real pity to miss this testimony of Simon Wiesenthal. The great Nazi hunter died in 2005. As for soap made from Jewish fat and other lampshades made from Jewish skins, curiously no star TV historian has mentioned them again for at least fifteen years.[331]

Here is a sixth variant: Jews murdered with quicklime. This version was written by the non-Jewish Pole Jan Karski, author of the book *Story of a Secret State*, published in 1944[332] and published in French in 1948 under the title *Mon témoignage devant le monde (My testimony to the world)*, from which we extract the following passage[333] : "The floor of the train (on which the Jews had been crammed) was covered with a thick layer of white powder. It was quicklime. Anyone knows what happens when water is poured on lime..... By contact with the lime, the flesh quickly dehydrates, it burns. The occupants of the train were slowly eating away the flesh from their bones... Dusk was setting in when the 45 carriages had been filled (I had counted them). The train, with its tortured cargo of human flesh, tilted and echoed with the heart-rending howls[334]."

In Auschwitz, the methods of execution were also diverse and varied, depending on the 'witnesses'. Eugène Aroneanu, a Romanian-born Jew who had been in the Auschwitz camp recounted one such method in his 'account of the events': 'About 800 to 900 metres from the place where the ovens are located, the prisoners climb onto trolleys that run on rails. At Auschwitz, they vary in size and can hold 10 to 15 persons. When the trolley is loaded, it is lowered down a slope and then runs at full speed down a corridor. At the end of the corridor is a wall and behind it is the

---

[330] Simon Wiesenthal, *Der neue Weg*, Vienne, 17, 18, 1946, in J. Graf, *The Holocaust under the magnifying glass*, p. 62.

[331] In 1988, world-famous celebrity Kirk Douglas still mentioned this story in his memoirs: "The atrocities committed in civilised Europe were of such a magnitude as to defy comprehension. It is hard to believe that human beings were able to lead other human beings into a room and in the guise of showering them to death by suffocating them with gas, then pull out their gold teeth, shave off their hair, and turn their corpses into soap and their skin into lampshades." Kirk Douglas, *The Ragpicker's Son* (1988), Cult Books, 2021, p. 173

[332] *Houghton Miffling*, Boston, The Riverside Press, Cambridge.

[333] Quoted by R. Faurisson, *Réponse à Pierre Vidal-Naquet*, 1982, p. 44, in J. Graf, *The Holocaust under the magnifying glass*.

[334] Jürgen Graf, *El Holocausto bajo la lupa*, Editorial Revisión, Buenos Aires, 1997, p. 62, 63.

oven door. The moment it hits the wall, the door opens automatically. He overturns the cart and throws his human cargo into the oven[335]."

Zofia Kossak 's testimony was equally moving. According to her, the Zyklon B introduced into the Auschwitz gas chamber was not "thrown", as some witnesses had claimed: "It rose from holes in the floor upwards: A shrill ringing of a bell, and immediately the gas began to rise through the holes in the floor. From a balcony, from which the door could be seen, the SS men watched with curiosity the agony, the terror and the spasms of those consecrated to death. For these sadists, it was a spectacle they never tired of...The death trance lasted between 10 and 15 minutes...Powerful fans expelled the gas. Now the members of the special commando team with gas masks appeared and opened the door in front of the entrance where there was a ramp with small trolleys. The team loaded the corpses onto the trolley, with the greatest haste. Others waited. And then it often happened that the dead were brought back to life. In this concentration the gas only narcotised and did not kill. Many times it happened that the victims came to their senses on the cars.... They would drive down the ramp at full speed and unload their cargo directly into the furnace[336]."

Several authors described how some eight hundred thousand corpses at Treblinka had been disposed of without a trace. The 'Russian' novelist Vassili Grossmann also revealed the Nazis' astonishing pyrotechnical skills in *Die Hölle von Treblinka*[337] : 'They worked day and night. People who had witnessed the cremations say that these ovens resembled gigantic volcanoes, whose terrible heat scorched the faces of the workers and that the flames reached a height of 8 to 10 metres...Towards the end of July the heat became suffocating. When the pits were opened, steam rose from them as if from gigantic boilers. The terrible stench and the heat of the ovens killed the smiling people who collapsed dead on the grills of the ovens as they wanted to drag the dead towards them."

Yankel Wiernik offered other "spicy" details: "The corpses were soaked in petrol. This caused significant costs and the result was unsatisfactory; the male corpses simply did not want to be cremated. Whenever a plane appeared in the sky, the work was interrupted and the corpses were covered with leaves so as not to be detected from above. It was a gruesome spectacle, the most horrible sight ever seen by human eyes. When the corpses of pregnant women were burned, the wombs burst and it was possible to see

---

[335] Aroneanu, *Camps de concentration*, Office français d'édition, 1945, p. 182, in J. Graf, *The Holocaust under the magnifying glass*, p. 88.

[336] Zofia Kossak *Du fond de l'abîme, Seigneur*, Albin Michel, 1951, p. 127-128, in J. Graf, *The Holocaust under the magnifying glass*, p. 89.

[337] Quoted from *Historische Tatsachen*, no. 44, in J. Graf, *The Holocaust under the magnifying glass*, p. 91, 92.

the embryos flaming in the mother's body...The gangsters stand near the ashes and are shaken by satanic laughter. Their faces glow with a truly diabolical joy. They toast the scene with schnapps and the choicest spirits, eat, joke and make themselves comfortable, warming themselves by the fire[338]."

Daniel Zimmermann warned us that his 1996 book, beautifully titled *The Year of the World*, was a novel. It is the story of François Katz, a brilliant student at the Ecole Normale Supérieure, just before the Second World War. François Katz came from a family of perfectly integrated Polish Jews, like all Polish Jews. He was a gifted little genius: "He won the General Competition in Greek and Latin. At the "*Normale Sup*", he chose Professor Levi as his thesis supervisor. He was an extraordinary man: everything about him is attractive, his *voltairian*, aged face, the breadth of his erudition, the subtlety of his humour, his frequent use of parables and metaphors when he pretends to question himself aloud...". Evidently, in the face of so much Jewish perfection, there was always some envious goy among the pupils to call him a "Talmudist Jew". But they were just bitter little goyim, and there was no reason to make a big deal out of them.

So François Katz was not Jewish at all. To his friend Jacques Ravanal, a Protestant from Cevennes, he assured him that he was "not Jewish at all". Moreover - we read in the first pages of the book - his father had been "categorically opposed" to his circumcision. For two generations, his family "had renounced this type of mutilation, perpetuated by obscurantist rabbis, just as they had renounced all religious practices".

Ten pages later, pointing out to his friend a group of Orthodox Jews in the street, François returned to this important point: "Do you understand, Jacques, why I claim not to be Jewish?" And Jacques replied: "But do you understand what they say? - Of course," François replied, "my mother taught me Yiddish. It's our secret code, because my father doesn't know it". Apart from this, François Katz was not Jewish. Besides, there is no "Jewish community" and Jews do not exist, as is well known, except through the eyes of anti-Semites.

François Katz was also very patriotic. He was very active in the patriotic Union of French Israelis. His father was Captain Katz, whose heroic attitude contradicted all the statistics of the time about his fellow soldiers: "Hero of Verdun, three times wounded, five decorations, Legion of Honour for exceptional exploits with arms[339]." A few decades later, one of the most beautiful private mansions in Paris would dedicate a permanent exhibition in memory of this handful of very special "patriots". But François, he, alas,

---

[338] Donat, *The Death Camp of Treblinka*, p. 170-171, in J. Graf, *The Holocaust under the magnifying glass*, p. 92.
[339] Daniel Zimmermann, *L'Anus du monde*, Le Cherche Midi, 1996, p. 24, 21, 17

a thousand times alas, was declared unfit for service in 1940, permanently exempted because of his "physical handicaps".

In 1940 the war broke out and the Jewish statute was promulgated. François was not Jewish, but, as we read on the cover of the book, "the Vichy regime and the Nazis proved him wrong": what bastards! Interned by the French police in the Drancy camp, he was caught up in a spiral that led him to participate in the unthinkable. "From Drancy to Treblinka, via Auschwitz, François is plunged into the concentration camp complex...This journey into the depths of darkness is also a journey of initiation...François becomes accustomed to horror and carries out the most abominable tasks." The book is "a relentless ascertainment of human nature. A deeply moving and unforgettable novel."

In Auschwitz, François Katz was to go through hell. To begin with, here is a scene of combat between prisoners. A boxing match organised by the camp authorities: "Without a referee, useless for an all-out pugilism, without rules", and the loser went straight to the gas chamber without even having had time to take a shower. Müller, a Jewish colossus, was settling scores with a muscular Pole who was probably very anti-Semitic. "He grabs him by the head and smashes it to pieces with a knee, before letting him collapse, dead... thus freeing himself from the gas chamber[340]." On leaving the ring, Müller is congratulated by an SS captain who had bet on him. The SS captain was happy: he had just won a thousand marks.

In the meantime - it must not be forgotten - the crematoria "smoked day and night". The cruel Doctor Mengele entered the scene: behind his "refined manners", he carried out all sorts of "terrifying experiments" on the prisoners. While François - who was also a wonderful violinist - played Fauré's *Berceuse*, Mengele stuck syringes into babies' chests [it's getting tiresome].

Here François had a vision of horror: in the dark room, he saw "dozens of human skulls with legends written in gothic calligraphy: 'Russian Jew, political commissar', 'Polish Jew, rabbi', 'German Jew, famous mathematician', etc. Behind each one, a jar of formaldehyde contains the corresponding brain." Mengele had also reduced some heads, in the manner of the Jivaro Indians. He had fixed them on small blocks of marble and used them as paperweights!

As soon as they arrived at Auschwitz, the prisoners were stripped of all their belongings. But Kramer, the camp commandant, was furious when he realised that the new consignment of French Jews had left very little gold behind. Mengele questioned François about it, and François replied that the French gendarmes themselves extorted money from the Jews before

---

[340] Daniel Zimmermann, *L'Anus du monde*, Le Cherche Midi, 1996, p. 105, 106

shipping them out: "The pigs, they poach in a guarded hunting ground. Mengele shuddered with irritation, in turn infecting Kramer who stopped beating Hans", the Jewish Kapo chief, who, to make amends, had asked to whip a newly arrived prisoner to death himself.

In the evening, Kramer, the SS commander, gave a "splendid party". He was "in high spirits", but François could not contain his indignation when he saw him "gently take Hans by the arm and lead him away to order a mink coat for his wife as a Christmas present[341]."

Auschwitz was a very lucrative business for the SS. The Auschwitz-Birekenaubank, we read, held "fabulous treasures from all over Europe". Gold wedding rings, teeth and dentures were melted down into ingots. Every week, under strict surveillance, an ambulance with the Red Cross emblem would go out to deliver the booty to the Bank of the Empire (page 104).... Admittedly, the Red Cross, and all crosses in general, do not bode well, it must be said.

The next shipment of Jews was scheduled to be taken to the gas chamber. François, who was a virtuoso violinist, took it upon himself to play some Yiddish melodies to reassure them as soon as they got off the train. The men and women were separated, and François Katz offered, out of gallantry, to carry the suitcase of a young Jewish woman. They hardly had time to get to know each other, as the prisoners were immediately sent to the collective showers. The young woman had noticed François: "If she is forced to undress in front of those gentlemen," she said, pointing to the SS crowded at the entrance, "she prefers that she also stays, because she trusts him.

The women looked worried, whispered among themselves and refused to undress in front of the SS. The young woman, who had caught François' attention, then understood what was going to happen. She began to undress slowly, and then an extraordinary, "unforgettable" scene took place: "...Her breasts appeared, splendid, without a bra. François would like to run away, but cannot, mesmerised.... The SS were also dumbstruck.... Even more slowly, the young woman pulls up her skirt, unhooks her stockings from the garter belt, takes them off and languidly removes her bare feet. She stands up again, booties in hand, jumps up like a cat and plants her stiletto heel in the eye of an SS. He snatches the pistol from him and shoots Schillinger. Schillinger collapses, shot in the skull. He shoots twice more before melting into the group of women. Terrified and not shooting back, the SS men flee towards the exit. François slipped between them. - Fire at will! The SS counterattack with machine-gun fire. Screams of terror, pain

---

[341] Daniel Zimmermann, *L'Anus du monde*, Le Cherche Midi, 1996, p. 113, 126, 116

and agony. The wounded are finished off. Silence[342]." Amazing episode, isn't it?

There were also SS women in the Auschwitz camp: "They are as cruel or more cruel than their male counterparts. One of them beats the hell out of an inanimate "Muslim" woman. In guard position, ten paces away, Hans uncovers himself and whispers:
- They call her the bitch. Every day she kills at least thirty people like this.
The SS turns the lifeless body over with its foot".

François Katz had a bad encounter with Mietek, known as the Bloody. Mietek was a Pole of the worst kind, a convicted common law member of the disciplinary command. On Christmas Eve, he had decided that no Jews were to be tolerated in positions of responsibility, except those who had rendered great services. And it so happened that he had a favour to ask of François: to hide a bag full of jewellery in Hans' room. To better convince François, he and his acolytes killed a recalcitrant prisoner before his very eyes: "Mietek the Bloody lifts up the prisoner, sits him on the red-hot cooker, he sizzles, his tormented body jerks, he stinks.... Mietek the Bloody disembowels him with a knife, eviscerates him with his bare hands, grunting with pleasure".

François had no choice. So he went to hide the precious bag under his friend Hans' mattress, but discreetly followed by an informer. The SS searched the room and Hans was arrested on the spot. In the evening, not a gallows was erected on the appeal square, but a cross. The SS commander read out the sentence. Daniel Zimmermann wrote: "...Hans allowed himself to be crucified without resistance. Without screaming, with little blood and, from the beginning, with violent contractions of all his muscles. In order to breathe, the colossus has to pull on his arms, which, according to Mengele, was proof that the cause of his death would indeed be a lack of oxygen, which would undoubtedly accelerate if his legs were broken, so that he could no longer support himself on them and, as a mechanical consequence, would quickly suffocate." Mengele told François: "I seem to remember, secretary, that this is what you Jews used to do. Moreover, I read that you administered a narcotic drink to the condemned before crucifixion to alleviate their suffering, if my memory serves me.... Ah, you didn't even know about these little humanitarian provisions? Well. Apart from that, how does it feel to see your best friend pinned down like a butterfly?"

Only François, Mengele and a guard were left beside the condemned man, who watched the agony of the wretch: "Kramer comes down from his

---

[342] Daniel Zimmermann, *L'Anus du monde*, Le Cherche Midi, 1996, p. 121.

pedestal, he returns home, his wife and children are waiting for him to celebrate Christmas, Heil Hitler![343] ".

François also saw with his own eyes the SS men crushing the heads of babies. Bielas, the second-in-command of the Treblinka sanatorium, was visiting Auschwitz. He asked his colleague, Dr. Mengele, to "lend" him this polite little violin genius. Mengele hesitated for a moment: "And then you will return his skull and brain to me? Deal!"

François was therefore sent to Treblinka. As soon as he arrived at the camp, he saw the Ukrainian guards busy with the poor Jews: "A bullet in the back of the head and the body is overturned, or pushed, into the incineration pit where a permanent fire, fuelled by sulphur, was burning. Soon only a forgotten, screaming baby was left. An SS man grabs him by the feet and smashes his head against the wall of a wagon[344]."

Here is another poignant scene: Prisoners stood firm in guard position. A Jewish boy, who had been taught by the SS to denounce his fellows, "points to a man who broke ranks to scratch his fingers". The dog jumps up, knocks down its prey, grabs it by the genitals and rips them off, then attacks the entrails. Bielas ironizes:

- The number of workers is wrong, dean of the field!
- Minus one unit, who died suddenly of haemorrhage, corrects Galewski, unperturbed[345]."

François Katz also learned to kill his own brothers: "On the floor, two men writhe in pain, holding their bellies. All around them, the inmates exult, betting on who will die first. They respectfully turn away when Galewski appears. He picks up a club from the floor and hands it to François:

- Kill them!
- Hitting them on the head?
- No, like this.

Galewski places the handle of his whip on the throat of the block leader. He climbs on top and alternates between left and right foot, swings: cracking, ready, now it's François' turn to do the same. A young man of his age, with a pained expression on his face, ready to die as a test. Success, François is an inveterate good pupil[346]."

The giant barbecue scene is also very memorable: Stumpfe, an SS, was nicknamed the Laughing Death. He used to throw live Jewish children on the stake (page 182). Above the gigantic pits, rails on concrete pillars

---

[343] Daniel Zimmermann, *L'Anus du monde*, Le Cherche Midi, 1996, p. 124, 128, 130, 131

[344] Daniel Zimmermann, *L'Anus du monde*, Le Cherche Midi, 1996, p. 153. It was probably an ancient Jewish custom with kidnapped Goyim babies.

[345] Daniel Zimmermann, *L'Anus du monde*, Le Cherche Midi, 1996, p. 156.

[346] Daniel Zimmermann, *L'Anus du monde*, Le Cherche Midi, 1996, p. 165.

"supported steel cross beams". It was a "cyclopean grill" that consumed thousands of corpses: "Under the effect of the heat, the corpses seemed to come back to life. Convulsions, contortions, they suffered again. Whistling, screeching, arms and legs twitched, trunks straightened. Skins blistered, faces wept. Deflagrations, wombs exploded, foetuses were expelled.

- Come on, come on, faster, faster!

... François was stoking the funeral bonfire... He would work among the bodies. He put melted fat on the bodies, as one would a leg of lamb in an oven: "With a bucket on the end of a pole, he extracted it from the bottom of the pit, in the cistern that collected human fat. Altered, blinded by the smoke, maddened by the whipping, suffocating, belching, vomiting, urinating and defecating standing up, he poured the boiling fuel on the places where the fire was least intense[347]."

In the face of so many horrors, François decided to be circumcised. Hadn't Abraham been circumcised at the age of ninety-nine? "So you finally agree to sign the Covenant Pact with the Holy One, blessed be He?" asked his friend Mosché. And François replied: "I don't believe in it and I never will. But I want to make an alliance with you, my brothers? The next day, the insurrection broke out". These were the final lines of this magnificent and moving story.

In the acknowledgements at the end of the book, Daniel Zimmerman explained that he had been "inspired mainly by the numerous testimonies of survivors of the Nazi extermination camps". He added that although the story was "fictional", writing it was a "very exhausting" experience. "More than half a century after Drancy, Auschwitz and Treblinka, had the time come for me to add the duty of imagination to the duty of memory?"

This is what the back cover of the book says: "In this book, fiction takes over from memory". And readers will also have noticed that Daniel Zimmermann is a pure literary genius: "Thanks to his sharp, hallucinatory writing, Zimmermann transcends the most unbearable facts and metamorphoses them into black diamonds".

We hope, however, that we may be allowed to say that we did not believe a single word of the story. Everything seems false: the death of the boxer, Dr. Mengele's skulls, the filmy episode of the stiletto heel, the bite of the German shepherd, the theatrical crucifixion and the children thrown on the stake, not to mention everything else. The fact that the leaders of the Jewish community allowed the publication of this novel, which calls into question all the suffering in the concentration camps, is astonishing.

---

[347] Daniel Zimmermann, *L'Anus du monde*, Le Cherche Midi, 1996, p. 183.

Hysterical fabulation III

The French academic Maurice Rheims was also a Holocaust survivor. He had known the notorious Danecker, Gestapo Oberfüher of sinister memory. Danecker was extraordinary, he wrote: slender, elegant, tall, good-looking, Aryan, in short. Very sincerely, he warned me: "You will never get out of Drancy, where I am taking you, unless you are dead. I will see to it myself!" He was a man who made no secret of his hatred of Jews[348]."

It is regrettable that Maurice Rheims did not explain to his readers the reasons for SS Danecker's hatred of the Jews. It would have been a most important testimony. But more important, of course, is that he returned alive from the hell of Drancy.

On 23 August 2008, *The Telegraph* published the umpteenth account of a Holocaust survivor, Eugène Black. He had just discovered in the Arolsen archives that his two sisters, whom he believed had been gassed at Auschwitz, had in fact died under Allied bombs while working in a factory near Buchenwald.

Emmaly Reed was another of these survivors. She had been separated from her Jewish mother, father and older siblings at the age of 3 [i.e. in 1933...], and sent to the Dachau concentration camp. At the age of 77, this woman was touring schools in the United States recounting the atrocities she had lived through. Under the headline *Twelve Years in German Concentration Camps: A Survivor Speaks Out*, the US weekly *The Western Times* on 27 March 2008 announced a lecture to be given by the Holocaust survivor at a Kansas high school. She was 15 years old when the French army rescued her: "It was the end of the war and the SS had to flee quickly, so they hung us against the wall. They put chains around our necks. If we breathed, we strangled and died. Almost 50% of the people died. If the French hadn't arrived at that time, I would have died too".

About Hitler, this woman said that she had seen him kill a child standing next to her: "(...) and I looked at his face. It was not the face of a human being, it was the face of the devil. These are scenes you don't forget. I still have nightmares about it at night and wake up screaming".

Jean-Jacques Servan-Schreiber, founder of the newspaper *L'Express*, was a third-generation French Schreiber, a descendant of Prussian Jews who sold cloth on the street. After the Great War, they made their fortune by creating the first newspaper dedicated to commerce and including advertising: *Les Echos*[349]. In his memoirs, *Passions*, published in 1991, he

---

[348] Maurice Rheims, *Une Mémoire vaganbonde*, Gallimard, 1997, p. 68.
[349] On JJSS: Christine Ockrent, *Françoise Giroud, une ambition française*, Fayard, Paris, 2003, p. 88, 89.

recounted how in 1938, when he was only thirteen, his father, a journalist, had taken him with him on a reporting trip to Munich. That was how the young Schreiber had the opportunity to get close to Chancellor Adolf Hitler in person:

"There, at the end of the bridge, a very long Mercedes is moving slowly, he wrote. All eyes are on it.... I stand there with my arms hanging down. The Führer, standing in his coupé, reaches me. A shout: Hitler's voice. He orders his chauffeur to stop and the car slams on the brakes. Hitler's eyes, two metres away.... I can still see them! They express the essence of this already fabulous character. They are light blue, streaked with black and yellow, and seem to have no look in them. He saw that I didn't raise my arm! In fact, I didn't even think about it. I wouldn't have done it, I want to believe, if it had occurred to me, but it simply didn't occur to me.... Hitler roars three or four sentences whose meaning I have no difficulty in understanding! I am hypnotised by the sound of that voice, which I hear live and not on the radio. It still doesn't occur to me to raise my arm, my body frozen and my gaze fixed on Hitler's fascinating eyes. Another shout to the driver and the car starts again. Then the roar of the crowd towards me suddenly turns into a storm.... Fortunately, two German policemen grab my arm and pull me out of the storm and take me back to the hotel, where I find my father[350]." Little Schreiber narrowly escaped!

This testimony is similar to that of writer Mark Halter. Marek Halter also had extraordinary stories to tell. During World War II, when he was still a child, he had the opportunity to meet Stalin, the "Father of the Peoples", in person. At the time, he was sheltering in the sun with his parents, in Uzbekistan, like hundreds of thousands of other Polish Jews: "My mother, he wrote, had a membership card of the Soviet Writers' Union...I was included in the delegation of the Pioneers of Uzbekistan who were to participate in the Victory Party in Moscow...At the last moment, I was appointed to offer Stalin the corsage of the Pioneers of Uzbekistan. I was so excited that they had to push me. Stalin took my flowers, ran his hand through my hair and said something that I did not understand from how disturbed he was[351]."

Marek Halter's tendency to make up stories is well known, having been thoroughly discredited by the weekly *Le Point* of 28 April 2005[352]. In this case, Servan-Schreiber's testimony was also highly suspect. As we can see, there are often similarities between the childhood stories of these Jews. Same feathers, same branches, as the good Mr Jean de La Fontaine would say.

---

[350] Jean-Jacques Servan-Schreiber, *Passions*, Fixot, 1991, p. 12.
[351] Marek Halter, *Le Fou et les rois*, Albin Michel-Poche, 1976, p. 26, 33
[352] In this regard, see *Planetary Hopes*.

Imre Kertesz, winner of the Nobel Prize for Literature, who was deported to Auschwitz at the age of 14, spoke in an interview with the magazine *Le Point* on 3 January 2008. He explained to readers the oppressive feeling that consumed him. He had been found half dead in a pool of ice water on the concrete of Buchenwald. He recounted:

"I still can't consider it rational that I was saved, why should I be saved, why not someone else? Imre used the occasion to warn us against the awakening of the monster: "Anti-Americanism and anti-Semitism are the fuel of the new dictatorships. Like Iran, which denies the Holocaust on the one hand but uses it to its own advantage when it suits it. So let us be vigilant; let the whole of Europe be vigilant". He further explained, "I simply refuse to give my testimony without further ado. When the survivors of the camps disappear, the experience of Auschwitz, if we believe Adorno, will be a dead memory. On the contrary, I believe that another generation will have to take up this subject and invent something new". Indeed, imagination is paramount to chase away the demons.

Here is an excerpt from Malinka Zanger's story, published in 2008 and entitled *Malinka*. It tells the story of a Jewish girl from Poland, about fourteen years old, whose family was annihilated and who miraculously survived: "Wladek, from his camp, was able to see the staging. When they arrived in Bobryk, they gathered all the inhabitants. Then they lined them all up against a wall. When the number of twenty-nine was reached, they all had to flee by order of the commanding officer. And so the manhunt began.... Among the victims were a baby and old people who could not move. They chased mother, aiming at her head several times.... My sister Luba was not among them at first, but she ran to be with mum. They shot her in the cheek and buried her alive.... The baby, who was smiling at the executioners, was the target of four rifles. An old woman, who came out of a burning house, was like a ball of fire. The hunt was over when they had counted twenty-nine victims."

In the preface to the book, the great Nazi hunter Serge Klarsfeld wrote: "The testimonies of Holocaust survivors are numerous. Of course, even so, we will always say that they are not enough. There is always a shortage of the kind of testimony that we think we have a right to expect from each survivor." And he added a little further on, "The story we are about to read is one of those that generate that hesitation that is often close to doubt."

In their book on the *Lobby*, John Mearsheimer and Stephen Walt quoted a 2002 article by one Leon Wieseltier in the weekly *New Republic*: "The community has become hypersensitive, submerged by an imaginary disaster it can no longer intellectually control. Death is at the doorstep of every Jewish inhabitant. Fear is everywhere. Reason has lost its mind. Anguish has become the supreme test of authenticity. Vague and provocative comparisons abound. The imaginary Holocaust is omnipresent[353]."

André Schwarz-Bart was best known for winning the Goncourt Prize in 1959 for his book *Le Dernier des Justes (The Last Just)*. The writer, who died on 30 September 2006, was of Polish origin. His father had begun studying to become a rabbi and then worked as a carny. On 3 October 2006, Robert Faurisson, the famous revisionist historian, wrote an interesting article about the author of *The Last Righteous*: "The success of *The Last Righteous* was resounding and brought its author considerable sums, wrote Faurisson. Hundreds, perhaps thousands of articles and studies have been devoted, in France and abroad, to what is now widely regarded as the first *great book* on the *Shoah*. But the author was a plagiarist, a literary fraud. This is the conclusion of a study published by Francine Kaufmann, professor at Bar-Illan University in Israel, in the *Revue d'histoire de la Shoah*, September-December 2002, p. 69-99. This text contains a list of Jewish authors systematically plundered by our forger: Martin Buber, Manès Sperber, Isaac Babel, Michel Borwicz and others. But André Schwarz-Bart also took advantage of a letter from Madame de Sévigné which relates how, in 1676, the Marquise de Brinvilliers was condemned by poisoning, beheaded and burnt. He had also reproduced word for word some lines from the novel by the Chinese author Lu Xun, *The True Story of Ah Q*. Venial sins, of course, since these robberies were committed with the pious intention of making us mourn for the Jews and their martyrdom".

The specialist on the subject, Robert Faurisson, concluded: "Concentrationary literature is full of such thefts, plagiarism and swindles. Firstly, as all these stories are largely fictitious, their authors proceed here and there with small thefts in non-Jewish literature, and then, secondly, these are in turn stolen by their fellow Jews. The result is an endless chain of stories, tales, novels, films and even supposedly historical works that do nothing but copy each other. This can be called "the circular circulation" (dixit Bourdieu) of the literary, artistic, cinematic or university trade in holocaustic lies and commerce. The unwary imagine that they are confronted with overlapping testimonies: the reality is that they are confronted with the inventions of liars and thieves. To give just one example, one could write a linguistics thesis on the character of "Dr. Mengele in Jewish concentration camp literature" alone. It would show the extent to which Jewish authors simply repeat themselves, sometimes without changing a single comma. They all evoke the figure of this alleged executioner of Auschwitz in the manner of the novelist or swindler

---

[353] John J. Mearsheimer / Stephen Walt, *Le Lobby pro-israélien et la politique étrangère américaine*, La Découverte, 2007, p. 210.

Schwarz-Bart, winner of the 1959 Goncourt Prize, whose stories, like those of his compatriots, are nothing but a series of clichés, implausibilities, absurd stories and Grand Guignol mixed with sperm, blood and faecal matter, all inspired by the Old Testament and the Talmud. In this sense, *The Last Righteous* is, a year after Elie Wiesel's autobiographical and mendacious account *The Night*, "the first great book about the Shoah"."

On 20 October 2006, on the Internet, Robert Faurisson returned to the fray and added, in addition to his article on Schwarz-Bart: "The juries of the Goncourt Prize have a certain weakness for holocaustic literature of the André Schwarz-Bart type. For 2006, they had to crown the novel by Jonathan Littell, the Jewish author of *Les Bienveillantes*". Faurisson quoted an article by Peter Schöttler published in *Le Monde* on 14 October: "The narrator, a sort of Tom Riley in SS uniform, does nothing but splash around in blood and shit (not forgetting the sperm, of course!), most of the time saying things as uninteresting as you find in a certain kind of airport literature."

Naturally, historians who dare to question the testimony of survivors are automatically wanted, extradited and sentenced. In 2002, revisionist René-Louis Berclaz was handed over by Serbia to Switzerland, where he was sentenced to 8 months in prison. Switzerland also imprisoned Gaston Amaudruz, who was over 80 years old at the time, as was Jürgen Graf, for a year.

Historian Ernst Zündel was handed over by the United States to Canada, and then by Canada to Germany, where he was sentenced in February 2007 to five years in prison, which he is serving in Mannheim. Belgian revisionist Siegfried Verbeke was handed over by the Netherlands to Germany, where he served nine months in prison. He returned to Belgium in 2006, where he was imprisoned for one year. In November 2005, the United States handed over German revisionist Germar Rudolf to Germany, where he was sentenced to three years in prison. In Austria, semi-revisionist historian David Irving, a British national, was arrested by police in November 2005 and imprisoned in Vienna for eleven months. Gerd Honsik, who had taken refuge in Spain, was arrested and extradited in October 2007 and imprisoned for 18 months. Engineer Wolfgang Frölich was sentenced to four years' imprisonment.

In January 2008, Sylvia Stolz, Ernst Zündel's lawyer, was also convicted and is serving a three-year prison sentence in Heidelberg. In October 2008, Australian revisionist Frederick Töben, a doctor of philosophy, was arrested in England and extradited to Germany, where he had already served nine months in prison for the content of his website. He was finally released a few weeks later. In December, the young Kevin Käthe was tried in Berlin and sentenced to eight months in prison.

In France, Robert Faurrisson has been severely fined on numerous occasions. Professor Jean-Louis Beger also received a one-month suspended prison sentence in 2000. Georges Theil received a six-month prison sentence and almost 60,000 euros in fines and damages. In June 2008, Vincent Reynouard was sentenced to two one-year prison sentences, in France and Belgium, and has since been on the run.[354]

On 1 November 2005, the UN banned revisionism.

"On 1 November, unanimously and without a vote, wrote Faurisson, the representatives of the 191 nations that make up the UN adopted - or allowed to be adopted - an Israeli draft resolution proclaiming 27 January "International Day of Commemoration in Memory of the Victims of the Holocaust". The draft also rejects any denial of the Holocaust as a historical event, whether total or partial. The existence of historical revisionism is thus recognised throughout the world," wrote Faurisson, "which proves its strength and its life, but, at the same time, this decision means that revisionists are subject to a moral ban by all the countries of the world.... The history of societies and religions is rich in prohibitions, proscriptions and excommunications, Faurisson continued, but whereas, until recently, the victims could, at least in principle, hope to find refuge outside their country or group of origin, here the condemnation is, for the first time in the world, of a universal character, which confirms that historical revisionism has an exceptional character and also that the Jews, once again, are able to obtain exorbitant privileges".

It is true that for Jews historical truth is of little importance. What matters to them is the myth that corresponds to their idea of their historical role and mission on earth. They write and interpret history solely in the interests of Judaism:

"Maimonides considered the study of history a waste of time, wrote Esther Benbassa. Later, Joseph Caro, author of the *Shulchan Aruch* (The

---

[354] Vincent Reynouard (b. 1969) is a French chemical engineer, mathematics professor, historian and author of several revisionist essays, videos and documentaries. In November 2015, Reynouard was tried before a Normandy court for denying the Holocaust in social media posts. Reynouard, who chose to represent himself in the trial, was sentenced to two years in prison; the sentence was increased due to Reynouard's previous convictions. Vincent Reynouard then went into exile in the UK from where he continued to publish his works and videos on the internet. In November 2022, Reynouard was arrested in Scotland. On 12 October 2023, the Scottish courts authorised his extradition which, after a legal battle, was confirmed on 26 January 2024, after Vincent Reynouard had exhausted all possible appeals. He was handed over to the French authorities on 2 February 2024, charged by an examining magistrate in Paris with "denial of war crimes", "denial of crimes against humanity" and "incitement to hatred". He was released under judicial supervision.

Table Served) and one of the leading codifiers of rabbinic law, forbade the reading of history not only on the Sabbath, but also during the week[355]."

So Israel Finkielstein, the renowned Israeli archaeologist and author of *The Bible Unearthed* (2001)[356], can prove through archaeology that the departure from Egypt could not have taken place: this is of no importance, because for the Jews myth is always much stronger than reality. They are a community with a fertile, even delusional imagination, which is constantly racking its brains.

Alexandre Minkowski illustrated this perfectly. In his 1980 book *A Not Very Catholic Jew*, he recounted his beginnings in the world of the "bustle and bustle". After the publication of his book, he was invited to a television programme, hosted by the star presenter Michel Drucker, one of his peers. He wrote: "It is enough for me to read or hear a story that is a little heroic or exemplary for my imagination to run wild and make me believe that I have lived it. That afternoon I was at once a mountaineer, a lonely sailor, a singer and a Nobel Prize winner in Biology[357]." And he continued: "It was thanks to a question, albeit a very anodyne one, and an act of audacity of which I would never have been capable in any other company, that I would be consecrated as a great sports expert. On that Sunday, a semi-final of the French rugby championship was being played. Drucker asked each of us for our predictions. I had never set foot on a rugby pitch, but on that particular day, it didn't matter. Nothing could stop me. And yet, frankly, I'm still not sure I fully understand the rules of the game. However, my knowledge of the technical vocabulary is sufficient to allow me to comment on a match in detail without my interlocutors suspecting for a moment that I barely know what I'm talking about. That is how, from that day on, I came to be regarded as a real connoisseur. The day after the programme, I received a voluminous letter that convinced me that rugby held no secrets for me[358]."

A few pages further on, Minkowski confessed his penchant for talking rubbish with the utmost aplomb and chutzpah. It is the famous *chutzpah* of which Jewish intellectuals are so fond of boasting: "I am capable of speaking confidently about what I know nothing about, especially if I am confronted with someone," he wrote. Fortunately, the RTL journalists had

---

[355] Esther Benbassa, *La Souffrance comme identité*, Fayard, 2007, p. 77.
[356] Norman Finkielstein, Neil Asher Silberman, *La Biblia desenterrada, Una nueva visión arqueológica del antiguo Israel y de los orígenes de sus textos sagrados* (2001), Siglo XXI, Madrid, 2003.
[357] "We are American Buddhists, Indian computer scientists, Arab ecologists, Japanese pianists, doctors without borders". Pierre Lévy, *World philosophie*, Odile Jacob, 2000, p. 42, in *Planetary Hopes*.
[358] Alexandre Minkowski, *Un juif pas très catholique*, Ramsay, 1980, p. 63-65.

the good idea to put me in direct contact with Mrs Veil, then Minister of Health... I respect Mrs Veil a lot, but some of her attitudes offend me. So, for once, I decided to make a plea for radically nationalised medicine.... I even went on a leftist diatribe and attacked "money", the notorious agent of corruption. And the more I spoke, the more I was surprised - even a little frightened - that I could defend with such ardour and conviction an opinion that was not entirely my own. After the programme, I received a lot of letters and phone calls of admiration, sometimes even dithyrambic. This convinced me that the only thing you have to do to be believed is to assert something with authority. No matter what you say, you have to be persuasive... You have to "show off", without mincing words or embarrassment... Then I began to talk about my trips to communist countries. I spared no detail, telling how I had met Castro, Pham Van-Dong and Zhou Enlai, including a little personal anecdote about each of them to make it clear that, although they were not close friends, I knew them quite well. Perhaps I was exaggerating a little, but it felt extraordinarily credible."

We can close this chapter with a quote from a film by Christian Merret-Palmair, entitled *Les Portes de la gloire* (*The Gates of Glory,* France, 2000). It is a story about door-to-door salesmen who go around the villages and towns of northern France cajoling their customers to sell them their trinkets. At the end of the film, one of these salesmen, nicknamed Balzac, recites his little verse: "If you compare the fate of two men, one of whom is endowed with true merit and the other who enjoys a false glory, you will have the feeling that the second is happier than his rival and almost always richer. Imposture excels and triumphs in lies. But without imposture, truth is nothing. This is not due, in my opinion, to some evil inclination of our species, but to the fact that truth is always too simple and too poor to satisfy men who demand, in order to be entertained or moved, a share of illusion and error. Nature is the first to deceive us in this way, for it is essentially through illusion and lies that she makes life pleasant or at least bearable for us."

The fabulist goyim: synthetic Jews

Jews are the population most affected by hysterical pathology. However, they are not the only ones who suffer from these psychic disorders. Hysterical delirium and sick imagination are also found in some non-Jewish authors. And when these authors speak of the misfortunes they suffered during the war, Jews instinctively recognise them as their own. They then benefit from all the publicity machinery and distribution networks that quickly catapultthem to worldwide fame.

The case of "Misha Defonseca" was quite emblematic. In an "autobiographical" book entitled *Surviving with Wolves*, published in 1997, 70-year-old Misha Defonseca told her extraordinary story. It tells the story of an eight-year-old Jewish girl who, in 1941, set off in search of her parents, who had been deported to Auschwitz. With the help of a simple compass, she left her native Belgium and walked across Germany and Poland to the Ukraine, hoping to find her parents. He travelled 3,000 kilometres. To survive, she stole food and clothes, and avoided men and their violence. In the forests, he joined a pack of wolves and became one of them.

In 2008, Misha Defonseca's book was adapted into a film directed by a certain Vera Belmont. The film is violently anti-German. The girl speaks with hatred of those "dirty Germans[359]", and Catholics also come off badly. We see, for example, a horrible harpy greeting the girl with a slaver's speech. A crucifix is prominently displayed on the wall. Indeed, Catholics are notorious for making money out of anything, even at the expense of a poor Jewish girl (quite the opposite of Jews, in fact).

On the Internet, the revisionist historian Robert Faurisson denounced the imposture, because in reality Misha Defonseca was not Jewish at all. Her name was Monique de Wael and her story was absurd. On 28 February 2008, the story finally came to light.

In the *Nouvel Observateur* of 10 January 2008, on the occasion of the film's release, Serge Aroles, author of *L'Enigme des enfants-loups (The Enigma of the Wolf-Children)*, gave his opinion: "Misha Defonseca's exuberant fiction, he said, repeats all the usual surrealist clichés, which science and archives have hopelessly destroyed every time he has investigated a wolf-child case: this child shares the life of a pack (6 adults and 4 wolf cubs), because she makes lupine companions by modulating the wolf's howl; her teeth (9 years old), her teeth, not her hands, tear the skin of a hare and crunch the bones of the prey (try it, even with adult teeth); Her tongue licks water effectively (again, try it!); He pacifies threatening male wolves by "immediately jumping on their backs" and whimpering "like puppies"; His wounds are healed by the (actually over-infected!) saliva of the entire pack that has come to lick his wounds, etc." And he continued: "But there are two inventions by Misha Defonseca whose excess is unparalleled; two fables that I have never encountered in a history spanning seven centuries (1304-1954): 1. On an "exceptional day", all the wolves of the pack go hunting, leaving him in charge of the cubs, even one of them wounded, which, according to the author, shows the great trust he had earned. 2. When, now a member of the pack, the little girl dares to

---

[359] *"Sales boches"* in French in the text.

urinate by raising her paw, she is "scolded" by the dominant she-wolf, who "orders her to bend down like the other females" to urinate (page 162). Paradoxically, in my book on the subject, I gave an irrefutable scientific explanation for the phenomenon of wolf-children: in the history of mankind, there have been cases exclusively of suckling cubs taken in by a solitary she-wolf in a state of pseudo-gestation (nervous pregnancy). The she-wolf suckles them and defends them, but their life expectancy is short".

The Belgian *daily Le Soir* published a statement by Misha Defonseca, in which he admitted that his story, presented as authentic, was a work of fiction and not an autobiographical account, as he had claimed for ten years. "I told myself a life, another life. I apologise," she declared. "I have always felt Jewish," headlined all the press the next day.

On 2 March, the website of the Belgian daily *Le Soir* reported that "Misha's" father, Robert de Wael, a member of a resistance network, had been arrested by the Nazis. He then denounced his comrades in order to see his daughter and took part in the interrogation of his former comrades-in-arms. His name - the height of ignominy - was removed from the stone stele in the Schaerbeek town hall that paid tribute to them.

"Yes, my name is Monique De Wael, but since I was four years old I wanted to forget it. My parents were arrested when I was four years old. I was taken in by my grandfather, Ernest De Wael, and then by my uncle, Maurice De Wael. They called me "the traitor's daughter" because my father was suspected of having spoken under torture in Saint-Gilles prison. Apart from my grandfather, I hated the people who took me in. They treated me badly. I felt different. It is true that I have always felt Jewish, and later in life I was able to reconcile with myself by being welcomed into this community. Certainly, I have always told myself a life, another life, a life that separated me from my family, a life far from the men I hated. That's also why I fell in love with wolves, why I entered their world. And I mixed it all up. There are moments when I find it hard to differentiate between what was reality and what was my inner world... I apologise to all those who feel betrayed, but I beg you to put yourself in the shoes of a four-year-old girl who has lost everything, who has to survive, who falls into an abyss of loneliness, and to understand that I never wanted anything other than to conjure up my suffering".

After these confessions, Serge Aroles, stupefied by the magnitude of the events, declared: "The case of Misha Defonseca is not in my book, it was so delirious that I did not dwell on it, thinking that everyone would quickly realise". And he repeated: "A she-wolf in need of adoption can develop a "nervous pregnancy" and end up with udders full of milk. It is very likely that, by statistical accident, some newborns hidden in the forest because of war, famine or neglect may have been breastfed for a short period of time. But this only applies to babies. And this, no doubt, has fuelled the myth of

THE MIRROR OF JUDAISM

wolf-children... [But] when Misha Defonseca explains that a she-wolf reprimanded her for urinating like a male when she raised her paw, or that she found herself babysitting in the pack, no one has ever gone that far in the delirium."

French publisher Bernard Fixot, who owns world rights to the book, said: "I asked Misha some questions a long time ago, in 1995. I was interested to know how he had survived.... Those stories about wolves, of course, surprised me a lot.... I knew Misha very well. I really trusted her. When you publish documents, you don't check everything. You check when it can cause harm to other people. In this case, no one. It was a very nice story that only harmed the Nazis". He then confirmed that he would not take legal action against the Belgian author.

Vera Belmont, the filmmaker who made the film *Surviving with Wolves*, said she was "a bit angry" with Misha Defonseca. "But she has built something, like a safeguard against sinking. So my heart aches for her."

The director said she had never had any doubts about Mrs Defonseca's supposed Jewishness, but she did not entirely believe the rest of her story about her journey with the wolves. "It's hard to be Jewish, so I never thought for a second that someone would take on that identity... If she had told me the truth, I would have done it anyway, because, being Jewish myself and wanting to talk about that time, I couldn't talk about it directly," she added. The director specified that the words "Based on a true story" would be removed from the credits of the film, which would nevertheless remain in theatres.

Maxime Steinberg, a "Belgian" historian of the Shoah, pointed out that the deportations of Jews began in Belgium in August 1942. There was therefore no reason for Jews to hide or flee in the spring of 1941. Misha Defonseca anticipated the facts by a year and a half...His crossing of Europe with no help but wolves is equally implausible. After a long legal and financial battle, which she eventually lost, the American publisher published on the Internet an extract from a record of the 1943-1944 school year, attesting that at the time when the heroine claimed to be in the forests of Poland, adopted by a pack of ten wolves, she was actually going to school in Schaerbeek. The document was accompanied by an extract from the Catholic baptismal certificate of 'Misha', who was born in 1937 in Etterbeeck, and was neither Jewish in father nor mother. The Schaerbeek school records also confirmed that during the 1943-1944 school year, Monique Dewael had attended school with Marguerite Levy, none other than her future husband's sister.

The case of the Swiss Binjamin Wilkomirski is also worth mentioning. At the end of 1955, Wilkomorski published a small 150-page book, *Bruchstücke aus einer Kindheit 1939-1948*, in which he recounted his experiences. The book was translated into a dozen languages and was a worldwide success. The French translation was published in January 1997 by Calmann-Lévy, under the title *Fragments / Une enfance 1939-1945*. The back cover read:

"Binjamin Wilkomirski does not know his date of birth, does not know his precise origins and has no relatives left. He was still very young when the round-ups of Jews in Poland intensified. His father was murdered in front of his eyes, he was torn away from his family and, at the age of four, he was deported to the Majdanek extermination camp. "My earliest memories resemble a field of ruins dotted with isolated images and events. Fragments of memory with hard, sharp edges that today I still cannot touch without hurting myself. Often in chaotic disarray and, for the most part, impossible to classify in chronological order. Fragments that obsessively resist the preoccupation with the order of the adult I have become and that escape the laws of logic". It is these fragments that the author reconstructs here through the eyes of the child he once was. An unforgettable book, a masterpiece of writing and emotion. Binjamin Wilkomirski currently lives in Switzerland. He is a musical instrument maker and clarinettist."

On 22 December 2002, Robert Faurisson summed up the matter in an illuminating article which we reproduce below: "In reality, this 150-page pamphlet is a masterpiece of non-writing and emotionlessness, Faurisson told us. It is a poorly crafted product whose author, at best, plays the bagpipes. Far from discovering "fragments of memory with hard, sharp edges", the reader finds nothing but blandness, incoherence, indefiniteness (in time and space), confusion, vagueness, smoke, vapour, fog and greyness. The action stagnates, the dialogue sounds hollow. The tone is wrong: the hero's constant cries, panics and tantrums are mostly tuneless. If everything is vague, it is on purpose. It is clear that the author has avoided giving details of places, times or characters because he feared cutting himself off with fragments. He claims to have been interned in Majdanek, but refrains from describing the camp, except by locating it on a hill which, in reality, never existed. He then implies that he was in Auschwitz, but does not write the name of Auschwitz, so he cannot be accused of being wrong about the camp. With rare exceptions, the characters do not really have uniforms, ranks, languages, precise jobs or even - and this is the last straw - truly distinctive features; they are no more than ghosts or cardboard bogeymen. The landscapes we traverse are everywhere and nowhere. This attention to erase any compromising detail is characteristic of the liar or the forger. It rules out good faith. It would be wrong to claim that the author ended up believing his own story. Our fraudster is constantly on the alert. He watches himself as liars do. He does not ramble, nor does he give in to illusion. He builds his story piece by piece, sentence by sentence, laboriously."

And Faurisson finished the job: "One hundred and fifty pages of such verbiage translated from German should have been a wake-up call for the most credulous. Everyone should have realised that Binjamin Wilkomirski belongs to the category of false witnesses who, having nothing to say about a lived experience, are reduced to piecing together a jigsaw of clichés, stereotypes, kitsch and prefabricated sentiments. Equally factitious is the account of the atrocities with which the author sprinkles his supposedly autobiographical narrative. In his book, the villains spend most of their time maliciously grabbing children to throw them through a window against a wall, smashing their skulls in, smashing a ball through their foreheads, burying them alive in mud, throwing them into a fire, to make "fuel" out of them (sic) or, more simply, to lift them off the ground by their ears, to lock them in kennels full of vermin, to make them walk on excrement up to their knees, to stick glass sticks "in the little boys' whistles" (p. 60). In a pile of corpses, we see a woman's belly swell and split open; our man can attest to this: "The abdomen tears open and a huge rat, all shiny and smeared with blood, rushes down from the pile of corpses. Other frightened rats emerge from the tangle of corpses and flee: I've seen them, I've seen them! Dead women give birth to rats! Rats! The deadly enemy of the children of the countryside. Rats attack us night after night, their bites inflict horribly painful and incurable wounds, wounds that nothing can heal and that make the children rot alive! (p. 84)".

"Despite its atrocious literary quality and inventions worthy of the Great Puppet Show, Faurisson continued, the book quickly became a bestseller. When it was published, the Shoah elite swooned in ecstasy. They choked with admiration at the strength of the testimony and the talent of the author. Lea Balint, an Israeli specialist on the children of the Shoah, Lawrence Langer, Daniel Goldhagen and Blake Eskin become champions of the cause, along with Wolfgang Benz, director of the Berlin-based Centre for Research on Anti-Semitism, and Annette Wieviorka in France. From the *New York Times* to the *Nouvel Observateur*, from the *Daily Telegraph* and the *Guardian* to *Le Monde*, the media shudders with joy and happiness. In the United States, the book was promoted by the *Holocaust Memorial Museum* in Washington and won the *National Jewish Book Award for Autobiography*, while the *American Library Association* included it in its 1997 "*Best Book for Young Adults*" list. In Britain, it received the *Jewish Quarterly* Literary Award and, in France, the *Mémoire de la Shoah* prize. B. Wilkomirski's oral testimonies have been carefully collected by Steven Spielberg's *Shoah-Foundation*, a foundation set up to collect 50,000 video testimonies in almost fifty countries in order to show the world that revisionists are falsifiers of history. Wilkomirski has travelled and lectured extensively, especially in schools. He amassed a fortune. His first miracle was to find his father in Israel, a Majdanek survivor named Jaakov Morroco.

Under the gaze of the cameras, father and son fell weeping into each other's arms. Second miracle: a Californian who calls herself Laura Grabowski and presents herself as an Auschwitz survivor claims to have met him in that concentration camp. Once again, the reunion took place in front of the cameras at Los Angeles airport. Laura Grabowski welcomed him with open arms, shouting: "He's my Binji!" For her part, she shows the scars of Mengele's media experiments. She is also music. Our clarinettist and his partner go on a lecture and concert tour. They make a pilgrimage to Auschwitz. And there, still in front of the cameras, our hero reveals that Mengele had inflicted medical experiments on him to turn the brown colour of his eyes blue, an episode he had never mentioned in his book. There is an incident that should have been a wake-up call: when asked to describe Mengele, B. Wilkomisrski refuses to do so (*L'enfant des camps de la mort: vérité ou mensonges*, documentary for British television by Christopher Oliglati, 1999).

"As early as 1995, a Swiss journalist, Hanno Helbling, head of the cultural department of the *Neue Zürcher Zeitung*, warned the German publisher Suhrkampf of the hoax. But Hanno Helbling was not lucky enough to be Jewish and was ignored as a vulgar revisionist. It was not until a Jew named Daniel Ganzfried, born in Israel and living in Switzerland, wrote in the Swiss weekly *Die Weltwoche* (27 August and 3 September 1998) that the process was set in motion, leading to a series of revelations about the impostor's true identity. Obviously, all the credit for the discovery goes to the Jew and not to the "revisionist" H. Helbling, whose name would quickly fall into oblivion.

"We learned that Binjamin Wilkomirski's real name was actually Bruno Grosjean. Born as the natural son of Yvonne Berthe Grosjean on 12 February 1941 in Biel (canton of Bern), he was entrusted by her to an orphanage. Adopted by a wealthy couple from Zurich, the Doessekers, he adopted the family name and became known as Bruno Doesseker. His mother died in 1981, receiving his meagre inheritance. He was never Jewish. His birth in Riga is pure invention. He spent his entire childhood in Switzerland, not in Majdanek, Auschwitz or anywhere else in Latvia, Poland or Germany. He never lived in an orphanage in Krakow. A genetic analysis proved that he is not related to Jaacov Morrocco. He only visited Riga, Auschwitz or Krakow as a tourist, long after the war.

"Laura Grabowski, on the other hand, is what you might call a con artist in a skirt. Her real name is Laura Rose Wilson; she was born in the United States to Christian parents in Auburn, Washington state. Ten years earlier, under the pseudonym Lauren Statford, she had written a book in which she presented herself as a victim of satanic rituals, showing scars that she later attributed to Mengele's experiments.

"The impostor starts by fighting the accusations. He mixes protests, threats and moans. In the absence of his real father, he meets his real uncle, who agrees to undergo a genetic test, but the impostor refuses. Testimonies begin to emerge from people who knew him well; it turns out that, from his youth, Bruno had a strong propensity to lie. We learn that a Jewish psychotherapist, Elitsur Bernstein, was involved in the forger's enterprise; a specialist in buried memories, he had helped the clarinettist reconstitute his identity as Binjamin Wilkomirski, supposedly born in Riga, then interned in a Kraków orphanage and deported to Nazi concentration camps. Some Jews then begin to distance themselves from this goy who has played at being a Jew and whose imposture, now all too evident, risks harming the entire community. Raul Hilberg and Yehuda Bauer express their scepticism. Jews like Judith Shulevitz in Canada, or Deborah Dwork and Deborah Lipstadt in the United States, persist in defending the impostor or his work; in their view, it matters little whether the story is authentic or not, for one must be careful not to play into the hands of the revisionists.

"In 1999, Elena Lappin, a Jew of Russian origin, devoted a study to the subject, *The Man with Two Heads*, which was translated and published in 2000 by the publishing house L'Olivier (general director: Olivier Cohen) under the title *L'Homme qui avait deux têtes (The Man with Two Heads)*. This time, the explanation is simple: for Elena Lappin, the author is sincere because he has a split personality. Jorge Semprun does not hesitate to express the same opinion (*Le Journal du Dimanche*, 6 February 2000, p. 27); he takes the opportunity to praise fiction, which, according to him, must "increasingly take over from history"; he states: "This has already happened in the cinema. Spielberg and Benigni have used fiction to go beyond reality, and it clearly works".

But more and more voices were raised to denounce the author's unwitting contribution to the rise of revisionism. Professor Faurisson's account is abbreviated as follows: One after another, the book was withdrawn from the market by the publishers, the Zurich courts took action, and a complaint of fraud was filed. In April 2000, we learned that the examining magistrate had decided to "close the investigation into the author of the false memoirs about Auschwitz". Here is the text from the Swiss Telegraph Agency: "...The Zurich court has closed the investigation into this case. The investigations have shown that there is no concrete evidence to suggest that the author of the book intended to "fraudulently" conceal his true identity.... Although the book has been shown to contain false statements, there is no evidence that its author lied."

"This court decision should have provoked an avalanche of commentary, Faurisson added, but it seems to have been followed by total silence. Today the Wilkomirski affair seems to be over, to the relief, no doubt, of many. And Robert Faurrisson concluded: "It is clear that when it comes to lies about the Holocaust, the Swiss judicial system does not reason any differently from the French, German, Austrian, Dutch, Canadian or Australian systems. It upholds lies committed in good faith, or even lies *possibly* committed in good faith".

But for Faurisson, "the king of impostors" remained Elie Wiesel: "In terms of false testimony," he wrote, "Elie Wiesel continues his career far ahead of Martin Gray, Filip Müller, Rudolf Vrba, Mel Mermelstein, Abraham Bomba, Fania Fénelon and the considerable multitude of other 'Holocaust' mythomaniacs. It remains to be said that one day their fame and fortune as Nobel Peace Prize laureates will not match those of the Rothschilds. For the time being, in his field, Elie Wiesel remains the king of impostors and next to him, let's face it, the goy Bruno Grosjean is almost insignificant".[360]

Misha Defonseca and Binjamin Wilkomirski, both orphans, were obviously pathological cases. As we know, hysteria is extremely contagious and, in this case, the pathology could also have been favoured by regular contact with cult members.

André Malraux was a well-known writer in the second half of the 20th century[361]. He was also General de Gaulle's Minister of Culture from 1959 to 1969. Roger Peyrefitte, another novelist, is certainly not a character we hold in high esteem, but his portrait of André Malraux deserves to be reproduced here: "He used communism, then Gaullism.... The only time I saw him, in the flesh, was thanks to Montherlant. When I returned from Athens, from the central administration, between 1938 and 1940, I was a regular visitor to the National Library... I often met Montherlant there.... We used to go out together and have lunch at the Louis XIV, Place des Victoires. One day he said to me: "Look, there goes Malraux... We didn't greet each other, Montherlant told me. I'm considered a right-winger, he's a red. A bad guy, but a great writer... I'll lend you *La Esperanza*". I gave him back the book a few days later: "I couldn't get past page 12. I admit he's a writer; there are some beautiful formulas, some flashes of brilliance. But reading it requires a constant effort...". In fact, Montherlant, like many

---

[360] Author Anne Kling has summarised several of these cases of Holocaust mythomaniacs in her book *Menteurs et affabulateurs de la Shoah*, Editions Mithra, 2013. (NdT).

[361] André Malraux (1901-1976) was a French novelist, adventurer and politician. He is representative of the French culture that revolved around the second third of the 20th century, and his life combines the novelistic elements of the writer with the expression of the public man, the propaganda of the politician and the reality of the historical events he lived through. This mixture has led some of his critics, such as the biographer Olivier Todd, to consider Malraux "the first writer of his generation to succeed in effectively building his own myth". His novel *La Esperanza (Hope)*, set during the Spanish Civil War, is famous. (wikipedia) (NdT).

others, had been impressed by Malraux's heroic comedy. He told me after the war: "I had the idea of rereading *La Esperance*. And he was right. Like you, I wasn't able to finish it...".[362]

"Malraux did not want his biography to be published. He would have preferred us to confine ourselves to consulting his work. Obviously, his biography is the destruction of his work! What does the *who's who* say, i.e. Malraux himself? Organiser and chief of foreign aviation in the service of the Spanish government. One need only read the memoirs of the commander of the Spanish Republican Air Force, published two or three years ago, to be convinced[363] : they did not know how to get rid of Malraux, inactive, incompetent, he disturbed all the activities of the group. Consequently, although he went to Spain, he did not play any decisive role there...

"Malraux colonel? He gave himself the rank, like Chaban gave himself the rank of general. Malraux in command of the "Alsace Lorraine" brigade? It was founded in June '44, what a good effort. I have the testimony of a man whom I revere and to whom I have already alluded and who was one of the thirteen chiefs of the resistance networks. What did you discover about Malraux? No feat of arms, only the formation of the famous brigade, two months before the liberation...

"Malraux claimed to have blown up a train, but he never gave the same place or the same date. And, I repeat, there is no trace of these supposed feats of arms. As a precaution, he always quoted the same witness, a reliable witness: his accomplice in the opium den, Emmanuel d'Astier de la Vigerie. Do you want another example? In his *Antimemoir*, he tells how he discovered the kingdom of the Queen of Sheba by plane. I knew that story. Jean Vigneau, my first editor, told it to me. As he made that famous

---

[362]Roger Peyrefitte (1907-2000) was a French writer and historian and an advocate of gay rights. Peyrefitte always proclaimed himself openly homosexual, or rather pederast: "I love lambs, not rams" (*J'aime les agneaux, pas les moutons!*). Even more than André Gide, and unlike Henry de Montherlant, whose friend and accomplice he was for a long time, Peyrefitte conceived his literary career as a militancy in favour of the love of ephebes (wikipedia). Henry de Montherlant (1895-1972) was one of the foremost French novelists, essayists and playwrights of his time. The author of some seventy books, he is best known for his novels *Les Bestiaires* (1926), *Les Jeunes Filles* (1936-1939), *Les Garçons* (1969) and his plays *La Reine morte* (1942), *Le Maître de Santiago* (1947), *La Ville dont le prince est enfant* (1951), *Port Royal* (1954) and *Le Cardinal d'Espagne* (1960). He was passionate about bullfighting, the Mediterranean world and the classical period in general, and was elected a member of the French Academy in 1960. After his death (suicide), his ambiguous sentimental and sexual life caused some controversy. (NdT).

[363]Peyrefitte is probably referring to Ignacio Hidalgo de Cisneros' memoirs published in 1961 and 1964 (NdT).

flight in the company of Corniglion-Molinier, I asked him about it directly.... He replied that he and Malraux had agreed to set up this farce and pretend that a few piles of sand were a kingdom that had disappeared...

"Malraux the art historian? When I was in the United States in 1967, a professor at Princeton told me that students got a zero when they referred to the unreadable *Les Voix du silence* [*Les Voix du silence*, an essay on Malraux's art, ndt]. Did he ever talk about love? Always about death. Did he ever smile? Look at his sinister face, which always appeared in sinister stories. His disappearance was presented in Giscardian France in much the same way as De Gaulle's had been presented in Pompidolian France. It is only natural that the official world, the creator of imposture, should want to honour the king of impostors[364]."

It should be noted that André Malraux shared his life with a certain Clara Goldschmidt, whom he had married in 1921, and whom readers of *Psychoanalysis of Judaism* have already met.

Jewish wives seem to exert a certain influence on some writers. Anatole France himself[365], for example, had also married a Jewess, an Austrian Jewess called Armande de Caillavet. Here is the testimony of Xavier Vallat[366] : Anatole France was twenty-four years older than him, but he had shown towards Vallat a certain sympathy; "a curious sympathy, tinged with protective consideration". It was the Dreyfus affair[367] that had separated them: "He had allowed himself to be drawn into Dreyfusism in order to have peace in his false marriage, Vallat wrote. But in private he was a healthy judge of the merits of the case. One day he said to me: "This will all end badly for the country[368] "."

---

[364]Roger Peyrefitte, *Propos secrets*, Albin Michel, 1977, p. 198-202. [Pompidoliana: from the presidency of George Pompidou; Giscardiana: from the presidency of Giscard d'Estaing. NdT.]

[365]Anatole France (1844-1924) was one of the great writers and literary critics of the Third French Republic, considered a moral authority of the first order. He was awarded the Nobel Prize for literature in 1921 for all his work.

[366]Catholic lawyer and extreme right-wing politician, anti-Semite and collaborationist during the Occupation (NdT).

[367]See footnote 63.

[368]Xavier Vallat, *Charles Maurras, No. d'écrou 8.321*, Plon, 1953, p. 20, 22. Xavier Vallat added: "However, once Madame Armande was buried, he published *The Gods are Thirsty*, which is a counter-revolutionary act".

3. The cosmopolitan mentality

The process of blaming the goyim

Blaming the "others" is a strong tendency among Jewish intellectuals. In 1946, Jules Isaac published a book entitled *Jesus and Israel* in which he said: "Some six million Jews murdered simply because they were Jews. To the disgrace, not only of the German people, but of the whole of Christendom. For without centuries of Christian catechesis, preaching and vituperation, Hitler's catechesis, propaganda and vituperation would not have been possible[369]."

All of humanity is guilty of what happened during the Second World War. This is what Elie Wiesel also wanted to tell us: "The world knew and kept silent", he said in a speech in Oslo[370]. Martin Gray also showed the same tendency to blame others: "The whole world is letting us die[371]"; "The whole world let us be murdered[372]...", he wrote.

Alexandre Minkowski, who declared himself a Christian at the beginning of his book, indulged in some less friendly remarks about Catholics in the "appended documents" at the end, and was pleased to publish a letter from a mysterious Catholic reader whose phraseology seemed rather Talmudic. It read: "Christianity has been guilty before God and history of immeasurable atrocities against the Jews. We have created a colossal taboo that is ruining the moral and spiritual health of the entire Western world..... There is only one possible remedy for all this: repentance. We must take seriously the warning of Jesus: "Unless you repent, you will perish" (Luke XIII: 3)...The hour of truth has come for the Christian Church, for the Christian, with regard to Israel. A historic *mea culpa* stands before us as a

---

[369] Jules Isaac, *Jésus et Israël, (1946)*, Fasquelle, Paris, 1959, p. 508; quoted in Léon de Poncins, *El Judaísmo y la Cristiandad*, Ediciones Acervo, Barcelona, 1966, p. 24-25. [A highly recommendable book because of the number of quotations from eminent figures in Judaism and their involvement in the reform brought about by the Second Vatican Council. Reissued by Omnia Veritas in 2015. (NdT)].

[370] Elie Wiesel, *Discours d'Oslo*, Grasset, 1987, p. 13, 22

[371] Martin Gray, *Au nom de tous les miens*, Robert Laffont, 1971, p. 109. (Translation omitted in Plaza & Janés, 1973, p. 102.)

[372] Martin Gray, *En nombre de todos los míos*, Plaza & Janés, Barcelona, 1973, p. 193.

challenge...The sick Church will only be healed and reunited when it has repented[373]."

Alexandre Minkowski's book ended with these lines. All that remains is to kneel before the Jews. But then again, these lines could well have been written by the author himself, usurping the identity of a Catholic to undermine Catholicism from within.

This constant denunciation of the foundations of European civilisation paved the way for the Second Vatican Council (1962-1965) and the reform of the Church, in which Jules Isaac had actively participated.

Naturally, Nahum Goldmann was also another fervent supporter of reform in the Catholic Church. In *The Jewish Paradox*, he explained the role of his fellow bishops in this change: "There is a mixed commission, composed of Catholics and Jews, which meets three times a year to eliminate or amend controversial passages in Catholic books, from the elementary catechism to the manuals used in Catholic seminaries and universities, not forgetting the liturgy and, above all, the Good Friday office. The work is very slow, because the independence of each bishop must be respected and there are hundreds of texts tainted with anti-Semitism; therefore, they must be removed country by country, language by language, and this will take years."

Nahum Goldmann had also met Pope Paul VI: "My position as President of the World Jewish Congress was an obstacle, because the Vatican said: 'We can negotiate with Judaism as a religion, but the Congress is a political organisation[374] '."

Elie Benamozegh was an eminent Italian Jewish rabbi and intellectual, who died in 1900, who also worked feverishly to reform the Catholic Church. He advocated Noachism, a surrogate universal religion for the Goyim envisaged in the Talmud. Gérard Haddad quoted him in one of his books: "Noachism is nothing other than the Catholic Church...but it carries within itself erroneous elements...It must renounce the divinity of Jesus, reinterpret rather than abolish the mystery of the Trinity and reconcile itself with the source from which it sprang. It is a matter of helping Christianity to complete its ultimate evolution" which was, he said, "a return to the principles of what he called the mother of the Churches, Judaism[375]."

---

[373] Alexandre Minkowski, *Un juif pas très catholique*, Ramsay, 1980, p. 289, 290.

[374] Nahum Goldmann, *Le Paradoxe juif*, Stock, Paris, 1976, p. 233.

[375] Gérard Haddad, *Histoire no. 3, Les Juifs en France*, Nov. 1979, special issue, p. 249-251. [Such was the Jewish conception of the world. In heaven one God, the common father of all men, and on earth one family of peoples, among whom Israel is the first-born, charged with teaching and administering the true religion of mankind, of which it is the priest". Elie Benamozegh, *Israël et l'humanité*, (*Israel and Humanity*), Albin Michel, Paris, 1961, p. 40, quoted in Leon de Poncins, *El Judaísmo y la Cristiandad*,

In the aftermath of the Holocaust, a new world religion, based on the suffering of the Jews, seems to be gradually taking root in people's minds, promoted relentlessly by the media system. Esther Benbassa, director of studies at the École Pratique des Hautes Etudes, wrote in *Another History of the Jews* (*Une autre histoire des juifs*, Fayard, 2007): "The Holocaust has been transformed into a veritable theology[376]... The genocide has been sacralised by the term Shoah since the 1970s, and history is now only read in the light of this tragedy...Making the Shoah an almost universal religion, recognisable to all, makes it possible [also] to compensate for the loss of traditions among those who are increasingly distancing themselves from Judaism[377]."

Gary Shteingart, a Russian émigré who had moved to New York in 1978, also expressed this idea in one of his novels, published in 2007: "The Holocaust, when judiciously exploited for purposes of guilt, shame and victimisation, can be an extraordinary tool for Jewish perpetuation[378]."

Naturally, Jewish filmmakers have made numerous films on this subject, to show the full horror that the Christians inflicted on the Jews. Here are some synopses published in *Le Guide des films,* an extensive three-volume work edited by Jean Tulard.

Lucie Aubrac (Fr. 1997) is a film in the glory of the French Resistance couple Lucie and Raymond "Aubrac" (born Samuel). On 21 June 1943, following a denunciation, Raymond Aubrac was arrested with Jean Moulin by the Gestapo. Lucie, his wife, would stop at nothing to free her husband from the clutches of the German police. The Germans are cruel to the point of exaggeration. This is a film by Claude Berri, whose real name is Langmann.

*Schindler's List (*USA, 1993) tells the true story of a German industrialist who saved deported Jews by employing them in his factory. The head of the concentration camp, Amon Goeth, brutally mistreats his Jewish maid

---

Ediciones Acervo, Barcelona, 1966, p. 204-205. And on Noachism see: (https://noahideworldcenter.org/. (NdT)]

[376]The new Holy Trinity, we would say: Auschwitz (Golgotha), the Gas Chamber (the Holy Cross) and the Jewish People (the Divinity Sacrificed for the sins of the world). (NdT).

[377]A 16 March 2016 Pew Research Center article entitled "*A Closer Look at Jewish Identity in Israel and the United States*" provided the results of a survey of Israeli and American Jews about their identity. Both surveys asked Jews about a list of eight possible behaviours and attributes that might be "essential" or "important" to their personal Jewish identity. In both countries, a majority said that remembering the Holocaust was essential to their Jewish identity (73% in the US, 65% in Israel). At https:// www.pewresearch.org/fact-tank/2016/03/16/a-closer-look-at-jewish-identity-in-israel-and-the-u-s/. (NdT).

[378]Gary Shteingart, *Absurdistan*, 2006, Ed. de l'Olivier, 2008, p. 336.

and shoots the prisoners from the balcony of his villa overlooking the camp. The prisoners live in daily terror. The savagery of the German soldiers contrasts with the weakness and innocence of the Jews. This is a film by Steven Spielberg, who also directed *Amistad*, a film denouncing the enslavement of Blacks, forgetting of course the appalling role of the Jewish shipowners.

The Burial of the Potatoes (Poland, 1990): In the spring of 1946, an old saddler returns to his home village after a long spell in the deportation camp and encounters the silent resistance of the other inhabitants. Gradually, he discovers that they are responsible for the death of his son and takes revenge by humiliating them. He ridicules the government representatives and denounces the peasants for their contemptible attitude towards the Jews. The film is by Jan Jakub Kolski, who is not a Polish peasant, of course.

Goodbye, Boys (*Au revoir les enfants,* France, 1987) is a famous film. It tells the story of the friendship between Julien, the son of a Lille industrialist, and Bonnet, a registered Jew with a false identity. The story takes place in a religious school on the outskirts of Paris in 1944. The kitchen boy, expelled from the school for dealing in blackmail, goes to the Gestapo to denounce the Jewish children and Resistance fighters hiding in the school. Bonnet's arrest put a cruel end to this friendship. Once again the finger is pointed at the French bourgeoisie, even though the director, Louis Malle, was also a son of the haute bourgeoisie, albeit Jewish. His film won a Golden Lion at the 1987 Venice Film Festival.

Sophie's Choice is a film by Alan Pakula (USA, 1983): Stingo, a young writer, meets Sophie, of Polish origin, who gradually tells him about her past. Naturally, she is also a survivor of the Auschwitz concentration camp. In a scene worthy of the Great Puppet Show, she recounts how, upon her arrival at the camp, in front of the cattle cars, an SS officer forced her to choose between her son and her seven-year-old daughter, who would end up vanishing in the gas chamber. The scene of suffering is interminable, but it still brings tears to the eyes of gullible viewers.

In Gérard Oury's *L'as des as* (1982), the Nazis are ridiculed by Jean-Paul Belmondo, coach of the French boxing team at the Berlin Olympics.

L'adolescent, by Jeanne Moreau (France, 1978): In 1939, just before the war, Marie, a young Parisian girl, comes to spend the summer holidays with her grandmother in a village in Auvergne. She falls in love with a young Jewish doctor with whom her mother has had a brief relationship. The screenplay is by Henriette Jelinek.

Marathon Man (USA, 1976) is another famous film: a Nazi criminal refugee in Uruguay arrives in New York to trade diamonds (the diamond business is typically Nazi, as we all know). Recognised by a former deportee, he slits his throat in the middle of the street with a knife hidden in his sleeve. There is also a scene in which a Nazi tortures a Jewish prisoner in a dentist's chair. The film is by John Schlesinger, who is not a Nazi.

A Sack of Marbles is a film by Jacques Doillon, based on the novel by Joseph Joffo (France, 1975). During the Occupation, a Jewish hairdresser sends his four children to the south of France. A teacher bullies the Jewish children, the caretaker sells his silence, smugglers take advantage of the situation, and the police and militia maintain order. In short, the French are bastards.

Crossroads of hatred (USA, 1974): After the war, a demobilised Jewish soldier is murdered. Captain Finlay leads the investigation which leads him to an anti-Semitic criminal, Montgomery. He will be killed by the police. No mercy for anti-Semites. A film by Edward Dmytryk, according to Richard Brooks.

Odessa, by Ronald Neame (UK, 1974): In 1963, Nasser sets out to launch plague bacillus rockets on Israel. He is helped by a German organisation for the reconversion of former Nazis, "Odessa". Based on a screenplay by George Markstein.

Michel Drach's *Les Violons du bal* (France, 1973) tells the story of the director's childhood during the war. "He learned the humiliation of being Jewish.... A very personal film, in which Michel Drach tells of his dismay at racial hatred, of his anguish and fears, but also of his immense love of life. He tells it all without false sentimentality, with great tenderness, generosity and restrained emotion". This was Claude Bouniq-Mercier's commentary.

In *The Army of Shadows* (France, 1969), Jean-Pierre Melville shows French Resistance fighters falling into the hands of the Gestapo. The Nazis organise a game of massacre. Simone Signoret plays the role of Lucie "Aubrac". The screenplay is by Joseph Kessel.

Tobruk, (USA, 1967): During World War II, a commando of German Jews in British uniform is tasked with destroying oil reserves in Libya behind German lines. This is not without friction with the old British officers with anti-Semitic prejudices. The film was not directed by an English officer: Arthur Miller, with a screenplay by Leo Gordon, who was also not an anti-Semite.

The Old Man and the Child is a well-known film by Claude Berri (France, 1966): during the Occupation, a young boy is sent to live with an elderly couple in the countryside. Yayo, the old man, is a petainist and an anti-Semite. Unaware that the boy is Jewish, he becomes attached to him. When the boy leaves by bus at the end of the war, the old man will not have noticed anything.

Jericho, by Henri Calef (France, 1946): In 1944, an attack is made on German soldiers in Amiens. The evil Germans gather the hostages in the church for their last night. The screenplay is by Claude Heymann.

Hitler's Madman, by Douglas Sirk (USA, 1942): *Reichsprotektor* Heydrich, commander-in-chief of the Nazi government in Czechoslovakia, is shot dead by two resistance fighters. Himmler decides to raze the village of Ldice to the ground. A horror. Based on a screenplay by Peretz Hirshbein and Melvin Levy.

Getting rid of the Jews would not help either. Let's look at *The City Without Jews* (Austria, 1924): To solve the unemployment and crisis, the chancellor of Utopia decides to expel all Jews in train convoys. A pamphlet is circulated, signed by "true Christians" but actually written by an underground Jew, demanding the return of the Jews. Thanks to a ruse, they soon return and everything returns to normal. The film was directed by a "true Christian": Karl Breslauer.

Actually, anti-Semites should commit suicide. It is the only good thing they can do to redeem themselves. This is what the director of the film *Partir, revenir* (France, 1985) wanted to tell us: When she published her first book, Salomé Lerner remembered....: During the last war, her Jewish father and mother had taken refuge in Burgundy with their friends, Hèléne and Roland Rivière. An anonymous letter (probably a French bastard) had denounced them. They were deported and died in a concentration camp, along with their son Salomé, a great pianist. Salomé was the only surviving member of the family. Roland Rivière took over the investigation and discovered that the culprit, the author of the letter, was his own wife. Hélène had denounced the Lerners for their jealousy; tormented by the weight of shame, Hélène committed suicide. Salome, appeased, was finally able to start writing her first book. According to Claude Bourniq-Mercier, this is a "sympathetic" film by Claude Lellouch.

Incidentally, it should be known that Jews have the right to kill their enemies (they have suffered so much). *La passante du Sans-Soucis (*1982) is a film by Jacques Rouffio: Max Baumstein, esteemed president of the humanitarian organisation International Solidarity, has just killed the Paraguayan ambassador. Arrested, he explains to his wife the reason for his action: in 1933, when he was still a child, he was martyred by the Nazis for being Jewish, and his father was shot dead before his eyes...[379]

The survivors of the extermination camps have been extensively compensated by successive German governments. Fifty years later, new compensation payments continue to be made. On 14 July 2000, for example, a decree published in the Official Journal of the French Republic

---

[379] In May 1926, the Jewish anarchist Samuel Schwarzbard murdered the Ukrainian nationalist leader Simon Petlioura in Paris in the middle of the street. The media hype surrounding the trial led to the founding of the League Against Pogroms, the direct predecessor of the LICRA. The Jewish community mobilised to defend the murderer. Schwarzbard was acquitted.

introduced a compensation measure for orphans whose parents had been victims of anti-Semitic persecution. Article 2 of the decree stipulated that the reparation measure would take the form, at the choice of the beneficiary, of a capital payment of 180,000 francs or an annuity of 3,000 francs per month (enough to rent a studio apartment in Paris in those years). By way of comparison, a war veteran received about 1,300 francs for six months, i.e. just over 200 francs a month. As for orphans whose parents had been "transformed into warmth and light" by American bombs (65,000 French victims), they did not benefit from such largesse either.

The reparations paid by democratic Germany to Jews around the world after the war are immeasurable compared to the stinginess of the French Republic, especially since the miraculous survivors of the death camps were innumerable. Simon Wiesenthal, in his book *The Murderers Among Us*, wrote after the liberation of the camps: "A turbulent stream of frantic survivors crossed Europe. They hitchhiked, made short jeep journeys or hung on as best they could from rickety train carriages without doors or windows. They sat huddled in hay wagons, and others just walked. They used whatever means they could to get a few kilometres closer to their destination[380]."

Nahum Goldmann, as president of the World Jewish Congress, had led the negotiations with Germany to assess the amount of compensation to be paid to the Jews. The journalist interviewed him: "Obtaining German reparations after the war was, by your own admission, one of your most essential achievements. Expelled from Germany by Adolf Hitler, you returned to talk almost on equal terms with Konrad Adenauer. How did your interviews develop?" Nahum Goldmann replied: "Obviously, since hundreds of thousands of survivors have settled in Israel, a very large part of the individual payments indirectly revert to the state: there are thousands of Israelis whose existential basis is made up of German payments. In another passage of his book, he was even more precise: "In 1945, there were almost six hundred thousand Jews, survivors of German concentration camps, whom no country wanted to take in[381]."

Obviously, the generosity of democratic Germany raised the hopes of the children of these "survivors", who soon expected to receive an annuity for the crimes committed against their parents. Apparently many of the sons and daughters of the deportees were themselves traumatised by such a tragedy, and it was only right that Germany should compensate the children of the victims. This led to the creation of the Fisher Fund, named after a

---

[380] Simon Wiesenthal, *The Murderers Among Us*, Editorial Noguer, Barcelona, 1967, (pdf), p. 38.

[381] Nahum Goldmann, *Le Paradoxe juif, Conversations en français avec Léon Abramowicz*, Paris, Stock, 1976, p. 156-164, 237.

lawyer who believed that "psychological or even psychiatric treatment" for 40,000 "mentally and psychologically affected" second-generation survivors should be compensated.

However, in May 2007, the German government made it known that it did not intend to pay these expenses, which did not "fall within the principles of international treaties on reparations[382]." In July of the same year, we read on the English-language website of the Israeli daily *Ynetnews* that the lawyer Gideon Fisher, the creator of the Fisher Fund, had decided to take the case to court. The revisionist information network "Bocage" translated part of the English text: "The undeniable proof that the defendant [Germany] intended to destroy the Jewish people, was that it had even planned to harm the second generation of survivors of the Jewish people knowing that if the final solution was not fully successful, the emotional damage caused to the second generation would be so severe and substantial that it would irreparably affect the Jewish race itself and destroy it completely. These deliberate actions have caused and continue to cause the claimants severe psychological and emotional damage, for which they must be compensated."[383]

The problem is that these psychological disorders had been observed in Jews long before the Second World War. This was precisely why Sigmund Freud, who came from a family of Hasidic Jews, developed psychoanalysis in the late 19th century: to try to cure his fellow Jews, who constituted almost all of his clientele. So it was certainly not the Shoah that disturbed these poor Jews.

On the other hand, it is perfectly legitimate to wonder to what extent these patients with an overflowing imagination - the hysterical phenomenon studied by Freud - can indulge in the morbid and mentally enrich an imaginary shoah from an already sufficiently painful history.

Humiliate and sully the opponent

Jews have a clear tendency to want to humiliate the enemy after they have defeated him[384]. Here, for example, is what Joseph Wechsberg wrote about

---

[382] On 3 May 2007, on the English-language website of the German daily *Spiegel Online International,* an article stated that - according to the spokesperson of the German Ministry of Finance - the German government had already paid about 64 billion euros to Holocaust survivors.

[383] Anne Kling also wrote a book on the astronomical reparations perceived by Jewish victims: *Shoah, la saga des réparations,* Editions Mithra, 2015. (NdT).

[384] In the year 2024, the stunned world watches as the state of Israel wages an inhumane and genocidal war against the Palestinian civilian population of Gaza. In the face of demonstrations of support and solidarity with the Palestinian people, Jews cry anti-

Simon Wiesenthal: "Soon after the war, when Wiesenthal was working for various American agencies, he accompanied American officials on their tours and on several occasions had to personally arrest SS accused of crimes. He saw in their eyes the same expression he had so often seen in the eyes of Jews arrested by the SS. But Wiesenthal noticed a notable difference: some of the Gestapo and SS supermen got down on their knees and begged for mercy, which the Jews never did. Wiesenthal had seen many Jews go to their deaths. Most of them were afraid, some were so terrified that the others had to support them. Some prayed and some cried. But they never begged for their lives[385]." The opposite was probably true.

Simon Wiesenthal himself recounted this highly suspicious testimony. In 1945, after the liberation of the Mauthausen camp, the SS had lost all pride: "Now they seemed afraid to pass me. One SS asked an American soldier for a cigarette. The soldier threw the cigarette he was smoking on the ground. The SS ducked, but another SS was quicker than him and picked up the cigarette butt. The two SS engaged in a scuffle until the soldier ordered them to leave."

Simon Wiesenthal soon had the opportunity to arrest his first Nazi. He was an SS guard named Schmidt. Wiesenthal was accompanied at the time by an American officer, Captain Tarracusio. This is what he wrote about the SS guard: He was an "insignificant little man, looking as anonymous as his name. I went up to the first floor, found him there and arrested him. He did not even try to resist. He was trembling. So was I, but for a different reason. I felt very weak after having climbed the stairs and because of the excitement. I had to sit down for a while... [Schmidt] sat in the jeep, between Captain Tarracusio and me, and begged for mercy. He was crying. He said he had been nothing but "a small fish". Why make him pay for it? He had done nothing wrong. He had been strictly following orders. He swore that he had helped many prisoners. I said to Schmidt: -Yes, you helped the prisoners. I saw you many times. You helped them to the

---

Semitism and protests in favour of the Palestinians are even legally repressed in the West. We have also seen how Tsahal (Israeli army) soldiers harass, abuse and humiliate Palestinians in the videos they post on their social networks. Some media outlets have echoed these humiliations perpetrated:https://www.eldiario.es/internacional/destruccion-humillacion-profanacion-tumbas-videos-muestran-abusos-ejercito-israeli-gaza_1_10856145.html;https://www.eldiario.es/desalambre/videos-odio-soldados-israelies-graban-comparten-redes-abusos-detenidos-palestinos_1_10694952.html. (NdT).

[385] Simon Wiesenthal, *The Murderers Among Us*, Editorial Noguer, Barcelona, 1967, (pdf), p. 17.

crematorium. Then he said no more. He sat there quietly, sunk into the back seat, wringing his trembling fingers until we reached the camp[386]."

Jewish novelists like to see the Goyim on their knees, trembling with fear before them. Arnold Mendel's novel *Tikoun* offers a good example of this. The setting is Paris in the 1930s. One night, in the Rue des Francs-Bourgeois, militants of the ACA (Alliance Against Anti-Semitism) caught red-handed a guy pasting an ignoble sign on a wall saying: "France for the French! Blum to the wall! Down with the Jews![387]" Arnold Mandel disembowelled: "The members of the ACA were neighbourhood kids, the sons of tailors and beanies, full of energy and not at all puny, dashing and with a heart full of hatred for the fascists. The French Action militant[388], with his bucket and paintbrush, was alone". He felt, Mandel wrote, "a most comical fear of anyone but himself. You could see his skinny buttocks quivering under the flannel of his student trousers and his forehead was beaded with sweat. Jewish boys surrounded him. They had ordered him to finish his homework, to have some fun, before knocking him out." They beat him to a pulp, but fortunately he was saved in time. Here the hero-narrator rose to defend the "rat-goy" in a long plea, in the name of fairness and the well-known moral principles of the Talmud: "They murmured, then laughed, and I won my case, perhaps also because a downpour fell and they were in a hurry to take shelter[389]."

The famous Holocaust eyewitness Martin Gray also had this inclination in his account *In the Name of All Mine*. In Leipzig, Germany, at the end of the war, he practised his longed-for revenge and "scouted the big game": the SS, all vile and "servile", who "begged for small advantages[390]." As did Wladyslaw Szpilman, in his story *The Pianist*, when he wrote: ""Quite a few people escaped alive during the war because of the cowardice of the

---

[386] Simon Wiesenthal, *The Murderers Among Us*, Editorial Noguer, Barcelona, 1967, (pdf), p. 35, 36-37.

[387] Leon Blum (1872-1950) was a socialist politician, one of the leaders of the French Section of the Workers' International (SFIO) and President of the Council, serving as head of government of the Popular Front. (NdT).

[388] Action *Française* (AF, *Action Française*) is a French nationalist and realist political movement of the "extreme right". It was founded in 1899, at the height of the Dreyfus affair, with the aim of carrying out an intellectual reform of nationalism. Originally structured as a republican nationalism, it quickly became monarchist under the influence of Charles Maurras and his doctrine of integral nationalism, which criticised the legacy of the French Revolution from anti-democratic, anti-Semitic, anti-secularist and anti-secularist positions. (wikipedia, NdT).

[389] Arnol Mandel, *Tikoun*, Mazarine, 1980, p. 43, 44

[390] Martin Gray, *En nombre de todos los míos*, Plaza & Janés, Barcelona, 1973, p. 296-297. [They swore for their children, for their mother. They were afraid and hungry. They were servile", p. 297].

Germans, who only liked to show courage when they knew they were far outnumbered by their enemies[391].""

In fact, these testimonies correspond perfectly to the Jewish spirit in general. In chapter XLII of his *Essai sur les moeurs et l'esprit des nations (1756) (Essay on the customs and spirit of nations)*, Voltaire had already written: "The Jewish nation...rampant in misfortune and insolent in prosperity".

It is also by the insults and slanders he utters that one can almost unerringly recognise a Jewish intellectual, whatever his name. Take, for example, how the well-known historian William Shirer scathingly portrayed the National Socialist dignitaries in his world-famous book *The Rise and Fall of the Third Reich*, published in 1960. Anton Drexler, one of the founders of the Nazi party: "A gaunt, bespectacled man, lacking proper training, with an independent way of thinking, but of narrow and confused convictions, a poor writer and a worse orator." Dietrich Eckart, one of the spiritual fathers of National Socialism, "acute journalist, mediocre poet and playwright... had led for some time, like Hitler in Vienna, the vagabond life of a bohemian became a drunkard, indulged in morphine and ended up confined in an institution for mental illness." Julius Streicher, one of Hitler's favourite companions, Gauleiter of Franconia: "This depraved sadist...was one of the most disreputable men around Hitler...His celebrated weekly magazine, *Der Stuermer*, fed on lewd tales of Jewish sex crimes and Jewish ritual murders; its obscenity produced nausea...He was also a notorious propagandist for pornography." Herman Goering, the famous aviation ace, "had spent most of his exile in Sweden since the 1923 *putsh*, was cured of his addiction to narcotics in the Langbro asylum" but "his epileptic wife, whom he loved deeply, had contracted tuberculosis and had become an invalid." Goebbels, the "atheist young Rhenish boy with a useless foot, a lively intelligence and a complicated, neurotic personality...was already a vehement, fanatical nationalist orator." "This little lame fanatic boiled over with ideas that were useful to the Führer." Alfred Rosenberg, "the important and dim-witted pseudo-philosopher who was one of Hitler's early mentors and who...had launched a veritable torrent of books and pamphlets of confused content and style culminating in a seven hundred page work entitled *The Myth of the Twentieth Century,* a ridiculous hodgepodge of his ideas about Nordic supremacy...Hitler always had a warm place in his heart for this dull, stupid, bumbling amateur philosopher." He also mentioned "the homosexual Roehm..." As well as Martin Bormann, "a sinister and servile individual...a sort of mole who

---

[391]Wladyslaw Szpilman, *The Pianist of the Warsaw Ghetto*, Turpial Amaranto, Madrid, 2003, p. 176.

preferred to hole up in the shady recesses of party life to forge his intrigues." Not forgetting Heinrich Himmler, "the poultry farmer [chicken breeder, ndt] who, with his spectacles, could be taken for a peaceful, mediocre schoolmaster[392] ", and Rudolf Hess: "The simian-fronted man, the Führer's alter ego in the Nazi party leadership, had a blind faith in astrology....nothing personally ambitious and loyal as a dog to the leader...confused mind, though less brutalised than Rosenberg, he flew to England in the illusory hope of negotiating peace there[393]." There was also "Dr. Robert Ley, a chemist by profession and a habitual drinker"; "Wilhelm Frick, the only grey personality. He was a typical German civil servant"; "the economics maniac Feder". And all of them led by "the former vagabond Adolf Hitler...".

"Such was the bizarre collection of unbalanced people who founded National Socialism...the conglomeration of men around the head of the National Socialists.

"In a normal society, they would surely have been cast aside as a grotesque collection of people who did not fit in. In the last days of the Weimar Republic, however, they began to appear to millions of confused Germans as genuine saviours[394]." The National Socialists thus had "abnormal brains", whereas the Jews, as is well known, are perfectly sane.

Since the end of the war, cosmopolitan propaganda has also imposed the idea that the French behaved en masse like bastards who denounced Jews to the German authorities. On closer examination, however, we realise that this wicked disposition was mainly on the part of certain Jews, who denounced their enemies to the public vindictiveness, such as Pierre Dac, for example, who broadcast on English radio lists of Frenchmen to be liquidated.

---

[392]William L. Shirer, *The Rise and Fall of the Third Reich, volume I*, Booket, Planeta, Barcelona, 2013, p. 67, 70-71, 86, 214-215, 184, 217, 218, 72, 218, 217
[393]William L. Shirer, *The Rise and Fall of the Third Reich, volume II*, Booket, Planeta, Barcelona, 2013, p. 284, 282, 280.
[394]William L. Shirer, *The Rise and Fall of the Third Reich, Volume I*, Booket, Planeta, Barcelona, 2013, p. 217, 72, 71, 218-219. [We must reproduce below a paragraph by William Shirer in which he demonstrates his great knowledge of Jewish biblical history: "Such were Adolf Hitler's ideas, laid out in all their terrifying starkness as he lay in Landsberg prison...He looked across the majestic Alps to his native Austria, dictating a torrent of words to his faithful Rudolf Hess and dreaming of the Third Reich he would build...and rule with an iron fist. That he would one day build it and win it was something he did not doubt in the least, for he was possessed of that burning messianic feeling common to so many geniuses who have come out of nowhere throughout history. He would unify a chosen people who had never before been politically a unitary whole. It would purify their race. It would make them strong. It would make its children the lords of the land." Rise *and Fall of the Third Reich, Volume I*, p. 140].

The Jan Karski Report confirmed this dismal trend. In February 1940, Jan Karski had written a report for the Polish government in exile, in which he mentioned Polish feelings towards the Jews, who actively collaborated with the Soviet occupiers in the East of the country: "It is certainly true that the Jewish Communists adopted an enthusiastic stance towards the Bolsheviks, regardless of the social class from which they came," he wrote. Saul Friedländer, who recounted this testimony, added: "Karski, however, ventured the explanation that the prevailing satisfaction, notable among working-class Jews, was due to the persecution they had suffered at the hands of the Poles. What he found astonishing was the lack of loyalty of many Jews, their readiness to denounce the Poles to the Soviet police and the like[395]."

We believe we again recognise another accusatory projection in Martin Gray's testimony. After the war, he left for America. In New York he was reunited with his family, who had not been exterminated. At first he worked in a butcher's shop: "I worked in the house of a butcher on 110th Street: I learned to cut meat, to press a pedal that falsified the weight when the package was put on the scales. The butcher paid well, to avoid complaints". But Gray had too many scruples and only stayed with the butcher for a few days: "Then he often gave the right weight. One day, just as I was going out, I went to see the master: 'Pay me,' I said, 'I won't come back. He swore in German, cursed the one who had recommended me". Martin Gray could not hide his disgust: "There, in the heart of New York, lived also that race of executioners whom he knew perfectly well. That race was everywhere: in Warsaw, in Zambrow, in Zaremby; it took the mask of an SS, of a Polish village mayor, of a Soviet colonel or of that thieving butcher. It was necessary never to make a pact with them, at any price, and to know how to renounce survival, to build one's own fortress, rather than be an accomplice. With them, whoever they may be, we must always be at war[396]."

In our humble opinion, it was probably a Jewish butcher who falsified the weights. We have read similar anecdotes in Yiddish literature. And in any case, it is hard to imagine a Jew like this Martin Gray handling pork in a goy (non-kosher)butcher's shop.

Haman's ears

---

[395] Saul Friedländer, *The Third Reich and the Jews (1939-1945), The Years of Extermination*, Galaxia Gutenberg, Barcelona, 2009, p. 90.
[396] Martin Gray, *En nombre de todos los míos*, Plaza & Janés, Barcelona, 1973, p. 321.

As we have seen, Jews always try their best to avoid military service, especially when the country in which they live resists their influence. But they can be fierce and fighters when it comes to securing the triumph of Judaism, particularly when it is at stake to promote the establishment of open and tolerant democratic regimes in defeated countries. Many of them, for example, joined the International Brigades in Spain, the French Resistance or the Red Army[397]. It would therefore not be surprising if, in the 16th century, after the expulsion from Spain, they formed "revenge groups" to fight alongside the Turks in the Mediterranean and Eastern Europe.

Let us not forget that the Ottomans had twice come to the gates of Vienna, in 1529 and 1683. Cerveny Kamen Castle, northeast of Bratislava, is located a few dozen kilometres east of the Austrian capital in Slovakia. This medieval fortress, built in the second half of the 13th century, was later transformed into a comfortable manor house. In one of the castle's rooms you can admire various weapons used in battles against the Turks. Behind a glass case is a curious machete taken from the Turks, which was used to cut off the ears of Christians. The metal weapon, which is about 40 cm long, is flat and rounded, but above all it has a hole in the centre in the shape of a drop of water, slightly larger than an ear. Three other holes have been drilled next to it, in the shape of three Stars of David, which is probably not a coincidence.

Jews have a long tradition of cutting off the ears of their enemies, judging by the celebrations of the religious holiday of Purim, when Jews all over the world eat cakes called "Haman's ears". Here is the story of this very famous episode in Jewish history:

The story is set in Susa, the capital of Persia, in the time of King Ahasuerus. One day, Ahasuerus gave the nobles of his kingdom a splendid banquet that lasted several days. On the seventh day, the king ordered Queen Vashti, adorned in her most beautiful clothes, to appear before him so that everyone could admire her, for she was very beautiful. But the queen refused to obey, and the king was so irritated that he disowned her. So they brought the most beautiful girls from all over the kingdom so that King Ahasuerus could choose a new queen.

An Israelite named Mordecai, who was raising his niece Esther, introduced her as his daughter. Esther, who was very beautiful, was chosen by the king, but, on Mordecai's advice, she carefully concealed her Jewish origins. So there was a crypto-Jew in the king's bed. Mordecai, having

---

[397]Read in *Jewish Fanaticism*. [In Spain, almost a third of the brigadists were Jewish. Another third were French. As for the "French" resistance, it was actually anti-fascist and not necessarily French, being composed mainly of Jews and Communists of all nationalities].

heard that two of the palace guards wanted to kill Ahasuerus, informed Esther, who told King Ahasuerus. The two guards were hanged, and the deed was recorded in the annals of the kingdom.

However, Ahasuerus had chosen as his favourite an Amalekite named Haman, who was then prime minister. The king ordered everyone to prostrate themselves before him, but Mordecai did not do so. Haman was filled with anger and swore that he would destroy not only Mordecai, but also all the Jewish people. He turned to the king and said, "There is a people scattered throughout your kingdom whose laws are different from those of your other subjects. If that is your wish, order this nation to be exterminated." Ahasuerus took the ring off his finger and handed it to Haman, saying, "Do as you wish with the Jews." And Haman sent sealed letters to all the provinces of the kingdom, ordering the slaughter of the Jewish nation on the 13th day of the month of Adar.

When Mordecai heard of the misfortune that threatened the Israelites, he tore his clothes, covered himself with sackcloth, sprinkled ashes on his head, and went out into the city, weeping and wailing bitterly, and all the Israelites fell into anguish. He told Esther of Ahasuerus' edict and urged her to go to the king and ask for clemency for her people. Esther replied, "Do you not know that it is forbidden for anyone, not even me, to appear before the king without being summoned, on pain of death? - What," Mordecai replied, "does Esther fear death when it comes to saving her people? God made her queen; who knows whether it was not that she might be the deliverer of Israel? Esther replied, "For three days and three nights let all the Jews of Shushan fast and pray for me, that God may show me favour in the sight of the king, and if I must die, I will die."

At the end of those three days, Esther, dressed in her best jewellery, appeared before the king. He was sitting on his throne. As soon as he saw her, he handed her the golden sceptre in his hand. She approached the king and knelt down. What do you have, Queen Esther," she said, "and what do you ask for? If it were half my kingdom, I would give it to you?

- King," said Esther, "if you have found grace in me, I beg you to grant me my life and the lives of my people, for we have an enemy who wants to take them away from us.

- Who and where is this man?" cried the king indignantly.

- It is that cruel Haman, here present; Haman wants to exterminate the Jews, and those people are my people. Haman was confused. One of his servants then told Ahasuerus that Haman had set up a gallows fifty cubits high in his courtyard to hang Mordecai. "Let him be hanged there," said the king. And this order was carried out immediately.

Ahasuerus then issued a new edict to annul the first, and the Israelites turned from mourning to rejoicing and celebrated feasts. In memory of this deliverance, Esther and Mordecai instituted an annual feast on the 14th of Adar: the feast of Purim.[398]

In the Old Testament, the book of Esther gives more details about the attitude of the Jews. "They wrote in the name of King Ahasuerus and sealed it with the king's ring. The letters were sent by couriers, riders on horses from the royal stables. In the letters the king granted that the Jews of all the cities might assemble to defend their lives, to exterminate, kill and annihilate the people of every town or province that attacked them with weapons, together with their children and their wives, and to plunder their goods, and this on one day, in all the provinces of King Ahasuerus, on the thirteenth day of the twelfth month, which is the month Adar.(Esther VIII: 10-12, Jerusalem Bible[399]) The Jews put all their enemies to the sword; it was a slaughter, an extermination: they did what they would to their

---

[398] According to *Histoire Sainte*, by M. Fresco, Editions Librairie Fresco, Paris.

[399] Translations at www.Bibliatodo.com. In the translation Biblia Kadosh Israelita Messianica, Esther VIII: 12, 13, a supposed letter of King Ahasuerus is reproduced:

" (...) *For Haman, a Macedonian [Amaleki], the son of Hamdatha, being indeed a stranger to Persian blood, and very distant from our kindness, and as a stranger received us, had hitherto obtained the favour which we showed towards all nations, and that he was called our father and was continually honoured by all the people near the king. But he, without showing his great dignity, devoted himself to deprive us of our kingdom and life; having by manifold and malicious deceits, sought for us destruction, as of Mordecai [Mordecai] who saved our lives, and continually sought our good, as also the blameless Esther, partaker of our kingdom, with all her nation. For by this means he sought, finding us destitute of friends, to have translated the kingdom of the Persians to the Macedonians. But we find the Yahudim [Jews], whom this wicked wretch had delivered over to their utter destruction, not evildoers, but living by the most righteous laws; and that they are children of the Most High and Almighty, the living Elohim, who has ordained the kingdom both to us and to our progenitors in the most excellent manner. Therefore, you would do well not to put into execution the letters sent to you by Haman the son of Hamdatha. For he who was the workman of these things is hanging at the gates of Shushan with all his family. Elohim who reigns over all things, will swiftly dictate vengeance upon him according to his due. Therefore, you will publish the copy of this letter in all places, that the Yahudim may live freely according to their own laws. And that you will help them, that even on the same day, being the thirteenth day of the twelfth month Adar, that they may be avenged upon those who in time of their affliction will lay upon them. For the Almighty Elohim has returned in joy the day where the chosen people should have perished. You, therefore, among your solemn feasts keep it on a high day with all feasting; that now and hereafter there may be safety for us and the stricken Persians; but for those who plot against us, a memorial of destruction. Therefore, every city or country whatsoever they be that do not do according to these things, shall be destroyed without mercy with fire and sword, and shall be rendered not only impassable to men, but also most hated by wild beasts and birds for ever.*" "*A copy of the edict was to be promulgated as a decree throughout the kingdom and proclaimed to all peoples, and the Yahudim were to be ready on that day to take vengeance on their enemies.*" (NdT).

adversaries...The Jews of the remaining provinces of the king gathered together to defend their lives and their safety against their enemies; they slew of their adversaries 75,000, but they did not plunder their goods. This happened on the thirteenth day of the month of Adar, and on the fourteenth day they rested, making it a day of joyful feasting (Esther IX: 5, 16-17, Jerusalem Bible).

This is the story of the Purim holiday, which Jews all over the world celebrate every year in February-March on our calendar: a bit like Ukrainians celebrating a bloody pogrom every year, but so what?

Purin means "chance" in Hebrew. The date of the extermination of the Jews, 13 Adar, was decided with the help of dice. For this holiday, all Jews dress up in costume, because it is said that God acted in the mask of Esther. The custom of dressing up as biblical characters is widespread among Jews. In Israel, a large costume parade is held in the streets of Tel Aviv. Children dress up as little Mordecai or Esther and shake their rattles. In schools, teachers strip off their dignity and go and sit at their pupils' desks while the pupils take their places. These joyous celebrations are preceded by a day of fasting, "the fast of Esther", because Esther had asked her people to fast and pray with her before she ventured to intercede for them with King Ahasuerus.

In the synagogue, the feast of Esther is celebrated with the reading of the Scroll of Esther, one of the five scrolls that make up the Hagiographa. On this day, it is permitted to express great joy, even within the walls of the synagogue. Loud whistles, percussions and the clanging of rattles punctuate the reading at the mention of the name of Haman or his sons.

The Talmud also recommends drinking and getting drunk during Purim, until one can no longer distinguish between saying "cursed be Haman" and "blessed be Mordechai" (the Hebrew language allows for this play on words). It is not a matter of wallowing under the table, but of reaching a level where concepts are understood beyond their mere enunciation.

Relatives and friends also give each other gifts and on this occasion eat doughnuts called "Haman's ears". These triangular-shaped doughnuts refer to the custom of cutting off the ears of "criminals".

After this, let us now look at the case of John Demjanjuk, known as "Ivan the Terrible", the Ukrainian-born Nazi who spread terror in the Treblinka camp in Poland. The man was arrested many years after the end of the war, in violation of all principles of the rule of law. An American citizen of Ukrainian origin, he was handed over by the US authorities to Israel, which brought him to justice as the "Treblinka monster". Legions of witnesses had described under oath the havoc wreaked by "Ivan the Terrible" at Treblinka.

The Swiss historian Jürgen Graf reported what these "witnesses" had said: "He had murdered 800,000 Jews with his own hands with the exhaust fumes of a ramshackle Russian tank. He cut off the ears of Jews and then gave them back to them in the gas chamber. With a bayonet he cut chunks of flesh from their bodies. With a sabre he cut open the abdomens of pregnant women before they were gassed. With his sword he cut off the breasts of Jewish women on their way to the gas chambers. He shot and beat to death, stabbed, strangled, flogged Jews to death or left them to starve to death slowly."

Demjanjuk was sentenced to death. In the meantime, Israeli judicial authorities acknowledged that the Ukrainian had probably never been to Treblinka. They then considered charging him with mass murder at the Sobibor camp (the only evidence against Demjanjuk was a valid Sobibor identity card, forged by the KGB; the paper of this document contained, according to an analysis carried out in the US, a photochemical component that had only been used since the 1960s). But the problem is that Demjanjuk was identified by a cohort of witnesses under oath as the "Treblinka monster", his case being an impressive proof of the value of witness statements in trials of this type[400]."

So this "Demjanjuk" had probably never cut off anyone's ears. As for the disembowelled women and the babies whose heads had been smashed against the walls, one could bet that once again it was a case of accusatory inversion. "The assailant screams for his throat to be slit. The trick is as old as Moses", wrote Louis Ferdinand Céline in *Bagatelles pour un massacre (Bagatelles for a massacre)*.

A pathological will to power

We know the fertile imagination of the children of Israel, self-absorbed for centuries. We also know their thirst for power. Indeed, Jewish suffering also finds an outlet in the quest for power, no doubt to protect themselves from the supposed hostility of the "others". While there are Jews living in poverty, there are also rich, very rich, immensely rich Jews, and their number among the world's billionaires (in billions) is completely disproportionate.

The role played by Jews in the creation of Hollywood is quite obvious, considering that Jews, the "priest-people" par excellence, have a message

---

[400] Jürgen Graf, *El Holocausto bajo la lupa*, Editorial Revisión, Buenos Aires, 1997, p. 71, 72. (Source: Rullmann, *Der Fall Demjanjuk* ["The Demjanjuk Case"]). Here is another example: on 1 August 2003, the Civil Court of Rome (Italy) convicted for defamation a certain Rosina Stame, daughter of Ugo Stame, for repeatedly claiming that her father had been tortured and that her torturer was none other than Erich Priebke, an SS officer; the accusations turned out to be totally unfounded (*Tabou*, volume 7, Ed. Akribeia, 2004, p. 60).

to convey to all mankind. It is therefore no coincidence that the Hollywood film studios were all founded by Jewish entrepreneurs.

Hollywood, Jacques Attali told us in *The Jews, the World and Money*, is a Jewish fiefdom: "Today's essential firms are: Universal, Fox, Paramount, Warner Bros, MGM, RCA and CBS are all creations of Jewish immigrants from Eastern Europe". "Adolf Zukor arrived from Hungary in 1890 (...) in 1917 he founded Paramount Pictures, which he put at the service of war propaganda". Carl Laemmle, a native of Laupheim in Württemberg, apprenticed to a tailor, founded Universal Studios in 1912. In 1923, the three Warner brothers, born in Poland, founded Warner Bros. Mayer, born in Minsk, founded Metro. In 1916, Samuel Goldfish founded Goldwyn, which he merged with Metro in 1924. The firm becomes Metro Goldwyn Mayer, "then MGM, which many translate in Yiddish - the language commonly spoken in Hollywood at the time - by Mayer Ganze Mishpoje (the whole Mayer family)[401] ". Although Dysney was not founded by a Jew, its current president bears the same surname as the famous Bolshevik leader: Eisner.

This information was confirmed by the supermarket writer Paul-Loup Sulitzer in his 1986 book *L'Impératrice*: In 1915, he wrote, "Hollywood became the Mecca of the film industry...Carl Laemmle's Universal, Zukor and Lasky's Paramount, and William Fox's Fox (a Hungarian Jew who started out as a suburban clown with a sidekick under the name of Schmaltz Brothers)...[402] "

In 1988, an American named Neal Gabler published a book on the subject: *An Empire of Their Own*, subtitled: *How the Jews Invented Hollywood*[403]. Neal Gabler took us into that world of "rogues, privateers and braggarts in the early film industry[404]." He left us with some interesting portraits of these Hollywood *tycoons*, who shaped so much of the Western imagination for several generations.

By the early 1930s, Louis Mayer's MGM had dethroned Zukor's Paramount. Louis B. Mayer "was always an extremist...Everything he did had to be bigger, a common enough affliction among Jews."

---

[401] Jacques Attali, *Los judíos, el mundo y el dinero*, Fondo de cultura económica, 2005, Buenos Aires, p. 416.
[402] Paul-Loup Sulitzer, *L'Impératrice*, Stock, Le Livre de Poche, 1986, p. 293.
[403] Neal Gabler, *Le Royaume de leur rêve, la saga des juifs qui ont fondé Hollywood*, 1988, Calmann-Lévy, 2005. Original title: *An Empire of their own, How the Jews invented Hollywood*, Crown Publishers Inc, New York, 1988, translated from English into French by Joahan-Frederik Hel Guedj. Neal Gabler, *An Empire of their own, How the Jews invented Hollywood*, Confluences, 2015.
[404] Neal Gabler, *An Empire of Their Own, How the Jews Invented Hollywood*, Confluences, 2015, p. 198.

Louis Mayer was a "*showman*" and obviously exhibited all the symptoms of a hysterical personality[405]. Neal Gabler recounted the impressions the character had left on some managers and directors: "A grandiloquent egomaniac"; "others saw his extremism as a kind of voracity"; "watching Mayer made me think of a praying mantis," said one director, "He is a predator... he preys on others and plays with them"; "others, even, thought his sentimentality was calculating and manipulative, expressed only to make an impression". And also: "Go see Louis B. Mayer," mentioned one director. Mayer," mentioned one director, "was always an experience. He was histrionic. He could lie on the floor, pray, sing and illustrate the kind of movies he wanted to make you see, sappy movies that no one would dare to make, and he could have monstrous rages"... Tears came easily to his eyes. He was famous for picking out reluctant MGM stars and pouring out sweet words of praise and affection until Mayer would burst into tears under the weight of his own performance. But it wasn't all mere showmanship. Mayer was a man who intoned his life in the highest emotional key, and he could also be just as emotional and sentimental in his private life. "As a man in touch with his emotions, he was capable of getting emotional in many situations, his grandson recalled. He would cry at the movies. The breadth of his emotions was not confined to feelings. Every emotion was enormous. Although it was difficult for him to get angry, he had a terrifying character...Sometimes he even resorted to force."

Here are some explanations that our readers will be able to decipher as they delve deeper into this book: His father, Jacob, who had emigrated from Russia, was a peddler. "Jacob was a failure in business and with his family. His refuge was religion...Jacob Mayer was among the righteous who placed the Torah...and was clearly one of the pillars of the Jewish community."

He was "described as "stingy and tyrannical", and there was certainly no love between father and son". "The family was terribly poor..... His father shamelessly exploited him...while his mother cried, fearing for his safety. At home he was the victim of his father's abuse and humiliation[406] ". His relations with his mother were very different: "During his formative years, his only point of reference had been his mother. He spoke of her with such idealism that even his grandson later wondered if Mayer was trying to compensate for some kind of lack or neglect. His daughter wrote that "he felt that everything good in him he had inherited from his mother"...As long as he lived, his mother's portrait hung above Mayer's bed[407]."

---

[405] Read *Psychoanalysis of Judaism*.
[406] Neal Gabler, *An Empire of Their Own, How the Jews Invented Hollywood*, Confluences, 2015, p. 164-168.
[407] Neal Gabler, *An Empire of Their Own, How the Jews Invented Hollywood*, Confluences, 2015, p. 173.

Harry Cohn followed in the footsteps of Louis B. Mayer to build up Columbia Pictures, which he ran with an iron fist. Cohn was the son of a German Jewish carver and a Russian Jewish mother. He had some of the same faults as his peers:

"According to one writer who worked hard there, Cohn ran Columbia like his own police state. He was tough, terrifying, ruthless and fearless, unbearably rude, foul-mouthed, flamboyant, a knuckle-headed power machine who had total financial and physical control of his self-made empire...He was said to have listening devices in every sound stage and could tune in to any conversation on the equipment, and shout over a loudspeaker if he heard something he didn't like."

"Among the untamed forces of Hollywood, Cohn, intimidating and disdainful, was probably the most fearsome... Cohn was fully aware of this effect; he was an eminence at Columbia Pictures, and he arrogated power to himself the way a monarch arrogates divine power." "It was nine yards from Cohn's office door to his desk, a walk visitors called the last mile. "Why do you have the table here, at this distance? - he was once asked by his friend, Columbia executive Jonie Taps - he said: 'By the time they get to the table, they're already defeated. Ever heard of psychology? He knew the effect it had. By the time they got there they'd shit their trousers[408] "."

Harry Cohn represented "the profane, vulgar, cruel, greedy, philandering tycoon". He was also "cunning and manipulative" and, "as with other Hollywood Jews, class, lack of education and religion conspired to do him great harm". "Cohn was consumed by his tough-guy pose...His obvious contempt and cynicism were the weapons of anger" and "" he instinctively believed that only through hostility, conflict and acrimony could superior work be done"." "The pathetic thing was that he was a man torn...between two different personalities which he felt he had to maintain. On the one hand, he wanted to be the toughest, most ruthless manager in Hollywood, the one everyone feared. On the other hand, he wanted to be seen as a man of taste and judgment, to be envied.

His extreme aggressiveness was undoubtedly due to problems in his childhood. This is what Neal Gabler wrote about it: "Cohn felt it necessary to distance himself from his past, as Louis B. Mayer did, because he saw it as a possible crack in his facade of invincibility. Mayer did, because he saw it as a possible crack in his facade of invincibility. He never told even his closest friends what demons haunted him as a child, or what abuse he may have suffered[409]."

---

[408] Neal Gabler, *An Empire of Their Own, How the Jews Invented Hollywood*, Confluences, 2015, p. 308, 248-249.
[409] Neal Gabler, *An Empire of Their Own, How the Jews Invented Hollywood*,

Naturally, some will explain his character by the suffering caused by the anti-Semitism he endured as a child. But our readers will soon know what to make of the traumas suffered by Jewish children.

Regarding the two Warner brothers, Jack and Harry, Neal Gabler provided the testimony of Universal executive Jesse Lasky's daughter Betty: "We went to the pool, and I remember two of the Warners brothers were there...I remember being terrified of them...They were two brutal guys. I wasn't used to guys like them...ghetto guys. That's what they looked like. They were very ugly [monstrous], but a different kind of ugly [a monstrosity], ghetto...It was like when a kid goes to the circus and sees a science fiction show[410] [and sees a monster[411]]."

They were also sexual predators: "Jack Warner flaunted his conquests as if they were trophies". But "the most notorious and insatiable sexual predator was Harry Cohn." Neal Gabler related this anecdote here: "Corinne Calvet, a pretty, generously proportioned young French starlet, was ordered by Cohn to come to his yacht to discuss a contract. That night Cohn, in his pyjamas, went like a bull to her room and attacked her. Calvet, who found him physically repugnant, managed to prevent him from going any further and hide until her boyfriend, actor Rory Calhoun, was able to arrive later that night to get her off the boat and to safety[412]."

In relation to a more recent era, Peter Biskind's 2004 book *Sex, Lies and Hollywood* also presented rather edifying accounts of the behaviour of personalities such as Bob and Harvey Weinstein[413], the founders of the

---

Confluences, 2015, p. 250, 251, 280

[410] Neal Gabler, *An Empire of Their Own, How the Jews Invented Hollywood*, Confluences, 2015, p. 355.

[411] Neal Gabler, *Le Royaume de leur rêve, la saga des juifs qui ont fondé Hollywood*, 1988, Calmann-Lévy, 2005, p. 282. (The translations differ. In general, we found the French translation more crude. N.T.)

[412] Neal Gabler, *An Empire of Their Own, How the Jews Invented Hollywood*, Confluences, 2015, p. 363, 364. This reminds us of what Louis-Ferdinand Celine wrote in 1937 in *Bagatelles pour un massacre (Bagatelles for a Massacre)*, his famous pamphlet: "You want a career? Pretty? You want to be flattered! Tell me... You want to be queen of the Jewish universe!... Do you want to be sovereign, little bitch?... World's favourite? All right!..."

[413] In October 2017, *The New York Times* and *The New Yorker*, published dozens of allegations of sexual abuse against Harvey Weinstein for harassment, sexual abuse and even rape. As a result, he was expelled from his company and the Academy of Motion Picture Arts and Sciences and his wife filed for divorce. Weinstein was arrested and charged with rape in New York on 25 May 2018...From the accusations of Rose McGowan and Ashley Judd, more than 80 women joined in, alleging repeated sexual misconduct by Harvey Weinstein, who took advantage of his power and influence to abuse them. This scandal led to the emergence of the so-called "*Me Too*" movement, a global movement under which thousands of women denounced situations of sexual

Miramax production company that emerged in the 1990s: "*Finesse* was never part of Harvey's arsenal. Look at his record: he ripped phones off the walls and threw them on the floor; he always slammed doors and overturned tables; anything within reach could be turned into a throwing weapon: ashtrays, books, tapes, the framed family photographs on his desk that Harvey would hurl at some hapless executive's head, only to watch them smash against the wall, shatter and send out glass shrapnel, because, in reality, they rarely, if ever, hit their target." Harvey Weinstein was uncontrollable: "When he lost control, he was capable of anything..." it seemed as if he was swelling, as if the barometric pressure had changed; you thought he was going to explode. And sometimes he would explode. His face would turn red, literally, and like stone. It wasn't like he was going to throw chairs, more like he was going to come at you, to strangle you." Miramax employees endured a lot of humiliation: "The Weinsteins took advantage of their instability, turned it into the bad cop/good cop routine they used to keep their underlings scared and shaking. "They drove everyone crazy," says Lipsky. "From the time I met them, their *modus operandi* was to stomp you down; then they'd help you up. First they'd walk over you and then apologise"...There were people who were simply too good to work there, and the Weinsteins tortured them[414]."

The Warners, like everyone else, despite their eccentricities, were naturally good Jews: "Jack Warner demanded that his Jewish employees donate a percentage of their salary to the United Jewsih Welfare Found. During a fund-raising drive, he summoned them to the studio cafeteria... "Warner walked in and, to our astonishment, recalled Alvah Bessie, brandished a rubber truncheon, which must have been a prop from one of the anti-Nazi films we were making...: "Everybody double your contribution here and now, or face the consequences!"...It was enough for him to say - admitted his son Jack junior - : "You won't come back to and work here if you don't give to the United Jewish Appeal[415]."

Neal Gabler mentioned the role of Edgar Magnin, "the rabbi to the stars" within the Hollywood world: "Calling someone an anti-Semite was the surest way to tarnish his reputation among Hollywood executives[416]. When RKO's production manager, George Schaefer, turned down Louis B. Mayer's offer to buy the negative of the film. Mayer's offer to buy the

---

abuse and harassment (wikipedia). (NdT).
[414] Peter Biskind *Sexo, mentiras y Hollywood, Miramax, Sundance y el cine independiente*, Anagrama, Barcelona, 2013, p. 92-96.
[415] Neal Gabler, *An Empire of Their Own, How the Jews Invented Hollywood*, Confluences, 2015, p. 421. [The French version in the text points to all their employees and not just their Jewish employees. NdT.]
[416] Just ask Mel Gibson.

negative of Orson Welles' masterpiece *Citizen Kane* (Mayer made the offer to destroy the film because it was loosely and unflatteringly based on the life of his friend William Randolph Hearst), Schaefer suddenly became the victim of a whispering campaign accusing him of anti-Semitism. Schaefer, determined to find the source, traced the rumours to a close colleague of Mayer. Of course, none of this prevented Hollywood Jews from practising reverse discrimination - "Those *goyim*!", Harry Warner used to shout in derision, or "He's a good boy for a *goy*", a Jew might say - but only in their sanctum sanctorum, when they were safe among fellow Jews, and only by word of mouth. Otherwise, Gentiles were feted and treated with deference[417]."

The American actor Kirk Douglas also had to adapt to the Hollywood environment to make the career we know. In his biography, rich in anecdotes about that world, he wrote: "People change when they get to Hollywood...It is the town where Cliff Robertson discovered David Begelman as a counterfeiter and thief, with the result that he was given a standing ovation in a Hollywood restaurant, while Robertson was blacklisted for four years[418]."

The American Jewish intellectual Walter Lippman came to this obvious conclusion: "The rich, vulgar, pretentious Jews of our great American cities are perhaps the greatest misfortune that has befallen the Jewish people. They are the source of anti-Semitism. When they run around in their cars, with their jewels and their furs, made up and so clean-shaven, when they build their French *chateaux* and their Italian *palazzi*, they stimulate latent hatred against pure wealth in the hands of shallow people; and that hatred spreads only[419]."

---

[417] Neal Gabler, *An Empire of Their Own, How Jews Invented Hollywood*, Confluences, 2015, p. 410. ["In pursuing an Americanized Judaism, Magnin was not only speaking as a fully assimilated San Francisco Jew. He was also adapting and sanctioning the views of his congregation. What German Jews wanted, what Hollywood Jews wanted, was a way to maintain their Jewishness (they couldn't help it) without being too aggressive about it or provoking the goyim...Mayer claimed that Edgar would fit in with any group. Magnin described himself as "a democratic person". He lived in Beverly Hills among the movie moguls in a Spanish hacienda that he designed himself because he believed that the Spanish period was the golden age of Judaism...All this made Magnin very attractive to Hollywood Jews, who had renounced the dogmatic Orthodox Judaism of his parents. Carl Laemmle, Harry and Jack Warner, Louis B. Mayer, Irving Thalberg, William Fox, and a host of film executives, directors, and actors became members of B'nai B'rith, but Magnin admitted that it was not the opportunity for religious practice that attracted them; if anything, it was the opportunity to secularize religion." Neal Gabler, *An Empire of Their Own*, p. 410-412. (NdT).]

[418] Kirk Douglas, *The Ragpicker's Son* (1988), Cult Books, 2021, p. 129

[419] Neal Gabler, *An Empire of Their Own, How the Jews Invented Hollywood*, Confluences, 2015, p. 353.

The masters of Hollywood were certainly caricatures of a certain form of Jewish domination. Martin Gray, a Holocaust survivor, also had something to prove to the world. After the war, he went to the United States, to New York, where he was reunited with his family, who, miraculously, had not been exterminated. "I multiplied my activities, games, sales, service, shows. I accumulated dollars. At night I collapsed in bed, exhausted." He then went into the antiques trade, particularly porcelain, feverishly buying everything he could find. He travelled to Europe, the continent had just emerged from the war in tatters: "I bought without haggling; haste was my strength. *Time is money*. On Monday I left for Frankfurt and Berlin. Soon I added London to my journey. I shopped, I phoned, I jumped from taxi to plane, I slept". A woman told him one day: "You have to take time to live, Mendle. Don't run all the time. Learn to be happy, Mendle. Don't always run away." But Mendle explained: "I preferred work to the peace she offered me. Perhaps, later on, a woman might somewhat slow down my career; perhaps one day I might at last find the taste of rest." (page 347). "In Berlin, the market was becoming difficult...All the antique dealers of America had fallen on Berlin, emptying the city and the whole of Germany of its porcelain...- Buy Tolek, buy everything, he said to his partner...And the dollars accumulated, and every thousand dollars was a wall of my fortress rising up...I piled up the dollars, invested, placed...I was already rich, an American citizen, importer, manufacturer, with a branch in Canada and another in Havana. I owned real estate, I put my money in the stock market. I went from one capital to another, my suburbs were called Paris and Berlin...". And again: "I was active, efficient; I didn't miss planes or sales... I cashed in, invested, bought, cashed out[420]...". And so it was that Germany, a defeated country, was plundered from top to bottom.

In her books, the writer Irène Némirovsky, who came from a family of bankers, also left us portraits of powerful people as she had seen them in her native Ukraine. In her novel *David Golder*, published in 1929, she told the story of a banker who, like her father, had emigrated to Paris: "In London, in Paris, in New York, when David Golder was named, people thought of a tough old Jew who had been hated and feared all his life, who had crushed everyone who had crossed his path[421]."

Golder frequented some of his peers, bankers and successful businessmen. Like this Fischl: "Golder regarded him almost with hatred, like a cruel caricature: a plump, red-haired, rosy-haired Jew with a comical, ignoble and somewhat sinister appearance...". He explained his travails: "Yes, I went through the courts... But, as you can see, I did no worse than

---

[420] Martin Gray, *En nombre de todos los míos*, Plaza & Janés, Barcelona, 1973, p. 332, 347, 348, 349, 351, 352, 357. Read further in *La Mafia judía*.
[421] Irène Némirovssky, *David Golder*, Salamandra, Barcelona, 2006, p. 125

at other times," Fischl listed with his fingers. Austria, Russia, France. I've been in jail in three countries. I hope it's over and they'll leave me alone. I hope they go to hell. I don't want to earn any more money, I'm old now..."

David Golder had also had business dealings with another Jew named Soifer: "They went out together, each leaning on his cane. Golder walked silently as his companion told him about a sugar deal that had ended in fraudulent bankruptcy. As he quoted the figures and the names of the shareholders involved, Soifer rubbed his trembling hands together with delight[422]."

Here is what kind of man this Soifer was: "Soiler, an old German Jew, an old acquaintance from Silesia whom I had lost sight of... I used to come and play cards with him. Soifer, once ruined by inflation, had made up for all his losses by speculating in the franc. However, he had been left with a permanent distrust, which grew from year to year, of a money that revolutions and wars could transform overnight into worthless paper money. Little by little, he turned his fortune into jewels. In a safe-deposit box in London he kept diamonds, magnificent pearls, emeralds so beautiful that even Glory in his best days would never have dreamed of owning them... However, he was stingy to the point of obsession. He lived as a tenant in a sordid furnished flat in a gloomy street in the Passy district. He wouldn't get into a taxi, even if it was paid for. "I don't want to get used to what I can't afford," he used to say. In winter, he would wait for the bus in the rain for as long as it took, and if there was no room on the second bus, he would keep waiting until there was. Years later, Soifer would die alone, like a dog, friendless, without a wreath on his grave, buried in the cheapest cemetery in Paris by a family who hated him and whom he had hated, but to whom he nevertheless left a fortune of over thirty million, thus fulfilling the incomprehensible destiny of every good Jew on this earth[423]."

At the beginning of the 21st century, the Jewish will to power can also be seen in one Sam Zell, an American billionaire; but there are many, many more. The left-wing weekly *Marianne* of 7 April 2007 published this brief article: "Sam Zell has made a fortune buying up buildings with old rents; he manages to subrogate the leases thanks to his political connections and then raises rents and evicts tenants, especially the elderly. He has just bought the *Los Angeles Times*, one of the most prestigious newspapers in the United States". And *Marianne* commented briefly, ironically, but without pointing out the real protagonists: "Long live the American model!" What bastards those "Americans", aren't they?

---

[422] Irène Némirovssky, *David Golder*, Salamandra, Barcelona, 2006, p. 46-47, 144
[423] Irène Némirovssky, *David Golder*, Salamandra, Barcelona, 2006, p. 140-141

In his book *The Jewish Paradox*, published in 1976, Nahum Goldmann had written: "Jewish life is made up of two elements: amassing money and protesting [424]." But Roger Cukierman, former President of the Representative Council of Jewish Institutions in France, was outraged at these prejudices and denied the obvious: ""Jews have money!"" Once again these terrible anti-Semitic prejudices, so trivialised that they always end up provoking the worst consequences[425]."

Finally, in his own way, Nahum Goldmann also denied the obvious. On page 39 of his book, he recounted an extraordinary anecdote, an interview with the Soviet Foreign Minister: 'Mr Litvinov, two months ago I met the Vatican Secretary of State, Cardinal Pacelli (the future Pope Pius XII), and Monsignor Pacelli spoke to me about the "world power of Judaism". I did not blame him: he is a Catholic, what does he know about Jewish life? But that you, Mr Litvinov, with your Jewish intelligence, should tell me such absurd things really makes me angry". I will never forget his reaction, Goldmann wrote. He remained silent for thirty seconds, then stood up, walked around the large table between us and held out his hand to me: "Let us shake hands, Mr. Goldmann; I said something absurd. Excuse me."[426]."

Fraudsters and traffickers

In our previous book, *The Jewish Mafia* (2008), we summarised the major swindles that had marked the history of the French Republic. As far as the Third Republic was concerned, we can also mention the following cases: the Sacazan case, which involved 23 cases worth 50 to 60 million, and which implicated Isaac Azan and the Levy brothers. There was also the Lévy-Goldenberg case, which amounted to 1 billion francs at the time. The Lloy de France-Vie case, which revealed the embezzlement of funds by Mr Haas, estimated at the time at 7 million francs. The Crédit Français case: four million embezzled by a certain Blumenfeld. The failure of Gaumont Franco-Films Aubert: a deficit of 400 million francs caused by the embezzlement of Heim and Goudchaux. The collapse of the Banque des Coopératives: a deficit of 10 million francs (director: Gaston Lévy). The Crédit Franco-Belge case (Sylvestre Blumenfeld); the Luxembourg Wulf Bank case (Abraham Adler); the Austrian Phoenix affair (Wilhelm Berliner); the Union continental carbonera case (Célestin, Ernest and Abraham Lévy). The Pathé-Nathan affair, a scandal that caused a lot of ink to flow from 1934 onwards and led to losses of 600 million. A few months

---

[424] Nahum Goldmann, *Le Paradoxe juif*, Stock, Paris, 1976, p. 67.
[425] Roger Cukierman, *Ni fiers, ni dominateurs*, Edition du Moment, 2008, p. 97.
[426] Nahum Goldmann, *Le Paradoxe juif*, Stock, Paris, 1976, p. 39.

earlier, another producer, the Tunisian Jew Jacques Haïk, had gone bankrupt, leaving a deficit of 103 million.[427]

Here is another famous scandal: Louis Louis-Dreyfus, the pre-war wheat king. In 1932, when the harvest was in surplus and prices were collapsing, he bought at 75 francs a quintal and stockpiled huge quantities. With the complicity of Minister Queuille - a future resistance fighter during the German occupation - he had the official price voted at 115 francs a quintal, which enabled him to supply the mills in Paris, Pantin and Strasbourg, which belonged to his co-religionists Baumann, Bloch and Lévy, at a profit of 40 francs. Louis Louis-Dreyfus also traded in Romanian wheat, which he had naturalised as "Moroccan", bought at 25 francs per quintal in Romania and sold for 115 francs in France.

During World War II, some Jews also made a lot of money trading with the Germans. In *The Jewish Mafia* we mentioned the two main dealers, "Monsieur Michel" and "Monsieur Joseph". But there were many others who made the news at the time for their involvement in the black market. The April 1944 document entitled "*Je vous hais!*" (*I hate you!*), from Léon Blum's famous cry to the Chamber of Deputies, quoted some of them: Abraham and Lesel trafficked in kilometres of cloth, quintals of flour and thousands of tins of tinned food (22 January 1943). Mrs. Salomouchitch stored a large quantity of cloth (25 April 1942). Mr. Raphael Worms hid enough coal in his cellar to supply a hospital in winter (27 February 1942). The leader of the gang, Simin Abelansky, was arrested on 13 June 1942. Elie Taïeb sold thousands of bread cards (8 March 1942). Joseph Hadjadj stockpiled hundreds of kilos of food for the black market (20 May 1942). The dealer Rozenstern was arrested with 300,000 francs in banknotes. A gang had sold 15,000 tons of rotten cabbage known as "Hungarian sauerkraut" (8 June 1942). Zahn and Grunberg were arrested for trafficking in food cards (27 November 1941). Marcel Weill had sold 4,000 kilos of wool at 434 francs per kilo (1 December 1941). Kroll and Kolcon were arrested for trafficking in textiles and poultry (1 December 1941). Goldberg, Feder and Moszek sold stolen leather worth several hundred thousand francs (19 February 1942). Lévy and Meyr trafficked pepper (26 June 1942). 700 packets of cloth, 15 packets of linen and 2700 bars of chocolate were seized from the house of one Baumgarten. Steinmuller was selling counterfeit food cards. Police confiscated cloth worth 220,000 francs from Jacob Pinto. Samuel Choima and Abraham Elefant had 269 pairs of shoes. Haïl and Lévy (arrested on 23 April 1941) had sold 700 kilometres of cloth.

---

[427] Review by Henry Coston, April 1944, in *Je vous hais!*, p. 82, 83.

In short, more than 4,000 Jews were arrested in the unoccupied zone for trafficking on the black market. One only had to open a newspaper.[428]

This was undoubtedly what inspired filmmaker Kurt Hoffmann to make his cult film in Germany, *Wir Wunderkinder (The Child Prodigies*, 1958): In the early days of Nazism, circumstances separate three young men who studied together. The first, Stein, is forced to flee because he is Jewish. The second, Hans Boeckel, loses his job as a journalist because he refuses to join the Nazi party. The third, Bruno Tiches, a careerist, joins the party. The three meet again after the war: Stein returns wearing an American uniform, Boeckel is a journalist, and the Nazi Tiches has become immensely rich on the black market. As is well known, it was the Nazis who profited most from the black market.[429]

Scams continue to occur regularly in all democratic countries in the West. In France, in December 2008, we learned that hundreds of complaints had been filed over the past year in connection with a scam set up by a Franco-Israeli network. The investigation began after two complaints were lodged in Dax (Landes) in December 2007. The investigations led to the arrest of four people in April and then around thirty in Israel at the beginning of December, where 700,000 euros, valuable jewellery and luxury vehicles were also seized. The fraudsters used faxes or telephone calls to offer advertisements to craftsmen, traders and associations on fake electronic directory services. After an initial free period, the victims, who had signed a contract that was difficult to read because it was sent by fax, received exorbitant invoices. To terminate the contract, they had to send a "deposit cheque" for a variable amount to be cashed by this network of fraudsters. For the 422 complainants last year, the losses ranged from 3,000 to 47,000 euros per victim.

But these criminals are in reality small fry compared to Bernard Madoff. This New York financier had been nicknamed "the Jewish Treasury Bond" by members of the American Jewish community because of the impression of security that the man and his financial products gave. In reality, the interest he distributed to his clients was not the result of his investments: he merely collected funds from new investors and distributed them to old ones (pyramid scheme). In December 2008, his company went bankrupt, ruining tens of thousands of savers. But we would later learn that the big

---

[428] April 1944, in *Je vous hais!*, p. 89, 90

[429] Recall that all Jews had been barred from leaving Germany: "Himmler ordered the cessation of all Jewish emigration from the Reich. The order, issued on 18 October 1941, was transmitted to all Gestapo stations on the 23rd." Saul Friedländer, *The Third Reich and the Jews (1939-1945), The Years of Extermination*, Galaxia Gutenberg, Barcelona, 2009 p. 387.

investment sharks were not the losers in this story. Fifty billion dollars disappeared. It was the biggest scam in human history.[430]

The enigma of anti-Semitism

Selective amnesia is one of the symptoms of hysterical pathology. Sigmund Freud, who had studied the phenomenon after attending Professor Martin Charcot's lectures at the Salpêtrière, wrote in 1916 about hysteria: "This latter neurosis is most often characterised by vast amnesias...As a rule, important details disappear from the complete picture of a recent memory of this kind, or are replaced by distortions of the recollection.Such impairments of the ability to remember are, as we have said, characteristic of hysteria; in hysteria they are presented as symptoms, states (hysterical attacks) which do not usually leave any trace in the memory[431].".

In *Planetary Hopes* (2005), we pointed out that most Jewish intellectuals denied the leading role played by their fellow Jews in the communist tragedy, often preferring, not without a certain shamelessness - the famous *chutzpah* - to pose as victims. Numerous pieces of evidence and countless testimonies do not prevent certain Jews from uttering monumental falsehoods. The Nazi hunter Simon Wiesenthal, for example, even tried to make us believe that, at the time of the invasion of Poland in 1940, the Soviets had pursued an anti-Semitic policy. Wiesenthal wrote: "But the last "liberators" had brought with them the NKVD, their security police, which set about arresting "bourgeois" Jews, merchants and factory owners, as well as the "intelligentsia": doctors, lawyers and teachers...Many Jewish "bourgeois" were given so-called "Paragraph 11" passports which made them second-class citizens, exempt from privileges, forbidding them to reside in the big cities or within a hundred kilometres of a border. They lost their good jobs and their bank accounts were confiscated."

At the end of his book, Simon Wiesenthal resumed his misleading lament: "During the Soviet occupation, from September 1939 to June 1941, many were arrested on charges of being "bourgeois" or of being members of the intelligence, or Zionists, or of possessing property...A few months later, all Jews in possession of "Paragraph 11" passports were deported to Siberia, where many of them died". However, we would learn that Wiesenthal had bribed an NKVD commissar, probably Jewish, and had thus managed to

---

[430] Read about it in Hervé Ryssen, *Israel's Millionaires*, OmniaVeritas, 2014: Carbon Tax Fraud, VAT Fraud, Madoff-type pyramid schemes, *Junk Bonds* and the bankruptcy of the Savings Banks in the 1980s, the real estate crisis of 2008 (FED policy, *Subprimes*, CDOs, CDS), etc, etc. (NdT).

[431] Sigmund Freud, *Collected Works, volume 16 (1916-17), Lectures on Introduction to Psychoanalysis (part III)*, Amorortu Editores, Buenos Aires, 1991, p. 259, 260.

obtain statutory passports for his wife, his mother and himself. And, at the end of the book, he paid lip service to the fact: "Unfortunately, there were some Jewish commissars among the Soviet officers[432]."

In reality, as we know, Jews were sent across the Urals for protection, and many spent the war in sunny Tashkent in Uzbekistan, a resort city known for its quality of life.[433]

Wiesenthal also told us of the ordeal of innocent Ukrainian Jews when the German troops arrived in 1941, without ever explaining that the Jews themselves, greatly over-represented in the communist regime and its repressive services at the time, had committed massacres against Ukrainian nationalists: "I know Jews who had been in Soviet prisons, who had managed to escape from them and were then murdered by Ukrainians 'because they murdered our own'. Whichever side the Jews were on, it always turned out to be that of the losers[434]." Jews, we must believe, are always innocent.

In his *Psychoanalysis of Anti-Semitism*, published in 1952, Rudolph Loewenstein showed the same shortcomings and lashed out at "prejudices": "Adherence to communism, he wrote, remained a marginal phenomenon among the Jewish public, contrary to the tenacious legend of Judeo-Bolshevism maintained to this day by the school of Ernst Nolte and his German and French disciples[435]."

Saul Friedlander, one of the great historians of the Holocaust, nevertheless acknowledged the role of his fellow Jews in the highest echelons of the Soviet regime: "There is no doubt that the percentage of Jews among the social and cultural elites of the Soviet Union was many times higher than their share of the country's population. This predominance was no less striking in the most sensitive areas of the state apparatus. According to historian Yuri Slezkine, 'by 1934, when the OGPU was transformed into the NKVD, Jews "of nationality" constituted the largest group among the "leading commanders" of the Soviet Secret Police (37 Jews, 30 Russians, 7 Latvians, 5 Ukrainians, 4 Poles, 3 Georgians, 3 Belarusians, 2 Germans, and 5 others from other groups)[436]. The high number of Bolshevik leaders of Jewish origin - especially in the first generation - was an obvious fact

---

[432] Simon Wiesenthal, *The Murderers Among Us*, Editorial Noguer, Barcelona, 1967, (pdf), p. 21, 173.
[433] We saw the testimonies of Samuel Pisar and Marek Halter in *Planetary Hopes* and *Psychoanalysis of Judaism*.
[434] Simon Wiesenthal, *The Murderers Among Us*, Editorial Noguer, Barcelona, 1967, (pdf), p. 173.
[435] Rudolph Loewenstein, *Psychanalyse de l'antisémitisme*, 1952, Presses Universitaires de France, 2001, p. 30.
[436] Yuri Slezkine, *The Jewish Century*, Princeton, 2004, p. 221.

which, of course, fuelled anti-Semitic propaganda, not only in the Reich, but throughout the West. Even Lenin - and this, on Stalin's orders, was kept a state secret - had a Jewish grandfather[437]."

However, Saul Friedlander had an interesting interpretation of the facts: "The crucial point missed by the anti-Semites, however, was the simple fact that Soviet Jews, at all levels of the system, were first and foremost Soviet citizens, devoted to the ideas and goals of the Soviet Union and unaware of their own origins.

To put it bluntly, the Jewish Bolshevik torturers were no longer Jews, since they were Bolshevik atheists. We have already pointed out these same tricks of other authors in our previous works. It is about the famous "barbapapa" Jew, who transforms himself according to the circumstances and is never a criminal[438]. "The 22 June 1941, Friedlander continued, transformed many of these "non-Jewish Jews" - to use Isaac Deutscher's famous expression - into Soviet Jews suddenly conscious of their origins and proud to be Jews[439]... In all sectors of Soviet society Jews were mobilised to the utmost to participate in the anti-Nazi struggle[440]." And here too, note well, they were no longer executioners or repressors, but liberators working to regenerate humanity.

However, Saul Friedlander presented a text that offered a slightly different interpretation of the causes of anti-Semitism. He quoted a pastoral letter of Cardinal August Hlond, the highest authority of the Catholic Church in Poland, dated 29 February 1936. Cardinal Hlond sought to stem the rising tide of anti-Jewish violence: "It is a fact that the Jews are declaring war against the Catholic Church, that they are immersed in freethinking and constitute the vanguard of atheism, the Bolshevik movement and revolutionary activity. It is a fact that the Jews have a

---

[437]Saul Friedländer, *El Tercer Reich y los judíos (1939-1945), Los años del exterminio*, Galaxia Gutenberg, Barcelona, 2009, p. 342. (Yuri Slezkine, *The Jewish Century*, Princeton, 2004, p. 245.) On Lenin's origins read further in *El Fanatismo judío*.

[438]Barbapapa is the name of the main character, the name of his species, and the name of a series of children's books originally written in French in the 1970s. Barbapapa (Barbapapa in French) is a pink character who was born from the earth in a garden; he can take any shape, though he is almost always pear-shaped, and stumbles into the world of humans despite trying to fit in. Barbapapa's name comes from French, meaning cotton candy (wikipedia, NdT).

[439]I grew up in a Russian city," proclaimed writer and journalist Elya Ehrenburg in a speech in August 1941. My native language is Russian. I am a Russian writer. Now, like all Russians, I defend my homeland. But the Nazis have reminded me of something else: my mother's name was Hannah. I am a Jew. And I say it with pride. Hitler hates us more than anything else. And that is an honour for us." (quoted in *The Jewish Century*, p. 288). (NdT).

[440] Saul Friedländer, *The Third Reich and the Jews (1939-1945), The Years of Extermination*, Galaxia Gutenberg, Barcelona, 2009 p. 343.

corrupting influence on morals, and that their publishing companies are disseminating pornography. It is certain that the Jews are perpetrating frauds, practising usury and dealing in prostitution..." Still, the Cardinal stood firm on the traditional principles of the Church: "But let's be fair. One may like a nation more or less, but we must not hate any nation. Not even the Jews... One can withdraw from the harmful moral influence of the Jews, keep away from their anti-Christian culture and especially boycott the Jewish press and the amoral Jewish publications. But it is forbidden to attack, beat, maim or kill Jews[441]."

At least we have here some lines of enquiry that would enable us to understand the levers of anti-Semitism. But among Jewish intellectuals, all this is evacuated from the field of their consciousness and, to use psychoanalytic phraseology, "repressed" in the dark regions of their subconscious.

So it is simply impossible to explain anti-Semitism. Martin Gray, in *In the Name of All Mine*, wondered about this incomprehensible hatred: "Why are they so strong, why are they the masters and we the slaves? Why this hatred against us? Why the death everywhere, threatening?" The poor Jews were "in the midst of rabid and mad beasts[442]..."

Take Adolf Eichmann, a senior Nazi leader, for example. Why did he feel the need to fight against Judaism? This was Simon Wiesenthal's explanation: "I made a mistake trying to find a motive in his childhood: there was no motive and no hatred. It was just a perfect product of Nazism". Apparently, anti-Semitism is simply madness, which led Wiesenthal to denounce the delusional paranoia of the Third Reich's dignitaries: "Hitler and his henchmen were convinced of the universal, all-knowing power of the *Wettjudentum* (Jewish world)[443]." Saul Friedlander also denounced "Hitler's lucubrations about the Jews".

---

[441] In Brian Porter, *Making a Space for Antisemitism: The Catholic Hierarchy and the Jews in the early Twentieth Century*, p. 420, quoted Saul Friedländer, *El Tercer Reich y los judíos (1939-1945), Los años del exterminio*, Galaxia Gutenberg, Barcelona, 2009 p. 64. [On the traditional policy of the Catholic Church towards the Jews, see Hervé Ryssen, *Historia del antisemitismo* (2010), p. 64].

[442] Martin Gray, *En nombre de todos los míos*, Plaza & Janés, Barcelona, 1973, p. 39, 126. ["He was a coward, despicable; that he belonged to the world of rabid beasts, which are killed because they are harmful, and that I and mine were - no matter what we had done... - I and mine were men with men's faces. And the rabid beasts could not defeat us, even if they killed us. I had but one regret: that I could not take part in the hunting cry when, at last, we rounded them up." Martin Gray, *In the Name of All Mine*, Plaza & Janés, Barcelona, 1973, p. 115].

[443] Simon Wiesenthal, *The Murderers Among Us*, Editorial Noguer, Barcelona, 1967, (pdf), p. 83, 82.

In a book published in 2008, originally entitled *Judaism for Dummies*, David Blatner, Josy Eisenberg and Rabbi Ted Falcon also explained to us learnedly that anti-Semitism is inexplicable. Listen to this: "No other human group has suffered as much throughout history (without disappearing) as the Jewish people. All those centuries of oppression and exile seem senseless, the fruits of incredible ignorance, sighing and fear. As Harry Cohen once wrote: "Let's face it, anti-Semitism cannot be explained: it can only be told."[444]."

Above all, it must be understood that anti-Semitism is a disease. In fact, chapter 16 was entitled *Curing Anti-Semitism*. The authors acknowledged that in ancient times, in the days of paganism, the poor Jews were already "accused" of separatism: they observed strict dietary rules, married only among themselves, had only one God, etc., etc., etc. Later, the accusations were raised to the level of "delirium": Christians accused them of having killed God, of poisoning wells, of practising ritual crimes, and so on.

And here is the luminous explanation of our three rabbis: "In fact, their neighbours tended to project onto them what they feared most. Thus, Jews were sometimes accused of being the seed of revolution and the promoters of communism, sometimes of being horrible capitalists; sometimes of being overbearing careerists and insinuating themselves everywhere, sometimes of living in seclusion; sometimes of being stingy, sometimes of spending without complexes.... As you can see, the rabbis concluded, Jewish existence has given rise to a whole series of fantasies and myths[445]."

In his 1952 *Psychoanalysis of Anti-Semitism*, Rudolph Loewenstein also pointed out the contradictions of anti-Semitic propaganda: "The Jews, he wrote, were portrayed both as capitalists gorging themselves on the blood of the "Aryans" and as communist revolutionaries. By persecuting them, the rich and middle classes hoped to exorcise the spectre of threatening revolution and at the same time get rid of their competitors. The workers believed they were freeing themselves from the yoke of their exploiters". And he repeated it 150 pages later: "In the eyes of some the Jews are linked with the capitalists, in the eyes of others with the communists[446]."

In his *Portrait of a Jew*, published in 1962, Albert Memmi also pretended not to understand: "German doctrinaires asserted, often on the same page, the existence of a Judeo-capitalism and a Judeo-Bolshevism. How can the two go together?... The belief that Jews are the masters of money and the

---

[444] Rabbi Ted Falcon, David Blatner, Josy Eisenberg, *Le Judaïsme pour les nuls*, First Editions, 2008, p. 208.
[445] Rabbi Ted Falcon, David Blatner, Josy Eisenberg, *Le Judaïsme pour les nuls*, First Editions, 2008, p. 210.
[446] Rudolph Loewenstein, *Psychanalyse de l'antisémitisme*, 1952, Presses Universitaires de France, 2001, p. 103, 251.

belief that they foment revolutions coexist in many minds without interfering in the slightest". Albert Memmi continued his attack: "The famous Protocols of the Elders of Zion, as we know, are the product of a hateful delusion, requiring answers other than those of reasoning."

In his book *Hitler's Willing Executioners*, published in 1996, the famous scholar Daniel Goldhagen also tried to explain to his readers the madness of anti-Semitism. The Holocaust was, according to him, "the most dreadful event of the twentieth century and the most difficult to understand in all of German history...The Holocaust and the change in sensibilities it brought about is beyond explanation...Explaining how the Holocaust came about is a daunting task empirically and even more daunting theoretically to the point that some have argued that it is inexplicable," he wrote in the introduction to his study. "The vicissitudes of anti-Semitism in nineteenth-century Germany were complex to the highest degree[447]."

Going back in history, one can see that Germans were deeply affected: "The corpus of German anti-Semitic literature in the 19th and 20th centuries (with its nonsensical and imaginary considerations about the nature of the Jews, their virtually unlimited power and their responsibility for almost all the evils the world had suffered) is so far removed from reality that any reader will be forced to conclude that it can only be the product of authors who were inmates of a madhouse[448]."

"Beliefs, as is often the case, contain hallucinatory elements...extravagant beliefs", wrote Goldhagen (page 72). Accusations of ritual crimes, in particular, persisted into modern times. Between 1867 and 1914, twelve trials for ritual crimes were still held in Germany and the Austro-Hungarian Empire. And, as Max Warburg, the prominent Jewish banker, put it, Germany "had disqualified itself from the ranks of the civilised peoples [*kulturvölker*] and had taken its place among the ranks of the countries where pogroms [*pogrommländer*] took place" (page 120).

Anti-Semitism is all the more inexplicable because Daniel Goldhagen makes no attempt to explain it. For example, only one sentence appeared in his text on the role of Jews in Bolshevism, on page 193: "Since Hitler believed that the Jews were all-powerful in the Soviet Union, it would be more appropriate to call Bolshevism "Judeo-Bolshevism" because, according to him, Bolshevism was a "monstrous product of the Jews"". Under these conditions, Goldhagen wrote, it was normal to consider that "the brutality of the Germans remains somewhat unfathomable."

---

[447] Daniel Jonah Goldhagen, *Hitler's Willing Executioners, The Ordinary Germans and the Holocaust*, Taurus, 2019, p. 22, 23, 83.
[448] Daniel Jonah Goldhagen, *Hitler's Willing Executioners, The Ordinary Germans and the Holocaust*, Taurus, 2019, p. 52.

Thus, Germans are evil and cruel by nature: "Anti-Semitism helps to explain their immense cruelty towards Jews which was almost always voluntary, initiated by each individual[449]." In contrast, the Jews were perfectly innocent: "Needless to say, the Jews of Germany wanted nothing more than to be good Germans, whereas the Jews of Eastern Europe had not previously experienced enmity towards Germans, but rather the opposite, since large sections of Eastern European Jews were Germanophiles." In reality, it was all the fault of the Germans and their delusional beliefs, of "their deadly racial fantasies." "The Germans' characterisation of the Jews and their beliefs about them were absolutely fantastic, the kind of beliefs that ordinarily only madmen have about other people[450]."

---

[449] Daniel Jonah Goldhagen, *Hitler's Willing Executioners, The Ordinary Germans and the Holocaust*, Taurus, 2019, p. 491.

[450] Daniel Jonah Goldhagen, *Hitler's Willing Executioners, The Ordinary Germans and the Holocaust*, Taurus, 2019, p. 508-509, 551. The lies that Jewish intellectuals spread in their writings are such that one sometimes wonders whether they write more to impress their own kind than to deceive the goyim. [Goldhagen's book caused great controversy and controversy, and was harshly dismissed by many authors and historians: "The book became a "publishing phenomenon" and achieved fame in both the United States and Germany, despite its scathing reception among historians, who condemned it as ahistorical and, in the words of Holocaust historian Raul Hilberg, "totally wrong about everything" and "worthless"." (wikipedia). The reader is referred to this article from *Slate* magazine of 8 April 1998 which summarises the controversy of the time: https://slate.com/news-and-politics/1998/04/goldhagen-s-willing-executioners.html. ("*The Attack on an Academic Superstar and How He Strikes Back*"). Goldhagen's book was intended to be a university study, with social science pretensions. In fact, he started it as a Harvard doctoral thesis. For our part, we skimmed the book and found it pedantic and fatuous. We reproduce a rather significant passage from Goldhagen's mystification: "In these pages we present a sociology of knowledge, an analytical framework for studying anti-Semitism (specifying its three dimensions of *origin, perniciousness,* and *manifestation*), and some fundamental notions about the character of anti-Semitism, because these elements, *whether expressed or not,* shape the conclusions of any study of this phenomenon. The importance of outlining the approach used in the study of anti-Semitism is all the greater because the data that provide the basis for the conclusions *are not exactly ideal* in a number of respects. Consequently, conclusions have to be defended *not only on the basis of the data and the use made of them, but also on the basis of the general approach taken* to understanding beliefs and cognitions, and anti-Semitism. It must be emphasised that the analysis conducted here *cannot be definitive, because the appropriate data simply do not exist.* The *deficiency of the data* is all the more evident because our purpose is not to investigate the character of anti-Semitism among political and cultural elites alone, but to gauge its nature and extent among all layers of German society." Daniel Jonah Goldhagen, *Hitler's Willing Executioners, Ordinary Germans and the Holocaust*, Taurus, 2019, p. 75].

Jean Michel Salanskis, a French academic, also set out in search of the truth. Anyone who really wants to understand the roots of anti-Semitic evil should read the powerful work of this Jean-Michel Salanskis, a mathematician and professor of philosophy of science at the University of Nanterre (France). His book, *Extermination, Law, Israel*, was published in 2003 by Éditions des Belles Lettres. To fully immerse oneself in the author's thought, it is absolutely essential to read the following excerpt very slowly and attentively. Very slowly, even word for word (pay attention to the commas!, ndt), otherwise you run the risk of not understanding anything. Ready?..... Here we go:

"Nazism declared unbearable as such a subgroup which, on the one hand, was of the same class, by the abstract legal definition to which it referred, as the large national democratic group, and which, on the other hand, by its way of inhabiting the democratically possible, had distributed itself in all individuation options according to possible contingent subgroups and had thus attained the optimal status of indistinguishability and proximity to all other components of the German people. So the metaphysical ostracism of the Jews constituted a very serious precedent: one that usually has no other meaning for the social subject than that a co-social other can suddenly, overnight, be declared abject. To a certain extent, then, anti-Judaism is expressed by its rejection of a certain ethically enforceable and absolute level of acceptance and acceptance of the other human being, as Levinas has put it. The acceptance of the other co-social human being cannot at all consist simply, as one sees and feels, in the merely rational principle of the a priori equal consideration of the subjects: it requires a certain concrete and sentimental openness, because what enables those who have been admitted to live easily is precisely a certain almost carnal benevolence, which dissipates as soon as one falls into exclusion[451]." That's clear, isn't it?

The great Jean-Michel Salanskis also wrote: "I would like, therefore, to contrast a perplexed unity of the Jewish fact with an imaginary-assumed unity of hatred. My conviction is that the perplexed unity is the truth, and the hateful-imaginary-presumed unity is the ordinary way of concealing that truth. The perplexed unity can be achieved, or rather experienced, through a phenomenological or rather "ethanalytical" reconstitution of the Jewish fact. The condition for the revelation of the phenomenon according to its dimensions, in this particular case, is none other than the suspension of the work of hatred, of the imaginary-presumed hateful projection of Jewish harmfulness[452]."

---

[451] Jean-Michel Salanskis, *Extermination, loi, Israël. Ethanalyse du fait juif*, Les Belles Lettres, 2003, p. 86, 87.
[452] Jean-Michel Salanskis, *Extermination, loi, Israël. Ethanalyse du fait juif*, Les Belles

Readers should know that Jean-Michel Salanskis has managed the feat of not slowing down at any point in his book. In all modesty, it is not the least of our merits to have managed to savour each of its 350 pages.[453]

For Rudolph Loewenstein, anti-Semitism is "neither paranoid nor phobic", but "simply a matter of criminology". And he continued his explanation, in a more classical vein: "Jews have been victims of sadism and political ambition, and have been allowed to be persecuted, plundered and murdered with impunity. They have often been hated for their vulnerability. Man is greatly attracted by the possibility of satisfying his instincts for cruelty on defenceless victims...The Jews, a weak minority attributed with 'dark and formidable power', offered the Nazi leaders the scapegoat they sought[454]."

Furthermore: "In the 19th and 20th centuries, Rudolph Loewenstein explained, it was mainly political and economic reasons that led to the persecution of the Jews. The tsarist government blamed them for general discontent and instigated pogroms aimed at diverting towards them the hostility that was about to break out against the established order, against a regime responsible for a tottering social and economic structure[455]."

The historian François Fejtö was a Marrano, i.e. a Jew who had falsely converted to Catholicism and declared himself a "citizen of the world". He too complained bitterly: "The multitudes, always deceived by promises impossible to keep, cry out for scapegoats. The Jew has played this role too often in the past". Especially since the Jews are innocent: "Why does God rage against the innocent?..... We are innocent, no one can rightfully forbid us to touch the fruits of the tree of life[456]."

Simon Wiesenthal had already told us that if the Jews had been persecuted for centuries it could only have been because of the folly of men: "Have we Jews not been suffering for thousands of years because we were said to be "collectively guilty"? All of us, including the unborn, guilty of the crucifixion, of the epidemics of the Middle Ages, communism, capitalism, adverse wars and adverse peace treaties? All the evils of mankind, from the plague to the atomic bomb, were "the fault of the Jews". We are the eternal *scapegoats*[457]."

Lettres, 2003, p. 42.

[453] Fortunately, the work of Jean-Michel Salanskis has not been translated into English. A priori, his thought - a mixture of Judaism and science - seems terrifying (NdT).

[454] Rudolph Loewenstein, *Psychanalyse de l'antisémitisme*, 1952, Presses Universitaires de France, 2001, p. 65, 103.

[455] Rudolph Loewenstein, *Psychanalyse de l'antisémitisme*, 1952, Presses Universitaires de France, 2001, p. 234.

[456] François Fejtö, *Dieu et son juif*, Ed. Pierre Horay, 1997, p. 67, 36, 49, 110. The tree of life is one of the most important kabbalistic symbols in Judaism.

[457] Simon Wiesenthal, *Los Asesinos entre nosotros*, Editorial Noguer, Barcelona, 1967, (pdf), p. 12. [We have replaced "scapegoats" in the Spanish translation by "chivos

It should be noted here, however, that the "scapegoat" is an image found very often in the Torah, being a figure dear to the Jews. The "scapegoat" was that beast burdened with all the sins of Israel which the Jews expelled by sending it to die in the wilderness[458]. A little more and we might think that the Jewish intellectuals here "project" their guilt onto the "anti-Semites".

The accusatory inversion

The mechanism of accusatory projection is well known to Jewish intellectuals. In his book *Psychoanalysis of Anti-Semitism*, published in 1952, Rudolph Loewenstein wrote: "A defensive mechanism against instinctual drives plays a fundamental role in the problems we are concerned with: it is "projection". This phenomenon, which is extremely frequent in both the normal and pathological psyche, is most clearly seen in paranoia and certain related pathological states. These patients imagine, for example, that someone has incited them to commit some sexual misdeeds. In reality, these are actions that they have actually committed or wanted to commit, and they are convinced of their own innocence. They attribute to others the role of tempters or instigators[459]."

According to him, "anti-Semites" have the following characteristics: "They are inaccessible to appraisal, to the test of reality, to the evidence of facts when these do not accord with their prejudices and preconceived ideas. The passions, motives and unconscious mechanisms at play in anti-Semitism, their hatred and fear, are too powerful to yield to reasoning or the facts of experience[460]."

Rudolph Loewenstein was a director of the American Psychoanalytic Association. He was also president of the New York Psychoanalytic Society from 1959 to 1961, and vice-president of the International Psychoanalytic Association from 1965 to 1967. So Loewenstein knew what he was talking about. For him, anti-Semitism was clearly a disease: "Delusional beliefs about Jews" have no basis in fact. "The accusation of taking diabolical pleasure in raping Aryan women", for example, was "part of these delusional beliefs". And he repeated: "The delusional beliefs of anti-Semites reflect the fear and hateful tendencies they feel against Jews".

---

expiatorios" to follow the French translation and the sense of Hervé Ryssen's text].
[458] Or on a cross?
[459] Rudolph Loewenstein, *Psychanalyse de l'antisémitisme*, 1952, Presses Universitaires de France, 2001, p. 79.
[460] Rudolph Loewenstein, *Psychanalyse de l'antisémitisme*, 1952, Presses Universitaires de France, 2001, p. 64.

Every effort must therefore be made to prevent further "outbreaks of delusional anti-Semitism", such as the one that had just "struck the world".

The problem is that anti-Semites are dangerously ill: "The delirious tenacity with which they maintain their most aberrant ideas about Jews, despite and against all the evidence" is truly "an enigma", as the essayist André Glucksmann would put it. The "anti-Semitic disease" is still very much alive. Hitler, wrote Loewenstein, was evidently a "sick man". "Hitler hated and feared the critical sense[461]."

In their 2007 book on the pro-Israel lobby, John Mearsheimer and Stepehn Walt quoted Mortimer B. Zuckerman, President of the Conference of Presidents, who, after referring to a "shameful epidemic of anti-Semitism" in the *US News and World Report* in October 2002, warned: "Europe is sick again".

In March 2004, *Boston Globe* columnist Jeff Jacoby had "devoted an article to the resurgence of the "cancer of anti-Semitism in Europe"[462]". These figures confirmed that anti-Semitism is essentially a disease, at least in the Jewish mind.

Rudolph Loewenstein, after many others, wanted to make this clear: "The Protocols of the Elders of Zion are a myth", an "absurd" plot. The Nazis "disguised and concealed their own plans for universal domination by projecting them onto the "Wise Men of Zion"... The Jew became the scapegoat for the whole world and was held responsible for all evils[463]". "Xenophobia, or hatred and fear of foreigners, is a phenomenon, if not widespread, at least very frequent," Loewenstein said. And perhaps even more so among Jews....

At the end of his book, he returned to the idea of the necessary struggle against anti-Semitism: "The search for truth is an integral part of this struggle. The present work is intended to contribute to it[464]." With these words he concluded his book.

In his 1962 *Portrait of a Jew*, Albert Memmi highlighted the very shortcomings of anti-Semitic thinking - or of the Jewish intellectual, if you prefer: "The more the non-Jew oppresses the Jew, the more he accuses him; the more he accuses him, the more guilty he feels towards him; the more

---

[461] Rudolph Loewenstein, *Psychanalyse de l'antisémitisme*, 1952, Presses Universitaires de France, 2001, p. 71-98, 102.
[462] John J. Mearsheimer / Stephen Walt, *Le Lobby pro-israélien et la politique étrangère américaine*, La Découverte, 2007, p. 205.
[463] Rudolph Loewenstein, *Psychanalyse de l'antisémitisme*, 1952, Presses Universitaires de France, 2001, p. 235.
[464] Rudolph Loewenstein, *Psychanalyse de l'antisémitisme*, 1952, Presses Universitaires de France, 2001, p. 107, 109, 113, 253.

guilty he feels, the more he has to declare him evil, the more he has to crush him...We are going round in circles".

Further on in his text, we read: "Anti-Semitism accuses the Jew of many machinations and attributes horrible traits to him. But a methodical examination of these traits shows that they are not specific, contradictory or excessively magnified. This portrait-accusation is no more than an accusation: it exists only in the mind of the anti-Semite. Far from enlightening us about the Jew, it allows us to infer the psychology of the anti-Semite[465]."

Daniell Goldhagen wrote brilliantly: "Anti-Semitism tells us nothing about Jews, but much about the anti-Semites and the culture that engenders them"; "Anti-Semitism draws basically on cultural sources that are independent of the nature and actions of Jews, and that Jews are then defined by the notions drawn from the culture that anti-Semites project onto them"; "Anti-Semitism arises from within the culture of anti-Semites and not from the character of the actions performed by Jews..."; "Anti-Semitism arises from within the culture of anti-Semites and not from the character of the actions performed by Jews..."."; the "underlying mechanism of anti-Semitism is seen in prejudice in general, although the impressive imaginative heights to which anti-Semites have repeatedly and routinely soared are infrequent in the vast annals of prejudice."; "Scholars of anti-Semitism should avoid the temptation to fixate on the handful of psalms of a prevailing anti-Semitic litany that seem to have a resonant reality, if only faintly, and to see in the actions of Jews some cause of anti-Semitism, for to do so is to confuse the symptom with the cause." Thus, "the hallucinatory accusations[466] " of anti-Semites are nothing more than the mirror of anti-Semitism.

---

[465] Albert Memmi, *Portrait d'un juif*, Gallimard, 1962, p. 166, 242.

[466] Daniel Jonah Goldhagen, *Hitler's Willing Executioners, The Ordinary Germans and the Holocaust*, Taurus, 2019, p. 65-67. [Some of Goldhagen's other reflections are worth quoting: "It is not possible to give any adequate theoretical explanation for the periodic outbursts of anti-Semitic expression that cause anti-Semitism to appear and disappear in a society"; "German anti-Semites had always been somewhat autistic in their conception of Jews. The autism was getting worse."; "(...)The will for a generalised slaughter of the Jews in all countries, despite the absence of any previous objective conflict with the Jews; this, because of the fantastic ideas they had of the Jews, demanded...total extermination...."Such brutality was, as a rule, voluntary, and the only master for whom it was carried out was none other than a German's own passions."; "Such cruelty, which was generally gratuitous and had no pragmatic, instrumental aim except the satisfaction and pleasure of the perpetrators....The only adequate explanation...holds that a demonological anti-Semitism, of the virulent racial variety, was the common structure of ideas held by the perpetrators and German society at large."; "The Germans' beliefs about Jews unleashed destructive and fierce inner passions which civilisation normally represses and tames."; "Germans used to kill Jews

In the cinema, this inclination towards inversion is quite common. There is no shortage of examples :[467]

In Joseph Losey's film *Monsieur Klein* (France, 1976), Robert Klein, a wealthy middle-class art dealer and opportunist, takes advantage of the German occupation to buy paintings cheaply from struggling Jews. But one day he receives a copy of the newspaper *Informations juives* at his home, even though he is not Jewish. He was soon accused of being Jewish and deported. To further muddy the waters, the director has cast Alain Delon, an actor with distinctly Indo-European features, in the lead role.

In the same genre, *Luna Park* (Russia, 1991): in Moscow, neo-Nazis are spreading terror. Jews, homosexuals and outcasts are mercilessly persecuted. But one night, Andrei learns that he is of Jewish origin. Dismayed, he sets off in search of his father, Nahoum Kheifitz, an old artist, and a strong friendship develops between them. In this way, Andrei becomes humanised. The film is by Pavel Lounguine, whose father was not a neo-Nazi.

The Fourth Dimension is a famous film by Steven Spielberg (USA, 1983): The racist Bill will be trapped in the skin of several characters persecuted by racists...

To fully understand Jewish intellectuals, one simply has to read them with a mirror. One realises then that they are incapable of talking about anything other than themselves.

On 19 September 2007, *Le Monde* published an article by Michel Tubiana, Honorary President of the League of Human Rights. In it, Michel Tubiana criticised Nicolas Sarkozy's immigration policy, which he considered too faint-hearted. Listen to this: "Since the creation of the Ministry of National Identity, we know that foreigners are no longer just men and women, but dangerous individuals who endanger the social, cultural and economic cohesion of our country". Foreigners "have become a kind of corrosive product that dissolves the national community through polygamy or the confrontation between Islam and the West". Tubiana took up the classic argument of the moralising Jewish intellectual: "This policy concentrates our fears and hatred on foreigners, transforms them into a danger and considers them inferior." And he continued: "State xenophobia imposes itself and is directed against all allogenic or supposedly allogenic people. France's message then loses its universality to the benefit of a

---

angrily, rage cruelly at them, degrade them, mock them and laugh at them like demons."; "The Germans used to kill Jews angrily, rage cruelly at them, degrade them, mock them and laugh like demons." *Hitler's Willing Executioners*, p. 71, 117, 510, 478, 479, 484, 489, 490].

[467] Read in *The Jewish Mafia* (2008).

conception of identity that excludes the other and encloses us in an immobile France, withdrawn in its anguish".

Again, one can only note that Jews never stop encouraging immigration, even if at the beginning of the 21st century, entire districts of the capital are populated by Afro-Maghrebi immigrants, and these immigrants are already imposing their law in many of the suburbs of the big French cities.

Michel Tubiana's text also presented the very specific characteristics of the Jewish intellectual who instinctively transfers his guilt to others. In this case, "the dangerous individuals endangering the social cohesion" of the country are not the immigrants, but Jewish intellectuals and decision-makers in the first place. It is Judaism that is the "corrosive product" that dissolves the national community, not the immigrant. And it is the Jews who most incite us to "a confrontation between Islam and the West". And who "considers others inferior", who "excludes the other", who "closes himself" and "withdraws into his anxieties", his "fears" and his "hatreds"? The Jew, of course. This text by Michel Tubiana showed once again the great homogeneity of intellectual Judaism.

In 1978, the writer Manès Sperber analysed the question in this way: "Hatred of Jews, he wrote, appeared to me very early on as an aggressive delirium of persecution... as a delirious fear of others, an anguish that the hater tries, however, to hide from himself. In his monomaniacal hostility, he convinces himself that he has an insuperable superiority over those he hates, that he must despise them, but also fear them because they are fiendishly malicious." He added: "Although this hatred is sometimes the worst danger to us, it is nevertheless your disease. It is the evil that afflicts you. No doubt it has caused us untold suffering, but we continue to overcome it without stopping[468]."

In Sperber's text, read with a mirror, we must first of all understand that it is indeed the Jews themselves who suffer "a delirium of persecution"; it is indeed the Jews themselves who display a "delusional fear of others" and a "monomaniacal hostility" towards the rest of the world; it is the Jews themselves who convince themselves that they enjoy an "insuperable superiority" and who "are diabolically malicious"; and, finally, it is the Jews themselves who are sick, profoundly sick. Their taste for provocation, their insolence, their morbid need to provoke the goyim, are part of their sickness. We might almost suspect that they wish to provoke the punishment they seem to be waiting for and which seems to give meaning to their existence. Certainly, according to some interpretations (*midrashim*) of Jewish eschatology, the Messiah will come when Israel is undergoing

---

[468] Manès Sperber, Être *juif*, Éd. Odile Jacob, 1994, p. 24, 31. Read in *Jewish Fanaticism*.

great tribulations, great suffering. At this point, we have the clear impression that the Jews are crying out to us for help.

In 1990, Alain Minc published a book entitled *The Revenge of the Nations*. In *Psychoanalysis of Judaism* we quoted some extracts from it, but - and this had escaped us - it now seems clear to us that, in Alain Minc's mind, the exact title was *The Revenge of Israel*. Rudolph Loewenstein wrote that anti-Semitism was "a criminology"... As for that Jeff Jacoby, as we have seen, he spoke of the "cancer of anti-Semitism"...

It is also necessary to read with a mirror the press director Jean-Jacques Servan-Schreiber, when he spoke of the "monstrous stupidity of the system of national sovereignty" which "brings with it war and hatred like storm clouds[469]". This was again a characteristic inversion. For it is Judaism that seems to bring war and hatred "like storm clouds".

On the other hand, we must also understand that for the Jews their rights over the entire planet are legitimate, as they are "God's chosen people".

In 1990, a minor novelist, David Vogel, had one of his characters say: "And do not forget that we Jews have to fight, not only against a specific enemy that threatens us today, but above all against the evil that has persecuted and tortured us in all generations and among all peoples. This gratuitous hatred against us must disappear from the face of the earth. I want to be confident that we will triumph over this enemy[470]."

As Elie Wiesel once wrote: Are we not at war with destiny, with the whole world[471] ? Edouard Valdman had the same characteristic Jewish mentality, which only reasons according to its own standards. The nations, he said, "project onto the Jew the fear within them, their own unknown. We must destroy, because we are afraid and cannot understand. This is how humanity, through the crime against the Jew from the origin, never ceases to destroy within itself the part of the foreigner, the part of the other, never ceases to destroy itself, simply[472]."

And here again we must understand that it is primarily the Jew who fears the foreigner, and not "the nations". And it is the Jew who "projects onto the nations the fear he carries within him", and not the other way around.

However, if we take the analysis of Edouard Valdmann's text to its logical conclusion, we are obliged to clarify his last sentence. Judaism is indeed "a crime against humanity" and "must disappear from the face of the earth". And Jewish eschatology can be clearly understood in this way:

---

[469] Jean-Jacques Servan-Schreiber, *Le réveil de la France, mai-juin 1968*, Denoël, 1968, p. 88.
[470] David Vogel, *Todos marcharon a la guerra*, Xordica Editorial, Zaragoza, 2017, p. 154.
[471] Elie Wiesel, *Célébration hassidique II*, Seuil, 1981, p. 182.
[472] Édouard Valdman, *Les Juifs et l'argent*, Editions Galilée, 1994, p. 68.

The Messiah will only come after the apostasy, after the disappearance of the last Jew. The drama of the Jewish condition appears here in broad daylight, in the reflection of the mirror.

It is therefore not surprising that Jews have encountered some resistance throughout history. Jewish historian Saul Freidlander had quoted Hitler's speech to party veterans on 8 November 1941: "I have come to know those Jews as world incendiaries (*Ich habe diese Juden als die Weltbrandstifter kennengelernt*)[473]." Friedlander also quoted in passing Goebbels' words, written by him in his notebooks dated 7 October 1940, during the offensive in Poland: "These Jews are no longer human beings. They are predators with a cold intellect, who must be rendered useless[474]".

The novelist Louis-Ferdinand Céline was also particularly indignant, and wanted to do away with the snake once and for all: "It's very simple: total fanatical racism or death! And what death! They are waiting for us! May the spirit of the mongoose animate us, inflame us[475]!"

Indeed, most of Europe's great minds were at one time or another enlisted in the ranks of the "anti-Semitic" or counter-Jewish resistance, from Tacitus and Cicero to Shakespeare, Voltaire, Dostoyevsky and Solzhenitsyn. And many more have spoken out against the folly of Judaism. Even Miguel de Cervantes had his good Sancho Panza say: "It is well true that I am somewhat malicious, and that I have my certain knave-like glimpses; but it is all covered and covered by the great cloak of my simplicity, always natural and never contrived; and when there was nothing else but to believe, as I always believe, firmly and truly in God and in all that the holy Roman Catholic Church has and believes, and to be a mortal enemy, as I am, of the Jews, should historians have mercy on me and treat me well in their writings[476]."

But the issue is not so much whether this or that great figure in history or literature was an "anti-Semite" as whether Judaism is the "mortal enemy" of the rest of humanity. The project of "Peace" and world unification promoted by Judaism can only be achieved through the ruin of all nations,

---

[473] Saul Friedländer, *The Third Reich and the Jews (1939-1945), The Years of Extermination*, Galaxia Gutenberg, Barcelona, 2009 p. 374, Annual address to the party's "Old Fighters" on 8 November 1941.

[474] Saul Friedländer, *The Third Reich and the Jews (1939-1945), The Years of Extermination*, Galaxia Gutenberg, Barcelona, 2009 p. 53.

[475] *Je Suis Partout*, 22 December 1941, in *Ecrits de guerre*, Nouvelles Editions, Paris, 1990, p. 26.

[476] *Don Quichotte*, Gallimard, Bibliothèque de la Pléiade, 1934, p. 475, in *L'Anthologie des propos contre les juifs*, by Paul-Éric Blanrue, Ed. Blanche, 2007. (Miguel de Cervantes y Saavedra, *Don Quixote de la Mancha, Part Two, Chapter VIII: Where he tells what happened to Don Quixote on his way to see his lady Dulcinea del Toboso*).

peoples and religions. Only the Jews and the "kingdom of David" will then remain on the face of the earth. The apparently peaceful slogans of militant Judaism, such as tolerance, human rights, democracy and equality, are in reality terribly effective weapons of war to subvert and destroy nations. But "Peace" - that word constantly on the lips of Jewish intellectuals - is undoubtedly the one they are unable to find within themselves.

PART THREE

PSYCHOANALYSIS OF JUDAISM

1. Sexual deviations

The ambiguity of Jewish identity is often reflected in its sexuality, judging by the cultural output of Judaism. Its tireless propaganda through the media has had an obvious impact on Western societies, to the extent that every year since the 1990s, hundreds of thousands of 'gays' and transvestites parade through the streets of European capitals. The omnipresence of Jewish intellectuals in television, cinema, bookshops, exhibitions and art galleries is the only explanation for this phenomenon of increasing homosexuality in all "democratic" societies. You can turn the problem around in every way: there is no other explanation.

Militant homosexuality

In her 1992 book, *Male Identity*, Elisabeth Badinter drew on Freud to convince us that homosexual tendencies normally exist in most human beings. Freud, Badinter wrote, "affirms that not only are we all capable of a homosexual choice, but that we have all, "at one time or another, practised it, even if, afterwards, some have relegated it to the unconscious and others defend themselves by maintaining an energetic attitude against it[477]." Once again, we see that it is a question of projecting a particular problem onto a universal plane. Elisabeth Badinter also stated: "We know, thanks to Freud,

---

[477] Sigmund Freud, *A Childhood Memory of Leonardo da Vinci* (1910), Idées / Gallimard, 1977, p. 92, in Elisabeth Badinter, *La Identidad masculina*, Alianza Editorial, Madrid, 1993, p. 132.

that male friendship has its origin in the sublimation of homosexual desire[478]." But we do not have to believe it.

Indeed, Dr Freud played a pioneering role in the normalisation of homosexuality. In 1930, he signed the petition for the revision of the Penal Code and the abolition of the crime of homosexuality between consenting adults.[479]

The psychoanalyst Elisabeth Roudinesco confirmed this: "As long as homosexuality was considered a degeneration," she wrote, "the question of its integration into the norm was not seriously raised. But from the moment Freud refused to classify it as a defect and turned it into a sexual disposition derived from bisexuality, the way was opened for all the questions that are raised today[480]." When homosexuality was no longer considered a sexual perversion, the door was opened to all other "abnormalities".

Naturally, it was Jews who were at the forefront of the gay movement. Classical" anti-Semites rightly accuse them of contributing to the dissolution of traditional society. But the truth is that this militant homosexuality, so present in Judaism, is above all a manifestation of a facet of Jewish identity.

In September 2006, Ted Pike, an American nationalist, cited the names of the leaders of the main "gay" associations in the United States: The Human Rights Campaign (Solomonese, Berman, Lieberman, Linsky, Perlman, Weiner, Schwartz); Human Rights Campaign Foundation Board (Oppenheimer, Rosen, Sharrin, Beesemyer, Bockelman, Ebert, Epstein, Fink, Freddman, Suber, Lappin, Zellner, Levin); Gay and Lesbian Alliance Against Defamation (Weinberger, Glukstern); etc. Another American nationalist, David Duke, also cited a whole list of leaders in his long article of 5 August 2007 entitled *From the Abyss*. Here are just three of them: Larry Kramer, co-founder of Act Up, a gay activist organisation; Alan Klein, co-founder of Queer Nation, and spokesman for the Gay & Lesbian Alliance Defamation (GLAA); Israel Fishman, founder of Gay Liberation in 1970, which later became the Gay, Lesbian, Bisexual, Bisexual, and Transgendered Round Table, and was the world's first gay organisation.

Take, for example, the biography of the great American poet Allen Ginsberg. In the United States he is best known for *Howl and Other Poems*, published in 1956. It is a long prose poem recounting his experiences, as well as a history of the Beat Generation, of which he was a founding member. The work provoked a scandal for its crude and explicit language,

---

[478] S. Freud, "On certain neurotic mechanisms in jealousy, paranoia and homosexuality", 1922, in *Névrose, psychose et perversion*, PUF, 1973, p. 281, in Elisabeth Badinter, *La Identidad masculina*, Alianza Editorial, Madrid, 1993, p. 147.

[479] Elisabeth Badinter, *La Identidad masculina*, Alianza Editorial, Madrid, 1993, p. 133.

[480] Elisabeth Roudinesco, *Pourquoi la psychanalyse*, Fayard, 1999, p. 168, 169.

and was temporarily withdrawn from sale for obscenity. In it, Allen Ginsberg went to war "against destructive materialistic values and American politics", according to sources consulted on the Internet. In 1961, Ginsberg published another important book, *Kaddish for Naomi Ginsberg*, which he had begun in 1957 in a Paris café, and in which he recounted "his mother's paranoid illness and their anguished relationship". It won't be long before you realise what those words mean.

In the 1960s, Ginsberg travelled to India in search of spiritual guidance, a period he recounted in *Indian Journals* (1970), and Tibetan Buddhism remained an important source of inspiration for him. Naturally, Ginsberg was awarded the highest literary honours in the United States: in 1972, his *The Fall of America* received the National Book Award for Poetry. Later, his *Cosmopolitan Greetings: Poems 1986-1992* was a finalist for the Pulitzer Prize. "Allen Ginsberg's poetry, spontaneous and free, is a blend of modernism, his Jewish origins, and his Buddhist faith".

The author of this review forgot to point out that Ginsberg was also a pioneer of the gay movement, and an active member of the North American Man Boy Alliance (Nambla), a paedophile advocacy organisation that was fashionable in leftist circles at the time. In 1994, the International Lesbian and Gay Association decided to expel Nambla. Ginsberg explained at the time that "the anti-paedophile hysteria reminded him of the anti-homosexual hysteria he had endured in his youth", and that he "chose to defend the association's right to free speech."

Advocacy of homosexuality seems to flow naturally from the Jewish spirit. The American actor Kirk Douglas, who was by no means homosexual, recounted in his memoirs the beginnings of his acting career. As a college student, he acted in a number of plays. One of them was called *Trio, the Whirlwind of Life*. "A play about a lesbian teacher who tries to seduce one of her young students". Kirk Douglas acknowledged, however: "Unfortunately, the subject matter was too bold for the time and we were forced to close on moral grounds[481]."

The industrialist Henry Ford - an automobile builder - had also been concerned about these constant attacks on traditional society and founded a newspaper, the *Deadborn Independent*, to denounce the role of Israelites in advocating sexual deviance: "The motion pictures are controlled by the Jews, not only partly, not fifty per cent, but wholly; with the natural consequence that the world is now up in arms against the trivialising and demoralising influence of this form of entertainment....It is the gift of this

---

[481] Kirk Douglas, *The Ragpicker's Son* (1988), Cult Books, *2021*, p. 108-109

race to create problems of a moral nature in any business in which they attain a majority[482]."

That was almost 100 years ago, in the 1920s. Fifty years later, all dams of containment were blown up and since then Jewish producers, directors and screenwriters have been having a field day flooding our television screens and newsstands with homosexuality and pornography.

There are countless television programmes and fictions that promote homosexuality, and this propaganda is obviously coordinated by who knows which conductor.

On 26 September 2007, for example, the Franco-German channel Arte presented an evening on the subject of "*ménage à trois*": At 10.30 p.m., Caterina Klusemann's documentary *"L'Amour à trois"* was followed by another documentary *"Jamais deux sans trois"* - *Une famille postmoderne*. The TV programme summarised the intrigue as follows: "In New York, two men who live together have a love affair with a woman who is going to give them two children...". And this is what the journalist wrote: "A pertinent documentary on the evolution of manners...". The director of this attack on the traditional family model was a certain Susan Kaplan.

On the same day, at the same time, Direct 8 screened *Coup de chance*, a film by Pierre Aknine (France, 1991): "François Kaplan, director of an insurance company, dies in an accidental fall after learning that his wife has left him to live with a woman...".

On the same day, the public channel France 2 broadcast a new programme produced and presented by Karine Le Marchand: *Tabous*. And this first programme was dedicated to homosexuality. A psychiatrist, Serge Hefez, explained that all this is perfectly normal and that we should be delighted to live in such an "open" society. Needless to say, Serge Hefez was a member of the community.

In December 2008, Arte aired *Clara Sheller*, a TV series by Alain Berliner (France, 2004). In the episode *Une Femme peut en cacher une autre*, Clara asks herself questions about Gilles, whom she suspects of dating another woman. Her friend JP tells her that he has a secret relationship with Pascal, a boy who lives with his partner. *Chrysantèmes pour Bernard* continues this story of a woman's affair. In *La porte de la tour bancale*, Gilles and JP are unable to commit to a real relationship. JP is now sure that Gilles is the one he loves and doesn't want to wait any longer to be happy. Thanks to Alain Berliner, French families can now watch two men in bed in *prime time at* night.

---

[482] Neal Gabler, *An Empire of Their Own, How the Jews Invented Hollywood*, Confluences, 2015, p. 407.

Let us now complete the list of films that trivialise homosexuality, which we presented in 2007 in *Jewish Fanaticism*.

Les yeux brouillés, by Rémi Lange (France, 2000): The actors play themselves. Rémi has been living with Antoine for three years and decides to take another lover. And here is Bouniq-Mercier's comment: "The film acquires an aura of authenticity that allows us to consider homosexuality as a normal relationship".

Faites comme si je n'étais pas là (France, 2000): Seventeen-year-old Eric can't stand his stepfather. From his room, he spies on his neighbours with his binoculars. These neighbours have very free morals, as Fabienne shares her flat with Tom, a homosexual. The film is by Olivier Dahan.

Drôle de Félix, by Olivier Ducastel (France, 1999): Félix, gay and HIV-positive, lives in Dieppe with his lover Daniel, a teacher. The film features some evil racist right-wing extremists.

Les Corps ouverts, by Sébastien Lifshitz (France, 1997): Rémi is eighteen years old. To relieve his boredom, he attends an audition. Marc, the director, is seduced by his charm and makes him his lover. Disconcerted by this homosexual experience, Rémi offers his body in various encounters, thus losing himself and perhaps finding himself again. A "dark" film, but also "endearing and certainly sincere", wrote Claude Bouniq-Mercier.

Pédale douce (France, 1996) is a film about the world of gay and transvestite clubs and the intrigues and misunderstandings that ensue. It was directed by Gabriel Aghion.

Mauvais genre, by Laurent Bénégui (France, 1996): Martial has just written his first novel. He is interested in Camille, but Camille prefers women.

Gazon maudit by Josiane Balasko (France, 1994) is another well-known film for French audiences. It tells the story of a lesbian who intrudes into a couple's life, and the husband eventually bows out, accepting this *ménage à trois*: "A provocative comedy of manners that challenges many preconceived ideas about love and sexuality," wrote Bouniq.

Muriel fait le désespoir de ses parents, by Philippe Faucon (France, 1994): 17-year-old Muriel becomes aware of her homosexuality when she meets the luminous Nora. The screenplay is by Catherine Klein.

Le Journal de Lady M, by Alain Tanner (France-Belgium, 1993): Lady M, a rock singer, meets Diego. She discovers that he lives with Noria, a beautiful black woman, with whom he has a daughter. The three of them start living together, but soon Lady M falls in love with Noria and Diego abandons the young women to his lovers.

Two boys, a girl, three possibilities, by Andrew Flemming (USA, 1993): On an American campus, Eddy, a reserved boy, shares a room with Stuart, an unrepentant flirt. Alex, a slightly androgynous girl, is his neighbour. Stuart likes Alex, who likes Eddy, who likes Stuart. Alex leads the two boys to come to terms with a sexuality that is not as determined as they think it is. The screenplay is by Alexandre Gruszynski.

Philadelphia (USA, 1993): A young lawyer is fired by his boss, officially for incompetence. In reality, it is because he has AIDS. With the help of his colleague, Joe Miller, they fight to defend themselves. "A flood of good feelings", wrote Jean Tulard about Jonathan Demne's acclaimed film.

See also *Mensonge*, by François Margolin (France, 1992): Emma is married to Charles. She soon discovers the sexual ambivalence of her husband, who has infected her with AIDS. This is not cool. A screenplay by Denis Saada.

Henry et June (USA, 1990): In Paris in 1931, Anaïs Nin is bored with her husband. When she meets the still unknown writer Henry Miller, she discovers an unknown Paris of artists and prostitutes. She has a sapphic affair with June, Henry Miller's wife. This is a film by Philip Kaufmann.

Prick up your ears (UK, 1987): In 1951, two students on a drama course come to terms with their homosexuality. They "get on perfectly", but one ends up murdering the other. "A cheeky, provocative and humorous play," Claude Bouniq-Mercier told us. The film is by Stephen Frears, a director of the most hysterical kind.

Le Chant des sirènes, by Patricia Rozema (Canada, 1987): Polly is hired as a secretary by the fascinating Gabrielle, director of an art gallery, and is captivated by her poise. The arrival of Mary, one of Gabrielle's homosexual relations, unsettles Polly for a moment. "A refreshing, poetic, humorous and irresistibly charming film," wrote Bouniq, whose glowing reviews confirmed the director's Jewishness.

Cent franc l'amour, by Jacques Richard (France, 1985): Jérémy, a poor photographer, gets Maurice, a homosexual antique dealer, to support him. But all he offers him is friendship, and at night he wanders from sex shop to *peep show*.

Another country, by Marek Kanievska (UK, 1983): a journalist in Moscow gets an interview with Guy Bennett, a spy who has left England. In the 1930s, he was a boarder at an upper-class school, but was publicly humiliated after an openly homosexual relationship. He decided to take revenge by joining his friend Judd, who professed Marxist ideas. "A document of English schools and the hypocrisy that reigns in the practices that govern them," read the *Film Guide*.

Pepi, Luci, Bom y otras chicas del montón (Spain, 1980) is Pedro Almodóvar's first film: Pepi grows marijuana on her balcony. Luci, the exemplary wife of a policeman, discovers homosexual and perverse pleasures with Bom, a punk singer, while smoking it. For once, Claude Bouniq-Mercier is critical: "The image is dirty, the direction is shoddy? A provocative film that, today, lacks any interest".

In 1975, the "French" filmmaker Claude Miller made a film entitled *La meilleure façon de marcher*. It is a story about holiday camp monitors for children. One of them is shy, taciturn and withdrawn, and has to put up with the teasing of his classmates. One day, one of them (Patrick Dewaere) enters his room without knocking and discovers him dressed as a woman. The secret is kept until the end of the holiday party. Everyone dresses up for the occasion and the repressed homosexual plucks up his courage and disguises himself as a woman. In a filmed interview, Claude Miller openly explained that he filmed his personal case.

In *Cruising* (patrolling and sexual encounters in gay slang, ndt) (USA, 1980,), several sadomasochistic homosexuals are murdered. A young rookie, Steve Burns, is charged with investigating in the gay milieus of Greenwich Village. The film is by William Friedkin.

Something Almost Perfect (USA, 2000): Abbie (Madonna) has never been lucky in love, but lo and behold, she gets pregnant by a homosexual after a night of drinking. A film by John Sclesinger.

Zig-Zig is a film by Laszlo Szabo (France, 1974): Marie and Pauline, two cabaret singers prostitute themselves to buy a chalet in the mountains. They discover that they love each other.

Bloody Mama (USA, 1970) narrates the misdeeds of the gang formed by Ma Baker and her four sons: Herman the sadist, Lloyd the druggie, Arthur the coward and Fred the homosexual. Crimes, rapes and overdoses. Finally they are cornered by the police and fight to the bitter end. A Roger Corman film.

Tell me you love me, Junie Moon, by Otto Preminger (USA, 1969): Junie, a young woman disfigured by a sadistic lover, Arthur, a tormented epileptic, and Warren, a homosexual paralysed in both legs, decide to leave the hospital where they are being treated to live together in a country house. "A little gem of real emotion... at times disturbing. Otto Preminger - says Guy Bellinger in the *Guide des Films* - gives his homosexual character great dignity".

Hunting scenes in Bavaria (FRG, 1968): Several marginal villagers are persecuted: a simpleton, a cripple, a prostitute and, above all, Abram, who has returned home after being convicted of homosexuality. The peasant bastards will kill him after hunting him down like a wild animal. The film is by Peter Fleischmann, who doesn't like peasants very much.

In *The Vampire's Ball* (UK, 1967), director Roman Planski depicts a blond, homosexual vampire: the small revenge of a short, wimpy brunette.

In the 1950s, one had to be a little more careful, as the goyim were still quite reactive and nervous at that time. Just watch *The Barefoot Contessa*, by the famous Joseph Mankiewicz (USA, 1954): Maria Vargas recalls her life: She was a cabaret dancer in Madrid when a Hollywood producer discovered her and made her a star. She met Count Toralto-Favrini, who married her, but whose impotence she discovered. Anxious to give him posterity, she found herself a lover. Mankiewicz declared, "In the end, Prince Charming should have turned out to be homosexual, but I couldn't go that far."

The Bamboo House, by Samuel Fuller (USA, 1955): Sandy Dawson, a homosexual, has created a criminal association of former soldiers in Tokyo.

Michael, by Carl Dreyer (Germany, 1924): Paris, 1900, a fashionable painter. "A work that deals with a homosexual affair with subtlety and discretion".

There is a strong tendency among Jewish intellectuals to project their neurosis on a universal plane. The novel by a certain Jean-Paul Tapie entitled *Le Garçon qui voulait être juif (The boy who wanted to be a Jew)* is a good example. The book was published in 2004 by the publishing house "H et O": "Arthur hadn't slept for a long time. Or very little. He didn't understand why he didn't sleep. Perhaps it had something to do with the fact that his father hated Jews and homosexuals? Yet Arthur had great admiration for his father, who had made him a healthy, sporty boy. So why go to Israel, why go to the kibbutz? In any case, if someone were to utter insults against Jews, Arthur knew that he would stand up proudly, that he would defend himself, and that many people around him, if not his father, would approve."

You've got it: Jean-Paul Tapie was evidently a homosexual Jewish writer who transferred his personal case into a goy. A "genius".

In *Les Bienveillantes* (Prix Goncourt 2006), Jonathan Littel also painted a picture of great Jewish suffering, through a rather unusual character: an SS officer during the Second World War who is homosexual, paedophile and has sexual relations with his twin sister: a typically Jewish script, as we are about to see.

The political advisors of the princes of the Republic, in the media, know how to skilfully dress up the militant homosexual discourse to make it acceptable to the mass of the goyim, always a little reluctant to accept the neuroses of the chosen people. In the weekly *L'Express* of 18 October 2004, the inescapable Jacques Attali lambasted the declarations of certain political personalities. Indeed, an Italian politician, Rocco Buttiglione, had declared before the European Parliament that homosexuality was "a sin" and that the purpose of marriage was "to allow women to have children and be protected by a man". This was too much for Attali, who was indignant, projecting the problem onto Europeans: "Everything is being set in motion, Attali wrote, to make homophobia once again a respectable opinion...The tragedy of the 1940s showed us that intolerance towards minorities, whatever they may be, is the breeding ground of dictatorships...If the West wants to save its values from external enemies, it will first have to rid itself of its own demons." But by this point in the study, the reader will have understood that what is at stake here are first and foremost the demons of Judaism.

The origins of feminism

Feminists fight for equality between the sexes, just as Marxists once assured us of the abolition of social classes and democrats now promise us a world without borders that will bring together a mixed and peaceful humanity. The aim is always to dissolve identities, be they sexual, social or national, and to coagulate the atomised particles in order to unify the world and work for the advent of a definitive "Peace" on Earth.

In his Moscow speech of 5 August 2007, entitled *From the Abyss*, American nationalist David Duke recalled the role of Jewish women in the origins of feminism in the United States: "The four most important leaders of radical feminism since World War II have been Betty Friedan, Bella Abzug, Gloria Steinem and Gloria Allred". And David Duke cited some examples of militant Jewish feminists since the 1960s: Heather Booth (abortion rights and anti-discrimination), Susan Brownmiller (author of *Against our will*, a book on rape); Blu Greenberg, Phyllis Chesler (Member of *Hashomer Hatzair* [483] and pioneer of women's psychology), Judy Chicago (feminist artist), Sonia Pressman Fuentes (feminist lawyer and founder of the *Now* movement), Nancy Miriam Hawley (feminist writer on health and sexuality), Alix Kates Shulman (feminist writer), etc.[484]

In France, Jewish women were also at the forefront of the movement. Elisabeth Badinter was one of its main representatives in the second half of the 20th century. She praised "the far-sighted discourse of the Viennese feminist Rosa Mayreder, who advocates a synthesis of masculine and

---

[483] Socialist Zionist youth movement.
[484] We have already addressed this question in *Psychoanalysis of Judaism* and *Jewish Fanaticism*. [This list can be completed: Ernestine Rose (first Jewish feminist, daughter of a rabbi and pioneer of the first wave in the 1830s-1870s), Rebeka Bettelheim Kohut (one of the first feminists, president of the World Congress of Jewish Women in 1923), Andrea Dworkin (radical writer, critic of pornography, Shulamith Firestone (second-wave radical feminist, author of *Dialectic of Sex*), Ellen Willis (writer and activist, co-founder with Firestone of the radical group *Redstockings* in 1969), Ruth Bader Ginsburg (US Supreme Court justice, lawyer and defender of women's rights in the United States), Shulamith Firestone (author of the book "*The Dialectic of Sex*") and Ruth Bader Ginsburg (author of the book "*The Sex Dialectic*"), and Shulamith Firestone (author of the book "*The Sex Dialectic*").(US supreme court justice, a career-long advocate of feminism), Judith Butler (philosopher and gender theorist, highly influential in third-wave feminism and queer), Naomi Wolf (preeminent and successful feminist writer), and others].

feminine for those individuals who have freed themselves from their sexual characteristics".

Elisabeth Badinter sought to wipe the slate clean by destroying the family basis of European civilisation: "Rethinking masculinity is an urgency that Americans have sensed before anyone else". She pretended to ignore the origins of "a much more radical and potent feminism for which the historical and psychological causes should one day be sought[485]."

But let us now turn to the interesting testimony of Gisèle Halimi, who was also one of the most prominent figures of militant feminism in France. Gisèle Halimi was born in 1927 in Tunisia, and was originally called Zeiza Gisèle Elise Taïeb. She first married Paul Halimi, divorced him and remarried Claude Faux, Jean-Paul Sartre's former secretary, to whom she was a friend and lawyer.

At the beginning of her biography, *Le Lait de l'oranger* (*The Milk of the Orange Tree*), published in 1988, Gisèle Halimi recounted her childhood in Tunisia and how she had rebelled against the position of women in the Jewish religion: "To earn divine favour, boys had to pray, she wrote. Girls - uninitiated in Hebrew and mere auxiliaries, almost domestics of the religion - were not to sin.... Very early on, perhaps at the age of ten, when I started secondary school at the Armand-Fallières secondary school, this trade-off struck me as suspicious. It was probably at the same time that my maternal grandfather explained to me that women, being impure, could not wrap the tefillin[486] around their arms during morning prayer. Besides, their function was not to pray, but to serve the man so that he would pray".

"Blessed be the Lord who did not make me a woman." This is how every faithful Jew begins his prayer and his day. Gisèle Halimi asked her grandfather: "And what do the women say? At this question, my grandfather nodded in the direction of the kitchen where my grandmother had disappeared: "A holy woman, but she doesn't have to pray. In fact, if she wanted to, she would simply reply, 'Blessed be the Lord who has made me as He willed.

This role assigned to us by God seemed to me to be very insignificant," continued Gisèle Halimi. So why should being born a woman be the misfortune of existence, a kind of fault to be paid for, to be redeemed? As much as my mother exaggerated the importance of the woman who, in the home, arranges the objects of worship, brings the man the water for the ritual ablution as soon as he wakes up and takes care to prevent the sins of her children, I persisted in thinking that God treated us with indifference...

---

[485] Elisabeth Badinter, *La Identidad masculina*, Alianza Editorial, Madrid, 1993, p. 34, 21

[486] Tefillin are leather wrappings or boxes containing Torah passages that pious Jews tie to their foreheads and left arms with leather straps during prayers.

In the synagogue, when I accompanied the men of the family, I was obliged, like all women, to go up to the balcony. From there, as mute spectators, we admired the courtyard where, around the Byzantine gold of the tablets of the Law, the men and boys enjoyed the privilege of addressing God directly... This segregation weighed on me and fed my resentment towards the Lord. When I went to class, I kissed the mezuzah[487] with increasing reluctance[488]."

It is a fact that, among the Jewish people, women have always been considered inferior beings, and it is probably no coincidence that most feminist harpies are Jewish by origin, and this since the beginning of the 20th century. Like their husbands, they too have a strong tendency to project their obsessive neurosis onto a universal plane, instead of considering the endogenous communal origin of their misfortune.

Gisèle Halimi had to face anti-Semitism at a very early age. At the age of eight, her teacher used to terrorise her, just for fun: "I was her favourite target for abuse. She would inflict a whole series of humiliations on me and sometimes even hit me. Why did she do that? I didn't understand. I still don't... When the bell rang for recess, I trembled with anxiety. The harpy would make me come to the edge of the platform: "Stay there," she hissed between her teeth. Without a word, her thin lips let out nervous little noises that sounded like burps, and her greenish eyes scanned the playground where my classmates were playing. With tears in my eyes, I then joined them, free at last. None of them said a word. They all knew, but none of them understood the reasons for this cruelty. As the days went by, the slaps left more and more visible marks on me, but I remained silent. One night, when the neuropathic teacher had been more violent than usual, I came home with red marks all over my face. Who slapped you? Who hit you? my father demanded to know. I ended up telling him everything: "When she sends me to the yard, she says to me, 'dirty Jewess' or 'dirty Moor', you are the Devil, all of you, you want to finish us off....

I sobbed at my own story, as if liberated: "It's so bad!" I still didn't understand anything. My mother cooled my face with a wet towel. "Can

---

[487] Mezuzah (from the Hebrew מְזוּזָה, "door jamb") is a scroll with two verses of Torah written on it, usually housed in a box or receptacle attached to the right jamb of the porches of Jewish houses and cities. (NdT).

[488] Gisèle Halimi, *Le Lait de l'oranger*, Gallimard, 1988, Pocket, 2001, p. 28. Kirk Douglas had six sisters. One day he had to leave home to go to college. On the day of her farewell "Ma's eyes filled with tears...She kissed me goodbye and in a low voice said in Yiddish something that startled me: "A boy is a boy, but a girl is a drek (shit)." "Poor Ma, she was left alone with six girls." Kirk Douglas, *The Ragman's Son* (1988), Cult Books, 2021, p.47 and Kirk Douglas, *Le Fils du chiffonier*, 1988, Poche, 1989, p. 62.

you believe it? A schoolteacher! She's crazy! She should be locked up in the Manouba!⁴⁸⁹ ""

We may be allowed to doubt this testimony. We are well aware of the propensity of Jewish intellectuals to use their imagination in every possible way, especially when it comes to recounting the harassment or persecution they may have suffered in the past. Moreover, we find it highly suspicious that an official of the French Republic could have harassed a student in this way without incurring the most serious penalties. We know that Jews are a particularly pampered population in the Republic, as can be seen every time a Jew is the victim of the slightest offence: the minister never hesitates to go to see the alleged victim. As early as 1866, the Jews of France seemed to be in a position to silence any manifestation of anti-Semitism on the part of petty officials. In 1869, Roger Gougenot des Mousseaux noted the regime's particular concern for the children of Israel and quoted this news item from the *Archives Israélites*: "A young boy of Jewish blood was offended in a school "by one of his companions, who did not fail to call him a Jew on every occasion. The father went to complain to the minister of public education and asked for protection. The minister himself immediately went to the school in question; he disciplined the class teacher, who had refused to intervene, and the teacher had to write a letter of apology to the father of the family, who was hurt in his religion[490] "."

Gisèle Halimi arrived in Paris in 1945, aged eighteen, amazed by the city. She went to live in Clichy, with the parents of one of her brother's friends - some goyim. André G. was the secretary of a communist cell in Clichy. With his wooden leg, he dragged Gisèle Halimi to political meetings: "The militants respectfully turned away", he wrote. André was nothing but tenderness for "his adopted daughter", until Gisèle demanded the money he had entrusted to her so that she could enrol at university. Gisèle was once again confronted with hatred and saw, behind the communist, the reddened face of the alcoholic and anti-Semitic goy:

"Suddenly, he tipped back in his chair, using only his leg and hands, he pushed his plate away with his elbow. "I'm sick, sick of you and your money... geez... who do you think you are... always asking for more.... That's enough... If you're not happy, you can get out, get out and that's it...!" Standing up, red-eyed, the grey moustache covered with spittle threatens me with his cane: "All the same, the Jews... that's all they think

---

[489] Gisèle Halimi, *Le Lait de l'oranger*, Gallimard, 1988, Pocket, 2001, p. 62, 63. La Manouba: psychiatric asylum located on the outskirts of Tunis, in La Manouba.

[490] Gougenot des Mousseaux. *The Jew, Judaism and the Judaisation of Christian peoples*, pdf version. Translated into English by Professor Noemí Coronel and the invaluable collaboration of the team of Nacionalismo Católico Argentina, 2013 p. 238. 238, (*Archives israelites*, XXII, p. 991; 1866).

about, money... filthy Jewess, you and your brothers, leeches, that's it, you're our leeches. "He screams like a madman, drooling from the corner of his mouth. I look at him, petrified. The man of all those generous speeches about equality, colonialism and racism? All that's left is a hate-filled lunatic pushing me towards the exit. But I have to check in, don't get me wrong. He doesn't understand, I don't understand anything, I'm stubborn. Get out of here," he shouts, "get out right now, not a minute more under my roof, Jewess...get out...I don't want to see you again..." And he pushes me with his cane towards the door".

Poor Gisèle barely had time to gather her things. As she knew no one in Paris, she immediately thought of the baker, with whom she had taken a liking. The baker introduced her to an old lady, Mme Darmour, who took her in with pleasure. Gisèle then enrolled in the Faculty of Law. Once or twice a week, Madame Darmour was visited by Madame Delrue, a widow. Gisèle was very unlucky, for it turned out that Madame Delrue was also a horrible anti-Semitic harpy. Unaware that Gisèle was Jewish, she willingly let off steam: "Madame Delrue displayed issues of *Je suis partout*, which contained, framed in red pencil, anti-Semitic caricatures. "Look at those noses and those hooked fingers... to take over the country... they dominate the real French, with their diabolical malignity and their money...". Sometimes he would get carried away and say: "Vermin that must be crushed[491].""

Gisèle Halimi became a prominent lawyer. She began as a communist, campaigned for Algerian independence and tirelessly denounced the French army, colonialism and the evil Whites. In 1971 she founded the feminist movement with Simone de Beauvoir and fought with Simone Veil for French women's right to abortion. She was also one of the founders of the globalist movement Attac. In 2006, like most Jewish activists, she was made an Officer of the Legion of Honour.

His book ended as it had begun: in the synagogue. Her father had died by then. In the Nice synagogue, she and her sister Gaby decided to stand with the men, not in the balcony reserved for women. There was a small incident when they were asked to remain in their place: "Gaby and I refused. We are equal before this God who takes away our father. The rabbi argues, but we don't move. The rabbi gives in. The ceremony goes ahead as planned, except for this exception[492]." In short, while the world of the goyim must be destroyed, "reinventing society" as Jews are wont to say, they, on the other hand, will go their own way to the end.

---

[491]Gisèle Halimi, *Le Lait de l'oranger*, Gallimard, 1988, Pocket, 2001, p. 82-88.
[492]Gisèle Halimi, *Le Lait de l'oranger*, Gallimard, 1988, Pocket, 2001, p. 438.

The destruction of patriarchy

The destruction of the family unit, the basis of traditional European society, seems to be another obsession of Jewish intellectuals. In her book *The Masculine Identity*, Elisabeth Badinter made this clear: "The questioning of intimate certainties is always long and painful... But this task of deconstruction is never random. It is only possible when the dominant model has demonstrated its limits. Such is the case of the traditional male model, out of step with the evolution of women and the source of a real mutilation of which men are beginning to become aware. The old man is dying to make way for another, different man, who is being born under our gaze and whose limits are not yet visible to us[493]." In 1917, the Bolsheviks were saying exactly the same thing.

Elisabeth Badinter cited the case of Otto Gross, one of his peers, who had an immeasurable hatred of European society: "Otto Gross calls for the advent of a matriarchy and the abolition of the law of the father...The brilliant Otto Gross was as fragile as Weininger. His life is a repeated settling of scores with his father and a constant manifestation of hatred of manhood, and his work is essentially a critique of patriarchy and traditional masculine values[494]."

In the Soviet Union, for example, the feminist activist Aleksandra Kolontái, who before the Second World War was the only woman to hold a high position in the Communist Party, had the heroine of one of her novels, *L'Amour libre-Trois générations* (*Free Love - Three Generations*), say: "For me, sexual activity is simply a physical necessity. I change lovers according to my mood. At the moment, I'm pregnant, but I don't know who the father of my future child is; I'm indifferent".

This obsession can also be found in Jacques Attali. In November 2007, Jacques Attali and his group of editors published their umpteenth book, *Amours, Histoires des relations entre les hommes et les femmes*. The presentation of the book reads as follows: "From society to society, every possible form of relationship between men and women has been tried out: the sharing of women, men or children; polyandry, polygamy, courtly love, long-term marriage, fleeting marriage, celibacy, multiple relationships. All sorts of prohibitions have been imposed, from incest and zoophilia to paedophilia and homosexuality, to name but a few. Conversely, none of these prohibitions have failed to be strongly recommended by other societies, glorifying marriage between brother and sister, father and daughter, between children. Today's technologies, with their potential for

---

[493]Elisabeth Badinter, *La Identidad masculina*, Alianza Editorial, Madrid, 1993, p. 14.
[494]Elisabeth Badinter, *La Identidad masculina*, Alianza Editorial, Madrid, 1993, p. 153.

virtual love, cloning and artificial wombs, open up dizzying new possibilities...This book, illustrated with numerous rare photos, is a journey through history."

We see in this text the clear will of the Jewish intellectual to destroy the European patriarchal family system, offering us as an alternative model all the evils engendered in the margins of other civilisations. And once again we see how Jacques Attali is literally obsessed with incest, as he talks about it in at least four other books in a very ambiguous way.[495]

In cinema, cosmopolitan directors have long been preparing the liberation of women from the shackles of the patriarchal family. Here are some of the films that have "liberated" European women:

Une femme d'extérieur, by Christian Blanc (France, 2000): Françoise, a thirty-five-year-old nurse, discovers that her husband Jacques is unfaithful. She throws him out and is left alone with her three children. Soon, she is indifferent to everything. She neglects her work, her home and her children, lives at night and indulges in chance encounters. The screenplay is by Roger Bohbot.

Striptease, by Andrew Bergman (USA, 1995): Erin has lost her job at the FBI because of her drug addict husband and has to dance in a strip club to make a living.

Le Rocher d'Acapulco (France, 1995): Sandrine, a shop assistant at the Tati shops, lives in a hotel. Gérald, her brother's old boyfriend, takes her in and goes to Acapulco. He encourages her to work through the pink Minitel and then to become a prostitute. Reluctant at first, she finally accepts. The film is by Laurent Tuel.

In *La Séparation* (France, 1994), Pierre and Anne form a couple that he believes to be united until the day he feels a crack open up. Their separation is inevitable and Pierre is left alone. The film is by Dan Franck.

Consentement mutuel is a film by Bernard Stora (France, 1994): A couple divorce by mutual consent. Jeanne gets custody of the child. The father does everything he can to destabilise Jeanne. "A feminist pamphlet", wrote Bouniq-Mercier in the *Guide des films.*

---

[495]Since Jacques Attali is so malicious towards us, let's be frank and not mince our words: a friend of ours, who a few years ago had worked in the "health care" department of the Ritz, in the basement of this great Parisian hotel, had seen several Hollywood beauties naked. He also told us that one day he had seen Jacques Attali naked as a worm. He had just taken off his dressing gown, about to get into the bathtub, and his p..., he said, was microscopic! Evidently, this story provoked a lot of laughter in our group. In any case, those who have read *Jewish Fanaticism* will see that what Dr. Valensin wrote is often true, at least in certain cases.

Tie me up, by Pedro Almodóvar (Spain, 1989): After his release from a psychiatric centre, Ricki dreams of leading a normal life with Marina Osorio, an erotic film actress with whom he had previously had an affair.

Mentiras piadosas (Mexico, 1987): Israel runs a small shop in Mexico City. With his homosexual friend Matilde, he has built a model of Tenochtitlan, for which he hopes to get a good price. Then he meets Clara. Israel and Clara leave their respective husbands to live together... "The traditional family has exploded, annihilated, prisoner of its own existential misery", wrote Bouniq-Mercier. A film by Arturo Ripstein.

Rendez-vous (France, 1985) is a film by André Téchiné, based on a screenplay by Olivier Assayas: Nina, a provincial girl, arrives in Paris with the intention of doing theatre. She meets Paulo, who falls in love with her, but she is attracted to Quentin, who is exhibiting in a pornographic *life-show*.

Femmes de personnes (France, 1984): Three women work in the same radiology office. Isabelle is tired of her husband and seeks solace in Julie, the receptionist. Cécile collects runaway lovers. Adeline, the secretary, sees her first love again and attempts suicide. A film by Christopher Frank.

In *L'Amour en douce* (France, 1984), Marc, a young lawyer, abandons his wife to pursue easy conquests. She has a lover who is into bodybuilding, while Marc is seduced by a call-girl. The film is by Edouard Molinaro.

What have I done to deserve this? (Spain, 1984): Gloria lives with an eccentric mother-in-law, a macho husband and her two sons: Toni, a small-time drug dealer, and Miguel, an occasional prostitute. She only survives on antidepressants. The film is by Pedro Almodóvar.

Coup de foudre, by Diane Kurys (France, 1982): In 1952, in Lyon, Lena is bored with her husband Michel. She meets Madeleine and leaves her husband. "A particularly interesting film", according to Claude Bouniq-Mercier.

Elle voit des nains partout, by Jean-Claude Sussfeld (France, 1981), is a parody of Snow White. Snow White is obsessed with sex. "A totally crazy and iconoclastic film that gleefully mixes the myths of our childhood in a spicy and delirious cocktail," wrote Bouniq.

Je vous aime (France, 1980): Alice has just broken up with Claude. She remembers that Christmas Eve when she reunited the men she had loved. "Claude Berri achieves the beautiful portrait of a free and independent woman".

Violette Nozière, by Claude Chabrol (France, 1978): The story takes place in the 1930s. To escape the mediocrity of her family life, Violette Nozière has affairs with students, prostitutes herself and contracts syphilis. For the love of a gigolo, she robs her parents and then poisons them. The screenplay is by Odile Barski, Hervé Bromberger and Frédéric Grendel.

In Claude Sautet's *Une Histoire Simple* (1978), Marie, about to turn forty, is divorced from Georges and has a sixteen-year-old son. She is Serge's lover and is pregnant by him. But she decides to have an abortion and leave him. The screenplay is by Jean-Loup Dabadie.

Le regard (France, 1976): in a museum, the camera carefully analyses Brueghel's work. At the same time, in a hotel room, the camera films a couple making love at length. Pornography and art. "Marcel Hanoun, as an artist and a poet, teaches us to look in order to better understand what is shown, to reach the truth".

Une chante, l'autre pas, by Agnès Varda (France, 1976): In 1962 Paris, Pauline dreams of becoming a singer. Suzanne is pregnant for the third time and is stranded when her father commits suicide. Pauline helps Suzanne to have an abortion. Ten years later, Suzanne is involved in family planning, while Pauline is bored with Darius, the Iranian man she loves. It was the time of feminist demonstrations. French society soon collapsed.

Histoire d'un péché (France, 1975): Eva, a pious and reserved young woman, has lived with her rich parents for a long time and has fallen in love with a young married man. She is going to kill the son she had with him. A film by Walerian Borowczyk that transgresses all moral laws.

Attention les yeux, by Gérard Pirés (1975). Mr. Rotberger is a film producer whose films don't work. To make ends meet, he decides to produce an erotic film with intellectual pretensions, but the film turns out to be a vulgar porn film.

Secrets of a marriage (Sweden, 1973): Marianne and Johann have been married for ten years and their relationship seems solid. But Johann falls in love with young Paula and they divorce.

Histoires d'A. (France, 1973): A worried couple go to a doctor's surgery because the young woman wants to have an abortion. They aspirate the foetus and that's it. The young woman comes out smiling and calm. The film is by Charles Belmont.

Sex Shop by Claude Berri (France, 1972): A penniless bookseller turns his business into a sex shop. In one scene, a customer explains to him (us) the benefits of all perversions: zoophilia, homosexuality, sadomasochism, necrophilia. The dialogue explicitly encourages sex with girls from the age of 12. It also glorifies the exchange of partners, adultery, homosexuality and feminism. Claude Langmann, also known as Claude Berri, who plays the bookseller, is in the film a man who has become impotent. Nor could he resist showing us a mixed couple: a blonde and a black man. The destruction of the goyim through miscegenation is a real obsession for them.

Such goods friends is a film by Otto Preminger (USA, 1971): After an operation, Richard Messinger, editor of a New York magazine, is in a coma. His wife Julie, who has two children, discovers her husband's dissolute life and his numerous love affairs, especially with his girlfriends. A masterpiece.

"A satirical comedy that harshly castigates the New York intelligentsia, its sexual manias and its artificial values", wrote Guy Bellinger.

Panic in Needle Park (USA, 1971): Helen has an abortion and runs off with Bobby, a drug addict. Helen, in turn, takes drugs and works as a street prostitute to earn some money. Bobby sometimes helps his older brother Hank, a thief, and ends up in jail. When he is released, he finds Helen in Hank's bed. Bobby becomes a drug dealer. The film is by Jerry Schatzberg.

Taking off (USA, 1970): Fifteen-and-a-half-year-old Jeannie runs away. Her parents join the Runaway Children's Parents Association. To help them understand their children's behaviour, they introduce them to drugs and sex. A film by Milos Forman.

The Happy Ending (USA, 1969): Nary Wilson has been married for sixteen years and has everything to be happy. But one day she collapses, leaves her husband and decides to start her life anew. Now that's feminism! A Richard Brooks film: now that's Judaism!

Les Amants, by Louis Malle (France, 1958): In Dijon, Jeanne is bored with Henry and the lifestyle of the city's haute bourgeoisie. By chance, she meets Bernard, a young nonconformist. On a warm summer night, she experiences with him the fullness of love. This film, which incites adultery, "remains a milestone in the liberation of manners," wrote Bouniq. The film won the Special Jury Prize at the Venice Film Festival.

A Summer with Monica is a film by Ingmar Bergman (Sweden, 1952): Monica is pregnant and marries Harry, but still dreams of other places. She resumes her independent life, leaving Harry with the child. An example for all truly free young women to follow.

Detective Story (USA, 1951) is a film that condemns puritanism. William Wyler, the director, makes it clear that he is a supporter of abortion. Jewish intellectuals have always been at the forefront in this field.

See also Frank Capra's *New York-Miami* (USA, 1934): A young heiress runs away from her familiar surroundings to join an aviator whom she wants to marry against her father's advice. However, she abandons him during the wedding ceremony to meet the reporter she has just met along the way. The scriptwriter is a certain R. Riskin: how they love to interrupt religious ceremonies...

The Austrian writer Josef Winkler may not be Jewish, but his case is quite emblematic: born in 1953 in Kamering, a village in Carinthia, Winkler faced the hostility of the rural world around him. The internet article by a certain Joel Vincent was very revealing of this pathological power of disintegration: "In his story, *Le Serf (The Servant), he* exposes the brutality and mental backwardness of the peasants, their hatred of Jews, homosexuals and anything that does not conform to the rituals orchestrated by the Catholic Church. Winkler's homosexuality is seen as a great provocation, a way of transgressing the established phallocratic order, which he sees as the very symbol of his father and the religious authorities."

Like many Jews, Josef Winkler also had a sick imagination: "Winkler gives us images of despair and nightmares, some of them surreal: frogs in uniform waiting to be eaten by officers, moles carrying coffins, pigeons nesting in barrels of cannon, himself looking like a dog burning at the stake. Even the dead, eager to take revenge on the Church, would rather rot in the cemetery than parade."

In *Le Cimetière des oranges* amères (*The Cemetery of Bitter Oranges*), Winkler, travelling in Italy, returned to his morbid visions: "A nun with a plastic baby Jesus inserted in her womb; fish disguised as convicts; a rat with a bishop's mitre following an empty hearse; a crucifixion crown woven by two nuns with eight crow's feet; or his father sharpening his scythe with the rib of a murdered Jew".

The writer denounced the Church and ancestral traditions "steeped in devotion and superstition": "The book opens with a long litany, dedicated to Jesus, recalling the tortures inflicted on so many innocents, and ends with Winkler's wish to see all the victims of the Church's power repatriated to the cemetery of bitter oranges: the two suicides of his village, Jacob and Robert, two young homosexuals led to their deaths by the villagers... and many other anonymous victims of the worst tortures. Winkler also imagines his own death, "carried off by transvestites and homosexuals, naked, in a sheet stained with lamb's blood", and buried in Naples under a lemon tree".

On 16 November 2000, *Le Figaro* published a glowing article by Claude-Michel Cluny on the publication of Josef Winkler's third novel, *Concert pour le temps dernier (Concert for the End Times)*, "brilliantly translated by Bernard Banoun". "A novel as beautiful and dark as a mountain storm", wrote Claude-Michel "Cluny, which places its author in "the front rank of the new literature in the German language" (readers now know what this praise means). It should be remembered that *Le Figaro* is a "conservative" newspaper, although it is true that its owner at the time was the arms manufacturer Serge Dassault, born Bloch.

In the Catholic daily *La Croix* of 9 November 2000, Jean-Maurice de Montremy noted the rise of the "extreme right" in Carinthia, Josef Winkler's home region, "geographically closed in on itself". And he explained very complacently: "In *Le Serf*, Winkler had already painted the Carinthian village that we see again in this new book: a village in the shape of a cross. Here, under the leadership of dreadful priests, stubborn, ruthless and silent peasants demand (and obtain) the maintenance of a religious order that has risen from the mists of time.... From baptisms to funerals, from masses to processions, the cross-shaped village finds itself under the sun of a Satan who usurps the name of Jesus." This new novel tells the story of the writer Maximilien, who returns to the village. Like Josef Winkler, he is homosexual and has a harsh and domineering father.

Joël Vincent continued his chronicle on the Internet: "Many others in Austria have already denounced the alienating morality of the Church. Thomas Bernhard, Elfriede Jelinek and Werner Scwab are the most virulent contemporaries. Others, such as Lilian Faschinger and Evelyn Schlag, attacked the religious institutions by raising the problem of female identity: through eroticism, the vital impetus and sensuality of free young women cast doubt and confusion on the priests.

While the first three authors mentioned are certainly Jewish, the last two may not be. In any case, we can clearly see here the convergences between homosexual militancy, feminism and the obsessions of Judaism.

Transvestites and transsexuals

For centuries, all observers of Judaism have pointed to the Jewish penchant for all kinds of sexual deviance. It is important to understand that this is not only a desire to pervert the Christian nations, as a certain somewhat simplistic anti-Semitic vulgate would have us believe, but also the expression of a characteristic neurosis.

In *Jewish Fanaticism*, we have listed some of the films in which the director delights in showing homosexuals, transsexuals and transvestites, and we have been forced to acknowledge that most of them were made by Jewish directors.

On 26 September 2007, the Arte channel broadcast the film *Wild Side*, by Sébastien Lifshitz (France, 2003): The film tells the story of Stéphanie, who is actually a transvestite: "She" lives in Paris, works as a prostitute in the Bois de Boulogne and spends the rest of her time with Djamel, a gigolo, and Mikhail, a Russian with a Chechen face who barely speaks French and works as a dishwasher in a restaurant. The young men have a three-way love affair. Everything in this film is sordid. The scenes of homosexuality are filmed with great complacency, and we will spare you the details.

But here is the review from the Arte channel website: "Our verdict: Sébastien Lifshitz films the search for happiness of a group of outcasts with grace and tenderness". And here is ours: "Homosexuality, mixed race and transvestites: this is clearly a Jewish film, directed by a Jew".

The newspaper *Direct Soir* of 2 October 2007 published this brief news item on page 19: "José Dayan, who directed *Les Rois maudits* for *France 2* and *Marie Octobre* for *France 3*, has just bought a documentary for *France Télévisions* on the subject of transsexuals. It is scheduled to be broadcast in 2008".

In *Les Poupées russes* (*Russian Dolls*, France, 2005), Cédric Klapish offers us a continuation of *L'Auberge espagnole* (*A Madhouse*). It still presents female homosexuality (between white women), but this time Klapish adds miscegenation (white man and black woman), cocaine consumption and a scene of transvestism.

Fantasy is an Israeli film by Avi Hershkovitz and Sharon Hammou. It tells the story of two transvestites: one is Jewish and the other is an Arab from Jaffa. Both are outcasts of society, rejected by their families and marginalised in the virile world of the Middle East...

A Raiz do Coraçao (*The Root of the Heart*, Portugal, 2000): In Lisbon, during the St. Anthony's Day festivities, transvestites join in the popular jubilation and militias are organised to hunt them down, resulting in the death of one of them. The film is by Paulo Rocha.

Ma vie en rose (France, 1997): The Fabres, a dynamic, close-knit couple and their four children settle in a residential area. Ludovic, the youngest, turns up at a party dressed as a girl. Ludovic's insistence that she is a girl in a boy's body, and his certainty that she will marry her boyfriend Jérôme, end up scandalising the neighbours and breaking the family's harmony. Panic-stricken, the parents decide to take their son to a psychologist... In reality, as you may have noticed, it was the director, Alain Berliner, who should have been consulted.

Ed Wood, by Tim Burton (USA, 1994): The life of the worst filmmaker in the history of cinema: Edward Davis Wood Jr, a man who loves to cross-dress as a woman and dress in angora jumpers.

The "American" comedy *Junior* (1994) deals with the issue of pregnant men: the authorities stop funding for Dr. Hesse's research on safe pregnancy. His partner, gynaecologist Larry Arbogast, suggests that he should see for himself the benefits of his treatment. Alex agrees to place a fertilised egg, already named Junior, in his abdomen. "Pregnant", Alex moves in with Larry, whose wife Angela is also expecting a child.[496]

Miss Doubtfire, by Chris Columbus (USA, 1993): The Hillards divorce, but the husband, who wants to see his children again, disguises himself as a governess and is hired by his ex-wife.

La Travestie, by Yves Boisset (1987), is the story of a young provincial lawyer, scorned and unloved. She goes to Paris and cross-dresses as a man. She successively meets a prostitute (who becomes her confidante), a middle-class woman (whom she seduces) and a macho schoolteacher. From drifting into murder, she ends up totally alienated. Yves Boisset was also the director of *Dupont Lajoie*, a very virulently anti-racist film, which is to say above all very anti-French.

---

[496] On the subject of the pregnant man read *Jewish Fanaticism*.

Levy et Goliath is a film by Gérard Oury (France, 1986): Moisés Levy is a traditionalist Jew from Antwerp who has broken up with his brother Albert. He arrives in Paris and unwittingly becomes involved in a drug affair that earns him the hostility of a gang leader, Goliath. He is saved by a fake transvestite, but a real detective.

In Pedro Almodóvar's *La ley del deseo* (Spain, 1986), Pablo's sister Tina is "a transsexual perverted by her father".

El lugar sin límites is a Mexican film from 1977. The brothel is the only house in a remote village that does not belong to the old deputy Don Alejo. He lost it in a bet with the landlady, who had an affair with Manuela, a transvestite. "A subversive script that questions the traditional foundations of a macho and patriarchal society," wrote Bouniq. The Mexican director in question is Arturo Ripstein, who, as we have seen, also directed a film that normalised homosexuality and denigrated the family unit.

The Ladder, by Stanley Donen (USA, 1969): Charlie and Harry, two homosexuals, live as a couple. Charlie is in a bad mood because he has to stand trial for transvestism and incitement to depravity.

The Major and the Minor, by Billy Wilder (USA, 1942): A comedy featuring men dressed as women and policemen as lords. It is not Wilder's only film to feature transvestites, although his films are admittedly much funnier than they are aggressive.

The TV magazine *Capital*, on the M6 channel, once did a report on the pleasures of nightlife in Istanbul, the Turkish capital. The journalists stopped at a transvestite nightclub, where the manager spoke French, with an accent similar to that of Roger Hanin, President Mitterrand's brother-in-law...

On 2 April 2007, we learned that the State of Israel had recalled its ambassador to El Salvador, Tzuriel Refael, who had been found drunk and naked in the courtyard of his official residence. In Jerusalem, the Ministry of Foreign Affairs confirmed that he had been recalled, without giving further details, but Salvadoran police said they had found the ambassador naked, drunk, bound and gagged, with a rubber ball in his mouth and sexual accessories thrown beside him.

We might also legitimately wonder whether the famous "Brazilian transvestites" are not simply Brazilian Jews, who are indeed very numerous in that country.

Before the Second World War, the forerunner of gay and transvestite studies was a sexologist named Magnus Hirschfeld (1868-1935). It was he who founded the first "gay" political movement in 1897. After studying medicine, he embarked on a career as a research scientist and, in 1920, founded a sexology institute in Berlin that became internationally renowned. He was called at the time the "Einstein of sex". Homosexual, Jewish and socialist, Magnus Hirschfeld had to flee Germany in the 1930s.

He died in Nice in 1935, after trying in vain to prevent the destruction of his sexology institute by Hitler's regime. In a film dedicated to him, Rosa von Prunheim revealed the personality of Magnus Hirschfeld, as well as the presence of his friend and guardian angel, the transvestite Dorchen.[497]

Let us end this chapter with Steven Cohen, a truly colourful character. Steven Cohen is a "South African" artist living in France, a homosexual and an anti-apartheid activist. Gérard Mayen described him briefly on the Internet: "A transvestite artist, creator of a "living art" that borrows equally from sculpture, contemporary dance and *performance*, Steven Cohen reflects on his testimonial condition as a homosexual, a Jew and a South African. With rawness and violence, he explores his complex identity and exposes his intimacy. With an exceptional sense of imagery and an uncommon sensitivity, he speaks of the indelible marks of history on the body. Disturbing, excessive, hypersexual and, at the same time, highly political, Steven Cohen tackles Judaism, the Holocaust and mourning - a deeply moving solo!"

In a long article entitled *The Art of Steven Cohen*, which we summarise here and put in order, we discovered the true nature of this "South African" artist. And indeed, we are going to see here that this Steven Cohen is profoundly "moving"; attention, we are going to go in crescendo:

We learn that Steven Cohen's "*performances*" "express issues of identity related to Jewishness, homosexuality and race. Cohen, who describes himself as a "queer Jewish freak", made a name for himself in South Africa and elsewhere with often controversial works. His creations were often found in art galleries, but also in public spaces such as taxi ranks, racetracks and town halls. In 1997 and 1998, Cohen and his partner Elu, a choreographer and dancer, produced a series of "living art" works that they presented in a series of impromptu events in public spaces.

In one of his "*performances*", they "kissed on a podium in front of a courthouse where an anti-homosexual law was being debated". Cohen's provocations were manifold: In 1998, for example, "he went to collect his FNB Vita Award finalist's cheque harnessed with blood-stained notes and

---

[497]Magnus Hirschfeld was to have a great posterity. In the 21st century, the LGBT movement experienced an astonishing exponential growth and became the new bastion of Western democratic values. In this respect, some of Hirschfeld's contemporary congeners can be mentioned: Mara Keisling (US transgender rights activist and founding executive director of the *National Center for Transgender Equality*), Eliza Byard (executive director of *Gay, Lesbian & Straight Education Network* until March 2021), Eli Erlick (activist, writer, academic and trans woman and founder of *Trans Student Educational Resources*), Dean Spade (US lawyer, writer, trans activist and associate professor of law and founder of the *Sylvia Rivera Law Project*), and Michael Silvermann and Jillian Weiss (founder and executive directors of the *Transgender Legal Defense & Education Fund* from 2003 to 2018). (NdT)

with his hands tied behind his back - an ironic comment on the artist's relationship with his patrons".

Even more powerful: Cohen paid an impromptu visit to an exhibition of wedding dresses, "the quintessential sentimental staging of heterosexuality". He was disguised as a transvestite, with a dildo in his anus: "the security staff quickly removed it, thus participating in the performance, before escorting him to the door".

In his shows, Cohen mixed dance and movement, dressed in elaborate costumes. He wore the Star of David on his face, head or chest, stained with blood, suggesting that it had been imposed on him by violence, "like cattle that are branded". It was applied to his nose and cock, "an essential part of the body in Judaism. The *brit milah*, the covenant of alliance with the god of Genesis through circumcision, is the mark that distinguishes Jew from Gentile."

His 1997 exhibition, *Concentration Camp*, included a photograph of Cohen at the age of six, in a girl's bikini, with make-up and pigtails: "This transvestite act of a child, a future artist, proudly posing for the photographer, is the starting point of a journey that leads directly from childhood to his work as a *performer*, using the gay tradition of drag to subvert it".

In *Tradition* (1998), performed to the tune of the Yiddish musical comedy *Fiddler on the Roof*, "Cohen is suspended from the ceiling as if dancing in the air and sprays a dark liquid emanating from his anus onto his partner, Elu, who dances beneath him. In *Taste* (1999), he uses the famous hymn to life *Lechaïm*. His face is covered, deprived of his identity, by a latex mask, and he wears a large polystyrene Star of David on his head, which he throws at the audience in a *striptease* gesture. At the same time, Cohen receives an anonymous message instructing him not to mock the Star of David. Cohen then removes his wig and pulls anal beads out of his sphincter. He continues with a rectal emission of black liquid into an antique glass container; some of the liquid is poured into a glass, which Cohen raises to the health of his horrified audience before drinking it. *Lechaïm* [Cheers! He thus demonstrates, the artist explains, that "the acceptance of the fag for himself is an acquired taste."

"In most of his solo performances, Cohen inserts dildos or other sexual objects into his rectum, where he keeps them for the duration of the often physically demanding performance, at the end of which they are ceremoniously removed by his assistant, Elu, in most cases. Cohen glorifies the anus both for its abjection and as a source of pleasure".

Since her first *performances*, Cohen has been wearing higher and higher heels, making it increasingly difficult for her to walk. "In 1999, with *Crawling...Flying*, the heels reached the size of oryx horns, a metre long, making it completely impossible to walk. Steven Cohen was forced to crawl, so he put on a show in public places, such as in front of polling stations where voters waited in single file to deposit their ballots in the ballot box during the 1999 elections: a jocular comment on those endless queues and South Africa's long march slowly crawling towards democracy. In 2000, he presented one of his reptation plays at Gay and Lesbian Pride... Cohen, in his oryx heels, seems to transcend the limits of the body and defy the laws of gravity".

Cohen had also gone to provoke the Negros. The show *Limping into the African renaissance* had started at 11pm on 31 December 1999. "The play refers to Thabo Mbeki's concept of "African renaissance"...The black octogenarian Dhlamini, with a globe on his head, walks in front of a limping Cohen into the future of Africa. Cohen did this *performance* in a dilapidated hut. He was acclaimed as a magician by the local audience, but also insulted and called a *stabane* (hermaphrodite). Unsurprisingly, he was dressed in "Eurocentric drag", with his face covered by a bondage mask and an erect black penis in place of his mouth; in fact, a dildo protruding from his mouth, a counterpoint to his own harnessed white penis. A prosthesis attached to one of his feet elongated the dancer's leg, hindering his movements. "Performing this piece is a triumph of execution and physical effort, a struggle akin to inserting the white body of the Jewish homosexual into the patriarchal and homophobic traditions of Africa."

"The Jewish body, as Professor Sander Gilman pointed out, is the site of multiple deviations from the imaginary of Western culture. The Jew is the essential other, disease-bearing, incestuous, bestial and cannibalistic. The Jewish body bears immutable signs of its identity: the nose was supposed to denote the Jew, but the Jewish foot was also thought to suffer from a congenital deformity. Cohen's apparent self-inflicted "deformities" (made-up nose, high heels) refer to these prejudices".

Sander Gilman underlined the obvious correlation between Judaism and homosexuality, but his diagnosis did not explain the causes: "Jewish identity, he wrote, poses a problem because it is expressed both in a discourse of self-hatred and in a stubborn self-defence, exploited by Cohen to subvert all identity politics.... Unlike the other, colonised or Oriental, for whom skin colour is an obvious racial marker, the Jew is not so easy to identify. In the white world, the Jew represents the other self - whose threat is precisely linked to the fact that he or she is easily overlooked in society. Similarly, the homosexual has often been presented as a secret, subversive presence that threatens social stability from within. In this sense, the figures of the Jew and the homosexual appear in Cohen's work not only as metaphor for the other in the social body, but also as the inner otherness, the hybrid self."

Rapists and unbalanced

In *Jewish Fanaticism* (2007) we have already seen numerous cases of American doctors and psychiatrists who raped their patients. In France there was the case of Gilbert Tordjman, a renowned sexologist who was the founder and "Pope" of French sexology. Gilbert Tordjamn was prosecuted in March 2002, and forty-four former patients came forward to testify before the judge, claiming to have been abused by this "specialist". We have also recalled, among others, the case of Thierry Chichportich, the "masseur to the stars", nicknamed "the man with the golden fingers" by the world's film elite. On 20 May 2006, *Le* Parisien reported that he had been sentenced to 18 years in prison by the criminal court of Nice for the rapes of thirteen young women whom he had previously put to sleep. Since then, there have been many other cases.[498]

On 7 February 2008, a Marseille gynaecologist, Patrick Azoulay, 48, was sentenced by the Marseille court to three years in prison, and was henceforth banned from practising any medical profession. The gynaecologist was accused of aggravated sexual assault by five of his patients. His victims complained of dubious back massages, scenes of onanism, incongruous rubbing, treatments that were not medical and often turned into humiliations. For a long time, they did not dare to say anything. The public prosecutor asked for a seven-year prison sentence, especially as Dr. Azoulay had already been sentenced in October 2002 to two years in prison, one of which was unconditional - a sentence that was never carried out. Patrick Azoulay did not appear in court. An arrest warrant had been issued for him in September 2003, and his whereabouts remained unknown.

---

[498] A striking case in point is Gérard Miller, a famous psychoanalyst and university professor, ubiquitous talk-show host and television icon, "media figure of the left", ironically nicknamed the "divan marquis" by *Libération* (the "*divin marquis*" was the Marquis de Sade, ndt) and the "red sequinned shrink" by *L'Express*. Miller was politically active on the extreme left between the 1960s and 1970s, before moving away from it and towards the classical left. For years, he walked freely, with his pursed lips, on television sets, peremptorily lecturing guests and preaching leftist orthodoxy. "In 2024, more than sixty women accused him of inappropriate behaviour, sexual assault and rape, mostly under hypnosis. *Elle* magazine published the accounts of 41 women, some of them minors at the time of the events, who testified about Gérard Miller's problematic behaviour between 1993 and 2020. Three of them reported rape and fifteen sexual assaults. The other twenty-three mentioned attempted assaults. They all described the same modus operandi: assaults committed most of the time after hypnosis sessions. On the 19th, four women complained in court that Gérard Miller had behaved inappropriately towards them. The next day, a 39-year-old woman filed a complaint with the Paris prosecutor's office for a rape committed when she was 17; according to her lawyer, the statute of limitations had not expired. On 23 February, the Paris prosecutor's office announced that it had opened a preliminary investigation on the basis of six complaints. On the 29th, France 2 broadcast the testimony of three women on its programme *Envoyé spécial* accusing Miller." (source wikipedia) (NdT).

According to the regional daily *La Provence*, which quoted a judicial source, the doctor had been on the run in Israel for several years.

There is also the case of Roger Chemoul, 61 years old. On 26 November 2007, he was sentenced to 5 years in prison by the Rhône Court of First Instance. Roger Chemoul was prosecuted for raping in 2003 a nurse who worked in the same old people's home as him, in Tarare. His defence did not convince the jurors. Chemoul claimed to be the victim of a plot: "In fact, it was Doctor Champin, director of the Montvenoux nursing home, who wanted to take revenge on me because I had provided *Lyon Mag* with information for its report on the nursing home scandal". After refusing Roger Chempoul's advances for a long time, the nurse finally gave in because he was her superior and threatened to make her lose her job. Chemoul then abused her on two occasions: once on a mobility table and a second time standing in the bathroom of a room occupied by a sick person. But at the hearing, a self-confident Roger Chemoul denied the facts, explaining that his penis was too small to allow standing sex with the victim. This line of defence was taken up by his lawyer, Alain Jakubowicz, but to no avail. The prosecutor demanded 7 years in prison.

On 3 November 2007, the weekly *Marianne* reported on the case of André Hazout, a famous Parisian gynaecologist who was also an international eminence in the field of in vitro fertilisation. The gynaecologist apparently carried out quite extensive gynaecological examinations. One patient reported that, during the consultation, the gynaecologist had pulled down his trousers and penetrated her until the phone rang: "He left to answer the phone, I was shocked", she told investigators from the criminal investigation department. About six patients who came to her practice with infertility problems filed complaints from July 2005 onwards, and many others were unable to do so because of the statute of limitations. The first complaints to the Medical Council date back to 1991. "These women were infertile, and he was their last hope. They trusted the doctor completely," said one of the victims' lawyers. "There was solidarity on the part of the medical staff to the detriment of the patients' bodies," said another lawyer indignantly. At the end of October 2007, the IVF specialist was placed under judicial supervision and banned from practising medicine.

On 16 June 2003, the daily *France Soir* reported the case of a rabbi from Perpignan. He was accused of rape by a 60-year-old woman who claimed to have been a victim of the rabbi for several months. According to the daily *Le Midi Libre*, the case began in March 2000, when the victim, who was trying to set up a commercial business, met the rabbi. He quickly forced her to have non-consensual sexual relations, threatening to derail her professional project. According to the 60-year-old, this harassment lasted until June 2001. In December 2001, she decided to report her aggressor for sexual and moral harassment. Then, in March 2002, a second complaint was filed, this time for rape. The woman had tried to keep the sheets stained with the rabbi's semen. While in police custody, the rabbi denied any sexual relationship with the 60-year-old woman, before recanting in the presence of the examining magistrate. The possibility of DNA analysis of the sperm on the sheets helped him to recover his memory.

Once again, we can see that sexual perversions seem to be a speciality of Jewish filmmakers. Here is Tom Kalin's *Swoon* (USA, 1992): in 1924, Richard Loeb and Nathan Leopold, scions of well-to-do Chicago families, are two brilliant eighteen-year-old Jewish intellectuals, bound by a homosexual relationship. They kidnap a fourteen-year-old boy, Bobby Franks, beat him to death and rape him. The film was based on a true story that attracted international attention at the time. The two teenagers were sentenced to life imprisonment. Richard was murdered and Nathan was released thirty-three years later.

There are also many prostitutes in cosmopolitan cinema: *La Vie devant soi* is a film by Moshe Mizrahi (France, 1977): In the Belleville neighbourhood, Madame Rosa is a sickly old Jewish woman, a former prostitute who takes in the children of street prostitutes. She is particularly fond of Momo, a fourteen-year-old Arab boy whom she has educated in the Hebrew religion. The screenplay is based on a novel by the famous Romain Gary (Roman Kacew).

Secret Ceremony, by Joesph Losey (UK, 1969): Leonora, a prostitute, visits her daughter's grave. She is followed by a strange young woman, a nymphomaniac, who indulges in perverse games.

Repulsion (UK, 1965) is the story of a neurotic girl who falls into a murderous madness. Carole has phobias. Every night she dreams that a man rapes her. Roman Polanski must have been inspired by several familiar cases.

In *Belle de jour* (1966), by the Mexican Luis Buñuel: a middle-class woman spends her evenings in a meeting house. There is a masochistic gynaecologist and a necrophiliac duke. The script is by Joseph Kessel.

It is clear that necrophilia does not leave some directors indifferent. *The Horrible Secret of Doctor Hichcock* is a film by Riccardo Freda (Italy-UK, 1962): In the London of 1885, Dr. Hichcock returns to his manor house with Cynthia, his second wife. Cynthia cannot stand the oppressive atmosphere of the house. One stormy night, she discovers the coffin of her husband's first wife. He turns out to be a necrophiliac. He uses the corpses of the hospital where he works to satisfy his sordid vice.

The Shadow of Night is a film by Ole Bornedal (USA, 1998): an old night watchman reveals to his replacement at the forensic institute that a former necrophiliac guard was raping the corpses of the women at the institute. At the same time, a serial killer stabs and scalps prostitutes. Soon strange things happen in the morgue. The screenplay is by Steven Soderbergh.

Santa Sangre (Mexico, 1989) again features a serial killer of prostitutes. Orgo runs a circus. Concha, his mystical wife, burns his penis when she discovers his infidelity. Orgo amputates both his arms before committing suicide. His son Fenix, disturbed by these atrocities, is committed to a psychiatric clinic. He escapes at the age of twenty and falls under the control of a possessive mother who uses hypnosis to force him to kill any woman who comes near him. The film was directed by a true Mexican: Alejandro Jodorowski. "It is a work of great visual richness, disturbing, atrocious and sublime, worthy of the best surrealist cinema. It may shock, but it will never leave you indifferent," wrote Bouniq, who gave the film four stars.

La Vie, l'amour, la mort is a film by Claude Lelouch (1968): François Toledo, a car factory worker, leads a quiet life with his wife Janine. He falls in love with Caroline, whom he meets in a hotel. One day he is arrested. He is denounced by his mother-in-law, who recognises him as a murderer of prostitutes. During fits of impotence, he strangled them to make up for his humiliation as a man. Although his state was more suited to psychiatry than to justice, he was sentenced to death and guillotined.[499]

The Night of the Generals (France-GB, 1966): In Warsaw in 1942, a woman is the victim of a sadistic crime. According to a witness, it is a crime committed by a German general. The film is by Anatole Litvak.

Throw Mom off the Train is a comedy by Danny de Vito (USA, 1987): Donner, a writer and teacher, hates his ex-wife, who has become famous by signing a novel written by him. One of his students dreams of killing his mother, whom he considers abusive. Why not exchange his crimes?

In *Rampage* (USA, 1987), a psychopath kills six times in gruesome ways, each time removing organs from the bodies of his victims. A William Friedkin film.

---

[499] Jack the Ripper, who terrorised London in 1888, was also a killer of prostitutes. On 14 July 2006, the very serious English newspaper, the *Times*, in its online edition, reported on this case, using the handwritten notes of the Scotland Yard policeman who led the investigation. The retired officer, Donald Swanson, gave the name of the man he believed to be Jack the Ripper: Aaron Kosminski, a Jewish hairdresser from Poland who lived in Whitechappel, east London. The police had identified him, and there had even been a positive confrontation with a witness. But this witness recanted when he learned that the culprit was also Jewish. Kosminski had been arrested after threatening his sister with a knife. Judged too mentally ill to be questioned, he was handed over to the care of his brother in a Scotland Yard house in Brighton. He was later committed to an insane asylum, where he died shortly afterwards. Read also about the case in *The Jewish Mafia*.

La Classe de neige (France, 1998): Nicolas, a shy and fragile boy, is taken by his father to a snow school. Soon a local boy disappears and it is discovered that men are trafficking in organs. The film is by Claude Miller. On the subject of organ trafficking, readers can consult our previous book on *The Jewish Mafia* (2008).

In *Viridiana* (Spain, 1961), Luis Buñuel reveals his sexual fantasies (fetishism, condemnation of chastity) and reaffirms his anti-Catholic hatred (the crucifix-knife). We also see an orgy of beggars parodying the Last Supper. The film won an award at the Cannes Film Festival.

Du Sang pour Dracula, by Paul Morissey (France-Italy, 1974): Shortage of virgin blood for Dracula: an increasingly rare species due to the relaxation of morals. Dracula is seen licking the blood of menstruations.

In *Crime City* (USA, 1984), Abell Ferrara films sadism, drugs, exhibitionism and voyeurism. William Lustig's *Maniac* (USA, 1980) is the story of a maniac who scalps his victims.

Halloween Night is a film by John Carpenter (USA, 1978): One Halloween night, a young man is driven into a murderous frenzy.

The Mad Bomber, by Bert Gordon (USA, 1972): A man whose daughter has died of an overdose punishes society by planting bombs in public places. Rape, cold-blooded murder, extortion of confessions, voyeurism, exhibitionism and much more.

Les Heroïnes du mal (France, 1979): Marceline loves making love to her white rabbit. Her parents make her eat it in civet. She takes revenge by giving herself carnally to a butcher who ends up hanging himself in front of her. She then slits her parents' throats with a knife. This play is Walerian Borowczyk. Claude Bouniq-Mercier wrote: "Boro goes a step further in the transgression of taboos and the search for pleasure, far from any repressive morality. In addition, he makes a beautiful film with a delicate and refined aesthetic".

Mister Frost is a film by Philippe Setbon (France, 1990): Inspector Detweiller arrests Mister Frost, a murderer of unknown origin who remains mysteriously silent. Two years later, Mister Frost finally agrees to talk to a young psychiatrist, Dr. Sarah Day. He claims to be the devil. Sarah succumbs to his evil charms, her reason falters and she commits the irreparable: she murders her patient. This film seems like a sinkhole for the suicidal desires of some.

Paedomaniacs

Paedophilia in the Jewish community is much more widespread than it seems. The French and international media are almost completely silent about this phenomenon and project the evil onto Catholic priests. In reality, the phenomenon is much more widespread within the Jewish sect, and in particular among orthodox Jews. Since the publication of *Psychoanalysis of Judaism* in 2006, the number of testimonies and court cases we have documented on this subject is now so large that we have decided not to publish them all.

In the United States, a website - *the awareness centre* - has been set up to record these embarrassing cases. The victims have come together in the Jewish Coalition Against Sexual Assault and Abuse (JCASA). For about ten years, this association has been fighting against paedophilia in Jewish religious circles in Israel, the United States and the rest of the world. Following investigations, a first list of 104 Israeli and American rabbis, most of whom had been prosecuted for sexually assaulting children, was published on the Internet. A second list of 267 names concerned teachers and leaders of Jewish youth associations. This was followed by another list of 93 paedophile cases, mostly committed by rabbis in Israel. But every week, new cases are reported in the American and Israeli press, to the point that we can no longer even publish the information on our website.

The case of Eugène Abrams of Long Island, New York, illustrates the phenomenon well: in 1974 he was sentenced to ten years in prison for 77 rapes, acts of sodomy and incest with children and obscenities with five girls, including his own. He was also convicted of running a nationwide child pornography ring from Long Island and Florida. After ten years in prison [only, ndt], he was convicted again of sexually assaulting a four-and-a-half-year-old girl.

An article by Elana Schor in the British newspaper *The Guardian* on 2 July 2008 pointed to one of the richest men in the United States, Jeffrey Epstein. He regularly spent his holidays with Prince Andrew and chartered his private plane to Bill Clinton, the former US president. But he had accepted an 18-month jail sentence in Florida after pleading guilty to making sexual advances on 14-year-old girls. Jeffrey Epstein, 55, was required to undergo HIV testing and to disclose his diagnosis to the families of his victims. In the mid-1980s, Epstein, a bank owner, had bought a Caribbean island and was well known in the financial world for his discretion with his clients. Florida authorities began tracking him in 2005 following a complaint from a young woman recruited by the billionaire.[500]

---

[500] The Jeffrey Epstein case became one of the biggest scandals of the decade in the US. The American Dylan Howard is the author of an investigative book: *L'affaire Epstein: Espionnage, caméras vidéos, prostitution de mineures et chantage*, Le Jardin des Livres, 2020. We reproduce below the introductory note to the book from the Amazon site: "For the first time, we present the dizzying life of billionaire Jeffrey Epstein, Bill Clinton's confidant, who for 20 years, on behalf of the Israeli services, deceived thousands of congressmen, senators, businessmen, journalists, movie stars, renowned scientists, university rectors and deans, prime ministers, princes and princesses

Goel Pinto, a gay journalist who had grown up in the Orthodox Jewish community in Jerusalem, went into exile in Tel Aviv and renounced the Jewish religion. He later claimed to have been raped as a child by an orthodox Jew in a *mikveh*, the ritual bath that purifies young boys. According to Jewish law - the *Halacha* - Jews who report such sexual assaults have the status of "*moiser*" (whistleblower) and can be assaulted or killed after a formal excommunication, the *herem*. Rabbi Nochum Rosenberg, who was part of the Hasidic community in Brooklyn, New York, was known for his energetic action around the world. He also crusaded against child rape in Orthodox Jewish communities. In July 2008, during a visit to the London community, he was violently assaulted by a group of Hasidic Jews. In the United States, the Chabad-Lubavitch sect, one of the main branches of the Hasidic movement[501], was represented and protected by Michael Chertoff, US Secretary of Homeland Security and close associate of US President George Bush.

It should be noted here that homosexuals are statistically more prone to paedophilia than heterosexuals. This was shown by a survey conducted in Los Angeles in 1983 among 3,132 adults. The survey revealed that 3.8% of men and 6.8% of women had been sexually abused in childhood. Ninety-

---

(including Prince Andrew), and even presidents with his network of young prostitutes. From his rise as a mathematics professor to his failed career on Wall Street, we follow him to his fame and downfall, including his momentous meeting with Ghilaine Maxwell, the daughter of another great Mossad spy, Robert Maxwell, who bought the British media on behalf of Israel. Although he claimed to be a millionaire thanks to Wall Street, in reality Epstein had become a pimp specialising in the ultra-rich and all-powerful, who demand only one thing: total discretion. He invited all the celebrities to his various luxury properties, both private and in Paris, where all the rooms were equipped with sound systems and very discreet cameras. By regularly supplying them with young girls, Epstein had created the largest international paedophile network, so much so that his plane was nicknamed "Lolita Express" by air traffic controllers, a plane on which Bill Gates and Bill Clinton regularly flew. He then sold the videos to the intelligence services. Arrested for the second time by US police for "child trafficking", he was found dead in spectacular circumstances in August 2019 in his cell at the Metropolitan Correctional Center in New York. A suicide that delighted all the celebrities whose names appeared in his famous "Black Book". This investigation, led by the great reporter Dylan Howard and assisted by two other American journalists, brings to light incredible revelations about the activities of Epstein, his "Madame" Ghislaine Maxwell and the way they enslaved these young women for the ultrarich, as well as the abuses they suffered. This book is uncensored and contains previously unpublished documents obtained by the author, who has followed the Epstein affair since his first prison stay in Florida. This did not stop Bill Gates, the man who wants to vaccinate everyone on the planet, from flying with him on the "Lolita Express" at least 4 times, long after his release from prison!". (NdT)

[501] On Hasidism and Chabad-Lubavitch read *Psychoanalysis of Judaism* and various cases in *The Jewish Mafia*.

three per cent of the perpetrators were male, and 35 per cent of them were homosexual. Another study by Dr. Freund and Dr. Heasman of the Clarke Institute of Psychiatry, conducted on 457 paedophiles, found that 34% of them were homosexual.

In France, the media's control over this issue is exemplary. The Leonid Kameneff case caused a certain stir because of its magnitude, but the Jewishness of the main protagonist was never revealed. In the 1980s and 1990s, Leonid Kameneff directed the association "*L'école en bateau*" (*School on a boat*). The former sea captain welcomed teenagers on his boat for stays at sea to help the "intellectual, psychological and social development of children". At each session, a dozen children between the ages of 9 and 16 embarked on an educational cruise under the authority of Captain Kameneff and his second-in-command. Over the past twenty years, three hundred pupils had been taught on board.

In 1994, Kameneff was first arrested in Martinique, but a procedural defect led to the proceedings being overturned and the predator was released after two months in prison. The man was accused of raping children under the age of 15 with abuse of authority between August 1979 and 1992. Several of his former pupils, minors at the time, had complained of sexual abuse. Some thirty young people who had sailed on the training ship had reported, among other things, massage sessions or collective masturbation, and fourteen of them had filed civil suits, since the facts reported by the other victims were time-barred.

In 2002, the case was reopened when a 26-year-old man filed a complaint, stating to the police that he had been sexually abused as a child. Further statements were subsequently taken. In January 2006, the press reported that "teachers and pupils conducted naked massage sessions, followed by fondling and sometimes sexual acts between adults and teenagers in the bunk beds". The matter was the subject of several television reports. The case was then transferred from Martinique to the metropolis. Of the 27 victims identified, twelve decided to file a complaint against Léonid Kameneff.

On 25 May 2007, the French judiciary issued an international arrest warrant for him, and in January 2008, at the age of 72, Léonid Kameneff was arrested in Venezuela and extradited to France, where he was immediately imprisoned.

On 16 April 2008, the weekly *Minute* published a long article on the subject, recalling another case, that of the Coral. In October 1982, a scandal hit the headlines when several public figures were accused of abusing young maladjusted children at the Coral, a centre created in 1975 by Claude Sigala near Nîmes. But the case did not reveal all its secrets.

In February 1997, Judge Jean-Paul Vallat, investigating the wiretapping scandal of the so-called Elysée anti-terrorist cell under President François

Mitterrand, discovered the hidden files of Christian Prouteau, former head of the unit set up in 1981. There he found the Coral file, proof that the case was closely followed at the highest levels. In April 1997, Captain Barril, who had worked under Christian Prouteau in 1982, confirmed this hypothesis: "I remember that we were alerted to stop the investigation into the Coral paedophile network because of the personalities involved".

At the origin of the whole Coral story, wrote the *Minute* journalist, was a certain Jean-Claude Krief. In October 1982, he had written a confession: "My name is Jean-Claude Kreif, I was born on 1 June 1961 in Argenteuil; the son of sick parents, I was in a DDASS institution for thirteen years, after which I decided to emigrate to Israel to take care of children".

Back in France, Jean-Claude Krief was introduced to the Coral through friends at the end of 1981: "I spent the holidays at the Coral and discovered that everyone there was a paedophile and that fucking children was not taboo. What I also discovered is that many celebrities regularly went there to indulge their sexual instincts, of course with young children who had no family and no voice". And he provided a list of visitors to the Coral. It included a minister in office at the time, the son of a former minister, a high magistrate, two famous writers, two psychiatrists, a journalist, a musician, two photographers and.... Léonid Kameneff, creator of the Boat School. Krief's accusations were never confirmed and, what's more, the man retracted them two months later, claiming to have been manipulated by the police as an extreme left-wing agitator. Krief then disappeared from view. For some, he was dead. For others, he was in Israel.

A film was even made about the Coral: *Visiblement, je vous aime* (France, 1995): Psychotics and juvenile delinquents live here "in total freedom and confidence, to better reintegrate into the social environment", wrote Bouniq-Mercier in *Le Guide des films*. He concluded: "A generous and fascinating work about freedom and the right to be different. The film is by Jean-Michel Carré, with a screenplay by Claude Sigala, who plays himself.

Twinky is a film by the very cosmopolitan Richard Donner (USA, 1991): a forty-something American author of erotic novels lives in London. He meets a sixteen-year-old schoolgirl and wants to marry her. It will be a failure. A predictable failure, like the one in the film.

Some Indian filmmakers also shared the same obsessions. *Split wide open* (India, 1999): Kepi is a slacker from Bombay. One day he is beaten up by the henchmen of powerful gangsters. He is in love with Didi, a ten-year-old girl, but one day she disappears, kidnapped by pimps to be given away for the pleasure of rich paedophiles. The film is by Dev Benagal, a real Indian by all accounts. But he didn't tell us anything about the true nature of these gangsters, kidnappers and rich paedophiles.

Betty Fisher et autres histoires is a film by Claude Miller (France, 2001): Betty Fisher is a successful writer. She has everything she needs to be happy, until the accidental death of her young son. His mother Margot, suffering from dementia, decides to kidnap a child to replace the missing one.

The Believers (United States, 1987). This one was to be expected: in New York, young children are kidnapped and ritually murdered. Psychologist Jamison discovers the existence of a sect, Santeria, which practices a Cuban variant of voodoo. The film is directed by John Schleisinger, who obviously does not belong to any voodoo sect.

In the same vein, there is also *The Man from Kiev* (USA, 1969): In Kiev, in 1911, a horrible pogrom takes place, and we don't know why (as usual). Having escaped the massacre, a Jewish craftsman comes to the aid of a rich Russian bourgeois, who takes him into his service. But when the craftsman rejects the advances of his boss's daughter, she accuses him of rape. Soon, the Jew is also accused of the ritual murder of a child by a fanatical Christian priest. He is horribly tortured in prison and sentenced to death. The Western democracies intervene and the world is on the brink of war, once again, to save a son of Israel. Fortunately, the poor Jew will be acquitted of such a horrible crime. The Jews are here collectively exonerated of the ritual crimes of which they are accused in almost every country in Europe and the Middle East. A film by director John Frankenheimer.

The Collector is a film by William Wyler (USA, 1965): A butterfly collector kidnaps a girl and keeps her in his house. When she dies, he chooses another.

The accusatory inversion is also evident in Peter Webber's film *Hannibal Lecter, The Origins of Evil* (2007), which reveals the childhood of the famous Hannibal Lecter, the psychopathic cannibal killer from *The Silence of the Lambs*: as a child, during the war in Lithuania, he saw his little sister being eaten before his eyes by hungry Russian soldiers. As a teenager, Hannibal seeks revenge and hunts down the criminals, one by one, to eat their brains. One of them has become a restaurateur in a French region, and Hannibal savours the fate that awaits him. He sits at a table and watches his future victim. We then learn that the owner of the restaurant, this child murderer is also a good Christian who wants his children to go to church.[502]

Another fairly typical example of accusatory inversion is American playwright David Mamet's play *Romance*, performed in Paris in 2006. An article by Pierre Karch, published in *L'Express* (online version) on 30 May, presented David Mamet's play: "His latest play, *Romance*, denounces the

---

[502] On the murder of Christian children, read Professor Areil Toaff's book, published in February 2007 and entitled *Pasque di sangue* (*Passover of Blood, Eastern European Jews and the Accusations of Ritual Crime*). Professor Toaff teaches at Bar-Ilan University in Jerusalem. Read in *Jewish Fanaticism*.

hypocrisy of political correctness. But he does it through laughter.... In this 75-minute play, performed without intermission, there is no respect for anything or anyone. The Jews mock the Christians, whose priests sodomise the altar boys, and the Christians bless heaven for not having been born Jews". The truth is that it is above all the Jews who are manifestly in the habit of sodomising their children, as we shall see later, and it is still the Jews who bless Yahweh daily for not having been born goyim or women. Naturally, the author of this work was also an apologist for homosexuality, as we can read in Pierre Karch's review: "The prosecutor has a lover, Bernard, whom he calls Bunny... The judge spent a week on the Spanish island of Ibiza with the usher...". The trial drags on because everyone brings their own personal problems to the table. "In one of his rare moments of lucidity, the judge, a paedophile and incestuous, declares that we are all guilty, for that is the Christian position, that of the "mea culpa" and that of the just man who sins at least seven times a day". Pierre Karch concluded that the play was "a masterstroke".

David Harrower's play *Blackbird* (2008) is rather suspicious. This was what one could read about it on the internet: "Can love exist between a twelve year old girl and a forty year old man? Uma was twelve at the time of this relationship with a forty-year-old neighbour. Questioned by the police, she was reluctant to denounce the man she considered to be her lover". The staging is by Claudia Stavisky, with a script in French by Zabou Breitman and Léa Drucker: "Actress Léa Drucker will try to succeed her cousin Marie Drucker for the title of "*Femme en or*" 2008."

All these sexual deviations are expressed in the Talmud, the holy book of Judaism, which contains the teachings of the rabbis and which Jews consider even more important than the Torah. We have already studied this issue in our previous books.[503]

Here is a summary of the gist: Sanhedrin 54b-55a explains how adults can abuse young children. As long as they have not reached sexual maturity, they are not physiologically capable of sexual intercourse, and they are not

---

[503] Read in *Psychoanalysis of Judaism*. Gérard Haddad wrote in his essay *The Talmudic Sources of Psychoanalysis*: "It is certain, however, that the interest of Hebraic thought in sexuality occupies a central place, by no means embryonic. It is, together with the midrashic art [the commentary and oral interpolation of the text of the Torah, ndt], the point at which the two systems of thought - Judaism and psychoanalysis - reveal this affinity, which stems from the very purpose of the two discourses. Psychoanalysis is undoubtedly the one that strives to come as close as possible to the economy of jouissance, a question that occupies precisely the primordial place in Judaism, even striving, according to Lacan, to give "the mode of employment". It is enough to convince oneself of this by rereading the Book of Ecclesiastes, - and the entire Talmud undoubtedly develops this path". In Gérard Haddad, *Les Sources talmudiques de la psychanalyse* (1981), Desclée de Brouwer, Poche, 1990, p. 244-245.

considered persons and therefore the laws on sodomy do not concern them. Many pages are devoted to the supervision of paedomania and "cohabitation" with young children. Sanhedrin 55a clearly states that a boy is considered sexually mature at the age of nine years and one day, and a girl at the age of three years and one day.

Ted Pike is a former director of the National Prayer Network, a Christian association in the United States. In an article entitled *Paedophilia, the Talmud's dirty secret*, published in October 2006, he quoted Shimon Bar Yochai, a famous first century AD rabbi, a major contributor to the writing of the *Mishnah* and, according to Tradition, the author of the book of Zohar, the 'bible' of Kabbalah: 'A proselyte under the age of three years and one day is allowed to marry a priest without being considered a prostitute (Yebamot 60b). For a young girl, the teaching of Bar Yochai is clear: sexual relations are permitted before the age of three, and marriage to a rabbi from the age of three and a day (Sanhedrin 55b, but also Yebamot 57b, Sanhedrin 69a, 69b, Yebamot 60b).

The name of Shimon Bar Yochai is still revered for such arbitrations by many ultra-Orthodox Jewish congregations. Sanhedrin Note 60b explicitly rejects the right of any rabbi to challenge his version. In the Israeli town of Meron, where Bar Yochai was born, a large pilgrimage takes place every year in which hundreds of thousands of Jews sing and dance for several days and nights in a row to celebrate the memory of the blessed rabbi. Shimon bar Yochai is still recognised as one of the greatest Talmudic sages and one of the most influential rabbis in history. In the 1936 English translation of the Talmud - the so-called Soncino version - it is simply mentioned at the bottom of the page that "marriages, of course, took place much earlier than today". (Sanhedrin 76a). It is true that Jews used to marry off their children very early. In his 1967 novel, The *House of Jampol*, Isaac Bashevis Singer confirmed this: "In former times, eight-year-old girls were already given in marriage[504]".

Freud, as we know, had studied the *Malleus Maleficarum*, the "Witches' Hammer", published in 1486. Ernst Jones wrote in his biography of the master: "Freud was especially impressed by the fact that the sexual perversions which the devil practised on his addicts were the same as the patients' accounts of their childhood, and it occurred to him to suggest that such perversions were relics of an inheritance from an ancient semi-religious sex cult of the Semites (24 January 1897)[505]."

---

[504] Isaac Bashevis Singer, *The House of Jampol*, German25 digital ed., p. 60. See other examples in *Psychoanalysis of Judaism*.
[505] Ernst Jones, *Freud (I)*, Salvat Editores, Barcelona, 1985, p. 259.

2. The incestuous sect

Jews have been obsessed with incest since the beginning of time. Direct testimonies are quite rare, as those affected remain very discreet about it, and very few incest victims file complaints against their own parents. But if we read the Jews with a mirror, one realises that this problem is still a major issue in the cultural production of Judaism.[506]

Between a father and daughter

Barbara was a well-known French singer in the 1960s and 1970s. After her death in November 1997, it was revealed that the Hungarian-born Jewish woman had been raped by her father. The secret had been kept hidden for a long time, but it was said that she "revealed it on stage to those who could hear". In one of her songs, *Au coeur de la nuit*, she alluded to this fact. "The analytical work she refused to do on a couch, she did on stage," wrote the weekly *Marianne* of 1 November 2007: "Barbara would return very elliptically to this trauma in her autobiography, *Il était une fois un piano noir*: 'One afternoon, I ran away to escape from my father. I couldn't take it any more. I walked, I walked. He told everything to the police, who advised him to return home, as he was a minor. But although the confession is brief, the wound festered in his most beautiful songs: *From Nantes* (1963) to *Aigle noir* (1970), the death of her father in 1959 accelerated the artist's transformation... This drama had to be exorcised". And *Marianne*'s journalist continued: "We almost forget that this woman used this intimate wound to revolutionise other taboos. In a totally assumed, almost provocative turn, Barbara sings of love affairs considered incestuous by society. *Marie Chevenance* tells the story of a love affair between a very young girl and a middle-aged man. "I have always thought that the most beautiful loves were incestuous loves".

Sophie Jabès is a "French" novelist born in Milan in 1958. After a childhood and adolescence in Rome, she moved to the United States and studied in Boston. There she developed a passion for cinema and became a television producer. She published her first novel in 2003: *Alice la Saucisse*. Here is a summary of her other novel, *Caroline assassine*, published in

---

[506] We have evoked this crucial question in *Psychoanalysis of Judaism* and *Jewish Fanaticism*.

2004: When her mother forbids her to read, Caroline decides to take revenge. She is only seven years old, and already she has "a pure work to do": to kill her mother and escape from a hellish family. While waiting to offer her the best possible death, she dreams of her absent father, whom she doesn't know but who will surely come to get her out of this madhouse. One day, he returns. But he is worse than the others. Alcoholic and incestuous.

And here is Karine Henry's comment on the Internet: "What could be no more than a tragedy is, believe me, funny, baroque and burlesque. A real jewel in the mélange of tones, a modern romantic tale without parallel in French literature. The second part of a trilogy on our taboos".

Here is an extract from Sophie Jabés' wonderful book, *Caroline assassine*: "The librarian hesitated. She was afraid for Caroline. She feared she would understand too much too quickly. She feared these readings for a seven year old. The girl insisted. Do you really think so? Yes. I really believe it. Caroline discovered evil. It fascinated her. She tried to look it in the face. Trying to tame her terror. Her compassion was immense... Writing led her to the infinite possibilities. Through the sufferings of these literary beings, a compelling desire for justice developed. Of course. Clear. Caroline felt she had a mission to accomplish, one that only she would have the strength and courage to see through to the end." This will suffice. The beauty of the style will not have escaped them: "a real gem."

In October 2008, a sordid event took place in Israel: Rose, a four-year-old French girl, was found dead in a river. Her father, Benjamin, was an Israeli who had met Marie in France. After Rose's birth, they decided to marry and live in Israel, but Benjamin abused the little girl and the couple fought over custody of the child. The father returned to France and Marie stayed in Israel, where she fell in love with Roni, Benjamin's father. She had two more daughters with him, aged one and two at the time. Marie was then 23 and Roni 45. We learned that it was the grandfather who killed Rose and threw her body into the river.

Fabrice Pliskin's novel *The Jew and the Half-Blood (Le Juif et la métisse*, Flammarion, 2008) should also be read carefully: David Lévy, a left-wing university student specialising in genocide, leads a quiet family life, steeped in virtuous multiculturalism and exotic fantasies. Until the day his next-door neighbour makes him a strange proposition: terrified at the thought of meeting his daughter, whose existence he has just found out, he convinces David to go to the rendezvous in his place. His daughter is Bintu, a racy twenty-two-year-old half-breed with false braids, endless legs and an almost devilish vitality. She is everything David is not: a former triple jump champion, an ambitious basketball player and right-wing councillor, a scholarship student as adept at defrauding welfare benefits as she is at rolling joints...".

Arthur Schnitzler was a well-known Austrian Jewish writer who lived in Vienna in the early 20th century. In one of his most famous novels, *Miss Else*, he portrays "a clearly neurotic and probably hysterical young woman who, in order to save her father from disgrace, submits to the old man's desire by presenting herself naked before him. But after doing so, she commits suicide". As we know, in 1928, Arthur Schnitzler's only daughter committed suicide with a revolver in Venice.

On the website of the Paris Psychoanalytic Society, for example, we read an article by a certain Jacqueline Schaeffer: "The ambiguity of the menstruation taboo can serve as an innocent ground for a father's incestuous transgression, she wrote. A Jewish patient tells how her father shared her bed during the period of impurity of her mother's rules. Another patient: her divorced father would take her in his bed, when her menstrual pains appeared, and put his hand on her belly: 'That's what I did to your mother when she was in pain'".

Once again, we can observe this phenomenon in cinema: *Four Minutes* (*Vier Minuten*) is a German film by a certain Chris Kraus (2006): For 60 years, Traude Krüger has been teaching piano to prisoners in Luckau prison in the former East Germany. When he meets Jenny von Loeben, imprisoned for murder, he soon realises that she is a young musical prodigy. Fascinated by this forgotten talent, the spinster wants to prepare her for the entrance exam to the Conservatory. But Jenny, violent and suicidal, resists the slightest discipline. The film has been hailed by critics as the best German film of the year, and "this virtuoso melodrama about music, prison, heavy inheritances and unspeakable secrets delves deep into the Germanic soul". And again: "Even if they are old archetypes, the confrontation between the Iron Lady and the young rebel (Hannah Herzsprung, a revelation) is fascinating. As for a clear tendency towards dramatic overload (was it really necessary to include false confessions, incest, lesbianism and the Nazi past in this story?), it is fortunately compensated by a truly brilliant mise-en-scène. Indeed, the film reveals that the young woman's hatred and violence are rooted in the fact that she has been the victim of incest. Gradually, a sapphic relationship develops between the young girl and her teacher...

In *Comme t'y es belle* (France, 2006), director Lisa Azuelos depicts the everyday life of wealthy, affluent Sephardic friends in Paris. During a family meal, a young girl innocently talks about a Jewish father who allegedly raped her children, which immediately causes unrest at the table.

The film *Arsène Lupin* (France, 2004) narrates the adventures of the famous "gentleman thief". Director Jean-Paul Salomé added some details: Arsène Lupin and his cousin are very attracted to each other. They have sex from the first day they meet and she becomes pregnant. Meanwhile, Arsène dates a woman much older than him... who slept with his father (as we learn at the end of the film) and who would also sleep with his cousin's son. The film is anti-monarchist and anti-Catholic: the French patriots of the *belle époque* are portrayed here as perverts and members of a conspiratorial organisation. Jean-Paul Salomé also directed *Femmes de l'ombre*, a film about the French Resistance against the Nazis.

Fiona (USA, 1998): Fiona was abandoned as a baby by her mother, a prostitute, and raped by her adoptive father. Her only way out is prostitution, where she will also come into contact with the world of drugs. A film by Amos Kollek.

Alone against all (*Seul contre tous*, France, 1998), by Gaspar Noé: A fifty-something butcher, unemployed and recently released from prison, arrives in Paris after beating his pregnant wife. All he has is his daughter, who is in a public institution. This monster with fascist, homophobic and racist tendencies loves his daughter incestuously. Everything in this film is dirty: empty streets, factory walls, etc. Gaspar Noé also directed *Carne*, in 1991: a butcher, abandoned by his wife, raises his daughter by himself, to whom he devotes his exclusive love. When he believes she has been raped, he reacts brutally by savagely wounding an innocent Arab. Thank you Gaspar Noé.

L'ombre du doute, by Aline Isserman (France, 1992): Twelve-year-old Alexandrine is sexually abused by her father. Her mother refuses to believe her. Alexandrine confesses everything to the police, triggering a family drama. Claude Bouniq-Mercier wrote: "The father is nothing more than an unfortunate and wounded being, as much a victim as a guilty one".

The Friends of the Heart (*Le Amiche del cuore,* Italy, 1992): Claudia, Morena and Sabrina are three childhood friends from the suburbs of Rome. Claudia wants to be a model. Morena studies nursing and takes the opportunity to supply her mother with drugs. Sabrina finds love with Lucio, but he leaves her when he learns of her incestuous relationship with her father. A film by Michele Placido, with a screenplay by Angelo Pasquini.

Roma, Roméo (France, 1991): This is what Bouniq-Mercier wrote in *Le Guide des films*: 'Twenty years later, David Waldberg returns to Rome for a love tryst with Countess Orsini. She is dead. Through Quentin, David meets a disillusioned French artist, Clara Orsini, daughter of the Countess. He feels the same passion for her, relives the same love and visits the same places with her. He learns that Clara is probably his own daughter". The film is by Alain Fleischer.

In 1978, Alain Fleischer directed *Zoo Zéro* (France, 1978): "Eva, a former singer, sings in a cabaret where all the customers are members of the same family. They leave the cabaret to tour a ruined city ravaged by epidemics. The family is soon decimated, except for Eva. She arrives at the zoo run by her father, named Yahweh. As a tape recorder plays an old recording of the *Magic Flute,* Eva and her father free the animals. They join in a final embrace before being struck by lightning. The animals occupy the territory of the humans". Claude Bouniq-Mercier added: "The quality of the sound and images adds to the formal beauty of this difficult and esoteric work, which describes a kind of apocalypse for our civilisation".

Twin Peaks, the famous thirty-episode series by David Lynch (USA, 1990). In Twin Peaks, a small American town, a terrible murder has been committed. Young Laura Palmer has been found dead and naked on the shore of a lake. And here is the solution to the riddle: it was the father who raped his own daughter.

Here is a brief summary of an episode of the medical series *House* (episode 13, season 2, *Skin deep*), which presents a case of hermaphroditism: The patient is a 15-year-old heroin addict and model who suffers from various disorders and ends up in Dr. House's consulting room. He discovers that she has been the victim of incest on the part of her father, who is also her manager. We later discover that it was the daughter herself who encouraged the incest and that, in order to succeed, she slept with everyone. After a few plot twists, House finally discovers that the model is actually... a man, as his testicles are hidden inside. We owe this masterpiece to one David Shore. We found some information on the internet about him: David Shore is the only one in his family who works for television. His twin brothers, Philip and Robert, are rabbis.

La fille de 15 ans is a film by Jacques Doillon (France, 1988): Juliette, fifteen years old, is in love with Thomas, a boy her age. Willy, Thomas's father, takes them to Ibiza and falls in love with Juliette, who gives herself to him.

Jacques Doillon also directed *La Fille prodigue* in 1981: Anne, in the throes of depression, leaves her new husband and joins her parents at their home in Deauville. She isolates herself with her father, driving away his wife and her lover. The relationship between father and daughter is ambiguous. At times, Anne behaves like a real child, capricious and cuddly at times; at others, she manipulates her father in a Machiavellian way. A strange tension develops between father and daughter. One night, after another argument, she loses her virginity in her father's arms. Jacques Doillon is also a professional anti-racist. Just like his daughter, who is devoted to cinema... like her father.[507]

---

[507] In February 2024, several actresses accused Jacques Doilon of rape, assault and sexual harassment, allegedly occurring between 1980 and 2010. On 6 February 2024, actress Judith Godrèche filed a complaint against him for rape of a minor under the age of 15 by a person in authority. The filmmaker is accused of having raped her on the sidelines and during the filming of *La Fille de 15 ans*. A few days after Judith Godrèche's statement, actresses Isild Le Besco and Anna Mouglalis in turn accused Doillon of sexual assault and harassment in an investigation by the newspaper *Le*

Charlotte for ever, by Serge Gainsbourg (France, 1986): Stan, an alcoholic screenwriter, has serious problems with his daughter Charlotte, who blames him for the death of her mother in a car accident. A film about a father's unbridled love for his daughter, with incestuous scenes. Serge Gainsbourg also wrote the song *Lemon Incest*.

The Color Purple is a film by Steven Spielberg (USA, 1986): The story is set in the heart of a black family in the American Deep South. Misery, ignorance and bestial brutalisation have replaced slavery. The heroine is a young black girl subjugated by her father, who rapes her and has two children with her. She is sold to a husband who makes her his slave, but she finds the strength to raise her head against those who exploit her. This screenplay by Alice Walker, a black woman, evidently inspired Steven Spielberg.

Hotel New Hampshire (USA, 1984): Win and Mary restore a school building and turn it into a hotel. They have several children: one of the boys turns out to be homosexual; the girl is raped, and there is even incest involved. The film is by Tony Richardson.

Un moment d'égarement (France, 1977): two fathers take their daughters in their twenties to San-Tropez. One of them is seduced by the other's daughter. A film by Claude Berri (Langmann).

Il faut vivre dangereusement, by Claude Makovski (France, 1975): Murdoc, a businessman, asks a private detective to follow Lorraine, a young woman he claims to be jealous of. The detective discovers that she frequents a brothel, where she is involved with a rich industrialist named Badinget. Now, Badinget and Murdoc are two brothers who hate each other, and Lorraine is Murdoc's daughter. The girl sleeps here with her father, and also with her uncle. The screenplay is by Nelly Kaplan, director of the very "cosmopolitan" film *The Pirate's Bride*.

*Contes immoraux (*France, 1974) is a succession of erotic stories. One of them is entitled *Lucrezia Borgia*. In 1498, while Savonarola was denouncing the dissolute morals of pontifical circles, Lucrezia Borgia was having sexual relations with her father, Pope Alexander VI, and her brother, Cardinal Cesare Borgia. Bounique-Mercier awards four stars to this film directed by Walerian Borowczyk. True or false, these alleged incestuous relationships raised suspicions at the time that the Borgia family was of marrano origin.

The Pleasure of His Company is a film by George Seaton (USA, 1961): Jessica idolises her father, the voluble and cynical Pogo, who is always away from home. When he reappears, she sets out to seduce him. The screenplay is by Samuel Taylor.

Monde, for events that occurred in 2000 and 2011 respectively. (wikipedia, NdT.)

Beggars of Life, by William Wellman (USA, 1928): In a panic, Nancy kills her father, a disreputable individual who is about to rape her. She runs away with a young drifter, disguises herself as a man and ends up in a railway camp. Based on a screenplay by Benjamin Glazer.

We reproduce below the testimony of a 56-year-old Jewish woman found on the Internet and published on 1 August 2007. We have translated it from English and summarised it. This woman claimed to have been a victim of incest in her Jewish family and to have been treated by a psychologist throughout her life. As a teenager, she thought she was Jewish, but later discovered that her mother was not Jewish when she was born. She therefore had to complete her conversion and purify herself in a ritual bath to become officially Jewish. She was married twice and had a child by remarriage. But before this second marriage, she was alone for ten long years: "I spent years telling myself that everything was fine, when the truth was that my mind was in total chaos. I lived in a kind of confusion between the truth and an imaginary world. I had nightmares, as if I was falling into darkness, and I would wake up before I hit the ground...".

When she was little, on Yom Kippur, she used to go to synagogue with Zada, her "wonderful grandfather": "I asked several of my friends, but none of them had any idea what was being said inside. In the synagogue, I would stand next to Zada and play with the fringes of his talit. I liked the singing, the quietness of the faithful... I didn't know what Zada had done with her daughter. I didn't know that incest could be passed on from generation to generation. I only knew that what happened at home should not be repeated to anyone. I was fifteen when Zada died. Life was turned upside down.

At his funeral, he discovered that Zeda was a Cohen. The Cohens are a model for the Jewish people. To be a Cohen is to be a direct descendant of Aaron, the brother of Moses, who was the first high priest of the Temple. Since the destruction of the Temple by the Roman armies of Titus in 68 AD, the Kohanim have maintained the purity of the lineage. This means that a Cohen cannot marry a divorced or converted woman, because her life before conversion was impure. "I also discovered that he had never been married to Bess because she had already been divorced, which did not prevent them from living together for twenty years." Kohanim must also avoid all contact with dead bodies in order to maintain a high degree of purity.

The status of Cohen is passed down through the male members of the family. "So, my father was a Cohen. I am a 'Bat Cohen', a daughter of Cohen, she explained. But according to Jewish law, I will not pass on the status of Cohen to my son."

And here he recounted his tragedy: "In the years following the death of his wife, the mother of his four children, Zada had slept with his eldest daughter as if she had been his wife. My father also abused his two daughters for years. The shame of incest has been with me all my life. From the age of seven until I was sixteen, I was continuously raped by my father. I never told anyone. I adored my father. He said that's what people do when they love each other, but I was not supposed to tell anyone. Today, I feel ashamed to come from a Kohanim family. My sister said that our father had abused us, but no one believed her."

These things should be kept secret: "The day she brought home a Catholic boyfriend, my father was furious. He tore off his shirt and declared her dead, according to the *shivah* rite. He ordered my mother and me never to speak to him again. When another aunt asked me if my father had abused us, I lied to protect him. Later, my sister converted to Catholicism at the age of 12. I now spent more time with my cousins. I would go to *shul* [synagogue, ndlr] with them. Now I want to take my maiden name and not be ashamed of it."

He added: "Incest exists in Jewish families. The long-term effects of childhood incest are fear, anxiety, depression, anger, sexual deviance, low self-esteem, tendency to take drugs and difficult relationships with the environment. Since the Talmud, there has been incestuous abuse in the Jewish community. This is nothing new[508]. We need to open our minds and hearts in the Jewish community to begin to understand the "incest survivors", like the Holocaust survivors. I know I am not alone[509]."

In a short novel entitled *The Diary of Yael Koppman*, published in 2007, one Marianne Rubinstein confirmed the harmful effects of incest on girls who may be inclined to indulge in every possible and imaginable experience in an attempt to forget the trauma. The cover of the book reads

---

[508] Rachel Lev, *Shine the Light, Sexual Abuse and Healing in the Jewish Community*, Northeastern University Press, 2002, p. 23. [Amazon book introduction note: "This is a journey into the stories, hearts, and minds of adult Jewish survivors of sexual abuse and incest. Rachel Lev, a therapist and incest survivor, blends her own experiences with those of other survivors and reflects on her personal relationships with the Jewish community, a community that can foster denial or be a place of healing. "Shine the Light" emphasises healing, which Lev believes can come through self-expression, creativity and, above all, feeling connected rather than isolated. The text includes first-hand accounts, poetry and evocative artwork. The 22 contributing authors and artists identify along the spectrum from "just Jewish" to "Hasidic" and represent a wide range of professions and ethnic backgrounds. Sexual abuse occurs in all religious and cultural groups, but Lev explains the particular difficulties of the Jewish community in acknowledging the problem, given its long history of victimisation and its need for a positive self-image. The author reveals that Judaism is rich in resources for healing as she explores Jewish law, tradition, and rituals that include the reflections of rabbis, lay leaders, and survivors." (NdT)]

[509] http://jewishincesthealing.blogspot.com/ The author provides a link to the website of the Awareness Center, which indeed presents hundreds of cases of paedophile and incestuous rabbis. TheAwarnessCenter.org/experience-god.html

as follows: "The life of an idle thirty-something, cultivating a troubled relationship with her mother, living and sharing a flat with her best friend, collecting men.... We argue often, he, planted on his hermetically sealed planet, and I on mine, madness and atavistic Jewish anxiety all clenched in a bundle[510]."

This analysis was also corroborated by Isaac Bashevis Singer. The novelist had moved to the United States in 1935. In *The Death of Methuselah*, a collection of short stories written between 1971 and 1988, a short story entitled *The Businessman* told the story of Manya, a Polish Jewess: 'By the age of 19, Singer wrote, she had already had a string of at least twenty lovers, including her own father, may he burn in Gehenna. She had also had some lesbian experiences and, in the end, had tried everything: sadism, masochism, exhibitionism, every possible kind of perversion[511]."

Aliza Schvarts is also, obviously, a daughter of Israel. This Yale University art student became known in April 2008 after, among other things, creating a painting using the blood from her menstruation or miscarriage, a final year work she entitled *Untitled [Senior Thesis]*. Aliza Schvarts obviously has a disturbed mind.

Here is an interesting anecdote found in September 2008 on the website *Les Intransigeants*: The narrator wrote that, a few days earlier, he had a drink with some friends and chatted with a girl he did not know. She told him about an old friend, a Jewish woman who, it seems, was not very mentally balanced: "Let me guess.... Was she a lesbian? - No, but yet she told me she was open to all sexual experiences, just to try them out"... I couldn't resist asking the ultimate question about the great secret shared by Jews: "And she wouldn't by any chance have had sex with members of her family?

- How did you guess? It's unbelievable, you're the first person to tell me! I've never told anyone before. But how did you guess... In fact, she was touched by her father! One day she collapsed in my arms and told me that she remembered it all. It had all happened when she was about six years old. She no longer knew if she had had sex or if it had just been touching.... She had erased these sad events from her memory and only remembered them for a few years".

And the author of these lines added: "Of course, some readers will reproach me for not publishing any proof of this conversation. But I swear that my testimony is true. If I had to prove it or present proof, I would simply say this: my religion forbids me to lie".

---

[510] Marianne Rubinstein, *Le Journal de Yaël Koppman*, Wespieser, 2007, p. 83.
[511] Isaac Bashevis Singer, *La Mort de Mathusalem*, Nouvelles, Stock, 1989, p. 153.

The Torah (the Old Testament) also presents an example of incest between a father and his daughters. The story of the daughters of Lot, Abraham's nephew, is well known. They had made their father drunk in order to copulate with him (Genesis 19: 30-38). Incest is excusable when it comes to procreation. "The Israelite tribe of Judah is supposed to be two-thirds descended from this kind of incest - cf. Genesis, 38; Numbers, 26: 19", wrote Maxime Rodinson, a community intellectual.[512]

Freud had evidently been inspired by the customs of the Jewish community to elaborate his theory of the "primitive horde". For only in the Jewish community does the father possess all women, including his own daughters, and nowhere else.[513]

Elie Wiesel also left some ambiguous comments on the subject of incest. In his book entitled *Hasidic Celebration II*, published in 1981, he spoke of the 'Besht', the founder of the Hasidic movement in Poland in the 18th century, once again expressing himself elliptically: 'There was a real friendship between father and daughter, wrote Elie Wiesel, a kind of complicity. One gets the feeling that the Besht was closer to his daughter than to his own wife[514]."

Between a father and son

Eve Ensler is an American playwright and author of a highly successful feminist play, beautifully titled *The Vagina Monologues* (1996). In 2004 she visited Israel with her partner Ariel Jordan. An article in the Israeli daily *Haaretz* on 2 February 2004 reported that both Eve Ensler and Ariel Jordan had been raped by their fathers as children. This is what was said about Jordan, who had travelled to Israel to see his mother and siblings again after a 15-year absence: "Jordan, a psychotherapist and filmmaker, was born in Kfar Blum.... When he was Israeli, his name was Ilan Tiano. "Carrying the name of my father, who raped me from the age of three to fourteen, was beyond my strength". Jordan encouraged Eve Ensler to reunite with her mother, whom she had not seen for years, "Ten years earlier, Eve had already forgiven her mother for turning a blind eye to her father's repeated incestuous abuse of her. "I decided to stop being a victim," the activist repeated. There you have the true origin of feminism.

An article in the *Haaretz* newspaper of 13 December 2006 reported some interesting statistics. It reported that in Israel, during the year, the

---

[512] Maxime Rodinson, *Peuple juif ou problème juif?*, La Découverte, 1981, Poche, 1997, p. 254.
[513] Read in *Psychoanalysis of Judaism*.
[514] Elie Wiesel, *Célébrations hassidique II*, Seuil, 1981, p. 76. On the Hasidic (mystic-kabbalist) movement, see *Psychoanalysis of Judaism* and *Jewish Fanaticism*.

Association of Rape Crisis Centers had received almost 2,000 complaints involving teenagers between 13 and 18 years of age. Ninety per cent of the victims had been assaulted by someone they knew, and 60 per cent of the cases involving children under 12 were incestuous relationships. As the age of the victims increased, the percentage of incest cases decreased, while the percentage of rape cases increased. Among young adolescents, 17% of the assaults took place in educational institutions, and of these, 11% in religious institutions. The *Haaretz* newspaper of 29 October 2007 quoted the National Council for Children in Israel as saying that reports of paedophile acts were on the rise. Thirty per cent of them concerned ultra-Orthodox communities, and more than half of the 9,000 cases dealt with in 2006 involved minors. It should be recalled that in the vast majority of cases, incest victims never file a complaint.

Andrew Jrecki's US documentary *Capturing the Friedmans* (USA, 2003) tells a story that caused something of a stir in the United States. In 1987, Arnold Friedman was accused in Long Island, outside New York, of raping dozens of very young boys who came to his house for computer classes. One of his sons, 18-year-old Jesse, was charged along with him, while his two other sons and his wife were unaware of what was going on in the house. Numerous paedophile magazines were found in their home. The Frideman's lawyer later admitted that the father had confessed everything to him: For years, he had been raping his son Jesse, before raping underage boys. Until the 51st minute of the film it was not clear that this was a Jewish family. But the final image showed the Star of David on the grave of the criminal.

War Zone (UK, 1999) is a film by Tim Roth. Tom discovers an incestuous relationship between his father and sister. And that is only the beginning. The horror ends when Tom and his sister stab their father. Tim Roth denounces the silence surrounding this violence, especially when he himself admits to having been sexually abused by his father. In *Little Odessa*, a must-see film, Tim Roth plays a Brooklyn hitman. His relationship with his father is extremely violent. Tim Roth also appears in Quentin Tarentino's *Reservoir Dogs*, playing the wounded man who turns out to be the mole undercover.

Festen is a film by Thomas Vinterberg (Denmark, 1998): On the occasion of his sixtieth birthday, a father gathers all his relatives in his manor house. His three children are there: Mickael, the youngest, a failed alcoholic; Hélène, the madwoman, who has come with her partner, a black man; and Christian, the eldest, who is still suffering from the suicide of his twin sister Linda. As they toast their father, Christian reveals a terrible secret: the incestuous acts his father committed with one of his sons.

In the cult film *They Live* (USA, 1988), the hero, John Nada, discovers through special glasses that a small part of the population is made up of perfectly normal-looking aliens. They form an elite that rules the world through lies. Nada has been the victim of an abusive father. The film is by John Carpenter.

Alejandro Jodorwsky is a "Chilean" author. In 1996 he published a novel entitled *L'Arbre du dieu pendu*. It is the fantasised story of the author's family, who leave the Russian ghettos at the beginning of the 20th century to land in Valparaiso. Fleeing the pogroms, the Levi family, renamed in the meantime with the more goy Polish name of Jodorowsky, left the Ukraine for lack of money to land by chance in Valparaiso and become Chilean. On 16 March 1996, the "reference" newspaper *Le Monde* praised this "Hasidic-Talmudic" masterpiece and introduced the characters: "Teresa Groismann, the terrible grandmother, curses the god of the Jews who took her son away from her and decides to become a goy flea trainer. Her husband Alexander, the shoemaker, is inhabited by a Caucasian rabbi who preaches wasteful charity". There is also "Abraham, the incestuous beekeeper; Salvador Arcavi, the tamer who learns to read the tarot cards in the eyes of his lions... all of them take us on a whirlwind of extraordinary adventures that lead them from the Russian ghettos to the Chile of the Great Depression". And the journalist concluded by putting his best foot forward: "A malicious and ironic piece of writing. A great baroque novel that will delight anyone who likes to be told stories". All that remained to be seen was how the story ended: with whom did this "Abraham" have incestuous relations: with his daughter, his son or his sister? Indeed, "transgender" relationships are cultivated in Judaism. One day we will also have to find out what really happened between Franz Kafka and his father.

Between a mother and her child

In November 2007, the National Theatre of Brittany, in the cities of Rennes and Quimper, hosted the 11th *Mettre en Scène* festival, an international meeting of stage directors and choreographers. The literary critic Mari-Mai Corbel wrote in her presentation of the event: "Two authors have chosen explicit texts on the meaning of the incestuous bond to express the madness of our time". First was *Incendies*, a play by Wajdi Mouawad (a "Lebanese"), directed by Stanislas Nordey. It was, according to the critics, a "contemporary re-actualisation of the Oedipal tragedy". In addition to the Oedipus myth," wrote Mari-Mai Corbel on the Internet, "we can also recognise, in the background, Marguerite Duras's *La pluie d'été*", behind the two protagonists who are the twins Jeanne and Simon. At first, Jeanne and Simon only know their father through the legend their mother tells them: that of a man passionately loved but lost, a hero killed in battle. "Laurent Sauvage, a faithful partner in Stanislas Nordey's productions, plays this desolate incarnation of the longed-for absentee, condensing the figures of lover, son and father, becoming father and brother to his children". The fathers are also brothers. To put it bluntly: the eldest son slept with his own mother. We have already seen something similar in Elie Wiesel's work[515].

Listen to this: "Incest is also present in Duras, but between the children...The first name "Simon" also evokes a deep and ancient Judaism, which is the argument from which Marguerite Duras' words emerge.... With this reminiscence of Duras, Wajdi Mouawad revives the climate of anguish and threat that weighs on Judaism". The underlying discourse here is typically Jewish: "Jeanne and Simon are presented as unconsciously threatened, in the same way that anti-Semitism proceeds, from the Inquisition to Nazism: a phantasmatic obsession with original ethnic purity. Hence the odious repression of Jewish origin by Christianity and Islam, and consequently the bastardisation of all peoples".

The other play was *Le Sang des rêves* (*The Blood of Dreams*), directed by Patricia Allio, based on Kathy Acker's novel *Sang et stupeur au lycée* (*Blood and Stupor at the High School*): "Patricia Allio chose to take a different, almost sadistic look at incest. The figure of the mother is eliminated, as is often the case with Sade. Janey's character knows she is in love with her father, when he is not unaware of what he is doing by taking her as his wife".

As we have seen, the singer Barbara had been abused by her father. But she also sang about incest between a mother and her son. In *Si la photo est bonne*, a young man is condemned for abusing his mother. In reality, it would rather be the Jewish mother who abused her son. This is also clearly suggested, for example, in the film *Prendre femme* by Roni Elkabetz (France, 2005).

Jacques Attali talks ambiguously about incest in at least four of his books. In his second novel, *Le premier Jour après moi* (*The First Day After Me*), published in 1990, Attali recounts the vision of a man who has just died and imagines that he is still alive. Strangely, he uses capital letters every time he speaks of "She". It is never clear whether it is his mother or his lover. On page 10, for example, he says: "To leave Sarah, to tell her I will never come here again; to leave, to go back to Europe, to see(Her) again, Ella". On page 14: "She will understand that it is all over between Sarah and me". On the following page: "She will laugh, throw her arms around my neck and say: "I love you". And on page 171: "Much later, after many checks, I understood that she was my mother.... And that that night had turned my father's life upside down.... Until the eve of his departure to the

---

[515] Read in *Jewish Fanaticism*.

Celebes, a few months after his arrival in the world[516]." In short, once again we see that Jacques Attali is obsessed with the question of incest.

In *The Khazar Empire and its Heritage* (1976), the former Jew Arthur Koestler claimed that the Jews of Eastern Europe were descended from the tribe of the Khazars, who came from the northern Caucasus and settled in present-day Ukraine, whose kings converted to Judaism in the eighth century. In the *Jewish Encyclopedia,* one can read that Heinrich Gratez, a great 19th century historian and theologian of Judaism, stated on page 141 of his *History of the Jews,* that "the Khazars professed an [immoral and] coarse religion, which was combined with sensuality and lasciviousness[517]."

Aldo Naouri is a paediatrician and author of the book *Adultères (*Odile Jacob, 2006). Alice Granger wrote a short review of this work on the Internet, which we summarise below. Her comments illustrate quite well the naïve foolishness of many goyim, who do not understand that Jewish intellectuals only talk about themselves and systematically project their neurosis on a universal level. Alice Granger has not understood that for them incest is not theoretical and that the "mother" to whom Aldo Naouri refers is above all the Jewish mother.

Listen to the lucubrations of this Alice Granger: "Aldo Naouri scrutinises, in the stories he loves to collect, detail after detail, the violation of the law prohibiting incest. He notes the almost systematic abuse of this law, and wonders why it is so fragile. His answer is: "It is the relationship between every mother and her child. A relationship that lends itself to incestuous drift".

Alice Granger continued: "In this book about adultery, the place of the mother is central. The incestuous mother. The mother who wants her child to lack nothing. Aldo Naouri writes: "No mother can spontaneously curb her incestuous propensity"...".

Now, if you don't mind, let's dive into the murky and nauseating waters of psychoanalysis: Ready? Here we go:

"There would be as it were an instance which, stronger than herself, would impel her to be able to do nothing but weave a virtual womb around her child, which would think of nothing else, with passion, making her child very afraid, afraid of her power to take everything from him, since she has the power to give everything to him, this for the boy as well as for the girl. Then the boy will then set about seducing his mother to make sure

---

[516] Jacques Attali, *Le premier Jour après moi,* Fayard, 1990, p. 171. ("La voir": see(La). NdT.)

[517] Heinrich Graetz, *History of the Jews IV,* Philadelphia, The Jewish Publication Society of America, 1894, p. 141. [H. Graetz, *Histoire des Juifs III,* A. Dularcher, Paris, 1888, p. 325.]

that she will keep him, he will be her phallus, so he will be less afraid of her, that she will no longer love him, and the girl will end up, in her strategy, turning to the father, she will seduce him, but in doing so she will again be afraid of her mother whom she is trying to take her man away from her. The boy who seduces his mother will be afraid of being castrated by his father. The girl who seduces her father will fear that her mother will stop loving her because she has set herself up as a rival to her father. A period of latency, followed by a violent upheaval in adolescence, when the boy hopes to meet a girl who resembles his mother: so, in this case, the mother, as "first", remains intact, the girl will be "second"! The girl, identified with her mother, will expect to meet a boy who looks like her father, and so she will be able to fit in with the mother like Russian dolls, from generation to generation. In this logical chain, as Aldo Naouri reminds us, the maternal instance remains really central"!

And poor Alice Granger concluded: "So I insist on what Aldo Naouri said: No mother can spontaneously curb her incestuous tendencies".

The US television series *Queer as folk* ran for five seasons. It follows the adventures of a dozen characters from the gay community: men, women and their friends. "It's super gritty," Julien emailed us. "You see them naked all the time.... It is surprising that it is only forbidden to children under 12, while erotic films in France, forbidden to children under 16, are much less daring than this... In short, the series defends adoption by homosexual couples, orgies and sexual freedom. Being gay is very fashionable. The gays are all nice, funny, tolerant, modern, handsome, sporty (the best ones, of course), artists...There is also multiracial propaganda (a black and white parent couple). And, of course, Christians are portrayed as horrible retards who reject progress...There is also an episode in which one of the heroines (lesbian and Jewish), whose German grandparents were deported, explains to her gay friend, who wants to marry a man, that she should find a Jew, as they are trying to forget "the incestuous relationship they had with their mother" (season 5, episode 9, around minute 5). In fact, the fag ends up finding a Jew, but, obviously, the latter discovers that he is not circumcised and explains to him that he cannot sleep with a goy...This series was broadcast in France on the channels *Paris Première* and *Pink TV*...". Julien, our correspondent, was familiar with the whole thing and explained, "The scriptwriters and producers are Ron Cowen and Daniel Lipman."

The series *Nip/Tuck* (USA, 2005) also featured a case of incest between a son and his mother, in episode number 13 (second season). The incestuous relationship is projected onto the Scots. Episode 14 is even more explicit: "On the McNamaras' side: Adrian goes to see Julia and confesses to her that he has slept with his mother on numerous occasions...". The series was directed by Michael Robin, with a script by Sean Jablonski and Jennifer Salt.

Another internet correspondent sent us a review of Alain Chabat's 2004 film *RRRrrrrr!!!*, which showed us once again that Jews are really worried about these incest stories: 37,000 years ago, in prehistoric times, two neighbouring tribes lived in peace... more or less a hair's breadth apart. While the clean-haired tribe lived out their days in peace, keeping the secret of the shampoo formula to themselves, the dirty-haired tribe mourned. So the dirty hair chief decided to send a spy to steal the recipe. This is what our correspondent saw: "The clean-haired tribe are dark, smart, nice, cool and... curly, while the dirty-haired tribe - the blondes - are made up of stupid people. However, one of the clean-haired ones was a bit different: he had blond hair, he was probably a "self-hating brunette"! After many twists and turns, we found out that this fake brunette would like to sleep with his brunette mother "when daddy dies"."

Captivity by Roland Joffé (USA, 2007) is the story of two brothers who capture famous women to torture and kill them. We later discover that their mother forced them into incestuous relationships when they were young. The screenwriter is Larry Cohen.

Du Poil sous les roses is a film by Agnès Obadia (France, 2000): Fourteen-year-old Roudoudou dreams of having big breasts and losing her virginity to a handsome stranger she met on a train. Fifteen-year-old Romain and his friend Francis believe their mothers have become lesbians. They set out to seduce them, hoping to lose their virginity to them. "The dialogue is crude, bordering on the obscene, but never vulgar... A stimulating film not for the prudish," wrote Claude Bouniq-Mercier in *Le Guide des films* de Jean Tulard.

The Hustlers, by Stephen Frears (UK, 1989): Lilly, in her forties, works for a bookmaker whom she occasionally swindles. Roy, her son, is a small-time crook who earns his living with very shoddy scams. When he falls in love with Myra, a rivalry arises between the two women, because Lilly is a possessive mother in love with her son.

Paul Schrader's semi-erotic film *La Féline* (1982) is a wacky tale of black panthers becoming men: Irena is reunited with her brother Paul in New Orleans. In the days that follow, a mysterious panther kills a prostitute (again, it's an obsession). The animal turns out to have a strange bond with Paul and Irena. The secret of the breed is discussed. "Because of the curse, we are an incestuous race, otherwise we metamorphose.... We need blood to live". The script is by Alain Ormsby.

La Luna, by Bernardo Bertolucci (Italy, 1979): In Parma, a teenager left to his own devices tries to get his mother, a diva, to take an interest in him. "The theme of incest is therefore the main theme of this film".

A 1973 collection of short stories by Isaac Bashevis Singer, entitled *A Crown of Feathers*, included a story entitled *The Dance*, in which the author returned to the subject of incest: In Warsaw, circa 1920, Matilda Bloch is a former dancer living in poverty. She comes from a family of Hasidic Jews, and has long since divorced a husband who beat her. He left for Paris and ended up committing suicide. Since then, Matilda lives alone with her son, who does nothing with his life. One day she offers the narrator, who is also destitute, a place to sleep. This is what can be read: "Mathilda gave me her room and said she would sleep on the sofa in the living room". The narrator woke up in the middle of the night and was shocked by what he saw: "The living room door was ajar. In the light of a red candlestick, mother and son were dancing, both barefoot, he in his pants and she in her nightgown. I could make out Izzy's bony neck, his prominent Adam's apple, his hunched back. It seemed to me that both mother and son had their eyes closed. Neither made a sound, as if they were dancing in their sleep. I stayed there for at least ten minutes, maybe much longer. I knew I had no right to spy on my hosts like that, but I was stuck there. Most likely they were waltzing, though I had trouble identifying their dance. No music, in complete silence. I held my breath and didn't move, stunned. Did the mother and son have an incestuous relationship? Had they both lost their minds[518] ?"

Elisabeth Badinter explained that all this was perfectly natural: "The erotic bond between mother and child is not limited to oral satisfaction. Through her care, she takes care to awaken his sensitivity, initiating him to pleasure and teaching him to love his body. A good mother is naturally incestuous and paedophilic. No one will dare to question that, but everyone - including the mother herself and the child - wants to forget it[519]."

In his *Introductory Lessons to Psychoanalysis* in 1916, Sigmund Freud also reasoned exclusively in terms of the customs of his community: "It is forgotten that if incestuous temptation really found insurmountable obstacles in nature, there would never have been any need to prohibit it, either by implacable laws or by customs. The truth is quite the opposite. The first object on which man's sexual desire is concentrated is always of an incestuous nature - the mother or the sister - and it is only by dint of very severe prohibitions that this infantile inclination can be repressed[520]."

---

[518] Isaac Bashevis Singer, *La Couronne de plumes*, 1973, Stock, 1976, p. 303.
[519] Elisabeth Badinter, *La Identidad masculina*, Alianza Editorial, Madrid, 1993, p. 67.
[520] Sigmund Freud, *Introductory Lessons in Psychoanalysis (1915-1917), Lesson XXI: Development of the libido and sexual organisations*, Collected Works, EpubLibre, Trans. Luis López Ballesteros y de Torres, 2001, p. 3140.

In the Old Testament, the laws prohibiting incest are indeed very explicit (Leviticus XVIII)[521]. However, it is narrated that Reuben, Jacob's eldest son, is said to have committed incest with Bilhah, his father's concubine (Genesis XXXV, 22).

In a book entitled *The Israeli women,* Lesley Hazleton, a Jew who had lived in Jerusalem and New York, drew an interesting parallel between incest among Jews and *aliyah,* the return and settlement of Diaspora Jews in Israel. The return to Zion, she explained, is like "the return of a son to his mother in a sexual union...The result of this union between the sons and their mother would be the rebirth of the son, which would also give new life to his mother by saving her from the injustices and suffering experienced in the Diaspora, and would restore her innocence and light as mother and giver of life". Lesley Hazleton went on to explain that the pioneers of Zionism were excited, in a sexual sense, by the idea of returning to the cradle of their history to impregnate their mystical mother, Zion.

Daniel Sibony is one of those little "French intellectuals" who abounded in France at the end of the 20th century. In a book entitled *Racism or Identity Hatred,* published in 1997, he wrote surreptitiously between two paragraphs: "The racist stumbles over the prohibition of incest[522] ". Daniel Sibony was also the author of another book entitled *Le Peuple psy (The Psychological People).* Perhaps he wanted to tell us something about a community of psychopaths?

Between brothers and sisters

In Jonathan Littell's 2006 Goncourt Prize-winning novel *Les Bienveillantes,* the hero is a gay SS officer who wants to become a woman and is madly in love with his twin sister Una. Listen to this: "She took a sculpted juniper phallus and took me as a man, in front of her large mirror that impassively reflected our intertwined bodies.... She used me as a woman, until all distinction was erased and I said to her, 'I am your sister and you are my brother' and she said, 'You are my sister and I am your brother'" (page 814).

This was obviously a projection, typical of the Jewish intellectual. Here is an extract from an interview with the author, published in *Le Figaro* on 29 December 2006:

"What would you say about your narrator today, what feelings would he or she inspire in you?

---

[521] Read *Psychoanalysis of Judaism* and *Jewish Fanaticism.*
[522] Daniel Sibony, *Le Racisme ou la haine identitaire,* Christian Bourgeois éditeur, 1997, p. 84.

- Jonathan Littell: It's hard to say anything good about such a despicable guy...
- Yes, but you lived with him for a long time.
- Jonathan Litell: I could say it's me".

In *Les Malveillantes - Enquête sur le cas Jonathan Littell* (Scali, 2006), essayist Paul-Eric Blanrue rightly wrote: "Aue is a mirror. First of all, of the author, who reflects himself in him by writing in the first person and bequeathing to him some of his peculiarities. Like Littell, Aue was born on 10 October; like Littell, he has spent part of his life in the south of France and abroad, and has lived through the separation of his parents...".

Colette Mainguy, a journalist at *Le Nouvel Observateur*, published a novel entitled *La Juive (The Jewess)* in 2001. Here is a review found on the Internet: "Ninth in a family of ten siblings, struggling with incestuous siblings, an older sister whom she admires but who manipulates her, an anorexic younger sister who makes her feel guilty, an abusive or ambiguous father and an emasculating mother, the author recounts the unspeakable suffering of an abused child. In the summer of her twelfth birthday, her older sister Beth, her tormentor, finds in her a "Jewish profile". Naturally, this situation was the starting point of a serious neurosis: "From then on, Colette became convinced that she was a foreigner, an "Anne Franck" isolated in an Aryan family. Her entire adolescence became a struggle and a torment, between the desire to throw off all ties with this family and the impossibility of tearing herself away from the clan. This book is a violent and often disturbing account of what can be the worst kind of tyranny: family."

Once again, the author projected his neurosis onto the Nazis. The back cover of the book reads: "In the summer of my twelfth birthday, I was born a Jew to an Aryan mother and a Kapo sister in a concentration camp. Prisoner number 9. I was the ninth child in a family of ten. Five girls, five boys. I rediscovered my Jewishness after five years of psychoanalysis. I had been having recurring Germanic dreams for so long. The Germans are chasing me. They machine-gun me and then I die lying under a tarpaulin in a lorry crossing the Vercors. I am arrested in the round-ups of Jews; I reproach my mother for abandoning me in a camp; I am a journalist and I tell what ghetto life is like before they lock me up in it; I give fellatio to Nazis, the Gestapo knocks on my door. I always run away. My hiding places are always dark cellars, sordid wardrobes or terrifying labyrinths; one night, I confront my sister Beth. She is the head of the Gestapo in a concentration camp".

The March 2008 issue of *Lire* magazine was devoted to Jewish literature. On page 26, an article introduces the writer Henry Roth. In an autobiographical book entitled *A Stone Trampoline over the Hudson* (1995), the protagonist, Ira Stigman, introduced Henry Roth himself. This is what the magazine said: "Ira confesses the unspeakable and literally immolates himself by confessing his incestuous relationship with his sister Mimmie". Naturally, Henry Roth was deeply traumatised by his hard life: "He had to face again anti-Semitism, humiliation and malicious insults...".

Hermann Ungar was a Czech writer born into a family of Jewish industrialists. He lived in Berlin, where he frequented his peers Joseph Roth and Franz Werfel. In one of his novels, *The Mutilated (Die Verstümmelten,* 1923), Hermann Ungar told the story of Franz Polzer, a miserable, paranoid office worker who falls under the domination of his overbearing landlady, Clara Porges, who eventually forces him to become her lover. Just as he was beaten by his father when he was younger, he is unable to free himself from this perverse relationship and mortifies himself with attitudes of self-flagellation. What can be read on the Internet is quite explicit: "This masochistic disposition seems to go back to the trauma of an original scene, in which, on discovering the incestuous links between his father and his aunt, he retains the fearful vision of his streak "between the black hair on the right and on the left". From then on, the female sex, this particular type of "streak", provokes in him not only a "bitter repulsion" ("the thought of this naked body that was not closed, of its horrible cavity open like open flesh", torments him), but also the fixed idea that he is repeating his father's incest. To this obsession... is added a latent homosexuality, in particular towards his childhood friend, the wealthy Jew Carl Fanta".

Here, Jewish self-hatred is taken to the max: "Carl, a legless cripple whose arm is soon to be amputated, is determined to flaunt his atrophies and to harass Dora, his wife, whose 'saintly' self-denial disgusts him. What is left of him in his putrefaction is a desperate determination to "stay alive, if only out of malice"... "I'm lying here like a dung tank and I stink. But I'm not dying," Carl scoffs..." Besides, what has been done with Carl's severed limbs? asks Franz, horrified.... Such is the dread that oozes from this bloody novel: to end up like the foul-smelling viscera of slaughtered animals that butchers throw into a pit. Discarded." Hermann Ungar died of acute appendicitis at the age of 36.

There are also many references to incest in cinema if you pay enough attention. Michel Lichtenstein's film *Teeth* (2008) is based on a very original script: Dawn, an able-bodied schoolgirl, does her best to repress all sexual desire. She is an active member of a group that advocates chastity until marriage. But this abstinence is severely tested. First by the handsome Tobey, with whom she falls in love. Then by the repeated provocations of Brad, her sexually extroverted stepbrother. Dawn's life is brutally turned upside down the day she discovers to her horror that, in case of attack, her vagina can become a weapon of defence thanks to the many sharp teeth lining the inside of it! There are some *gore* scenes in the film, for example one in which the carnivorous beauty's incestuous brother is emasculated (with bits of penis scattered on the floor). *Teeth* is, it seems, "a delicious revenge of the female gender against the prevailing male coarseness".

Désengagement is a film by Israeli director Amos Gitaï (2007): a French-Israeli and a Dutch-Palestinian meet in a train corridor. They chat and share a cigarette. "The two characters embrace and, in doing so, abolish borders", wrote Yasmina Guerda on the internet. The audience is then transported to Avignon. This is what the review says: "A father has died. His daughter Ana is almost ecstatic and talks about leaving her husband to her half-brother Uli, who has come from Israel for the funeral. From the beginning, the atmosphere is heavy. It is suffocating. We feel Ana's discomfort as she sings, fusses, giggles like a child and verges on incest with her brother."

Stèphane Kurc is the director of *Terre de lumières* (France, 20008), a heavy telefilm in four episodes. We have only seen the fourth episode, entitled *La Terre des secrets*, which was broadcast on television in September 2008. The story is set in a Moroccan town during the Occupation. The characterisation of the characters reveals the cosmopolitan stamp: there are, of course, the Jews, persecuted for no reason; the poor Jewess is played by a beautiful blonde with Nordic features, just to throw the unwary off the scent. The Arabs, on the other hand, are proud and dignified, while the French fall into two categories. A French woman, for example, is pregnant with an Arab child and gradually abandons her French husband, whom she despises. At the end of the film, she gives birth to little Hassan, whom she raises alone, as the Arab father prefers to fight against the bad guys for his country's independence.

Another French woman has two children by a former soldier - the hero of the film - who was wounded and disappeared ten years ago. Taken in by Bedouins, he converted to Islam and went on to fight against his own countrymen. As such, he was imprisoned and sentenced to death for treason by the Vichy authorities. His daughter, who recognised him, managed to free him thanks to her brother, the chief of police, a moderate collaborationist compared to the other bastards in the French police - apart from the Gaullist of the day, of course.

Meanwhile, the Americans have landed in Morocco and liberated the country. The end of the film further confirms director Stéphane Kurc's Jewishness: we learn (we will spare the details) that it was the police chief, as a soldier, who had once tried to kill his sister's lover during a mission in the Djebel... because he was secretly in love with her; in love with his own sister! So, once again, it was a story of incest that a Jewish director had projected and foisted on his goyim characters.

In any case, it is clear that Stéphane Kurc does not like the French very much, otherwise he would not have insisted on putting their wives in the arms of Arabs, making a hero of a Frenchman who has converted to Islam, tearing their families apart and systematically making them feel guilty. Another French couple also appeared during the liberation of Morocco: the wife learns that her husband has collaborated. She despises him to the point of pointing a loaded pistol at him, before expressing her disgust for him, although in reality it was nothing more than Stéphane Kurc's disgust for the native French. The interminable doleful soundtrack makes this unbearable dreck frankly unbearable. But we saw it through to the end... well, almost to the end.

In *The Pact of the Wolves* (France, 2001), Christophe Gans depicts the rape of a sister by her brother. The film is also very anti-racist: an Indian beats up French peasants in the middle of the 18th century!

There is also *Select Hôtel* (France, 1996): in the Pigalle district, the Select is a brothel. Twenty-year-old Nathalie survives as best she can: a drug addict and prostitute, she relies on the protective love of her brother, Tof, a young delinquent. Bouniq-Mercier wrote: "A powerful and disturbing work, crude and prurient, atrociously dark and yet luminous". The film is by Laurent Bouhnik.

In *Kika* (Spain, 1993), a comedy by Pedro Almodóvar, a man obsessed with sex has a habit of sleeping with his own sister. Escaped from prison, he goes to visit her at his bosses' flat, where she works as a maid, and takes the opportunity to rape the mistress of the house...

The Cement Garden (UK, 1992): A modest family lives in a grim and isolated suburban dwelling. The parents die one after the other and the four children are left alone. Jack has an incestuous love for his sister. The film is by Andrew Birkin.

La mujer del puerto (Mexico, 1991): El Marro, a sailor, meets a beautiful prostitute, Perla, in a cabaret in the port and falls in love with her. Perla's mother, Tomasa, recognises him as the son from whom she was separated in tragic circumstances. From that moment on, the incestuous love between Perla and her brother seems doomed to failure. A film by Arturo Ripstein (him again!).

On ne meurt que deux fois (France, 1982): Charles, a young student from a good family who lives alone in Paris with his hysterical and possessive sister, sets out to find his father's former lover. In a cabaret in Pigalle, he discovers a teenage girl, Clémentine, with whom he falls in love. She turns out to be his stepsister. A film by Caroline Roboh.

L'invitation au voyage, by Peter del Monte (France, 1982): Lucien cannot accept the death of his twin sister, who was electrocuted in the bathtub. He hides her body in a double bass case, attaches it to the luggage rack of his car and hits the road. Finally, he burns his sister's body. The story of a "mad, incestuous love".

Chère inconnue (France, 1979), based on a screenplay by Bérénice Rubens: Gilles is a paraplegic who can only get around in a wheelchair.

Louise, his sister, takes care of him with devotion, but suffers from his emotional loneliness. They live in an isolated house on the Brittany coast, where only Yvette, the baker, comes to break the monotony. Louise places an advert in a local newspaper looking for a soul mate. Soon, from the information given to her by her correspondent, she realises that it is indeed her brother who answers. When Gilles wants to meet her, Louise hires a comedienne. The film is by a certain Moshe Mizrahi, who is certainly not Breton.

Caligula, by Tino Brass (Italy-UK, 1977): Caligula, after the assassination of Tiberius, is named emperor of Rome. Advised by his sister Drusilla, with whom he has an incestuous relationship, he soon becomes a bloodthirsty tyrant. Caligula believed himself to be God and gradually fell into madness. When his sister dies, he despairs. The screenplay is by Gore Vidal.

My God, how I have fallen so low! by Luigi Comencini (Italy, 1974): At the end of the 19th century, Eugenia, a young Sicilian noblewoman, marries Raimondo, a wealthy bourgeois. But on the wedding night she receives a telegram revealing that her husband is her brother. As compensation, she allows herself to be raped by his chauffeur...

*The Great Bourgeoisie (*Italy, 1974) is a film by Mauro Bolignini: At the end of the 19th century, Tulio, Linda's brother, who is a militant for his socialist ideas, loves his sister with an almost incestuous love.

Au long de la rivière Fango, by Catherine Sigaux (France, 1975): Jérémie and Bild, two horsemen, arrive in a community living on the banks of the Fango River. It was founded by Mathilde, a woman who left her husband and baby to escape urban society and buy this land. They all live happily apart from the world, with no thought of work or money. Bild believes he is Mathilde's abandoned son, while Jérémie is attracted to her daughter Maurine. When Bild dies, Jérémie learns that he is Mathilde's son and that Maurine is therefore his sister. The film also presents several clichés against capitalism.

The Abduction of Bunny Lake (UK, 1965): Ann Lake has moved to London with her illegitimate daughter, Bunny, and her brother. One day, the girl disappears from her school. The police come to doubt the girl's very existence, as all evidence has disappeared. Ann seems to suffer from psychiatric problems. "Could Ann be having an incestuous relationship with her brother?" A film by the famous Otto Preminger.

Sandra (Italy, 1965): Sandra, whose father died in deportation, has married an American academic. She learns from her brother that it was her mother who betrayed her father. A kind of incest develops between brother and sister. The film is by Luchino Visconti.

Mort d'un tueur, by Robert Hossein (France, 1963): Massa, a gangster, has spent several years in prison following a denunciation. He returns to

Nice to take revenge. His sister Maria, whom he loves from a shady love affair, has become the mistress of Luciano, the man who betrayed him.

As in a mirror (Sweden, 1961): Karin has moved to an island to spend her holidays with her husband Martin, a doctor, her brother Frederik and her father, a widowed writer who is always travelling. She suffers from mental problems and practices incest with her younger brother. The film is by the inimitable Ingmar Bergman.

Royal Wedding, by Stanley Donen (USA, 1951): Tom and Ellen Bowen are siblings and form a fashionable dance couple. They become aware of the depth of their feelings. The screenplay is by Alan Jay Lerner.

Scarface (USA, 1931) is the story of a gangster in love with his sister. The film was directed by Howard Hawks, with a screenplay by Ben Hecht and Seton Miller. In 1983, Brian de Palma directed another version, based on a screenplay by Oliver Stone and starring Al Pacino.

Freud had read the works of Conrad Ferdinand Meyer, the great Swiss writer, and always had a great predilection for this author. In her 1964 book *The Judge (Die Richterin)*, Marthe Robert explained at the foot of the page in her work on *The Psychoanalytic Revolution*: "It is undoubtedly a romanticised rejection of a memory of the writer's relations with his sister... On the one hand, this novel flatters megalomania; on the other, it is a defence against incest[523]."

Sander Gilman of the University of Chicago had researched the subject himself. In *Sibling incest, madness, and the jews*, he described how Jews in 19th and early 20th century Europe were often associated with certain forms of sexual deviance. He noted that "inbreeding within the Jewish community had fostered the idea that incest between brothers and sisters was a common practice in that community[524]."

The prolific Yiddish novelist Isaac Bashevis Singer, winner of the Nobel Prize for Literature, also unashamedly projected his guilt onto Christians. In his novel *Krochmalna No. 10*, one could read: "In Argentina, Peru, Bolivia, Chile and elsewhere, daughters are raped by their fathers, brothers sleep with their sisters and a mother has sex with her own son. People are not always arrested for these crimes. They go to the priest, confess and, with a little holy water, he absolves them[525]". Once again, we must see here a classic accusatory inversion.

Nor is David's story in the Bible very moral by our European standards. His adultery with Bathsheba is followed by the murder of her husband, Uriah. His eldest son, Ammon, committed incest with one of his sisters.

---

[523] Marthe Robert, *La Révolution psychanalytique*, Tome I, Payot, 1964, p. 137.
[524] Journal *Taxonomy and deviance*, 1998, vol. 65, no. 2, p. 401-433, New School University, New York, NY (1934).
[525] Isaac Bashevis Singer, *Le petit monde de la rue Krochmalna*, Denoël, 1991, p. 54.

Ammon was murdered by his brother Absalom, who, having regained the king's favour, began to plot against his father, waging war against him and taking his concubines.

In 2008, a programme on the History Channel (*Banned from the Bible*) dealt with the Bible and the selection of sacred texts. Among the books that had not been preserved in the canonical version was the Book of Jubilees, which is said to have been written in Hebrew to complete the story of Genesis (around 100 BC). The biblical text mentioned only two sons of Adam and Eve: Cain and Abel. The question then arose among Jewish scholars as to whom Cain might have married, since there were no women. The Book of Jubilees had clarified the question by stating that Adam and Eve had had three sons and six daughters. Therefore, humanity had developed through incestuous relationships between brothers and sisters. A rabbi explained in the documentary that the Jews of the time could not accept the idea that Adam and Eve were not the only (and therefore perhaps not the first) and, above all, they were reassured to know that the Jews - God's people - had not had to marry foreigners of impure blood.

Surely we should also read with a mirror the text of a small book of about forty pages, written by a certain André Benzimra and published in 2007: *The prohibition of incest according to the Kabbalah*. The book, published by a small publishing house, was reserved for members of the community. André Benzimra explained that the Scriptures had silenced "the incest that the first people had to commit in order to populate the earth. This was because they wanted to take away an argument from those who put no brakes or barriers to the pursuit of their pleasure".

We learn that Rebecca may have been Isaac's own sister: "Concerning Abraham's descendants, there is a hidden legend in the Bible that Bahir 78 reveals, not without resorting to the cipher method of proceeding by allusions of allusions. This text states that Abraham had a daughter and suggests that she was none other than Rebecca, the same one who was to marry his son Isaac. The first assertion is based in particular on a passage in the Talmud. The second is based on some uncertainty about Rebekah's origin: throughout Genesis XXIV she is presented as the daughter of Bethuel, son of Nahor. However, in verse XXIV, 48, she is incidentally given as the daughter of Nahor himself, Abraham's brother[526]... God needs a daughter, His *Shechinah*, to transmit His influence and His blessings, just as Abraham needed a daughter to beget his spiritual posterity...The fact that Rebecca was Isaac's sister and wife is, moreover, an additional mark of her kinship with the heavenly *Shechinah*, which synthesises various family ties

---

[526] In notes, at the end of the book, one can read: "Bethuel and Nahor were undoubtedly Rebekah's parents". In other words, Betuel slept with his own mother.

with those who are attached to her. Thus Wisdom (another name for the *Shechinah*) was successively Solomon's mother, wife and daughter, for Solomon learned everything from her, lived in her intimacy, and finally rose above her".

And André Benzimra continued: "Yes, Abraham's descendants come only from Abraham's seed. But this whole story was kept secret to avoid giving credence to the idea that, after the love affairs between Isaac and Rebecca, incest is permitted to everyone. It was kept secret from Isaac himself: that is why Rebekah was brought up away from him until the time came to celebrate their nuptials. Afterwards, the truth was probably revealed to him and the need to marry this distant sister[527] ".

Abraham therefore had a daughter, and "she was none other than Rebekah, the future wife of his son Isaac. Without the union of Abraham's sons with their sisters, humanity would not have fulfilled the divine mandate to grow and multiply, and would have died as soon as it arrived on earth".

Before Abraham, Adam himself was obliged to give his own daughters to his sons: "The intertestamental writings mention twin sisters who were united to Adam's sons and through whom they were able to reproduce".

Incest is thus a crucial issue in the history of Judaism (and humanity!). "According to the Kabbalistic tradition, wrote Benzimra, the mysteries of incest are even more important than those relating to any other question: "The chapter relating to incest is the quintessence of all the Scriptures, says the Zohar III, 81a. Indeed, as we shall see, the question of incest is closely linked, on the one hand, to the question of the reigning Order in the Cosmos, and, on the other hand, to the doctrine of God in His highest aspects[528]."

In the footnotes, Benzimra also evoked "God's union with the community of Israel (Zohar, III, 7b)", which is here his sister: "Leviticus XX, 17: "If a man marries his sister, it is a grace (*khessed*). The Man designates God; his sister designates the Community of Israel[529]."

As we can see, incest is a real obsession for Jews, an almost central issue. Mother and son, father and daughter, father and son, brother and sister, uncles and nieces... It is what we call inbred families, where they all fit together like pipes, from generation to generation. There is no doubt that a

---

[527] André Benzimra, *L'Interdiction de l'inceste selon la Kabbale*, Archè Edizioni, Milano, 2007, p. 13, 7-9.

[528] André Benzimra, *L'Interdiction de l'inceste selon la Kabbale*, Archè Edizioni, Milano, 2007, p. 25, 12

[529] André Benzimra, *L'Interdiction de l'inceste selon la Kabbale*, Archè Edizioni, Milano, 2007, p. 33. In the Bible, one can read: "The man who takes his sister as his wife...is an ignominy". However, "*Khessed*" (pronounced *Chessed* in English) has a double meaning for Jews: it is "ignominy" and "tenderness"; on these Kabbalistic aspects and the *Sechinah* (the Community of Israel), read *Psychoanalysis of Judaism*.

large-scale official investigation into this problem would be urgently needed, and for our part, we are not far from thinking that, in the interests of the Jews themselves, children should be separated from their parents from early childhood to protect them and to break the process of incestuous generations. This was perhaps the aim of the kibbutz in Israel, where the emphasis was on communal living.

In any case, it is clear that it is no longer a question of the notion of a "chosen people" at all, but of a relevant medical diagnosis. Freud undoubtedly understood that the origin of Judaism was not religious, but sexual. But he did not have the courage to reveal to the whole world that the famous "Oedipus complex" was in reality only the "Israel complex", and preferred to project the neurosis of Judaism onto the rest of humanity. Jewish intellectuals should always be read with a mirror. Always.

3. The myth of the Oedipus complex

The father of psychoanalysis based his theories on the study of hysterical pathology, which was obviously no accident. On the basis of his own personal case and the study of his Viennese colleagues, he demonstrated that incest was the main cause of hysteria, before suddenly inverting the problem and "projecting" it onto a universal plane: the mysterious "Oedipus complex" was born.

The development of psychoanalysis

Professor Jean Martin Charcot was the forerunner of studies on hysteria at the end of the 19th century. In 1882, he opened what was to become the largest neurological clinic in Europe at the Salpêtrière hospital in Paris. A renowned professor, he attracted students from all over the world. Under his influence, mental illnesses began to be systematically analysed and hysteria began to be distinguished from other disorders of the mind. Charcot remained convinced that the fundamental cause of hysteria lay in a hereditary degeneration of the nervous system, and he was the first to use hypnosis as a means of treatment, with a view to discovering an organic basis for hysteria.

Sigmund Freud attended Dr Charcot's lectures from October 1885 to February 1886. In *Life and Work of Sigmund Freud*, Ernst Jones, who was Freud's first major biographer, explained:

"What impressed Freud most in Charcot's teachings was his revolutionary conception of the problem of hysteria... Hysteria, up to that time, was considered either a matter of simulation, or at best of "imagination" (which after all would be more or less the same thing), which was in no way worthy to occupy the time of a respectable physician, or else a peculiar disorder of the uterus which could be treated - and often was treated - by the removal of the clitoris. The displaced uterus could also be brought back into place by the administration of valerian, whose aroma is unpleasant to it. And so it was thanks to Charcot that, almost overnight, hysteria became an entirely respectable disease of the nervous system... He made a systematic and extensive study of the manifestations of hysteria, a study which allowed a more precise diagnosis of the disease, and at the same time demonstrated the hysterical character of many conditions to which another nature had been attributed. He also insisted that hysteria could also affect the male sex, which should no longer surprise anyone since it was included among the diseases of the nervous system".

Professor Charcot further demonstrated "that he could provoke by hypnotism, in predisposed subjects, hysterical symptoms, paralysis, tremors, anaesthesia, etc., which coincided, down to the smallest details, with the symptoms of spontaneous hysteria, as they appeared in his other patients and as they had been described in detail in the Middle Ages, when they were attributed to demon possession[530]."

Charcot had observed that hysteria affected Jews in particular. In *Psychoanalysis of Anti-Semitism,* published in 1952, Rudolph Loewenstein wrote: "In his *Tuesday Lessons* at the Salpêtrière, Charcot had made numerous allusions to the pathological genealogies of Jewish families, applying to one patient the diagnosis of "travelling neuropath", a transparent allusion to the tradition of instability, wandering and nomadism attributed to the Jews (the tendency to hysteria was linked to medieval persecutions). To Freud, who was beginning to express some doubts about the doctrine of hereditary aetiology and the theory of the "neuropathic family", which had become dear to a teacher of whom he had been a pupil in 1885 and 1886, Charcot replied bluntly on 30 June 1892: "Well, you find out, especially in Jewish families, exploration is easy[531]"."

At the same time, in 1894, Cesare Lombroso, an Italian Jew, published in Turin *L'Antisemitismo e la scienza moderne,* a work in which he set out to refute the arguments that "the Jew" was endowed with a different nature. However, Lombroso took up Charcot's thesis that Jews suffered from specific mental disorders (hysteria or locomotor ataxia). But he sought the cause in persecution and history, not in a deviant nature.

Doctor Charcot also had a presentiment that hysteria could be caused by traumas of a sexual nature. Freud was naturally very interested in studying this pathology, for the simple reason that he felt directly concerned by it. At the Salpêtrière, wrote Ernst Jones, "he heard Charcot state categorically to his assistant Brouardel that certain cases of neurotic disorders were always attributable "to the genital thing[532]"".

---

[530] Ernst Jones, *Vida y obra de Sigmund Freud, volume I,* Anagrama, Barcelona, 1981 (abridged edition), p. 230-231.

[531] Michel Bonduelle, *Charcot, un grand médecin dans son siècle,* Paris, Editions Michalon 1996, p. 269-275, in Rudolph Loewenstein, *Psychanalyse de l'antisémitisme* (1952), Presses Universitaires de France, 2001, p. 18.

[532] Ernst Jones, *La Vie et l'oeuvre de Sigmund Freud, tome 1,* 1953, PUF, 1958, p. 274. "The second anecdote refers to an explanation that Charcot gave his assistant Brouardel, very emphatically - and which Freud was given to hear - to the effect that in certain nervous disorders it was always a question of the *chose génitale."* Ernst Jones, *Life and Work of Sigmund Freud, volume I,* Anagrama, Barcelona, 1981 (abridged edition), p. 250.

Freud later demonstrated, based on what he had observed in the Jewish community, that hysterical pathology had its origin in the practice of incest. Elisabeth Roudinesco, in her 1999 book *Why Psychoanalysis?* explained that the word "psychoanalysis" had appeared in 1896 in a text written in French by Sigmund Freud himself: "A year earlier, with his friend Josef Breuer, Freud had published his famous studies on hysteria, in which he recounted the case of a young Viennese Jewish girl suffering from a strange illness of psychological origin, in which sexual fantasies manifested themselves through contortions of the body. The patient's name was Bertha Pappenheim and her doctor, Breuer, who treated her with the cathartic method, gave her the name of Anna O." Under hypnosis, the patient answered the doctor's questions. Breuer observed that her symptoms gradually disappeared. The cure was based on the spoken word. The essential message that remained was that the word heard and shared led to healing. The fact of verbalising suffering, of finding words to express it, made it possible, if not to cure, at least to become aware of its origin and thus to come to terms with it.

Anna O was a very intelligent and attractive young woman, but she suffered from various nervous disorders, paralysis, contractures, language and sight problems, all of which appeared after her father's death. In her 1964 book, *The Psychoanalytic Revolution*, Marthe Robert told us: 'Breuer once found her in hysterical labour, the logical result of an imaginary pregnancy that had gone unnoticed and which had occurred in response to Breuer's treatment. Although deeply distressed, Breuer calmed her down by hypnotising her, and then, in a cold sweat, left the house[533]." Elisabeth Roudinesco observed, however, that the patient had not been cured: "By consulting the archives, modern historians have shown that the famous case of Anna O., presented by Freud and Breuer as the prototype of cathartic healing, did not actually result in the healing of the patient. In any case, Freud and Breuer decided to publish the story of this woman and to present it as a princeps case in order to better vindicate, vis-à-vis the French psychologist Pierre Janet, the priority of the discovery of the cathartic method. As for Bertha Pappenheim, although she was not cured of her symptoms, she became another woman. A militant feminist, pious and rigid, she dedicated her life to orphans and victims of anti-Semitism without ever mentioning the psychological treatment she had undergone in her youth, which had turned her into a myth[534]."

In 1896, Freud definitively abandoned hypnotism and switched to the "free association" method. Ernst Jones wrote that a patient, Mrs. Emmy

---

[533] Marthe Robert, *La Révolution psychanalytique, tome I*, Payot, 1964, p. 118.
[534] Elisabeth Roudinesco, *Pourquoi la psychanalyse*, Fayard, 1999, p. 29, 30.

von N., had once reproached Freud for interrupting her by asking her about her thoughts. According to Jones, this marked the beginning of psychoanalysis: "The forging of this method is one of the two great feats of his scientific life. The other is his self-analysis, thanks to which he learned to explore the early sexual life of the child, and within this, the famous Oedipus complex[535]."

In 1896, Freud argued categorically that the specific cause of hysteria was to be sought in a disorder of sexuality. Thirteen analysed cases had allowed him to reach this conclusion. Hysteria, he claimed, was caused by a serious incident of a passive sexual nature occurring before puberty. It was in children of three or four years of age that this incident produced the greatest effects. "The favourite age for such an episode was three or four years, and Freud supposed that, occurring after the age of eight or ten, it did not lead to a neurosis[536]," Jones wrote.

He added: "Until the spring of 1897 he still firmly maintained his belief in the reality of these childhood traumas, so powerful was the effect of Charcot's teachings about traumatic experiences and so sure was the confidence with which they were reproduced by patients' associations[537]."

What Ernst Jones wrote next is very instructive, once one realises that it was only about the Jewish community: "From May 1893, when he first announced this to Fliess, until September 1897... he held the view that the essential cause of hysteria is a sexual seduction of an innocent child by an adult person, usually the father. The evidence of the analytical material seemed irrefutable. He held to this conviction for four years, although he was increasingly surprised at the frequency of these alleged episodes. It began to appear that, in a high proportion, fathers were the protagonists of

---

[535] Ernst Jones, *Vida y obra de Sigmund Freud, volume I*, Anagrama, Barcelona, 1981 (abridged edition), p. 242.

[536] Ernst Jones, *Life and Work of Sigmund Freud, volume I*, Anagrama, Barcelona, 1981 (abridged edition), p. 263. Note that this age corresponds to that fixed by the teachers of the Talmud. [At the bottom of every case of hysteria one must find one or more premature sexual experiences, which correspond to the first years of childhood and which can be revived by analytic work even when whole decades have passed". *Life and Works of Sigmund Freud*, p. 263-264. (NdT)]

[537] Ernst Jones, *Life and Work of Sigmund Freud, volume I*, Anagrama, Barcelona, 1981 (abridged edition), p. 265. ["If we review the evolution of Freud's views on sexuality and childhood up to the time of his self-analysis, taking as a basis both his publications and his correspondence with Fliess, we must come to the following conclusions. His understanding of the problem was much slower and more gradual than is often supposed. Some things that are clear today were quite obscure at the time. He had necessarily to start from the conventional view of childish innocence, and when he encountered the shocking accounts of seduction by adults he also preferred the conventional view that this represented precocious stimulation." *Life and Works of Sigmund Freud, Volume I*, p. 319-320. (I, p. 319-320].

such incestuous attacks. Worse still, they were usually episodes of a perverse nature, with the mouth or anus as the point of choice. From the existence of certain hysterical symptoms in his brother and several of his sisters (not himself, mind you) he deduced that even his own father should be accused of such acts[538]."

On the website dedicated to the psychoanalyst Françoise Minkowska, the latter confirmed: "Sigmund Freud came to believe that almost all the patients he treated or observed at the time had in fact suffered sexual abuse or maltreatment during their childhood and that their disorders were essentially due to these traumas. Their memories and testimonies overlapped with a disconcerting regularity that deeply shocked the young physician and theorist. He mentioned them in his notes and expressed his astonishment and his questions, especially in his correspondence, partly hidden by the Freudian archives and recently brought to light by Jeffrey Moussaief Masson[539]."

However, in 1897, after the death of her father at the end of October 1896, Freud abandoned the theory of "seduction" and adopted that of "fantasy": the hysterical woman had no longer been the object of incest as a child, but it was now she who had fantasised about her father! The father was absolved, free of suspicion. The parents were no longer guilty. Now it was to be assumed that the children were in love with their opposite-sex parent and desired incestuous relations with him. Ernst Jones wrote here: "In the February following his father's death, Freud mentioned the fact that he had accused him of acts of seduction, and three months later he announced his own incestuous dream, which put an end, he said, to his doubts about the matter of seduction[540]."

In his letters of 3, 5 and 15 October 1897, Freud recounted the progress of his self-analysis and apparently acknowledged his father's innocence. Ernst Jones was satisfied with this explanation: "He had already realised that his father was innocent and that he had projected onto him ideas of his own. Childhood memories of sexual desires towards his mother had arisen from seeing her naked[541]." Jones further wrote, supporting the Freudian thesis: "Freud had discovered the truth of the case: that irrespective of incestuous desires of parents towards their children and even of occasional acts of that kind, what was really at issue was the existence, as a general

---

[538] Ernst Jones, *Vida y obra de Sigmund Freud, volume I*, Anagrama, Barcelona, 1981 (abridged edition), p. 320-321.
[539] See Jeffrey M. Masson, *The Assault on Truth: Freud's Suppression of the Seduction Theory - Le réel escamoté: Le renoncement de Freud à la théorie de la séduction*, Editions Aubier, 1984.
[540] Ernst Jones, *Freud (I)*, Salvat Editores, Barcelona, 1985, p. 246.
[541] Ernst Jones, *Freud (I)*, Salvat Editores, Barcelona, 1985, p. 247.

matter, of incestuous desires of children towards their parents, and specifically towards the parent of the opposite sex...The incest desires and fantasies would be later products, probably situated between the ages of 8 and 12 and referred to the past, masking them behind the screen of early childhood[542]."

There you have it written down in all its letters, that was it: the birth of infantile sexuality and the Oedipus complex.

Françoise Minkowska confirmed this analysis: "A little less than a year later, in 1897, Freud stopped believing in his neurotic, i.e. original trauma hypothesis, and in a short time developed the Oedipus complex, which would henceforth advantageously replace the "theory of seduction" developed by dint of observations during the preceding years". But Françoise Minkowska rightly pointed out that "Freud was not very generous in explaining the reasons for such a change of heart. But why? An extract from a letter Freud sent to Fliess on 21 September 1897 mentions the explicit reason for this U-turn: 'The surprise of finding that in every case the father had to be accused of perversion, without excluding my own'". In the same letter, Freud added: "Such a generalisation of the acts committed against children seemed hardly incredible".

"Little credible': that was the only reason Freud invoked for his theoretical shift. Françoise Minkowsak wrote: "We can understand such surprise, the need for scientific caution and the dread of such a conclusion, but this reticence alone was enough to invalidate a hypothesis that was the result of multiple observations and cross-checks".

All psychoanalysts accepted this idea - or pretended to accept it - to explain the transition from seduction theory to fantasy theory. Ernst Jones was clearly satisfied with Freud's explanation, and we have searched in vain for the biographer's comments on the change of mind of the founder of psychoanalysis. In 1897, Freud "admitted his error," Jones wrote. "The year 1897 was the climactic year in Freud's life[543]."

---

[542]Ernst Jones, *Freud (I)*, Salvat Editores, Barcelona, 1985, p. 244-245. [The most he would come to admit was that young children, even as young as 6 to 7 months (!), had the capacity to register and grasp, albeit imperfectly, the meaning of the sexual acts of adults which they had come to witness or hear (2 May 1897). Such experiences would become significant only at the moment when their memory was revived years later by fantasies, desires or acts of a sexual nature. There is no doubt, therefore, that for a period of about five years Freud regarded children as innocent objects of incestuous desires, and that it was only very slowly - and no doubt at the cost of considerable inner resistance - that he came to recognise what has since become definitively known as infantile sexuality." *Freud (I)*, Salvat Editores, p. 245].

[543]Ernst Jones, *Vida y obra de Sigmund Freud, volume I,* Anagrama, Barcelona, 1981 (abridged edition), p. 320, 268.

Marthe Robert, for her part, had not suspected anything either and fainted with admiration: "The letter of 3 October 1897 marks a historic date, she wrote: It contains the first allusion to Freud's most sensational discovery: the one that gave him the key to the secret drama of every childhood, a long-forgotten and yet fatal drama, which he named the Oedipus complex after the Greek hero[544]."

For Melanie Klein, everything was quite clear: 'Freud was convinced that the memories of hysterical patients, the reproduction of scenes of infantile seduction, were not based on real experiences but on fantasies. In fact, this observation...marks a decisive turning point in psychoanalytic theory[545]."

Elisabeth Roudinesco also supported the Freudian thesis, being careful to avoid any reference to the very special customs of the Jewish community: Freud, she wrote, "developed his famous theory between 1895 and 1897 according to which neurosis originated in real sexual abuse. It was based on both social reality and clinical evidence. In families, and sometimes even in the street, children are often abused by adults. The memory of this brutality is so painful that everyone prefers to forget, ignore or repress it. Listening to hysterical women at the turn of the century who told him such stories, Freud was satisfied with their discourse and developed his first hypothesis: that of inhibition and sexual causation of hysteria. Since they have actually been seduced, Freud believes that hysterics suffer from neurotic disorders. As a result, he began to doubt the parents in general, and Jacob Freud in particular, but also himself: had he not had guilty desires towards his daughter Mathilde?"

Elisabeth Roudinesco added: "It was through contact with Wilhelm Fliess that Freud abandoned his theory of seduction. He knew that not all fathers were rapists, but at the same time he recognised that hysterical women were not lying when they claimed to be victims of seduction. How to explain these two contradictory truths? Freud sets out to do so by starting from the obvious. He realised two things: firstly, that very often women invent the attacks in question without lying or pretending; and secondly, that when the event occurs, it does not explain the outbreak of neurosis. Freud replaced the theory of seduction with that of fantasy, and in the same process solved the riddle of sexual causes: they are phantasmatic, even when there is real trauma, because the reality of fantasy is not the same as material reality. The abandonment of trauma as the sole causality goes hand in hand with the adoption of a psychic unconscious. Indeed, the Freudian

---

[544] Marthe Robert, *La Révolution psychanalytique, tome I*, Payot, 1964, p. 143.
[545] Mélanie Klein, Paula Heimann, *Développements de la psychanalyse*, Presses Universitaires Françaises, 1966, 1991, p. 166.

theory of sexuality assumes the primary existence of a sexual drive and phantasmatic activity[546]."

In 1895, Freud published his first book, *Studies on Hysteria*. The book had a print run of 800 copies and in thirteen years Freud had only managed to sell 626 copies. After that, the general media hype transformed the character into a genius of mankind.

Freud had undoubtedly been under strong pressure from his entourage and prominent members of his community not to reveal Jewish customs. According to Françoise Minkowska, his first aim was to exonerate his own parents, and in particular his father: "Of course, we will not have failed to note with astonishment that Freud included his own father among those whom he himself considered 'perverts'. In fact, the deepest emotional reason for this sudden change is probably that Freud's original observations led him to accuse his own father, who had recently died in October 1896, as this extract from a letter sent to his good friend Dr. Wilhelm Fliess also shows: "Unfortunately, my own father was one of those perverts. He is the cause of the hysteria of my brother and some of my younger sisters. The frequency of such relationships often gives me pause for thought".

"The night after his father's funeral," continued Françoise Minkowska, "Freud had a dream tinged with guilt in which he read a sign: 'Please close your eyes'. Please close your eyes to what? Freud can close his eyes on his deceased father, of course, but he can also close his eyes on his deceased father's guilt, one supposes".

In short, wrote the psychoanalyst once again very correctly, "the Oedipus complex formulated by Freud in 1897 abruptly and almost completely eliminated the responsibility and guilt of adults in the genesis of psychological disorders". The blame henceforth lay with the "Oedipus", i.e. the sexual fantasy developed by the child and projected onto the parent of the opposite sex. The cause of psychological disorders was now shifted to the Oedipus complex, a complex that could remain unresolved for rather mysterious reasons.

But Françoise Minkowska forgot her maternal responsibility. At the age of forty-two, Freud continued his self-analysis. In Marthe Robert's book, *The Psychoanalytic Revolution*, we find an interesting passage: "He then discovers within himself...his hostile feelings towards his father, his incestuous tenderness towards his mother, his death wishes, his elusiveness...His reluctance to divulge the secret of the dark world into which he has just entered is such that, in letters to the only friend to whom

---

[546] Elisabeth Roudinesco, *Pourquoi la psychanalyse*, Fayard, 1999, p. 86, 87.

he confesses the results of his analysis, he relates his memories of his mother writing in Latin[547]."

In *The Interpretation of Dreams*, Freud had written: "Perhaps it was reserved for all of us to direct towards our mother our first sexual impulse and towards our father our first feeling of hatred and our first destructive desire. Our dreams bear witness to this. King Oedipus, who has killed his father and taken his mother in marriage, is but the fulfilment of our childish desires. But happier than him, it has been possible for us, in later childhood, and as long as we have not contracted a psychoneurosis, to divert our sexual impulses from our mother and forget the jealousy that the father inspired in us...Like Oedipus, we live in ignorance of those immoral desires that nature has imposed on us, and in discovering them we would like to turn our eyes away from the scenes of our childhood[548]."

In fact, it was Freud himself who preferred to "avert his eyes", so as not to reveal the dark secret of Judaism to the world. Evidently, he had come under heavy pressure from his peers while developing his theories on the origins of hysteria. By inventing the theory of the Oedipus complex, he concealed the reality of incest in Jewish families and exculpated Jewish parents. And in the process he was erasing the trail, projecting this Jewish specificity onto a universal plane through a Greek hero.

Psychoanalysis in question

Psychoanalysis has completely ignored the actual abuses suffered by children, particularly Jewish children. Abuse and abusive attitudes were even widely justified by a number of specialists and non-specialists under the guise of avant-garde practices and theories during the 1970s, as did, for example, the famous psychoanalyst Françoise Dolto, a woman raised in a Catholic family. In an interview with the feminist magazine *Choisir la cause des femmes* in 1979, she replied:

"Choisir: But there are rape cases, aren't there?

- Françoise Dolto: There is no rape. There is consent.

-*Choisir*: When a girl comes to you and tells you that, as a child, her father had intercourse with her and she felt it was rape, what do you tell her?

-F. Dolto: She did not feel that it was rape. She simply understood that her father loved her and that he consoled himself with her, after his wife did

---

[547] Marthe Robert, *La Révolution psychoanalytique*, Tome I, Payot, 1964, p. 41.
[548] Sigmund Freud, *La Interpretación de los sueños I*, Biblioteca Nueva, Madrid, p. 294-295, and in Marthe Robert, *La Révolution psychoanalytique*, Tome I, Payot, 1964, p. 171.

not want to make love to him...In father-daughter incest, the daughter adores her father and is delighted to be able to defy her mother.

- *Choisir*: In your opinion, isn't there such a thing as a vicious or perverse father?

-F. Dolto: It is enough for the daughter to refuse to sleep with him, saying that this is not done, for him to leave her alone.

-*Choisir*: But can you insist?

-F. Dolto: Not at all, because he knows that the child knows that it is forbidden. And the incestuous father is afraid that his daughter will talk about it. In general, the daughter doesn't say anything, at least not immediately[549]."

"When one knows the considerable impact that a psychoanalyst like Françoise Dolto has had on many educators and parents, wrote Françoise Minkowska, one shudders to think of the consequences of such comments. This impact is even greater for patients who have had to give up their childhood memories and emotions under pressure from a therapist reluctant to listen to the truth. Here it is also important to realise how the psychic defences developed by a victim of incest can be partly manipulated in the course of a treatment that conforms to the dogmas of classical analysis. In fact, most memories of traumatic scenes only manifest themselves to victims in the form of physical symptoms, sexual disorders, cryptic anxieties, fantasies, dreams or regressions unrelated to a trauma that the subject has consciously remembered. It is therefore easy for a therapist to tell a patient that these images and emotions are oedipal fantasies, unreal and without historical support in the patient's life, insofar as these censored memories are effectively lived, defensively, as unreal by the patient's psyche."

And Minkowska concluded: 'The ultimate goal of an analysis has long been, and often still is, to free parents and adults from all responsibility for the child, from all blame for the harm done to the child, or to forgive them immediately and then blame the analysand himself, placing the ultimate cause of the harm experienced in an inexplicable "poorly resolved Oedipus complex". Most professionals remain faithful to the dogmas of Freudian theory and do not allow a patient to evoke his memories without questioning their reality or giving them a negative reception (which patients have no problem in doing themselves).... It is also evident that the vast majority of specialised psychoanalytic literature is often silent or cryptic about incest, which is regarded as nothing more than an infantile

---

[549] *Choisir la cause des femmes*, autumn 1979. The interview with Françoise Dolto was part of the report *Les enfants en morceaux (Children in pieces)*, a study by Annie Brunet, Béatrice Jade and Christine Pecqueur. Interview quoted in *Le Viol du Silence (The Violation of Silence)* by Eva Thomas.

fantasy. This blindness, the denial or questioning of the traumas suffered, is unfortunately still common today, is practised daily in therapy and is still taught to students in psychology faculties. Thus, the frequency of incest remains a taboo subject among psychoanalysts: we know today that only an infinitesimal fraction of abuse is reported. This is because a child is always incapable of defending himself and is almost never free to speak". Françoise Minkowska added: "We now know that children can become ill not only by repressing hidden desires or impulses, but also simply out of love, to protect their tormentors, who are often their own family members or close environment. However, these discourses remain confidential and little known to a public that is otherwise quite familiar with the classical Oedipus thesis". But what Françoise Minkowska did not mention is that the "executioners", in this case, are often mainly Jews.[550]

However, from the very beginning of the psychoanalytic movement, some therapists and theorists took seriously the words of patients who shared with them their emotions and intimate memories: Sándor Ferenczi and Wilhelem Stekel, in particular, became dissidents of the psychoanalytic movement.

Sándor Ferenczi came to be regarded for a time as the spiritual heir of the father of psychoanalysis. He was marginalised precisely because he was reluctant to question the reality of the traumas reported by his patients. Some of his texts and speeches, such as *The Confusion of Tongues between Adults and Children*, described the psychological consequences of sexual and incestuous abuse. Ferenczi stated: "The Oedipus complex may well be the result of real acts committed by adults...The objection that these were the child's own fantasies, i.e. hysterical lies, is losing force because of the considerable number of patients in analysis who themselves confess to having assaulted children".

But these considerations were dismissed and forgotten by the psychoanalytic movement, then in full swing. Analysts who wished to join the movement had to confirm the main theses by incorporating the Oedipus complex.

Awareness came later, in the second half of the 20th century. Françoise Minkowska welcomed this: "There are now quite a few therapists, psychoanalysts or not, who recognise the reality of childhood trauma in the genesis of psychological disorders and give it their full attention. Among the best known specialists who have spoken out clearly on this subject are Alice Miller and, more recently, Susan Forward".

---

[550] A website (theawarnesscenter.org) specialising in reports of paedophile rabbis estimated that 1.3 million of the 5.5 million Jews in the United States were sexually abused. This meant that one Jew in four would have been raped as a child; in proportion, this is as if 75 million Americans had been raped. Read in *Psychoanalysis of Judaism*.

In *Why Psychoanalysis,* Elisabeth Roudinesco gave us an overview of the changes that had taken place in the interpretation of psychoanalysis: "The revisionist historiography that appeared from 1978 onwards was initially very creative, she wrote. Researchers who claimed to be heirs of the great historian Henri F. Ellenberger produced remarkable works, notably Frank Sulloway, author of a monumental work on the origins of Freudian thought *(Freud, Biologist of the Mind: Beyond the Psychoanalytic Legend).* These historians rightly questioned the canons of official history, inherited from Ernst Jones and above all from Kurt Eisler, the main organiser after the Second World War of the Sigmund Freud Archives deposited in the Library of Congress in Washington. But after a few years of relentless combat against Freudian orthodoxy, the revisionist movement became so anti-Freudian that it abandoned scholarly studies and threw itself fanatically into the debate of ideas[551]."

Elisabeth Roudinesco thus denounced Peter Swales, who in 1981 "already claimed - without the slightest proof, of course - that Freud had had sexual relations with his sister-in-law Minna Bernays". He allegedly got her pregnant and then forced her to have an abortion.

In France, psychoanalysis was attacked by both the communists and the Catholic Church. In 1972, Pierre Debray-Ritzen, a child psychiatrist and hospital doctor, published *La Scolastique freudienne,* which met with considerable success. For Elisabeth Roudinesco, his position was "as fanatical as that of his American counterpart", Adolf Grünbaum. On the communist side, hostilities ceased between 1965 and 1970, thanks to Louis Althusser, who revised the orthodox positions.

The 1980s saw a "scientific drift": "In 1980, Kurt Eisler, director of the Sigmund Freud Archives, and Anna Freud decided to entrust the complete publication of Freud's letters to Wilhelm Fliess to an American scholar duly trained by the International Psychoanalytical Association (IPA). Jeffrey Moussaief Masson took note of the files and, Roudinesco wrote, interpreted them in a wild way, with the idea that they contained a hidden truth, a shameful secret. He thus claimed, without the slightest proof, that Freud had abandoned the theory of seduction out of cowardice. By not daring to reveal to the world the atrocities committed by all adults with all children, Freud would have invented the notion of phantasy to mask the traumatic reality of the sexual abuses that are at the origin of neuroses. Therefore, Freud would have been simply a falsifier".

In his 1984 book *The Assault on Truth,* which was one of the *best-selling* American psychoanalytic books of the second half of the century, Jeffrey Masson again accused Freud and the orthodox of fantasy theory of being

---

[551] Elisabeth Roudinesco, *Pourquoi la psychanalyse,* Fayard, 1999, p. 118.

the allies of a power based on oppression: the colonisation of women by men and of children by adults.

Logically, feminists should harbour an undying hatred of Sigmund Freud, who transferred guilt from fathers to daughters, in order to avoid evoking the great taboo of Judaism. The famous feminist lawyer Catharina MacKinnon would also adopt the idea of the Freudian lie, and in 1992 Judith Herman published a book in which she reviewed the history of hysteria in view of a revaluation of trauma[552]. In the wake of this scandal, the American revisionist movement began to destroy Freudian doctrine and the reputation of Freud himself, who "had once again become a diabolical doctor guilty of abusive relationships within his own family".

Yet we owe it to Freud to have raised this question of incest, which was the great hidden secret of Israel. All that remained was to present this "psychoanalytic science" in a mirror in order to understand that, deep down, *Judaism was the illness that psychoanalysis had tried to cure.*

4. The accusatory reversal

We have already noted in the course of this study, and in our previous books, the strong inclination of Jewish intellectuals to project their own guilt onto others, and to accuse their opponents of acting in this way. The phenomenon of accusatory inversion is indeed very classic in intellectual Judaism. Thus, we must always read what Jews write with a mirror in order to understand that whatever they may say about others is in reality an expression of what lies deep within themselves. From there, everything becomes very simple.

The incestuous genesis of a genocide

In his *Psychoanalysis of Anti-Semitism*, published in 1952, Rudolph Loewenstein, like Sigmund Freud, projected the incestuous tendencies of Judaism onto the whole of humanity: "In today's civilised societies, he said,

---

[552] Elisabeth Roudinesco, *Pourquoi la psychanalyse*, Fayard, 1999, p. 114, 115, Catharina MacKinnon, *Feminism unmodified, Discouses on Life and Law*, Harvard University Press, Cambridge, 1987. Judith Herman, *Trauma and Recovery*, New York, Basic Books, 1992.

sexual relations between children and parents and between brothers and sisters are strictly forbidden. However, we know that these prohibitions do not prevent the existence of more or less well repressed incestuous desires. A large part of human neuroses are based precisely on the psychic conflicts associated with them[553]."

A certain Roger Zagdoun, a psychoanalyst by profession, was much more caricatured, if that is possible. In 2002, he published a 274-page book on the origins of the Hitler phenomenon. The title of his book was quite revealing: *Hitler et Freud, un transfert paranoïaque ou la genèse incestueuse d'un génocide* (*Hitler and Freud, a paranoid transference or the incestuous genesis of a genocide*, Editions L'Harmattan). Here is what you could read on the Internet about this Jewish intellectual: "The psychiatrist and psychoanalyst Roger Zagdoun takes a unique look at the tragic episode of Nazism and, more specifically, at the Shoah. Following Freud's work on the psychology of the masses, Roger Zagdoun applies psychoanalytic theory to the study of human collectivities, developing the concepts of Collective Subject, Collective Unconscious, and Collective Neurosis. In this work, he uses these concepts to analyse the Nazi collective delirium".

Listen to this: "The German collective Subject experienced an uprising of the repression of the unconscious desire for incest, which is a desire to return to the nothingness before birth. It set this desire in motion after projecting it onto the minority constituted by the Jews...Roger Zagdoun's thesis is that the Shoah was more than a murder, it was an annihilation, which the author interprets as the return of a repressed collective incestuous fantasy, that of Germany. Roger Zagdoun analyses the Holocaust as the delusional act of a group of paranoid psychopaths, and Nazism as the historical product of a Germany depressed after its defeat in 1918".

The Jewish magazine *Passages* published an interview with the immortal author of *The Paranoid Transference*. In it, Bertrand Delais interviewed the aforementioned Roger Zagdoun: (Hold on).

"Roger Zagdoun: What seems to me important in Hitler's case is that, in an oedipal context, he wants to kill the father. He wants to kill him as the father-ancestor, and the Jew is the ancestor of the Christian. It is a cultural murder.[554]

---

[553] G. Kurth, *Le Juif et Adolf Hitler*, Psa. Quart. XVI, 1947, in Rudolph Loewenstein, *Psychanalyse de l'antisémitisme*, 1952, Presses Universitaires de France, 2001, p. 121.
[554] This is what Rudolph Loewenstein said in turn: "The conflict between the Jews and Christ, which took place more than nineteen centuries ago, reflects in the more or less conscious imagination of Christians their own ancient conflicts with their father, and becomes the unconscious symbol of the Oedipus complex. (*Psychanalyse de l'antisémitisme*, 1952, Presses Universitaires de France, 2001, p. 86).

-Bertrand Delais: You go so far as to describe interwar Germany as a historical personality caught in a dilemma, with paranoid delirium on the one hand and depression on the other, which you contrast with this paranoid functioning. What can we say about this opposition you establish between paranoid delusions and depressive tendencies?

-Roger Zagdoun:... It is the question of projection and internalisation as described by Freud... What also seems to me to be very important is the question of projection and internalisation of guilt. The paranoid person projects his guilt outwards, it is always someone else's fault, it is never his own fault and under no circumstances. The depressive, on the other hand, assumes it. The guilt is theirs. In fact, the paranoid and depressive postures follow one after the other in the development of the child... From a depressed mother, a paranoid son results, a depressed son. For the mother, her child is the complement of her personality, it is what she does not have and what she is not, or what she does not want to be. The child identifies with something of the mother's desire that is what she lacks. It becomes its opposite, like the finger of a glove turned inside out. The paranoid mother projects her unconscious guilt onto the child, who becomes depressed and internalises this projection because it is what his mother desires. Conversely, the depressive mother internalises guilt, so the child becomes paranoid because he has a mother who offers herself to his projection and allows him to project his guilt, which he then displaces onto others to protect her.

-Bertrand Delais: You mention the idea of German paranoia. But in your opinion, are the reasons historical - the Treaty of Versailles - or cultural, for example, German romanticism as an expression of a depression?

-Roger Zagdoun: It is undeniable that the Treaty of Versailles was too hard on the Germans. As for the economic crisis of 1929, it was really the first great depression in the Western world. And Germany was hit harder than the rest of Europe. German society functioned like a depressed mother who abandons her child and turns it into a paranoid...On the one hand, there was a depression that triggered a reactionary paranoia, so the Germans came out of the post-Versailles depression and the crash of 1929 with a paranoid system that took the form of fascism. Projection is a very important element for a group to get out of its depression. The depressed find a paranoid to guide them, and the slaves find masters while waiting for the executioners to find victims. But, on the other hand, if a depressed mother has a paranoid child, I also believe that a depressed society produces a paranoid society, as a mutation of the personality, just as a mother gives birth to a child with a personality opposite to her own. When Germany was building its unity, and if we go back to the earlier kingdoms, Bavaria was ruled by a melancholic and suicidal king. All Bavarian melancholy could produce was paranoia and a Hitler to embody it. Bavarian melancholy produced a Wagnerian and paranoid Hitler.

-Bertrand Delais: Since the work of Claude Levi-Strauss, we know that what distinguishes human societies is above all the prohibition of incest. Moreover, Nazism had a particularity that distinguished it from any other fascist regime: the methodical and organised preparation of the Final Solution, the Shoah. You also have this singular opinion: the Shoah is incest. What do you mean by this? Is it the weight of the forbidden that is signified in this way?

-Roger Zagdoun:....I make the connection between the Shoah and incest precisely by looking at things from the angle of incest. The child cannot want to penetrate the vagina from which it comes. So the death drive is not biological, but is the return of a repressed desire for incest. The child cannot desire the vagina from which it came, and it is the marginalisation of this sexual thought that originally creates the unconscious. In fact, Freud perfectly demonstrated the functioning and reality of the unconscious, but at no point did he define its cause. The sexual thought of the male child in relation to his mother is, in fact, synonymous with death, since it represents a return to nothingness, because it means returning to the place from which it comes: it is, therefore, the unthinkable, since death cannot be thought. And this is the beginning of the creation of a psychic space for the discarded thoughts, the place of the original repression. And if we accept the idea that incest is first and foremost the incest of the child, the child, having become a father, projects his desire for incest onto his daughter. He wants to annihilate himself in his daughter as he wanted to annihilate himself in his mother".

This is what psychiatrists call the phenomenon of "incestuous generations".

And this Zagdoun once again projected his own guilt: "The Jews were actually the object of Germany's unconscious desire for annihilation, like an incestuous daughter who wanted to annihilate her father, hence the Shoah, annihilation in Hebrew".

The diabolical Jew

Norman Mailer was an "American" writer who benefited during his career from all the loudspeakers that the "international media community" makes available to members of the "hyperclass", as Jacques Attali calls it. His latest novel, published in 2007, is entitled *A Castle in the Forest*. It is a book about Adolf Hitler's childhood. This was the review in the newspaper *Le Monde* on 11 August 2007:

"At 84 years of age, the celebrated American author seems to be able to prove with this book that he has lost none of his audacity.... The novel covers the period 1837-1903, the life of Hitler's father. When Alois died, Adolf was 14 years old and a mediocre schoolboy. So far, so normal. But Mailer is not content with a third-person historical account, but tells the story of the background and childhood of possibly the most evil man who ever walked the earth. He has chosen to entrust the narrative to a demon. A subaltern demon sent by Satan: Dieter, an SS who worked under Heinrich Himmler."

Dieter has secret information about Adolf Hitler's origins. He recounts his childhood and describes his family, showing how the dictator "developed his obsessions". In one passage Norman Mailer has Alois Schiklgruber, the father of the young Adolf, speak; Alois is in a tavern in Braunau (Austria) and openly shows his hatred of the Church while drinking his beer:

"Do you know that, in the Middle Ages, prostitutes were more respected than nuns? They even had a guild of their own! I read about a convent in Franconia that was so stinking that the Pope had to investigate. Why? Because the Franconian prostitutes' guild complained about illegal competition from the nuns.
- Come on," said two drinkers in unison.
- It is true. Yes. Absolutely right. Herr Lycidias Koerner can show you the text. Hans Lycidias nodded slowly, thoughtfully. He was a little too drunk to know for sure who should favour his authority.
- Yes," said Alois, "the Pope says, 'Send a monsignor to find out'. I ask you: what does the monsignor's report say? That half of the nuns are pregnant. That is the bare fact. So the Pope investigates thoroughly in his monasteries. Orgies. Homosexual orgies.

He said this with such force that he had time to take a long drink from his mug.
-Which should come as no surprise," said Alois, having also taken a breath of fresh air. To this day, half of the priests are still in a rut. We know that[555]."

Naturally, everyone will have understood that it was Norman Mailer who was expressing his own hatred of the Catholic Church. The novelist also suggested that Hitler was born of an incestuous marriage, for Alois, his father, would also have been the uncle of his wife Klara Poelzl. Little Adolf had just been born, and "The Master", as the demon Dieter called him, had already discovered a promising recruit: "While the Master was not often sympathetic to breast-feeding, since its absence could stimulate ugly energies that we would later use, he was more tolerant of cases of incest in the first degree. So he wanted the mother to be close to the child - so much

---

[555] Norman Mailer, *El castillo en el bosque*, Editorial Anagrama, 2007, Barcelona, p. 103.

the better for us! (A monster is much more effective when he can appeal to maternal love to seduce new relations)".

Mailer continued, scatologically, through the voice of his diabolical character: "Excretory dramas also offer advantages. A dirty baby's bottom sends a signal: the mother is a potential client of ours. The opposite is also useful. Klara is an excellent example in this respect. She always kept a clean house. Her lodgings at the Pommer Inn were then as immaculate as a household run by several good maids. The furniture sparkled. So did Adi's tiny anus, which his mother kept spotless as an opal, small and shining, which I also approved of: an incestuous son must always be aware of the importance of his excrement, even if it is reduced to a tiny arsehole that is always being polished[556]."

In the weekly *L'Express* of 4 October 2007, François Busnel interviewed the "great American writer": "There is no human explanation for the horror of what Hitler did, explains Norman Mailer...Hitler was weak, as all the witnesses say. He was a total failure, even emotionally...He was chosen by the devil from among several candidates. And the devil - quite logically - appointed a devil to watch over him from the moment he was created by his father Alois."

François Busnel continued his interview with Norman Mailer: "You favour the incest theory...". To which Norman Mailer replied: "Historically, it is a very real possibility. Hitler's father, Alois, married a woman who we know was his niece and who we may fear was his daughter...I imagine the devil present on the night Hitler was conceived.... For me, Hitler's childhood is a metaphysical saga".

It was not the first time Norman Mailer invoked the presence of the devil to explain historical or contemporary events. Here is what he wrote in 2003 in a book entitled *Why We Are at War*: "That is why I am inclined to think, Mailer wrote, that the best explanation for 9/11 is that the devil won a great battle that day. Yes, Satan was the pilot who guided those planes into that atrocious outcome[557]." In it, Norman Mailerm also denounced the terrible influence around US President George Bush of all the fundamentalist Christians who had gotten America into the war against Iraq. For everyone knows that it is Christians who are responsible for all the wars that the West has waged in the last 150 years, and certainly not the Jews, who are always innocent. In any case, we can believe that Satan was close to Norman

---

[556] Norman Mailer, *El castillo en el bosque*, Editorial Anagrama, 2007, Barcelona, p. 100.

[557] Norman Mailer, *¿Por qué estamos en guerra*, Editorial Anagrama, 2003, Barcelona, p. 121.

Mailer and followed his thinking very closely. Perhaps he even preceded him.[558]

For the rest, we see once again that the Jewish intellectual is merely transferring his own faults to the Goyim in a classic accusatory inversion. It cannot be stressed enough: Jewish intellectuals must always be read with a mirror. One understands then why many of these subsidised cultural associations systematically lump "racism, anti-Semitism and paedophilia" together as crimes that should be banished from society forever.

On 15 November 2007, the weekly *Le Point* published an article by Emmanuel Carcassonne in tribute to Norman Mailer, who died recently on 10 November 2007. Norman Mailer was apparently considered a beacon of literature, a super-powerful genius, a Jewish light in the darkness of goy gentility. Compared to his immense oeuvre, William Shakespeare and Victor Hugo had become minuscule. "America has lost its democratic king', wrote Emmanuel Carcassonne.

But let us listen to the last words of Norman Mailer, who, before his death, still managed to distil a little of his venom, while correcting with his publisher a book of interviews on the question of God: "To shock people, I could have made lovers of John the Baptist and Jesus Christ," he declared.

"He was looking for a title and asked us point-blank: "All priests are liars" - that's not bad, is it? And Mailer added: "My publisher thinks that attacking religious fundamentalism will sell better than my novels". To change literary register, Norman Mailer could also have attacked Jewish fanaticism. He would then have shown - simply and genuinely provocative, of course - how Moses, long before Freud, had been groped by his own mother, and how the rabbis had ex post facto magnified the story of that hysterical family.

The sick become doctors

Clearly, Freud was affected by the evil that had so much retained his attention. Ernst Jones, Freud's first biographer, had written: "According to all probabilities, very few neurotic manifestations were evident in his behaviour in relation to all those around him - with the single exception of Fliess. His sufferings, however, were very intense at times, and during those ten years there must have been very few and isolated moments when life was worth much in his eyes.... It was, however, in the years which mark

---

[558] Joseph Roth, another "genius writer", who lived in Germany at the beginning of the 20th century, had already revealed to us in a veiled way the "diabolical" nature of certain Jewish intellectuals (The Sabbateists), but projecting the evil onto the anti-Semites, who, according to him, embodied the Antichrist (read in *Psychoanalysis of Judaism*).

the culmination of his neurosis - 1897 to 1900 - that Freud produced the most original part of his work...Freud recognised, of course, his neurosis, and in the correspondence he uses the term several times to describe his state. There seem to have been no physical symptoms of "conversion[559]", and he would undoubtedly later have regarded this state as a hysteria of distress. It consisted essentially of extreme mood swings...His moods end between periods of *elation*, excitement, and self-confidence, on the one hand, and on the other, periods of severe depression, doubt, and inhibition[560]."

Freud himself spoke of his excessive impressionability and inclination to complain: "'I have a great talent for complaining,' he once said, and went so far as to declare that in the last fourteen months he had known only three or four days of happiness[561]." Apparently, Freud was an emotionally unstable man and certainly suffered from several physical ailments during his life that he complained about, although he usually overcame them: "During his life, Freud suffered from frequent attacks of headache that rendered him incapable of everything, and which were entirely refractory to any treatment. It is not yet known whether these complaints were of organic or functional origin...These annoying complaints, however, made him suffer much less than those of psychological origin, which tormented him during the first twenty years of his adult life[562]". "In spite of being

---

[559]'Conversion' symptoms are psychosomatic disorders. In the film *Hollywood ending* (2002), for example, Woody Allen plays a neurotic and hypernervous Jewish film director who suddenly goes blind during the shooting of his film. His psychoanalyst assures him that it is a temporary disorder.

[560]Ernst Jones, *Freud (I)*, Salvat Editores, Barcelona, 1985, p. 231-232. [The only forms of localisation of his anguish were his occasional attacks of fear of dying (*Todesangst*) and of anguish at travelling by rail (*Reisefieber*)... In periods of depression he could neither write nor concentrate his thoughts (except on his professional work). He would then let hours of inaction pass, dominated by boredom, passing from one thing to another, amusing himself with opening new books, contemplating maps of ancient Pompeii, playing solitaire or chess, but unable to concentrate on anything for long periods of time. In a word, a kind of restless paralysis. He sometimes suffered attacks during which there was a marked restriction of the degree of consciousness, a state difficult to describe, in which he felt like a veil giving rise to an almost twilight state of mind (6 December 1897). He was visibly inclined to complain to Fliess about his unhappy moods. It is very surprising to note this fact, so strange to the real Freud. He had to endure many things in later years: unhappiness, afflictions and severe physical suffering. But he endured all this with the greatest stoicism." *Freud (I)*, p. 232].

[561] Ernst Jones, *La Vie et l'oeuvre de Sigmund Freud, tome 1*, 1953, PUF, 1958, p. 188.

[562] Ernst Jones, *Freud (I)*, Salvat Editores, Barcelona, 1985, p. 144. ["In 1923, he learned that he had cancer of the jaw. He underwent thirty-three operations, all very painful, and for sixteen years he had to live in pain, often terribly intense". *Freud (I)*, p. 25].

endowed with a robust constitution, I have not been in good health for the last two years[563] ", he wrote to his beloved wife.

His mother wrote to him in a letter of 27 June 1886: "First of all, regain a certain degree of calm and tranquillity, which at present you lack to such a deplorable degree. You have no reason for this moodiness and despair, which border on the pathological. Put aside all such calculations, and become, first of all, a sensible man again[564]."

Concerning the mysterious Mr. Y, mentioned in a short article entitled *Ueber Deckerinnerungen (1899)* (*About Screen Memories*[565]) inserted in *The Interpretation of Dreams*, Ernst Jones wrote: "The precautions he took did not prevent some of us from realising that the patient of whom he spoke was none other than himself. Jones quoted another letter of 14 November: "I told you that my most important patient was myself. It was after my trip that my self-analysis began[566]." And also, "In a letter of March 2, 1899, we learn that the analysis had done him much good and that he was evidently much more normal than he had been four or five years before[567]."

Early in his career, Freud had praised the benefits of cocaine, which helped him to cope with his malaise: "Depression, like all other neurotic manifestations, diminishes the sense of energy and virility: cocaine restores it....Two years later, he was to be scorned for having introduced, thanks to his indiscriminate propaganda for a "harmless" wonder drug, what his detractors called "the third scourge of mankind[568] "."

Mikkel Borch-Jacobsen, co-editor of *The Black Book of Psychoanalysis*, had conducted extensive biographical research on Freud using the archives to which he had access. Some of these archives remained curiously protected from the gaze of historians who questioned the scientific qualities of Freud's work. In fact, Freud had a clear tendency to construct theories

---

[563] Ernst Jones, *Freud (I)*, Salvat Editores, Barcelona, 1985, p. 144. ["As my person has become more important, even to me, since I have won you, I think more of my health than before, and I do not want to wear myself out. I would rather set aside my ambition, make less noise in the world, and be less successful, than damage my nervous system. As long as I must remain in hospital I shall live like the *goyim* [non-Jews, ndt], modestly, learning the ordinary things and not endeavouring to make discoveries or to go deeper into things." *Freud (I)*, p. 145].
[564]Ernst Jones, *Freud (I)*, Salvat Editores, Barcelona, 1985, p. 129.
[565]"Freud's article on screen memories (*Ueber Deckerinnerungen*, 1899), contains a delightful and remarkable dialogue between Freud and "a man of thirty-eight, academically trained," who had overcome "a slight phobia through psychoanalysis.""
 At
https://web.archive.org/web/20210922055220/http:/www.lacanianworks.net/?p=7604.
[566]Ernst Jones, *La Vie et l'oeuvre de Sigmund Freud, tome 1*, 1953, PUF, 1958, p. 28.
[567]Ernst Jones, *Freud (I)*, Salvat Editores, Barcelona, 1985, p. 247.
[568]Ernst Jones, *Freud (I)*, Salvat Editores, Barcelona, 1985, p. 88.

based on his own problems. Borch-Jacobsen referred to Mitchell to show that the Oedipal theory was the product of Freud's repression of his own hysteria[569]. This is what anthropologist Illel Kieser El Baz wrote in his 2007 book *Incest and paedocriminality, crimes against humanity* :[570]

"He manipulated his patients' confessions and widely publicised cures that were, in fact, often imaginary. In this way he interpreted his results (or lack of them) and persuaded his patients. He was particularly adept at disguising therapeutic failures as scientific progress. "I thought it, so it must be true," Freud said, quoted by Jung in his correspondence."

Ernst Jones also echoed this: in 1900, before he distanced himself, Fliess accused him of being "a "thought reader", and, moreover, that he "read his own thoughts in patients[571] "".

The founder of psychoanalysis certainly had things to hide. In the preface to *The Life and Work of Sigmund Freud*, Jones wrote: "Freud took meticulous measures to keep his private life secret, especially his early years. On two occasions he completely destroyed his correspondence, notes, diary and manuscripts." In 1885, at the age of 29, he burned all his private papers and wrote to his fiancée: "I cannot grow up, nor die, without worrying about who will come and rummage through these old papers[572] ". Freud had confessed to Fliess that his father had abused his brother and sister, but it is very likely that he was also a victim of his incestuous father. Freud's close friend Wilhelm Fliess, with whom the founder of psychoanalysis had corresponded for many years, was himself an incestuous father, as his own son Robert Fliess would later testify.

The members of the circle that Freud had created around him seemed to suffer from the same malady. The famous child psychiatrist Bruno Bettelheim wrote: "Those closest to Freud, like Ferenczi, the most intimate of them all, were unfortunately known to be terribly neurotic[573] ".

Wilhelm Stekel had first been a patient of the father of the psychoanalytic movement, before becoming a disciple: "The colleague to whom Freud attributes the initiative of the first grouping is Wilhelm Stekel, a doctor

---

[569]"He himself referred to the priceless and virtually magical gift of his mother's special veneration: "The man who has been the undisputed favourite of his mother retains in life the attitude of a conqueror, that confidence in triumph which often leads to real triumph"; as Freud would later write: "When a man has been the undisputed favourite of his mother, he manages to retain throughout his life a feeling of victor, that confidence in success which often leads to real success". Ernst Jones, *Freud (I)*, Salvat Editores, Barcelona, 1985, p. 20-21, 34.

[570]Illel Kieser El Baz, *Inceste et pédocriminalité, crimes against humanity*, Fondation littéraire Fleur de Lys, 2007.

[571]Ernst Jones, *Freud (I)*, Salvat Editores, Barcelona, 1985, p. 237.

[572]Marthe Robert, *La Révolution psychoanalytique, Tome I*, Payot, 1964, p. 152, 29

[573]Bruno Bettelheim, *Le Poids d'une vie*, 1989, Robert Laffont, 1991, p. 67.

suffering from severe neurotic disorders who, around 1901 or 1902, had come to him for treatment[574]."

In a tribute to the psychoanalyst Melanie Klein, entitled *Development of Psychoanalysis* and published in 1966, Paula Heimann took up the Freudian thesis of the infantile desire for incest. The sick delusions of these neuropathic Jews were here manifested in broad daylight, through the looking glass: 'At the time of the fully developed classical Oedipus complex,' she wrote, 'the prohibitions are directed against the passionate desires for one parent and against the murderous rivalry for the other, as Freud first discovered. In the anal phase, sadistic-anal drives and in the oral phase, sadistic-oral drives are forbidden by the corresponding type of superego. We may recall here that Abraham drew attention to the inhibition of voracity in early childhood, and that Ferenczi introduced the notion of "sphincteric morality"... While the child, in his genital sensations, experiences masculine impulses to penetrate the mother (direct Oedipus complex), he also feels her as a rival with respect to his female receptive goals, which are directed both towards the father and towards the mother endowed with the father's penis[575] ". Undoubtedly, this Paula Heimann had also been a victim of incest.

Freudian psychoanalysis had obviously had perverse effects. After Freud, numerous therapists and psychoanalytic theorists developed theses that placed the child's perverse desires at the centre of psychic illness and the problem of incest. Freud had already described children as 'perverse polymorphs', identifying violent and savage sexual desires in many of their normal gestures and attitudes.

Melanie Klein, for her part, had developed the theory of the 'cruel infant', eager to sadistically devour the mother's breast, and had succeeded in locating the Oedipus complex in the first months of the child's life. Thus, a whole series of infantile attitudes could be interpreted not by what they manifested (sadness, joy, anger, fear, anxiety, excitement, curiosity, etc.), but by strategic Oedipal whims or manoeuvres aimed at satisfying inevitable sexual desires and rivalries.

"If Freud was the first to discover the repressed child in the adult, wrote Elisabeth Roudinesco, Melanie Klein was the first to reveal what was already repressed in the child: the infant.... The Kleinians thus opposed the classical oedipal model to a pre-oedipal model, referring to the anguished universe of a great symbiosis with the mother: a wild world, inaccessible to the law, no longer given over to paternal despotism but to the cruelty of

---

[574] Marthe Robert, *La Révolution psychoanalytique, Tome I*, Payot, 1964, p. 216.
[575] Mélanie Klein, Paula Heimann, *Développements de la Psychanalyse*, Presses Universitaires de France, 1966, 1991, p. 128, 156.

maternal chaos. Melanie Klein probably had a disturbed mind. Professor Debray-Ritzen thought she was simply insane.[576]

Sabina Spielrein was another such patient who later became a doctor. She was born in Rostov-on-Don in 1885 to a wealthy and educated Jewish couple. Both her grandfather and great-grandfather had been respected rabbis. But during her adolescence, Sabina Spielrein suffered from schizophrenic disorders, a severe hysteria accompanied by schizoid symptoms. In August 1904, her parents took her to Zurich for treatment at the Burghölsli Hospital. There she became Jung's patient and they became lovers.

Jung and Freud corresponded about Sabina Speilrein. Jung's second letter, dated 23 October 1906, read as follows: 'I regularly treat a hysteric according to your method. A difficult case, a twenty-year-old student of Russian origin, ill for six years. The first trauma occurred between her third and fourth year. She saw her father whip her older brother's bare bottom. A deep impression. Later he could not help thinking that he had defecated in his hand with his father. Between her fourth and seventh year, she convulsively tried to defecate on her own feet, one foot under her, the heel pressed against her anus, and tried to defecate while preventing defecation. She often retained her faeces like this for a fortnight! She has no idea how she has come to behave this way.... The main symptoms are the idea of defecating on his father? I would be very grateful if you could tell me in a few words what you think of this story".

Sabrina Spielrein married a Russian Jew named Pavel Scheftel in 1913. In 1925, when psychoanalysis was no longer officially accepted in Soviet Russia, Spielrein left Moscow and moved to Rostov. It was there that her husband began to suffer from psychotic disorders, from which he died in 1930. Sabrina Spielrein then moved to Zurich, where she became a doctor treating mental disorders: "An original thinker whose ideas were later to play an important role in the Freudian system[577] ", wrote Bruno Bettelheim.

Janusz Korczak, whose real name was Henryk Goldszmit, was the scion of generations of Jewish scholars. He made his career at the Warsaw Pedagogical Institute in the first half of the 20th century and distinguished himself for his work on behalf of children: "I am the son of a madman and I want to be the Karl Marx of children," he had declared. He was only eleven years old when his father began to suffer from severe mental problems that eventually necessitated his admission to a psychiatric hospital.

---

[576]Elisabeth Roudinesco, *Pourquoi la psychanalyse*, Fayard, 1999, p. 159, 128.
[577]Bruno Bettelheim, *Le Poids d'une vie*, 1989, Robert Laffont, 1991, p. 92-113, 83, 84

He published his first novel in 1905, *The Children of the Street*, followed in 1928 by *King Matthias I*. It is the story of a boy who becomes king when his father dies. His first concern is to reform the kingdom for the greater good of adults and children. The little king is none other than Korczak himself, embodied in a child who fights bravely against all the injustices of the world.

Korczak 's book reflects the "anti-racist" obsessions of Judaism: the adult king who implements the reforms decided by the little king is, in fact, a black king. "Only the black kings are the true friends of Matthias, and they are ready to sacrifice their lives for him, while the white kings, despite their beautiful promises, end up abominably betraying him[578] ".

The novelist Isaac Bashevis Singer also lived with "the Jewish disease". In 1935 he had left his wife and five-year-old son in Warsaw for the United States. His biographer, Florence Noiville, did not, however, give any explanation for this. But this is what she wrote about him: "Burning, passion, pride, shame, despair.... In the early 1930s, all these sensations intertwined in Singer to such an extent that he wondered whether he was mad or possessed by a *dybbuk*. He suffers from nightmares, reads books on psychiatry and delves into the works of Freud, Jung and Adler to understand how he can go from depression to extreme euphoria in a matter of seconds. Once again, he feels like a double, convinced that inside him coexists a young man full of ambition and another, melancholic, who gives himself "to his last pleasures before he is buried"... "One day, Singer wrote, in a book or a magazine, I came across the expression "split personality", which applied perfectly to my state[579]."

Bashevis was his mother's first name: "This pseudonym, once again, is a tribute to this woman he admires so much". His father, on the other hand, was an insignificant Hasidic Jew. As for her sister, Hinde, she had been an epileptic since childhood. She also suffered from severe anxiety attacks, which later developed into persecutory insanity.[580]

Isaac Bashevis Singer always remained a Jew conscious of his "mission". In 1944, he wrote to his son: "Victory over the enemy is drawing nearer and nearer". He was also "frightfully stingy", wrote Florence Noiville. His son Israel had come to see him in New York after a twenty-year absence: "A dollar a day was all he gave Israel. The latter, dumbfounded, did not dare to ask for anything. "Very soon, he concludes, I felt I didn't belong here, next to my father. He didn't know what to do with me. He had no time. He had no money."

---

[578]Bruno Bettelheim, *Le Poids d'une vie*, 1989, Robert Laffont, 1991, p. 250-259.
[579]Florence Noiville, *Isaac B. Singer*, Stock, 2003, p. 91, 72
[580]Florence Noiville, *Isaac B. Singer*, Stock, 2003, p. 82, 175

In 1967, Isaac Bashevis had published a novel entitled *The House of Jampol*: the story takes place in pre-war Poland. Bonifratov Hospital was an asylum for the insane. Among them were, wrote Isaac Bashevis Singer: "...the peaceful madmen who spent the day dreaming; the furious, who had to be straitjacketed; the melancholic, sunk in invincible sadness; the paranoid, convinced that they had inherited immense fortunes, that they had great buried treasures or that they belonged to the royal family...Among the Jewish patients there was an incredible number of Messiahs. Women were more prone than men to erotic disturbances. Insanity was basically a mental illness, but it was more closely linked than other illnesses to social, cultural and religious factors[581]."

The historian François Fejtö went so far as to express the problem in these terms: "It seems natural that it is "the sickest of peoples" that has produced so many great doctors, just as it is also "the most accused of peoples" that has produced so many lawyers to plead not guilty, even in the most desperate cases[582]." Indeed.

---

[581] Isaac Barshevis Singer, *The House of Jampol*, German25, p. 295-296.
[582] François Fetjö, *Dieu et son juif*, Éditions Pierre Horay, 1997, p. 112.

5. The liberation of the Jew

At the individual level, hysteria is common in the Jewish community, where incest seems to be practised more than in any other community. But the truth is that everything in intellectual Judaism corresponds to the manifestations of hysteria: histrionics, egocentrism, fabulation, selective amnesia, duplicity, paranoia, great emotional fragility, a sense of mission, etc......

The Jewish prison

There are many Jews who suffer from belonging to the sect and who would like to find in themselves the strength to free themselves, to break down the walls of their prison in order to become part of humanity. The constitutive ambivalence of Jewish identity can be interpreted as an oscillation of identity, a pendulum swing between the weight of genealogy and the desire for normality.

Militant Jewish intellectuals and rabbis, the guardians of tradition, naturally see things from a different angle and speak here of denial, betrayal and "self-hatred". Here, for example, is what the philosopher Bernard-Henri Lévy wrote in *Récidives* in 2004:

"I have known Jews who were ashamed of their Jewishness. We have all known families in which, like Bloch in *In Search of Lost Time*, they blushed when they heard the word Jew at the dinner table. I have had friends who, like Bloch, whom Proust tells us spent his youth, and even his maturity, "cleansing his being and almost his face of anything that might give away his Jewishness", went to great lengths to hide, one an accent, the other a family, the third this or that stigma that might indicate that he did not belong to eternal France. Not to mention the extreme left of my twenties, that of those Jewish militants in the big Trotskyist or Maoist organisations, who made it a point of honour to erase, if not all Jewish traces, at least all Jewish concerns: revolutionary universalism, they thought, was at that price! None of this was my business. As far as I can remember, I have never participated in any such form of Jewish self-denial[583]."

It is understandable that it is not easy to be born and to be a Jew, and that Jewishness can be experienced as a disgrace by some Jews, who go to great

---

[583] Bernard-Henri Lévy, *Récidives*, Grasset, 2004, p. 389.

lengths to hide their origins in order to be accepted by the Goyim and to integrate among them. But we must not lose sight of the fact that, for centuries, Jews have practised the marrano tradition of disguise, which consists of consciously moving behind a mask in order to subvert the nations from within. While Marcel Proust's "Bloch" may be sincere, the communist revolutionary cited by Bernard-Henri Lévy is a very dubious example. Indeed, communist ideology corresponded exactly to Israel's egalitarian fanaticism and its universal messianic hopes. By relegating Jewish religious traditions to the wardrobe, the communist Jew was simply pursuing the aims of the Jewish people in a different, secularised garb.

The story of "Joseph the Dreamer", as told by the "English" novelist Israel Zangwill, is another illustration of the identity tearing of the Jewish personality and the desire of certain Jews to tear down the walls of the "Jewish prison[584] ": In the Rome of 1600, Giuseppe de Franchi was clearly an anguished Jew. His people were languishing in ghettos, stubbornly rejecting the Christian culture that was then flourishing magnificently in all areas. After much reflection, he finally accepted the obvious and decided to convert: "When we are Christians, the ghetto gates will fall," he said. But his mother and sister were not of the same opinion: "Christians," Rachel and Miriam repeated in horror.

After converting to Christianity, Joseph was ostracised from his community and excommunicated. He began to preach to his former fellow Jews and also tried to convince the Pope to convert the Jews. During the carnival in Rome, when the famous Jewish race was being held, he passionately exhorted the crowd of Christians to love the Jews. But he got carried away with his passionate exhortations, even insulting the Pope: "He, the vicar of God? I should be the vicar of God. God speaks through my mouth. He is "neither the spiritual emperor nor the vicar of Christ, but the Antichrist himself".

Friar Giuseppe quickly tied the pallium to his crucifix and, waving the piece of red cloth over his head, exclaimed: "...".
-Here is the true banner of Christ, the symbol of the martyrdom of our brothers! As you see, its colour is that of the blood that He shed for us. May those who are with Jesus follow me!"

Of course, poor Giuseppe aroused the indignation and anger of the Christians. He was seized by the soldiers and imprisoned. "The only doubt was whether he would be considered a rapist or a spy. In either case, he deserved the death penalty."

On the other hand, for his former co-religionists, relatives and friends, Giuseppe remained a traitor: "The Jews rejoiced at the vengeance meted

---

[584] The expression is by Jean Daniel (Bensaïd), read in *Psychoanalysis of Judaism*.

out on the renegade". Giuseppe was burned at the stake. "In the house of Manasseh, Joseph's father, there was great rejoicing. Musicians had been hired to celebrate the death of the renegade, as tradition demanded". Where his remains had been buried, there was a pile of stones. "They had been thrown by pious Jewish hands, symbolising, according to the Old Testament, that the renegade should have been stoned to death".

Giuseppe had not managed to free himself completely from the clutches of Judaism. Naturally, Israel Zangwill took pleasure in telling this story to his Jewish audience, in order to make them understand that it is impossible to get out of the Jewish prison.

This was also the aim, for example, of Henri Bean's film *The Believer* (USA, 2001)[585]. In New York, Danny Balint is a young skinhead, ultra-violent and furiously anti-Semitic. He wants nothing to do with his family, with these "people", with this inept religion. He is a determined neo-Nazi who proudly wears his swastika T-shirt. Until, of course, the day his identity conflict resurfaces and drives him inexorably to suicide. It is a must-see film that evokes what is commonly referred to as "self-hatred", which in reality is nothing more than a salutary awareness of the fundamentally hostile nature of Judaism towards the rest of humanity[586]. Given that the director himself belongs to this community, it is not surprising that Danny's attempt to free himself from the tyranny of Judaism is doomed to failure. It is important to understand that the film is primarily addressed to Jews themselves, to warn them against such temptations. The message of the film can be summarised as follows: "It is useless to try to leave Judaism, you will not succeed".

Frank Capra's *The New Generation* (USA, 1929) had the same objective: in the Jewish quarter of New York, an ambitious young Jewish man, who has made it as an antique dealer, disowns his parents and his name. But in the end he is reconciled with his family. The script was by S. Levien: you can't get out of Judaism.

The novelist Isaac Bashevis Singer published a short story that perfectly illustrates the point: *The Feather Crown*. It is the dramatic story of a Jewish woman from a Polish shtétlj who has left Judaism and married a Christian, but inevitably returns to her original community to die.

Jewish intellectuals, who complain incessantly about the racism to which their fellow Jews have fallen victim since the dawn of time, also regularly maintain the myth of an unchanging Jewishness, which can never dissolve into the nations. According to them, a Jew who had forgotten his Jewishness would inevitably see it resurrected sooner or later, even several

---

[585] Read in *Psychoanalysis of Judaism*.
[586] Read the chapter on "self-hatred" in *Psychoanalysis of Judaism*.

generations later. This is what we might call "the myth of the incubating Jew".

In *Psychoanalysis of Judaism* we saw an example of this Jewish obsession in a story by Pierre Paraf entitled *The General von Morderburg*: the son of this Prussian general, married to a daughter from Israel, who had also become an officer, had no idea of his Jewish roots. However, he was different from the others and was mysteriously attracted to the Jews. And what was meant to happen happened: he rediscovered his Jewishness. The novelist also develops a theme dear to the hearts of Jewish intellectuals: revenge against the Goyim.

Here is another example from André Spire's book *Quelques juifs et demi-juifs*, published in 1928. Here again, the story tends to establish the idea that, in a Jew, Jewishness can never be definitively forgotten; that it may remain unconsciously buried for a long time, but that it will in any case reappear in broad daylight, even several generations apart. André Spire summarised the novel *L'Imagerie du Cordier*[587] by a Provençal Jew named Armand Lunel:

Isaac, whose parents had fled from a Rhenish Jewry at the end of the 18th century, was taken in by the nuns of Carpentras. Thanks to the zeal of a preacher named Nicolo, he was baptised and educated in Catholicism. His name was now Lucas-Mateo Peccavi. He later married Nicolo's niece and became an honest merchant in Carpentras. His only flaw was that he was an anti-Semite. In 1815, at the time of the Restoration, he openly expressed his views against the Jews of the city, and throughout the 19th century, the Peccavi sons and daughters were good Catholics, grew up in the favourable shadow of the bishopric and were married by their bishop. Two generations later, at the dawn of the Dreyfus affair, Lucas-Mateo Peccavi's grandson, Augustine, as furiously anti-Semitic as his grandfather, naturally became the leader of the anti-Dreyfusards. But here, Armand Lunel's imagination changed the course of events. Suddenly the story of the Peccavi family was unravelled, and everywhere it was whispered that Augustine the anti-Semite was in reality nothing more than a dirty Jew. For Augustine Nicolo-Peccavi, the situation was obviously dramatic, for, one might say, he had discovered that he was Jewish-positive! It was a terrible catastrophe. His customers went elsewhere for supplies and his business declined rapidly.

The incubation period was over: "Defeated by his repressed Jewish soul... Nicolo Peccavi, deceived, ruined, wounded, was abandoned by his compatriots, Christians and Jews alike". "Like his great-grandfather, Mémucan, the merchant of Saracen amulets ended up in an itinerant trade,

---

[587] *Nouvelle Revue Française*, 1926.

despised and unstable, city commissionaire, porter at the Carpentras station[588]".

In his book, André Spire also presented the example of Otokar Fischer, "a Czech national poet and a Jew". He was born in 1883 in Kolin (Bohemia) to Jewish parents "completely detached from Judaism". "His parents protected him from all Jewish contact" and he later married a Christian woman "of pure Slavic race". But one does not get rid of the "virus" so easily: "he thought he could be a national Slavic writer," wrote André Spire. And here, too, his origins were to emerge.

Otokar Fischer published several collections of poems between 1911 and 1921, until one day some Jewish poems fell into his hands. It was a revelation to him and, "like Henri Heine, he felt himself a Jew again, a Jewish poet". In 1923 he published another collection of poems, entitled *Les Voix (The Voices),* which, as André Spire wrote, revealed "those dark movements which we can repress for a time from the field of our consciousness, but which watch relentlessly in the deepest part of us, in our very marrow".

He was no longer just a Czech poet: "He was a Jewish poet who added a Czech voice to the many accents of this modern Jewish poetry which, from San Francisco to the Urals and the Caucasus, from Lebanon to the banks of the Jordan, sounded on three continents, in the languages and literatures of twenty countries". Otokar Fisher had thus become a champion of the unification of the world, of the intermingling of peoples, of the disappearance of nations and of "Peace" on Earth, so that Israel would triumph in the end.

Thus, Jewish intellectuals and rabbis do their utmost to make Jews understand that it is completely useless and illusory to want to leave the community, and that sooner or later they will be swept away by the magnetic and almost supernatural force of Judaism, of "this Jewish soul, as André Spire wrote, which it is impossible for us to renounce, even if we had the baseness to wish to do so, to renounce[589]".

The legend of Moses also serves to maintain the myth. Moses, a baby, was abandoned in a basket, floating on the waters of the Nile. He was rescued by the Pharaoh's daughter Baita, who discovered the child, took him in and brought him up in the palace. As an adult, "he began to dazzle the king and his courtiers[590]", wrote Elie Wiesel. Later, he too would return to the community to which he belonged.

These stories were written precisely to encourage Jews to stay in the fold, because since their release from the ghettos, Jewish intellectuals have had

---

[588] André Spire, *Quelques Juifs et demi-Juifs*, Grasset, 1928, p. 27-32.
[589] André Spire, *Quelques Juifs et demi-Juifs*, Grasset, 1928, p. 37-41.
[590] Elie Wiesel, *Célébrations biblique*, Éditions du Seuil, 1975, p. 142.

no choice but to note that hundreds of thousands of their fellow citizens have chosen to leave the Jewish prison and forget Judaism for good.

In these conditions, anti-Semitism is very useful, almost indispensable, as it helps to close ranks and bring the community together. François Fetjo put it this way: "Have we not lived apart from all nations to the point of attracting universal hatred? It is the hatred of the nations that has ensured the preservation of the Jews. It is persecution that has kept them, segregation that has hardened the heart against the blows of fate[591] ".

It is also a question of drawing into the fold of Judaism any individual who happens to discover a drop of Jewish blood in his veins. Augustin Peccavi, for example, was no longer a Jew at all, since he was an anti-Semite, and it is strictly impossible to be both at the same time, unless, of course, one is an infiltrated Jew, which raises the problem of *Marranism*. Only the novelist's imagination had brought him back to Judaism, for there is no known example in history of an anti-Semite suddenly worshipping the chosen people after discovering a distant Jewish ancestor. In reality, the result of such a discovery in one's family tree would above all predispose one to a radicalisation of anti-Semitic sentiments. Hitler, for example, said of Reinhard Heydrich, a high Nazi dignitary: "I trust him, because I know that he wants to kill the Jewish blood in him". And if Heydrich had been a Jew, as they say, we would know it.

The suicidal Jew

It is not surprising then, with such jailers, that some Jews have preferred to take refuge in suicide rather than remain prisoners of this sect of delusional lunatics, whose aims of "universal and final peace" poorly conceal a project of subjugation of humanity. As far as we know, there are no statistics on this question, but the examples we have found in the literature suggest that the Jewish community is by far the most suicidal community in the world.

In our previous books we have already mentioned the cases of some well-known literary figures: the famous Stefan Zweig took his own life in Brazil in 1942, and the Nazis had nothing to do with it. The same was true of the philosopher Walter Benjamin, who committed suicide in 1940 in Port-Bou after crossing the Spanish border. Also during the war, the revolutionary Ernst Toller, who had played an important role in the communist revolution in Bavaria in 1918, committed suicide. He hanged himself in New York. Also worth mentioning are the German playwrights Kurt Tucholsky, who committed suicide in 1934 after taking sleeping pills, and Ludwig Fulda,

---

[591]François Fetjö, *Dieu et son juif*, Éditions Pierre Horay, 1997, p. 65.

who committed suicide in 1939. The "Austrian" novelist Ernst Weiss committed suicide in 1940 by slashing his wrists in the bathtub. In the same year, the composer Gustave Brecher took his own life in Belgium by throwing himself into the sea.

Jewish intellectuals have a habit of blaming the Nazis as a scapegoat. If Jews commit suicide, it is their fault and their fault alone[592]. In reality, Jews did not wait for the Nazis to commit suicide.

The phenomenon already existed before the war: the "Italian" philosopher Felice Momigliano committed suicide in 1924. The Viennese physicist and philosopher Ludwig Boltzmann hanged himself in 1906. The Austrian philosopher Otto Weininger shot himself in the heart in October 1903.

In 1928, as we have seen, the only daughter of the Austrian novelist Arthur Schnitzler committed suicide in Venice, shot by a revolver. She was nineteen years old. The eldest son of the Austrian poet Hugo von Hofmannsthal committed suicide at the age of twenty-six, also with a revolver. So did Karl Marx's two daughters. The daughter of the Chief Rabbi Weil threw herself from the Eiffel Tower. Albert Memmi also quoted "Israel Zangwill's hero Zangwill at Had Gadya, letting himself be carried away by the waters of the Thames", and "Ludwig Levisohn's Adam[593]".

In the early 20th century, Kafka evoked the strangeness and pathological despair of his Jewish classmates at the German school in Prague. "Many of them, he said, committed suicide during his student years[594]".

Let us also examine the work of Yossef Haim Brenner. Brenner was a novelist born in the Ukraine in 1881. With his first two novels, *In Winter* (1904) and, above all, *Around the Point* (1905), he made a name for himself. In 1905 he moved to London, where he contributed to the weekly *Jewish Chronicle*. In 1909 he settled permanently in Palestine, where he published numerous essays on Hebrew writers and translated Russian literature into Hebrew, in particular Dostoevsky's *Crime and Punishment*. In 1921 he was murdered by Arab rioters in Jaffa. This was what one could read about him on the Internet: "The autobiographical element is apparent in several of his novels. Like him, his heroes are uprooted people, unable to accept themselves and to escape a fate forged by the heavy heritage of the ghetto. The two heroes of *Around the Point* succumb to despair; one commits suicide, the other takes refuge in madness". And also: "*Mourning and Failure*, his last novel, is the long confession of a sick and tormented man who, having failed to fulfil himself through physical labour, slowly sinks into a joyless life".

---

[592] On suicides see also *Psychoanalysis of Judaism* and *Jewish Fanaticism*.
[593] Albert Memmi, *La Libération du Juif, Portrait d'un Juif II*, 1966, p. 230.
[594] Marthe Robert, *D'Oedipe à Moïse*, 1974, Agora, 1987, p. 18.

The novelist Romain Gary also committed suicide in 1980, as did the philosopher Albert Caraco in 1971[595]. The well-known "Italian" writer Primo Lévi also committed suicide in 1987, after a lifetime of bearing witness to his experiences in the "death camps". Jerzy Kosinski, another fabulist "witness", also committed suicide in 1991, taking barbiturates. Death camp historian Joseph Wulf took his own life in 1974.

In 1970, the painter Rothko ended his career in abstract painting by cutting his wrists. It was also in that year that the German-Jewish poet Paul Celan threw himself into the river Seine. The mother of the Israeli writer Amos Oz committed suicide in January 1952, aged 39. Jean Daniel, a prominent newspaper editor, recounted his childhood in Algeria and spoke of his cousin David, who committed suicide at the age of 20[596]. And, as we know, there was a real hecatomb in Elie Wiesel's entourage.[597]

Boris Fraenkel was one of the founders of the International Communist Organisation (ICO), one of the many Trotskyist sects. A German Jew, born in 1921 in Danzig, he arrived in France in 1938 and introduced the Freudian-Marxist literature of Herbert Marcuse and Wilhelm Reich, as well as the revolutionary works of Leon Trotsky. Boris Fraenkel was a man in the shadows. But he suddenly hit the headlines in 1995 when he revealed the Trotskyist past of former socialist Prime Minister Lionel Jospin. It was he who had introduced him to Trotskyism in the 1960s: "It was an extraordinary opportunity to penetrate the high civil service," he told *Le Nouvel Observateur*. Fraenkel remained in the shadows until the end of his life. He committed suicide on Sunday 23 April 2006 by throwing himself into the Seine.

Mourir à trente ans (France, 1982) is a film by Romain Goupil that follows the life of Michel Recanati, a Trotskyist leader in May 1968 who committed suicide in 1978. On 18 November 2008, the French daily *Libération* published the testimony of a former Maoist, also Jewish, who claimed that there had been many suicides of militants in his group in the 1970s: about fifteen out of a total of thirty-five.

Bruno Bettelheim had also committed suicide. The world-famous child psychiatrist had run the orthogenetic school in Chicago for some thirty years. He had worked in particular on infantile autism and always remembered that 80% of his inmates left the orthogenetic school cured. He claimed to have treated hundreds of schizophrenics. However, as Jacques Bénesteau wrote in his 2002 book *Mensonges freudiens* (*Freudian Lies*), "only a minority of the 220 patients in this institution were schizophrenic".

---

[595] On the philosopher-prophet Albert Caraco read *Jewish Fanaticism*.
[596] Jean Daniel, *Le Refuge et la source*, Grasset, 1977, Folio, 1979, p. 108.
[597] Read in *Planetary Hopes*.

Nevertheless, the small international media community had turned him into a star who aroused the admiration of the crowds.

In the medical world, however, he was best known for his brutality. He was a "real bastard", said psychoanalyst Kenneth Colby in the *Washington Post* of 26 August 1990. "One of the worst people psychoanalysis has ever produced". In *Newsweek*, on 10 September 1990, Darnton called him "Beno Brutalheim". His famous book, *The Uses of Enchantment*, published in 1976, was a blatant and indisputable plagiarism of a book by Julius Heuscher. In *Freudian Lies*, Jacques Bénestau wrote: "He was a tyrant, but also, as biographical research by Paul Roazen in 1992 and Richard Pollak in 1997 would reveal, a mythomaniac and a mystifier". He played the role of Jewish resistance fighter and took the liberty of lecturing his allegedly passive comrades during the war, accusing them of having been accomplices of their executioners. "He would have been captured during an escape attempt, in a plane with its engines running, and tortured for three days," wrote Jacques Bénesteau. In reality, "he had not left Austrian territory, and was more occupied with obtaining a diploma essential for an academic career he had been thinking about since 1926".

In addition to his fabrications about the conditions of his imprisonment, he claimed to have been a student at the University of Vienna for fourteen years: "He only exaggerated ten years to cover the period during which, without interruption, he actually replaced his father, who died in 1926, in a timber trading business. He claimed to be a doctor in philosophy, art history and psychology, with *summa cum laude* honours, but in May 1937 he only obtained a diploma in landscape aesthetics (supposedly inspired by Freudianism) without any distinction[598] ". Bruno Bettelheim committed suicide in March 1990 by suffocating himself in a plastic bag...

On 15 November 2007, the French daily *Libération* devoted an article to a certain Olivia Rosenthal, on the occasion of the publication of her latest book, *On n'est pas là pour disparaître*. Winner of the 10th Wepler-Fondation la Poste prize, Olivia Rosenthal, 42, declared: "The protagonists of my books are often people who have an altered contact with reality.... In *Mes Petites Communautés*, in 1999, I evoked the relationship between two sisters. Here, it was above all about my sister's suicide... I wonder what my life would have been like if my sister hadn't thrown herself out of the window". In fact, we would have liked to know why Olivia Rosenthal's sister committed suicide - a story of incest, perhaps?

In any case, all these suicides are precisely the proof of their humanity. But in the interests of humanity, it would be preferable for Jews to testify

---

[598] Jacques Bénesteau, *Mensonges freudiens*, Éditions Mardaga, Bruxelles, 2002, p. 328-334.

rather than take refuge in death. For Françoise Minkowska, psychoanalysis retained its therapeutic efficacy. Psychoanalysis, she explained, remains one of the most effective theories "for uncovering childhood traumas". The psychoanalyst only has to "test himself against the reality of incest".

If they want to heal themselves, and humanity, Jews must begin to speak openly about the dark secret of Judaism, to begin at last "a cure through words".

Forgetting Judaism

Despite their financial might, despite all the honours, some financiers also ended up committing suicide, as if driven by a fatal destiny. In 1996, 41-year-old Amschel Rothschild hanged himself in his Paris hotel room. His grandfather, Charles, had already cut his own throat with a razor. In 2000, a descendant of the family, Raphael, was found dead after a party in New York.

The historian François Fetjö acknowledged that some Jews could be driven by an insatiable thirst for gold: "You were the first to practice this hunt for profit, for the power of money, the first to recognise it as a dynamic principle of progress and transformation". And he continued, confirming the words of Irène Némirovsky: "We have exchanged the Song of Songs for the cries of the Stock Exchange. We are now capitalists... We buy castles. We are powerful. We enter the government and the Jockey Club. We have horses and mistresses...And yet.... Rich, powerful, now hunters instead of hunted, often exploiters instead of exploited, friends of the king instead of his enemies, we are not happy. A restlessness gnaws at our insides. A secret shame, a remorse. As if simple happiness were not within our reach... Our power is respected. So why this uneasiness, this feeling of dissatisfaction... Where does this feeling of powerlessness that torments us come from?" François Fetjö wondered: "Are we innocent, do we not have a clear conscience? Unfortunately, no, our conscience is not clear. We have a guilty conscience. But whose fault is it? Who disturbs our peace, who quarrels with us? Whose fault is it that, in full creative fever, in full growth, in the very heart of happiness, we suddenly feel alienated again, split in ourselves, alien to ourselves?[599] "

So he admitted that he felt powerless to answer this question. For him, as for other Jewish intellectuals, Judaism remained a mystery: "We find ourselves locked in a vicious circle, he wrote... Defeated and sick, we fear

---

[599] François Fetjö, *Dieu et son juif*, Éditions Pierre Horay, 1997, p. 104, 72, 73, 75

the laughter of others.... The Jew is enclosed; as in a citadel, as in a sanctuary, in his fidelity to the Law, to the texts of the Law[600]."

In his *Portrait of a Jew*, Albert Memmi, a Tunisian Jew and non-believer, also allowed himself some confidences: "The Jewish condition, I lived it first of all as a condition of misfortune.... Are there no happy Jews? Aie, I am tempted to answer: no!.... In reality, I don't know many Jews who are happy to be Jews. Jews who are happy in spite of being Jews, perhaps". And he continued: "Anxiety is a mark of Jewish nature.... Very few of us knew, for example, how to sit quietly in the sun, stretched out on the grass or dreaming in an armchair, as I saw non-Jews do with envy. We couldn't sit still. Every weekend we would get into a car and drive a hundred kilometres or so; we would have a bad lunch somewhere and then, with just enough time to smoke a cigarette, we would set off again on the pretext of having a coffee thirty kilometres away, or seeing some famous site that we would absentmindedly glance at, only to realise that it was getting dark and that it was time to go home, that is, to get back into the car and start again....the truth is that we were only at ease on the move.... I found the same restlessness, perhaps aggravated, among the Jews of Europe[601]."

In volume II, published in 1966 and entitled *The Liberation of the Jew*, Albert Memmi wrote: "The Jew does not live, he survives. He is not a normal being, but a historical ghost". And he observed "an undeniable correlation between neurosis and Judaism. "Is it a mental illness to be a Jew?" was the almost serious headline of a leading Jewish magazine a few years ago. Fortunately, not all Jews are psychologically fragile...But it is too much: the number of psychological disorders, certainly neuroses rather than psychoses, is certainly much higher among Jews than among non-Jews. Even taking into account the fact that they are more likely to seek treatment, i.e. that they declare themselves ill to a greater extent. A psychiatrist who had practised for twenty years in Tunisia summed up his experience to me as follows: "The specific illness of Jews is anxiety and, correlatively, depression". And I would not have needed much research to agree with him. I certainly did not have many examples of calm and serenity in my environment[602]."

The famous Jewish psychiatrist Bruno Bettelheim had spent his whole life trying, in vain, to understand this phenomenon: "I have devoted most of my life to studying why certain people accept to sink into mental illness instead of fighting for the freedom of their spirit. I have also been very

---

[600] François Fetjö, *Dieu et son juif*, Éditions Pierre Horay, 1997, p. 102, 93, 47.
[601] Albert Memmi, *Portrait d'un juif*, Gallimard, 1962, p. 30, 38, 39.
[602] Albert Memmi, *La Libération du Juif, Portrait d'un Juif II*, Gallimard, 1966, p. 25, 230.

concerned with the problem posed by those millions of Jews who did not cower in the face of death, but refrained from fighting for their lives[603]."

Elie Wiesel had also written: "I belong to a traumatised generation that has experienced loneliness and abandonment[604]."

But the trauma of the Jews, as we all know, does not date back to the Second World War. Jews had already been traumatised for a long time. In fact, the 1904 edition of the *Jewish Encyclopaedia*, published long before the Second World War, stated:

"Acute psychoses in infants are more frequent among Jews than among non-Jews[605]." And also this: "Jews are more prone to diseases of the nervous system than non-Jews. Hysteria and neurasthenia are also more frequent[606]."

In an article on the expulsion of the Jews from Spain in 1492, published in *Le Monde* on 2 August 2007, Henri Tincq characteristically pointed out that Spaniards were traumatised by the event. And not without reason he underlined the "paradox", a term much used by Jewish intellectuals: "A wave of anti-Semitism without Jews will sweep over Spain, incapable of chasing away its ghosts. An unprecedented paradox, wrote Henri Tincq: the more Spain parks, hunts and burns its Jews at the stake, the more it corrodes itself with the obsession of knowing who are the real or false Jews, the true or false converts. Behind every face, in the church or in the street, the doubt insinuates itself: is this person who claims to be a Christian really one, is he not a "crypto-Jew" who secretly keeps the Sabbath on Saturdays, cooks according to the rules of *kashrut*, celebrates the Jewish festivals and performs the funeral cleansing according to Jewish ritual? A trauma was born that would plague Spanish society for three centuries... Purity of blood became a subject of terror both for the convert who sincerely lived his Catholicism and for the façade Catholic who remained faithful to the Law of Moses. They were subject to the same regime of suspicion, to the same threat of the Inquisition. Every convert was a Jew and therefore a potential enemy of the Catholic faith. It was the beginning of a neurosis: Jewish and heretical contamination came through blood, milk and seed".

Evidently, Henri Tincq reversed the situation and very classically projected his unease onto others, for it was in fact the Jews who were literally traumatised by the energetic Spanish reaction and their expulsion from Spain.

Here is what Esther Benbassa wrote in 2007, for example, in her work entitled *Suffering as Identity*: "The banishment of the Jews of Spain, Sicily

---

[603] Bruno Bettelheim, *Le Poids d'une vie*, 1989, Robert Laffont, 1991, p. 325.
[604] Elie Wiesel, *Discours d'Oslo*, Grasset, 1987, p. 14.
[605] *Jewsih Encyclopedia*, Vol. VI, 1904, p. 556, 603-604
[606] *Jewsih Encyclopedia*, Vol. IX, 1905, p. 225.

and Sardinia, the forced conversion of all the Jews of Portugal, the expulsion from Navarre, Provence and the Kingdom of Naples, created an immense trauma subjectively comparable to that of the Holocaust". And again: "The expulsion from Spain was to remain for many an original trauma constitutive of the Jewish experience in the East[607]."

The expulsion from Spain raised questions among Jewish intellectuals, who could not understand why the "chosen people" were treated in this way:

"The psychic and spiritual shock of the expulsion and its cohort of pains, which affected the Sephardim for several generations, were, if not the only factor, at least one of the many that contributed to nurture, throughout the 16th and 17th centuries, a powerful mystical and messianic current of diverse origins[608]."

Indeed, "psychic shock" had set brains on fire, and the Sephardic diaspora had seen the birth in its midst of several self-proclaimed messiahs, such as David Reuveni and Salomon Molcho in the 16th century, and above all the famous Sabbatai Zevi, who was at the origin of a formidable messianic movement.[609]

However, Jewish neurosis had other sources besides this trauma. Rudolph Loewenstein was aware of certain problems that undermined the Jewish sect and observed "major psychological disorders" in many Jews. One chapter of his book is in fact entitled *Psychoanalysis of the Jews*. To understand the trauma of the Jews, Rudolph Loewenstein explained, one had to go further back in history:

"It is true that the most serious traumatic event for them was the destruction of the Second Temple and the destruction of Jerusalem in 70.... The loss of Jerusalem and Palestine was to the Jews what the loss of a beloved parent or a happy home is to the individual. The result for the Jews was a permanent state of mourning[610]."

In the Middle Ages, the Jews suffered a second great trauma: first the persecutions of the first Crusade, then life in the ghettos, which obviously did them no favours: "From the 14th to the 18th century, this internalisation even intensified to the point that, for many of them, it had pathological

---

[607] Esther Benbassa, *La Souffrance comme identité*, Fayard, 2007, p. 82, 89.
[608] Esther Benbassa, *La Souffrance comme identité*, Fayard, 2007, p. 91.
[609] On the Sabbatees, the Donmehs, the Frankists, and the Messianic Kabbalah, see *Psychoanalysis of Judaism*.
[610] Rudolph Loewenstein, *Psychanalyse de l'antisémitisme*, 1952, Presses Universitaires de France, 2001, p. 211-213. See also in *Psychoanalysis of Judaism*. Let us recall here the medical diagnosis of hysterical pathology: "Freud's patients were often in a state of real mourning and/or permanent amorous disappointment" (in Psychoanalysis of Judaism). (in *Psychoanalysis of Judaism*).

consequences. Intellectual isolation led to a predisposition to neurosis and neurotic character disorders".

In fact, Jews see their history as a succession of traumas: "If the great trauma suffered by the Jewish people as a result of the loss of Palestine was not enough to create all those traits that are considered typical of Jews, the accumulation of traumas due, over the centuries, to the persecutions of the Middle Ages and the regime of internment in the ghettos, left a much deeper imprint on their psyche[611]."

For Rudolph Loewenstein, this was the origin of Jewish neurosis: "If there are a relatively large number of neurotics among Jews, it is due precisely to this process. For him, it was merely a consequence of the aggressiveness of others against the Jews, who were always persecuted for no reason: "In their struggle for survival, he added, the Jews acquired certain neurotic characteristics which gave the persecutors some more pretexts[612]".

François Fetjö showed a little more frankness, furtively evoking "our "Oedipus complex". But he did not dwell on it too much, as if suffering from vertigo in the face of emptiness. Twenty pages further on, he again approached the precipice and preferred to turn to God: "It is not by chance that a Jew is at the origin of psychoanalysis," he wrote. This dark, carnal drama that unfolds between father and son - this drama woven of love, rivalry, aggression and sin - the Jew is particularly sensitive to it, for he has a very strange family relationship with God. He who has always suffered from an Oedipus complex with regard to God".

Thus, it was better to limit oneself to the general assessment of the benefits of psychoanalysis: "By helping us to understand this situation, to unravel our growth crises, to tame our inner monsters, psychoanalysis can free us from much of our anguish, give us back a little of our original innocence, our freedom[613]."

Freud had understood that the origins of Judaism were of a sexual nature before fleeing in haste from the precipice to which he had come too close. A minor author like Michel Herszlikowicz is, as far as we know, one of the very few Jewish intellectuals who have dared to approach and look into the abyss. In his *Philosophy of Anti-Semitism*, he wrote, also furtively, as if frightened by such a bold step: "Psychoanalysis overcomes anti-Semitism when it looks for a non-Jewish origin to the Jewish people[614]."

---

[611] Rudolph Loewenstein, *Psychanalyse de l'antisémitisme*, 1952, Presses Universitaires de France, 2001, p. 220, 221.
[612] Rudolph Loewenstein, *Psychanalyse de l'antisémitisme*, 1952, Presses Universitaires de France, 2001, p. 226, 235.
[613] François Fetjö, *Dieu et son juif*, Éditions Pierre Horay, 1997, p. 91, 109, 113.
[614] Michel Herszlikowicz, *Philosophie de l'antisémitisme*, PUF, 1985, p. 154.

But in reality, psychoanalysis is more akin to *Judeotherapy*[615]. The whole thing, let us repeat it once more, can be summed up in these ten words:
Judaism is that disease that psychoanalysis claimed to cure.
François Fetjö, as a good Jew, nevertheless had unshakable confidence in the future. Soon, he was sure, the Messiah would come and free the Jews from the evil that gnawed at their insides: "The most anguished, the most tormented of all peoples, we are also the most optimistic, the most certain of the final healing[616]."

Albert Memmi was also confident that the Messiah would bring healing to the Jews: 'One day, he will bring peace to this troubled people...'. As far as I can remember, he wrote, I always find the Messiah, the *Mashiach*, half character, half event, familiar and mysterious, faceless, but capable of extraordinary words and deeds: When will the *Mashiach* come? He (literally the saviour, the Lord's anointed), will shower us with blessings, revive the dead, take vengeance on our enemies, return us to Jerusalem.... [and it will be] the end of the yoke of the nations that weighed upon our lives."

Albert Memmi therefore refused to see the real causes of the Jews' misfortune and blamed the eternal scapegoat of "anti-Semitism": "To this intolerable condition, to the obstinacy of a monstrous persecution, the Jew can only relentlessly oppose a past of glory and a future of triumph, which reassure him and intimidate his aggressors. Against the persistence of an incomprehensible accusation, he can only tirelessly repeat his defence, to the point of delirium, to the point of the crispness of body and mind." Such was the "tormented fate of this people[617]."

The Jews are the "chosen people of God": this is the only possible explanation for the uniqueness of Judaism. Everything else must be expelled from the consciousness of the Jew, "repressed", to use psychoanalytic terminology.

In *The Gates of the Law*, published in 1982, Chief Rabbi Ernest Gugenheim recalled the founding events of Jewish mythology. In the wilderness of Sinai, God made a covenant with Israel and Moses received the tablets of the Law. "There, in the solitude of the desert, in the deep silence that fills the wilderness, God and Israel celebrate their mystical marriage. I will make you my wife forever..." (Hosea, II, 19). (Hosea, II, 19-20). And Gugenheim added: "The angels themselves remain motionless and silent at the moment when God unites with Israel. Then he gives to his

---

[615] The word belongs to Pierre Guillaume (1940-2023), an ultra-left militant and revisionist.
[616] François Fetjö, *Dieu et son juif*, Éditions Pierre Horay, 1997, p. 92.
[617] Albert Memmi, *La Libération du Juif, Portrait d'un Juif II*, Gallimard, 1966, p. 133, 130, 136.

young bride the act that consecrates their union, the divine Torah, so that she may keep it preciously, as the apple of his eye, and never be unfaithful to him..... From then on, the community of Israel is indivisibly united to God[618]."

The Jewish community, we must understand, is a woman: the bride of God.

We find this image again in François Fetjö, who began by lamenting the misfortunes of Israel: "That we are slandered, that we are despoiled, that we are persecuted, that our children are snatched from our arms to be massacred, that we are the most persecuted of all men and the most humiliated, it is not He who is responsible for this, but the goyim, the gentiles, those who do not know God, those who do not know what the love of God is. And so, unperturbed, through centuries of shame and misfortune, the Jew has stood firm, [the Jew] has not broken the contract. He stood like a wife abandoned by her husband[619]."

André Neher gave us the following explanations: "The Bible compares the Covenant concluded between God and Israel to a marriage, which allows Moses, the prophets and the singers of the Canticle and the Psalms to describe the history of this Covenant as the history of Love that passes through the most diverse and moving phases: awakening, first meeting, courtship, union, birth of children, but also jealousy, quarrels, separation, divorce, widowhood and, finally, a passionate return and reconciliation. From this perspective, Israel is God's female partner".

The creation of the State of Israel in 1948 could thus be integrated into Jewish religious eschatology. This radical ambiguity, which we consider to be the main characteristic of Judaism, was echoed by André Neher when he wrote: "In another perspective, more in keeping with reality," he wrote, "Israel is the virile being. What then will be the female partner of this Israel-man? Precisely *Erets*, the Land, which is waiting to be loved and betrothed? This Land was not "conquered" by Israel, contrary to what national history with its war stories from the time of Moses and Joshua might suggest. Long "promised", it was "offered" by God to Israel. God entrusts this jewel, this pearl of great price, guarded by Him, and asks Israel to be the faithful companion of this peerless bride[620]."

Judaism is thus, in a sense, hermaphroditic. The Jew settled in Israel is the male Jew, guardian and husband of the Promised Land, while the Jewish community of the Diaspora is a woman who is to beget the Messiah: it is the "birthing of the Messiah", Jewish intellectuals invariably write when they speak of the coming of the Messiah.

---

[618] Ernest Gugenheim, *Les Portes de la Loi*, Albin Michel, 1982, p. 41.
[619] François Fetjö, *Dieu et son juif*, Éditions Pierre Horay, 1997, p. 47.
[620] André Neher, *L'Identité juive*, 1977, Petite Bibliothèque Payot, 2007, p. 123.

Let us recall here what we have already seen in *Psychoanalysis of Judaism*: every misfortune that strikes the community, every cataclysm, is compared by rabbis and Jewish intellectuals to "the birth pangs" of the Messiah - the *Hevlei Mashiah*, in Hebrew.

Elie Wiesel, for example, had one of his characters, a Hasidic Jew from Poland, say at the time of the French Revolution: "Why not take the initiative and hasten liberation... The Jews need the Messiah more than ever? Since he is so near, why wait passively for him, why not go out to meet him? Undoubtedly, the times are ripe and the time is ripe. These wars, these convulsions are the *Hevlei Mashiah*, the torments and anxieties of messianic liberation. All the symptoms, all the signs are here[621]."

However, no Jewish intellectual has realised that this "mystery" of Judaism, like this ambiguity, is typically hysterical in nature. Jewish mission, fabulation, selective amnesia, egocentrism, exacerbated emotionality, megalomania, etc., reveal the same clinical picture. The "divine choice" is also a manifestation of the pathology studied by Dr. Freud. As for the "birth of the messiah", it corresponds to nothing other than the classic nervous pregnancy of the hysterical woman referred to by psychiatrists. "The" Jewish community is thus a hysterical woman who imagines she can give birth to a messiah. We can never thank the founder of psychoanalysis enough for having opened our eyes, knowing that we only had to read his books with a mirror.

Jews are hardly fascinated by the beauty of the world. Their penchant for permanent militancy, fuelled by messianic obsession, simply prevents them from seeing the world as it is. The fact is that, after three thousand years of history, their artistic output has remained insignificant and mediocre. Those who have tried in recent decades, transgressing the biblical proscriptions ("thou shalt not make idols"), have offered us nothing but deformities, which correspond to the very essence of their unbalanced nature. Their sculptures are all more twisted than one another; their paintings, atrociously deformed. That is why, evidently, they took refuge in abstract art.

The purpose of Jewish art is thus not to deliberately denature or defile European or "Aryan" art, but to reflect a spirit, a mental universe and an imaginary that is very much "the community's" own. This should be seen much less as a desire to "pervert" the beautiful than as the expression of its neurosis. Anti-Semitism stems from this misunderstanding of the depths of the Jewish soul, and feels as an aggression what can also be perceived as a call for help. Naturally, there is also an element of malice in the literary

---

[621] Elie Wiesel, *Célébration hassidique II*, 1981, p. 124, 125.

production of Judaism, which pursues its historical "mission" against all odds.

The question is whether the Jew can free himself from his evil and thus free humanity as well. The cover of Albert Memmi's book *The Liberation of the Jew* reads: "Albert Memmi dismisses all false solutions to the Jewish drama: name changes, intermarriage, assimilation, conversion to Christianity, secular universalism, socialist revolution, return to the Jewish religion and traditional values".

From the very first sentence of the book, Albert Memmi asked: "Is there a way out of the Jewish condition? Throughout his history, the Jew has almost always hoped for a solution to his problem, whether in assimilation or in the myth of 'next year in Jerusalem'". But he was pessimistic: "I hardly believe in the possibility of recovery from such a long illness[622]".

In 1898, the "English" novelist Israel Zangwill wrote in *Dreamers of the Ghetto*: "The chosen people, indeed! It was exhausted by the great effort of centuries, the long series of inbred unions, so many periods of persecution, so many adopted customs, languages and nationalities[623]."

It was at this time that Theodor Herzl and others began to encourage Jews to settle in Palestine. Evidently, the aim was not only to create a Jewish state there, but also to cure the Jewish neurosis by returning to the land and to healing manual labour. Marshal Philippe Pétain had already said: "The land, it does not lie". Very few intellectuals have understood and expressed the true motivations of Theodor Herzl and the founders of Zionism.

Albert Memmi clearly saw the return to the land as the best solution to the Jewish problem: "Since it is impossible for the Jew to live fully among the others, the Jew must be removed from the midst of the others (or, of course, merged with them, if assimilation had been possible).... The Jew must be made a people like the others, a nation like the others...Oppressed as a people, and living as a people, the Jew must be liberated as a people," he wrote. "This national liberation of the Jew is called the State of Israel...Only Israel will put an end to the negativity of the Jew and liberate his positivity[624]."

Unlike the rabbis, Albert Memmi accepted the idea that a Jew might want to leave Judaism: 'Assimilation must be a legitimate way out for any Jew who wishes to do so', he wrote. But it was the state of Israel that should liberate the community: "It is the existence of a Jewish nation that will finally allow the painless fading of Judaism. In fact, misfortune and myth

---

[622] Albert Memmi, *La Libération du Juif, Portrait d'un Juif II*, Gallimard, 1966, p. 12, 13.
[623] Israël Zangwill, *Rêveurs de ghetto*, Éditions Complexe, 2000, p. 287.
[624] Albert Memmi, *La Libération du Juif, Portrait d'un Juif II*, Gallimard, 1966, p. 243, 248, 243, 253.

stood in the way: with a Jewish nation, misfortune will cease and the myth of mission throughout the world will be dispelled...Only Israel, at last, will restore our dignity[625]."

The writer Arthur Koestler lived for several years in Palestine before committing himself body and soul to the USSR and international communism. The great Moscow trials and his own experience of the Spanish Civil War later led him to reject Marxism and emigrate to England during World War II. In 1941 he published *The Zero and the Infinite*, a book that had a great international impact and in which he denounced the excesses of the Soviet system. When *The Zero and the Infinite* was translated and published in Paris at the end of the war, French communists lashed out at him, slandering him and covering him with opprobrium and dung. The newspaper *L'Humanité-Dimanche* had published a map of Fontaine-le-Port, on the outskirts of Paris, marking the exact position of the house where Koestler lived and noting that "the General Staff of the Cold War met there," where "armed militias were trained."

In 1952, Koestler was still pinning all his hopes on the Zionist movement. In his autobiography, *Blue Arrow*, he wrote: "(...) I had become impatient, and really allergic, to all pretensions of belonging to a chosen race...The more I learned about Judaism the more discouraged I became; and the more fervently Zionist. The Jewish State was the only cure for that disease which I could neither name nor define; but which seemed to me intimately connected with the Jewish peculiarity of having no country and no flag[626]

---

[625] Albert Memmi, *La Libération du Juif*, Gallimard, 1966, p. 243-259.

[626] Arthur Koestler, *Arrow in the Blue (Autobiography)*, Vol. 1 (1952), Alianza Editorial, Madrid, 1973, p. 151. ["For centuries and centuries Jewish children had been educated in the Yeshiva, the Talmudic school, where their intellects were nourished by scholastic exercises based on commentaries on commentaries on commentaries on commentaries on the Bible...The Mosaic rite had degenerated into a complicated system of "interpretations" whose purpose was to overcome the original laws. For generations Jews were taught in Talmudic schools to interpret *yes* as *no*, and to understand white where it said black; until at last this technique became a conditioned mental reflex. To what extent this mental corruption in matters of religion was a consequence of the social pressure which forced the Jews to live outside the law, and to what extent the Talmudic mentality in turn worked upon the pattern of their social conduct, it is not easy to say. The result, in any case, was a vicious circle, a *perpetuum mobile* generating anti-Semitism, linking persecution and evasion in an alternating and monotonous rhythm...I had no idea of my revulsion at a form of worship that seemed to consist in mocking the Lord and one's own conscience. I knew the practices of the orthodox Jews during the feast of Pessach, when the Law requires one to eat unleavened bread and not to have crockery in one's house that has been in contact with leaven. "*In his house*", the sages declared, means "*in his possession*". Therefore, the thing to do on the eve is to go to the house of a non-Jewish neighbour and enter into a nominal contract with him; to sell him the crockery, on the assumption that he will buy it back from him, after Pessah, for the

". And he further added: "I am not sure that the Jews of Palestine are less neurotic than Jews anywhere else; but they are certainly less conscious of their neurosis, and if they are they do not care...This may be regarded as a gross generalisation, but the strikingly "non-Jewish" aspect and mentality of the native generation seems to allow it[627]."

His book *The Thirteenth Tribe*, published in 1976, attempted to prove that the Ashkenazi Jews of Central Europe were no more and no less than the descendants of the Khazars, a Turko-Mongolian tribe that converted to Judaism in the early Middle Ages. It was certainly not a thesis that was likely to receive a very favourable reception in the Jewish world. At the time, Koestler seemed to have succeeded in abandoning Judaism for good.

Undoubtedly, many Jews also wish to escape from the Jewish prison. This is no easy task, given the weight of heritage, atavism and the imaginary created by generations of novelists and rabbis who have consciously built the walls of their own prison. Jean Daniel, editor of a leading left-wing weekly in France, believed that Judaism should be able to be "effortlessly abandoned[628]". But he made a difficult condition to accept: "If anti-Semitism disappeared, he wrote, if it only became comparable to the generalised xenophobia that certain peoples, communities and groups intermittently arouse, I could freely choose whether or not to affirm my membership, or rather my adherence, to Judaism".

In short, considering that anti-Semitism reinforces Jewish identity, Jews should be given full freedom of action in the hope of a hypothetical assimilation.

Many Jews have not felt the need to make such requests and have simply abandoned Judaism without looking back. Despite the efforts of the rabbis, Judaism is, in fact, perfectly soluble in the nations. Of course, it is not easy to leave Judaism, and most Jews live with their ambivalence and torn identity for the rest of their lives. But it is possible, and it is much more common than one might think.

As Robert Munnich said in 1979, in a book of interviews with Jewish personalities: "If you want to live more comfortably, you can always escape,

---

same sum. It is not necessary to take the crockery to one's neighbour's house; it may remain where it is because as it is no longer one's possession, the Lord is considered satisfied...Similarly, lighting a fire on the Sabbath is a sin; but paying a non-Jewish servant to commit that sin is the accepted orthodox custom. A large part of Jewish ritual seemed to consist of such subterfuges, and to have degenerated into manoeuvres to circumvent the Law." Arthur Koestler, *Arrow in the Blue (Autobiography), Volume 1* (1952), Alianza Editorial, Madrid, 1973, p. 150-151. (NdT)]

[627] Arthur Koestler, *Flecha en el Azul (Autobiography), Vol. 1* (1952), Alianza Editorial, Madrid, 1973, p. 216-217.

[628] Jean Daniel, *La Blessure*, Grasset, 1992, p. 258-260.

stop being Jewish: change your surname, have an intermarriage and end up forgetting that you are Jewish[629]."

Nahum Goldmann also said: "If a Jew no longer wants to be a Jew, if he disavows Judaism, if he does not give his children a Jewish education or baptise them, then he can cease to be a Jew. That is why so many Jews have disappeared over the centuries; otherwise there would be hundreds of millions today[630]."

That is why, in spite of everything, we must love the Jews: to help them out of their isolation. It is not easy when you know them; but it is not easy to be a Jew either.

Let us recall here the wise words of the gentleman Roger Gougenot des Mousseaux, who wrote in 1869, at the time of the "emancipation" of the Jews in Europe: "Almost all these men are lost, but they are not evil. We even like some of them, and their nature is excellent; we only find their doctrines detestable. A pitiful environment, a vitiated education, a certain poverty of intelligence which makes them insensitive to the world have made them what they are [and what so many others would have become in their place]. Likewise, let us beware of despising or hating them; and, except for a very special reason, it is enough [to pity] them, even if all that remains is to fight them. This movement of fraternal compassion is [truly] the only one inspired by him whom we call a *Jew*; and we shall never tire of repeating it[631]."

Naturally, Gougenot des Mousseaux was referring only to individuals, and not to the "doctrine" of Judaism. At that time, some observers had already foreseen the catastrophes that would befall Europe and humanity in the following century. It would be the time of the great cataclysms, totalitarianisms and World Wars, before the advent of the atomic age. The death toll would no longer be counted in tens of thousands, but in tens of millions. Materialism would soon spread across the globe, drying up traditional cultures, dissolving nations, uprooting individuals and throwing them into huge and chaotic migratory flows. It was said that great pandemics would reappear on Earth during the age of ecological catastrophes. Humanity had never known such dangers. Jewish messianism, above all, would take the form of tireless planetary propaganda, pervading the entire media system. Soon - *"it was written"* - a great "Peace" would reign in the world, all conflicts would disappear and humanity would

---

[629] André Harris, Alain Sédouy, *Juifs et Français*, Grasset, 1979, Poche, p. 252, quoted in *Jewish Fanaticism*.

[630] Nahum Goldmann, *Le Paradoxe juif*, Stock, Paris, 1976, p. 81, 82.

[631] Roger Gougenot des Mousseaux, *The Jew, Judaism and the Judaisation of Christian peoples*. Pdf version. Translated into Spanish by Professor Noemí Coronel and the invaluable collaboration of the Catholic Nationalism team. Argentina, 2013. p. xxxviii

finally be unified, led by Wise Men who would be recognised by all as God's "chosen people".

The hysterical contagion is now spreading everywhere, on all fronts, in all nations, in all homes, threatening all cultures, all religions, all identities. Nothing seems to be able to stop this unifying, anti-racist, materialistic and ultimately destructive cosmopolitan frenzy. Messianism thus represents a serious threat to the whole of humanity. But if we look more closely, we realise that the universal, total, absolute and final "Peace" dreamt of by the prophets of Israel is above all the Peace that the Jews are unable to achieve within themselves. Using a mirror, we can read these hackneyed words: "Crime against Humanity". And it is again the mirror that allows us to straighten out and make sense of Jewish eschatology:

The Messiah will only come after the apostasy, after the disappearance of the last Jew. This is the existential tragedy of every Jew on this earth. Invested with the mission to save humanity, he has no choice but to work to destroy it or to destroy himself.

Paris, February 2009
Second edition, March 2019

Other titles

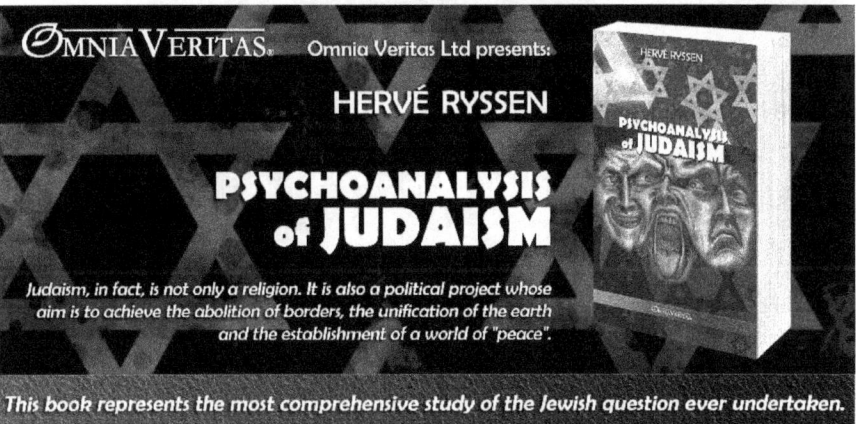

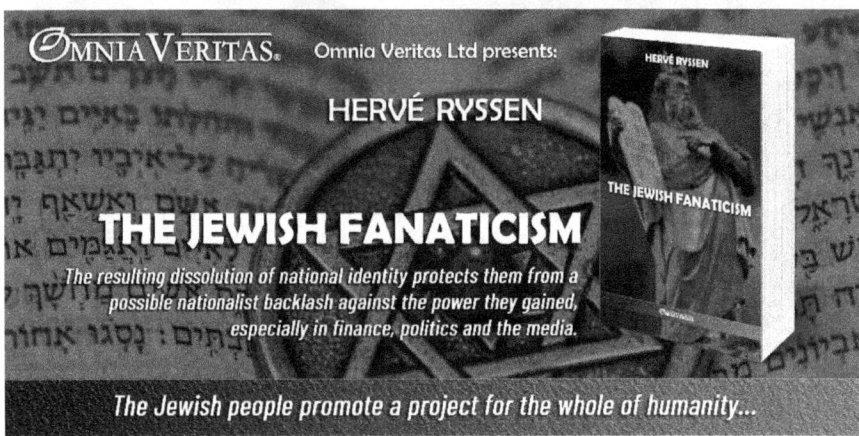

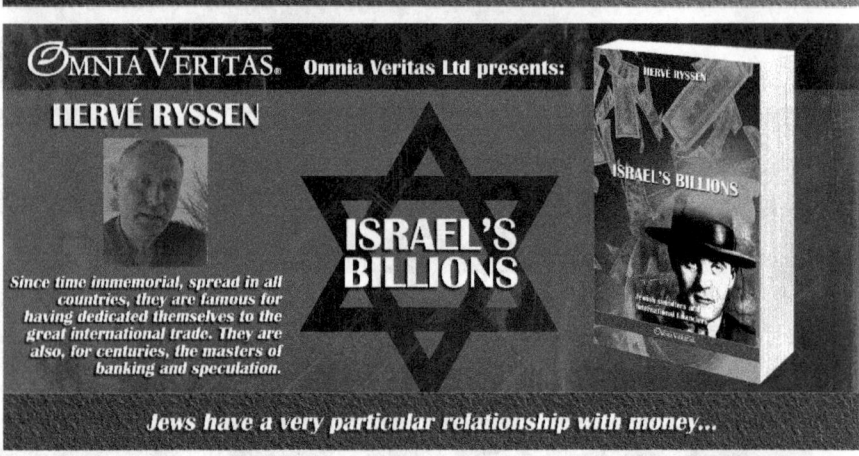

THE MIRROR OF JUDAISM

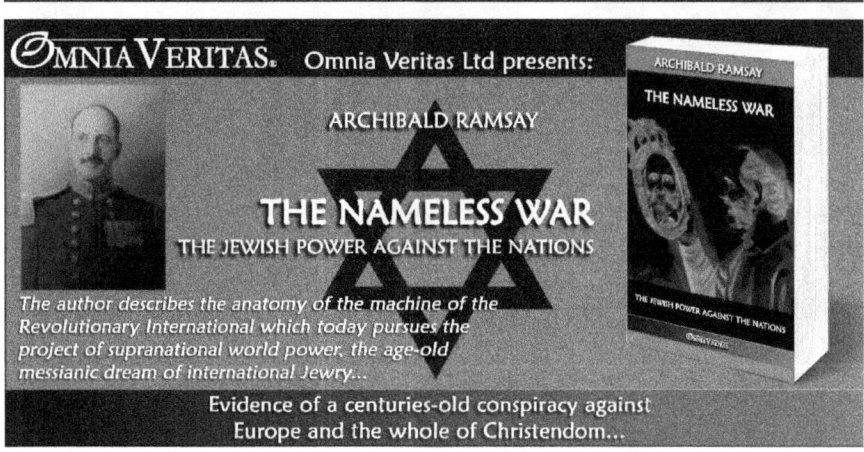

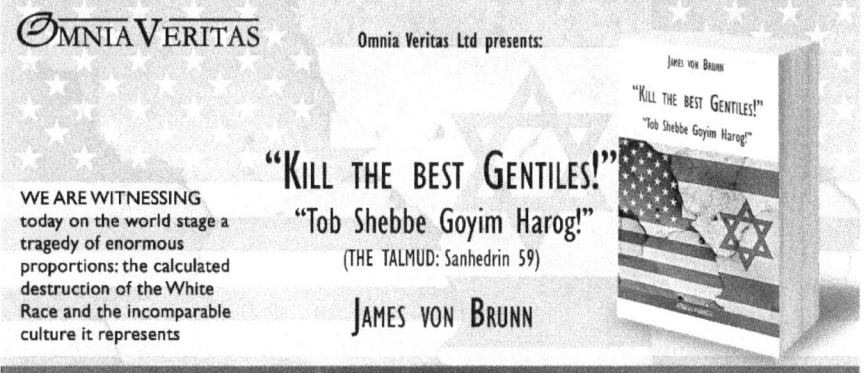

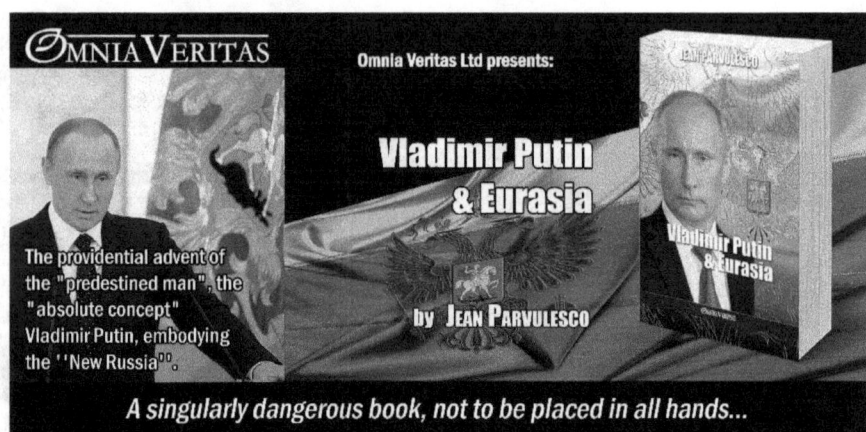

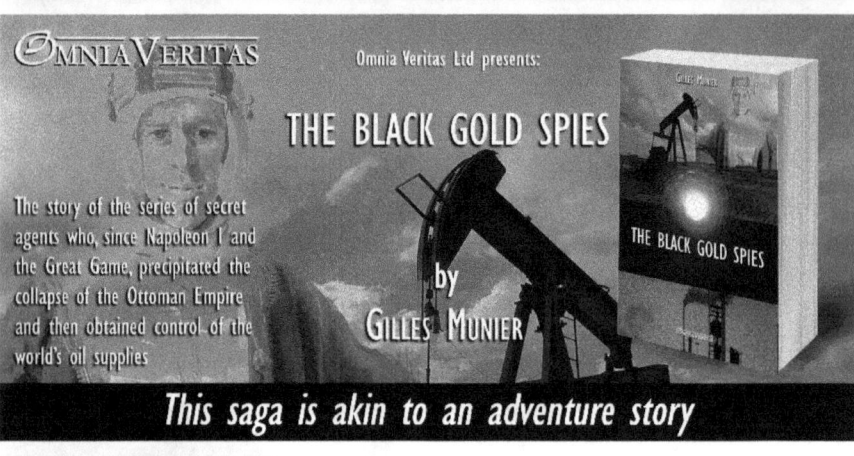

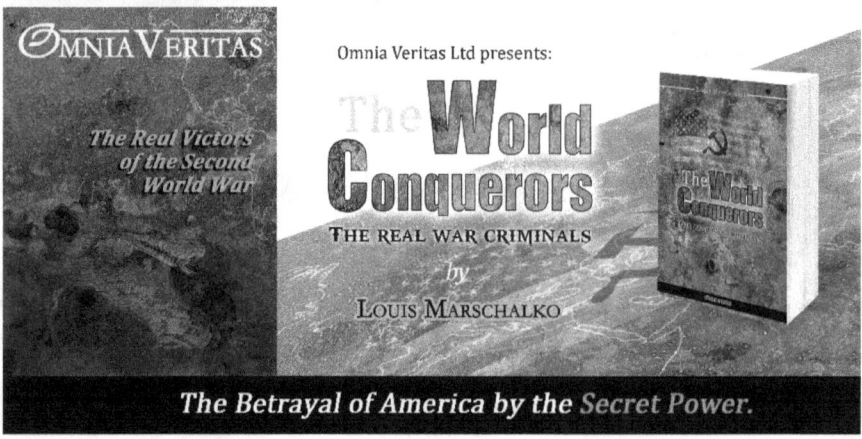

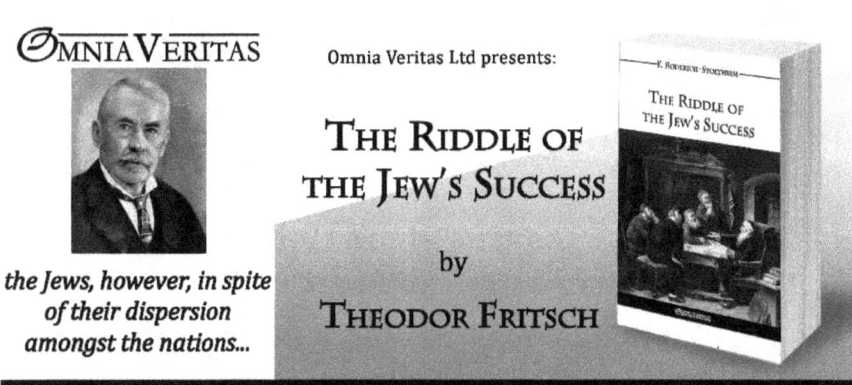

THE MIRROR OF JUDAISM

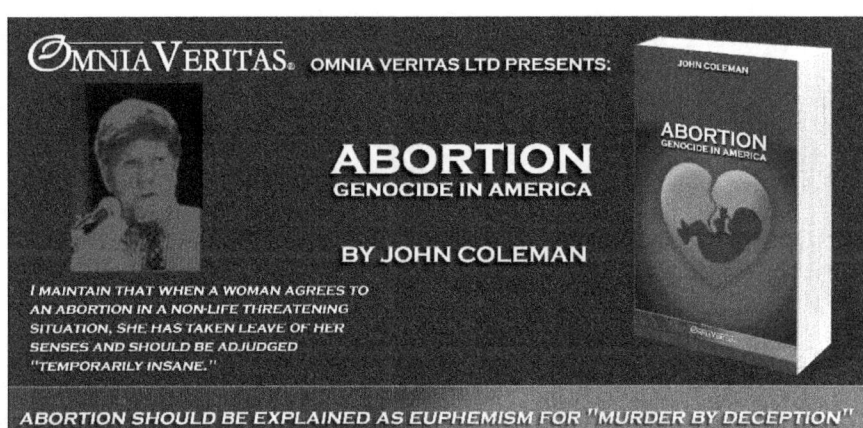

THE MIRROR OF JUDAISM

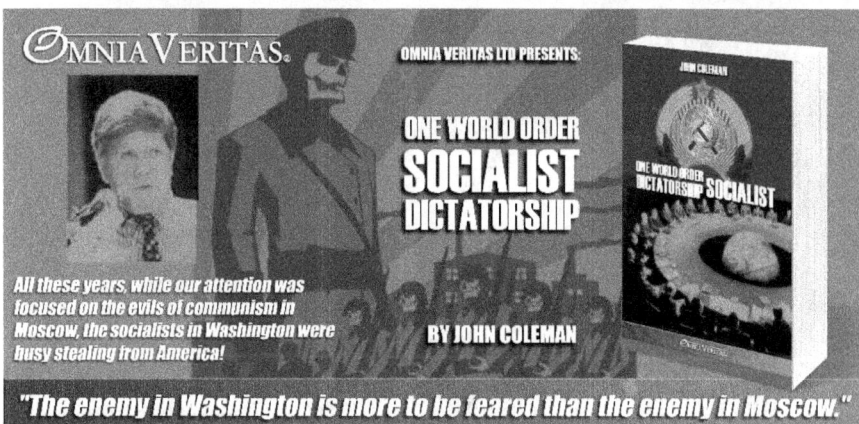

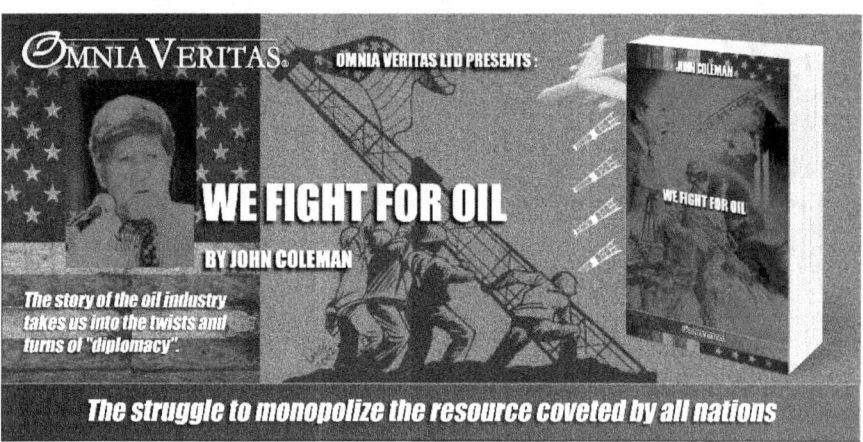

www.ingramcontent.com/pod-product-compliance
Lightning Source LLC
Chambersburg PA
CBHW071313150426
43191CB00007B/609